MIDWAY

PACIFIC

WAKE I.

HAWAII

OCEAN

SOLOMON
ISLANDS

FIJI
ISLES

NEW
CALEDONIA

BANE

920
M12

AMERICA
PRESS
LIBRARY

Douglas MacArthur

DOUGLAS

NEW YORK : HENRY HOLT AND COMPANY

MacARTHUR

AMERICA PRESS LIBRARY

Clark Lee and Richard Henschel

Copyright, 1952, by Henry Holt and Company, Inc.

*All rights reserved, including the right
to reproduce this book or portions thereof in any form.*

FIRST EDITION

*Printed in the United States of America
by H. Wolff, New York.*

This book is dedicated, with love, to
L.K.L. and M.C.H.

Contents

Douglas MacArthur

An Informal Biography by Clark Lee

Douglas MacArthur

A Pictorial Biography

Edited and with captions by Richard Henschel

Acknowledgments

WE WISH TO EXPRESS OUR SINCERE GRATITUDE TO THOSE WHO HAVE GENEROUSLY contributed to this book by providing access to correspondence, records, photographs, and personal information about Douglas MacArthur and his family, or by aiding in the research and preparation of the manuscript.

For their kind assistance we wish to mention, especially, Mrs. Mary H. McCalla MacArthur, Col. Warren J. Clear, Dr. Louis Morton, Maj. Gen. Patrick J. Hurley, Col. George Cocheu, Charles L. Kades, Howard Handleman, Governor John J. Dempsey, Miss Virginia Lee, Leonard Lyons, Mrs. Elizabeth Lee Pettig, Rex Smith of American Airlines, John J. Alicoate, Miss Maggy Fisher, John Monyhan.

Also Theodore Miller and the Milwaukee Historical Society, Frank Taylor and Patrick O'Rourke of the Milwaukee *Sentinel*, Robert Lassiter, Mrs. Mary Nelle Morris, Edward F. Dziadzio, Lt. Col. W. J. Morton, Dr. Sidney Forman, Lt. Col. James Leer, Capt. William Ochs.

Also Malcolm MacArthur, Bowman MacArthur, George Seamon and the Rainbow Division Veterans' Association, Maj. Gen. Courtney Whitney, Mrs. Marie Beard Glenn, Mrs. Mae Wachs, Walter B. Wolf, Brig. Gen. Henry J. Reilly, M. Manning Marcus, Edward Folliard, Harold Rodier, and Frank Hewlett.

Also Mrs. Mitchell Mackie, Mrs. Martin Fladoes, H. O. Wood, Miss Peg Hehmeyer, Mrs. George Miller, Solon J. Carter, Byron Boruzek, William K. Winkler and Mrs. Margaret Clark Henschel.

Also Mrs. Donna Traxler and the staff of the Signal Corps photographic library, Maj. Marshall Berard, Maj. John Bardwell, Lieut. W. B. Stanard, Lieut. Donald F. McConville, Miss Muriel Seelye, Robert Berger, Thomas Stowe, James Brustares, Mrs. James Jordan, Andrew Bradley, Frank Gay, Frank Bobowski, James Carnahan, Capt. Clovis Crummett, Lieut. Gaetano Faillace, Saul Flaum, Thomas Carolan, Ira Rosenberg, Bart L. Stafford, Sgt. FC Kenneth Wipperman, Frederick Hill Meserve, Capt. Irwin Forman, Conklin Mann, and Lieut. Joseph Boyle.

Acknowledgments

The following agencies and organizations have supplied photographs for this book: International News Photos, Keystone View Co., European Picture Service, The American Olympic Committee, The American Red Cross, The United States Military Academy, The National Archives of the United States, The Milwaukee (Wis.) *Sentinel*, The New York *Herald Tribune*, The Harris and Ewing News Photo Service, The United States Air Force, Navy, Coast Guard, Marine Corps, and Army Signal Corps.

Clark Lee and Richard Henschel

New York City

An Informal Biography

I

Introduction and Action

C H A P T E R

1

To Set the Stage

IN THIS YEAR OF GRACE IN THE EARLY 1950'S, THIS YEAR of alternate shooting and talking in Korea and uneasy cold war elsewhere, the United States has nearly as many generals in high places in its councils as does a Central American republic immediately after a revolution.

There are generals to right of us, generals to left of us, generals to east of us, generals to west of us. There are generals in and out of uniform, generals on inactive service who are extremely active, and, sometimes, vice versa. Generals write our best sellers and our peace treaties, and generals serve as our diplomatic and geopolitical experts. They spend most of our tax money and—not content with advising the President what to do—at least two of them would very much like to be presidents themselves. One at a time, of course.

Fortunately for the rest of us, our generals are good generals when it comes to fighting wars—our current crop has fought three, winning those in 1917-18 and 1941-45 and getting a draw in Korea in 1950-51. Perhaps unfortunately, they cannot agree about *where* to fight them, and at present they are engaged in a bitter controversy over this matter. Pending a settlement of this dispute, private citizens can only hope that it will not terminate in a compromise that will have the Europe-first generals fighting in Europe and the Asia-firsters battling away in Asia, while the global strategists fight all over the globe and the rest of us dodge atom bombs at home.

This is a startling possibility and a terrifying one, but at the same time there is something relaxingly ridiculous in the picture of our generals bickering among themselves like noisy fishwives. The public had not had time to digest all the volumes recounting their fraternal squabbling in World War II when their current policy battles broke into the open and they sailed into each other in full sight of the whole world and revealed the depth of their disagreements.

One doubted that "time was on our side" in the air and atomic race, another said, "Definitely, it *is* on our side." One said we had a "shoestring" air force after spending billions for planes and pilots, another declared we had a fine air force. They disagreed on how well prepared we were, disagreed over what we should do in the Far East, disagreed as to Soviet Russia's likely intentions, disagreed as to whether or not war was inevitable, disagreed about our foreign policy, and disagreed on practically everything. On only one point were they in agreement—that they should be given more money. The Secretary of State joined the argument with a fascinating explanation of how our brilliantly conceived foreign policy had somehow brought about disastrous results, and the President chimed in with a series of warnings intended to terrify the nation into supporting the generals in their unified demands for more money.

The net effect of this spectacle was something less than reassuring, but at least it demonstrated that the generals are essentially like the rest of us. Far from knowing all the answers, they are not even in accord regarding the management of their own business.

This book is about one of these contending generals—General Douglas MacArthur. He is certainly the most controversial of all of them and perhaps the most difficult to write about, which explains this somewhat light approach to a subject which is more serious than facetious.

What makes MacArthur a difficult subject is the fact that nearly everything he has ever said or done can be judged in two ways. If a person thinks he is essentially a good man, then his words and deeds fit into that picture, but if the bias of the viewer is essentially against him, the same words and acts can be interpreted to conform to that basic prejudice. The net result is that there is only one thing reasonably certain about a book concerning Douglas MacArthur—it won't change anyone's opinion about him.

The controversial storm that followed his dismissal is nothing new in MacArthur's life. So strong and heated are opinions about his personality and his views that only a cool-headed minority has been able to judge him on a basis of impartiality and logic; usually opinions are swayed and confused by the legend and symbolism that surround him.

At several periods in the past 20 years the mere mention of the name "MacArthur" has been enough to start violent discussion in parlor, barroom, or on the floor of the Senate. To millions he is great, dedicated, infallible, living on a plane far above ordinary mortals. "A reincarnation of St. Paul," as former President Hoover said, "come out of the East." And come to lead us—behind The Cross and The Sword—to eventual peace on earth.

Others fear him as a representative of the forces of dark reaction, a dangerous man-on-horseback with dictatorial ambitions; a narrow-minded general, imperious, so self-centered that through his own lack of vision he would plunge the world into atomic warfare.

Regardless of these conflicting viewpoints, there is no dispute about the fact that MacArthur has devoted a vigorous and uncompromising lifetime to the service of his country. He possesses extraordinary mental powers and great integrity; his courage is formidable and his physical and mental endurance close to phenomenal. As a general, he depended as much on intuition as on textbooks, and in all his battles he skillfully avoided needless slaughter of his own men. His qualities of leadership and statesmanship are vast, and his name is stamped indelibly on the history of the Pacific for some centuries to come.

It would be entirely fitting that such a figure should have less attractive qualities in proportion to his virtues. But despite all that has been said and written about him to the contrary, such is not the case with MacArthur. That he is ambitious, optimistic, and highly self-confident is true, but such qualities are not usually considered faults in a leader. Less attractive is his extreme sensitivity which in recent years makes criticism unbearable, if not to him personally, then certainly to the extraordinarily sensitive men who usually surround him. Perhaps his least admirable tendency is to claim for himself full credit when things go right, and to point out quickly that others are at least equally responsible when a mistake is made. He is open to censure also for the fact that the men around him have tended to color fact with fancy in order to embellish his record, and that they frequently have sought to make things so simply by saying they were so.

It is relatively easy to continue to catalogue the further characteristics, both admirable and otherwise, of MacArthur. As a figure, he is remote, austere, and lonely. But in private relationships he is thoughtful, considerate, humorous, interesting. He has great vision and knowledge. He is emotional and sincere, with a tremendous capacity for work. He is religious, something of a mystic, fatalistic, and inspirational. He has held great power, but has never used it for its own enjoyment nor for its own sake, but instead for the things he believes in and for whose preservation he has offered his life innumerable times on the field of battle—human freedom and the old, timeless virtues.

The circumstances of his career, half of which was served outside of his own country, frequently forced upon him the making of sweeping political and military decisions. He eagerly welcomed this responsibility; his decisions usually proved correct and were eventually applauded. The result of these experiences was that when he found himself, in the final showdown that led to the termination of his military service, once more faced with indecision and vacillation among his superiors, he not only insisted on expressing his own views but continued to do so in contradiction—certainly of the spirit, if not the express language—of their directives and orders to him.

For most of his adult life, MacArthur has been a symbol and a legend. In World War I he was the hero general, valorous, victorious, ascetic, and incredibly handsome. Later, as Chief of Staff, he sought to prepare the country for inevitable war and became to his haters a symbol of the militaristic, blood-lusting warmonger.

In the great depression of the early 1930's, after public rebellion against economic paralysis had expressed itself in the Bonus March—which he dispersed by the display of force—he was a symbol of all the inadequacies of the Hoover administration, and hatred of the regime was largely concentrated against him.

At the start of World War II, in a time of black defeat, despair, and even cowardice, he rose from the remote jungles of distant Bataan as a towering symbol of future victory. He became the Savior of Australia, Liberator of the Philippines, and finally Conqueror of Japan.*

During the five and one-half years he ruled Japan he became to the Japanese a symbol of benevolent conquest, of peaceful revolution. Americans regarded him as a solid rock, a secure island in a restless world, a bastion standing firm against the forces of communism.

When President Truman dismissed him from high office, he became a symbol of dissatisfaction against a seemingly hopeless war and against the confused and uncertain foreign policy of an administration already in disfavor because of its shoddiness and aura of corruption.

In a sense, MacArthur's career started long before he was born; for 90 years the name MacArthur has been on the lips of the American people in times of great crisis, conflict and controversy.

The first legendary MacArthur was the father of Douglas. Then only 18, Arthur MacArthur seized his regimental colors at Missionary Ridge in the Civil War and dashed through heavy fire to the top of Confederate breastworks, winning the Congressional Medal of Honor for heroism and immortality as "The Boy Colonel of the West." For 25 of the next 30 years he was a frontier soldier, fighting campaigns against the Apaches and Sioux and helping to pacify with saber and carbine the last great continental areas to be taken into the United States.

When the Republic burst its western continental boundaries at the turn of the century and reached out across the Pacific to take the Philippines, there was the same MacArthur, still vigorous and bellicose, carrying democracy to the Filipinos at the point of a bayonet. Douglas MacArthur, destined for fame from the time of his birth in 1880, made his own career a deliberate projection and extension of his father's.

Arthur MacArthur subdued the Philippines and began the first faltering steps toward making them democratic; his son first lost and then rewon those same islands and went on to subdue a second Asiatic country, Japan, and take giant strides toward its democratization. Subsequently, he became the first military leader of the United Nations, the first world organization to resort to force in its efforts to eradicate the settlement of disputes by force.

Seen together, the careers of Arthur MacArthur and of Douglas MacArthur synthesize the westward expansion of America. Between them,

* I am speaking here, of course, in symbolic terms, without reference to the parts played in the actual fighting of World War II by the Navy, Marines, Air Corps, and others.

they led American armies which overwhelmed the civilizations of two Asiatic nations and substituted, or attempted to substitute, the main features of American civilization.

In a material sense, they carried America across the Pacific militarily, economically, and politically. In ideological terms, they introduced Christian democracy to the Orient with bayonet and atom bomb. The expansionism which they represented differed from the old imperialism in that it sought to assist rather than to exploit the vanquished and occupied nations. But regardless of its aims, it is still expansionism.

And in 1950, this American expansionism came into head-on collision with another expansionist movement. This new force is antireligious communist ideology, expanding from West to East behind Russian military, economic, and political power and expressing itself through puppet armies of the Asiatic mainland. In one of the last corners of the vast Asiatic continent not yet in the Russian orbit—in the small southern half of Korea—the two forces met in armed conflict in the last week of June, 1950.

The resultant explosion blew Douglas MacArthur out of his posts of supreme command in the Far East and into a suite in the Waldorf Towers in New York. In one sense, the firing of MacArthur was absolutely necessary. In another, it was a confession by the men who fired him that they could not (any more than MacArthur) find any easy and sure solution to the problems confronting the world. Firing him did not, nor could it, decide the terrible question of whether armed democracy and militant communism can eventually settle down to live together in the same world, or whether much of that world will be destroyed in a cataclysmic conflict. But his dismissal and his subsequent homecoming did give his fellow citizens a chance for a closer look at him than they had had for some years, and it also made him, for the foreseeable future, a force to be reckoned with in the life of America.

In his memorable homecoming address to Congress, MacArthur announced that he was "fading away" as a soldier, but it soon became apparent that he was simply exchanging his warrior's uniform for the toga of an elder statesman. In this latter capacity he has been traveling about the country and exercising his right as a citizen of the Republic to speak freely, critically, and often. He has spoken clearly and forcefully, and his words reveal a different man than the distorted and mythical figure he had been during his long absence. But even so, the legends and myths die hard, and the interpretations of what he says are still colored by preconceptions and prejudices based in large measure on incomplete understanding of the events of his life.

One fact that certainly has not escaped MacArthur's fellow Americans as they hear him speak is his preoccupation with history. It is constitutionally impossible for him to say, "We had a tough fight." Instead he will say, "We had the toughest fight in history." His sentences are replete with historical comparisons: "No commander in the history of warfare

. . . ," "History does not record a more glaring example . . . ," "In all history there is not a parallel . . ."

This intense interest in history extends not only to the remote past with which MacArthur is so intimately familiar through his encylopedic studies, but also to his immediate ancestry. To understand this is to make more comprehensible many of his actions, his decisions, convictions, and even his mannerisms and choice of words. Because this is so, it is pertinent and necessary in this book to tell something of those active and interesting ancestors in whose lives there are many striking similarities to the events of MacArthur's own extraordinarily eventful career.

CHAPTER

2

Some Older MacArthurs

"THE FIRST RECOLLECTION I HAVE," DOUGLAS MACArthur is fond of saying, "is the sound of Army bugles."

MacArthur conveys to these simple words such portentous meaning that his listener sees a Western epic unrolling before his eyes—a whole era of American history comes alive; covered wagons rocking over sun-baked plains, the smell of sweated horses and leather, and the bright notes of a bugle through the thin desert air.

In the dim memories of childhood and the stronger ones of boyhood, all those things are real to MacArthur. He lived on their fringes nearly 70 years ago, and he lives them again when he sees a Western movie; Westerns, quite naturally, are his favorites. He was born in an Army post at Fort Dodge (now part of Little Rock), Arkansas, and lived with his soldier-father and his mother in a succession of posts in the states and territories, some of them actually in Indian territory.

On one trip from the nearest railhead to a fort in New Mexico, the mother and her sons made a long, jolting journey in a covered wagon. Far from formal schools at this time, Mrs. Mary MacArthur used books from her husband's extensive collection, and herself taught Douglas and his older brother, Arthur. Their quarters at this fort and even in the relatively more urban surroundings of posts in eastern Texas resembled a school room. The father considered reading (and talking) on all subjects the most delightful form of occupation; he was a self-educated man and won a degree in law. Like his son in later years, he could talk with informed interest on almost any subject.

Only once was Arthur MacArthur known to have been stumped for words. The occasion, when the older MacArthur was stationed at Fort Leavenworth, which was the Army's first school, was so unusual that Douglas MacArthur recalls it well and enjoys retelling it. "My father," he says, "came home one night in the greatest possible anger. My mother said, 'Arthur, what is the matter with you?' He said, 'Well, I have just been assigned to make the discussion at next week's Lyceum.' And my mother said, 'Why, you should be very proud to get an opportunity. What is the subject?' And my father said, 'That is the trouble. The subject that was assigned to me was this: The Spirit of the Age—What Is It?' "

As youngsters, Douglas and his brother Arthur were intelligent and quick to learn. Douglas was an avid reader of military and historical volumes, he rode a horse and shot a rifle like a cavalryman, and the last words he heard each night were those of his mother, telling him he would "be a great man like his father some day." From his earliest years he was a fastidious dresser, and his mother claimed that this was his inheritance from the gentlemanly plantation owners on her side of the family.

A close relationship developed between mother and son that lasted throughout her life. From hearing her talk of her own ancestors, from hearing the soldiers repeat tales of his father's bravery in battle, and from his reading, Douglas MacArthur developed that kinship with the past and sense of historical continuity which is one of his marked traits today. It is doubtful that even his mother or father knew the details of the family genealogy but the boy came to understand that his was a distinguished heritage whose traditions he must carry on. Young Arthur MacArthur is being inculcated with the same feeling of family continuity today.

MacArthur's own ancestors were actors in many exciting historical events; an Italian king who was murdered; a MacArthur beheaded by King James I; Revolutionary War leaders who fought in New England and Virginia. On his father's side, his descent is straight from the highlands of Scotland through both grandfather and grandmother, both of them members of the MacArthur family whose clansman ancestors have been prominent in Scots history for 1,000 recorded years; a Scots proverb states, "There is nothing older, unless the hills—MacArthur and the Devil." The MacArthurs were a branch (and for some 150 years eight centuries ago, the chiefs) of the Clan Campbell, they fought beside Robert the Bruce at Bannockburn in the decisive battle for Scots independence and as a reward were given large grants of lands forfeited by the MacDougalls. Farther back, MacArthurs fought in the Great Crusades, and there are still tombstones of Crusaders buried under a foot or two of earth on an island in Loch Katrine, in a district where the family is famous in romance and history. More recently, two MacArthurs died at Culloden, two others escaped the disastrous defeat of the Highlanders by the British, and one went to Australia to found a prominent and wealthy family.

From his paternal grandmother, Douglas MacArthur inherited both English and French blood, the latter traceable directly back to Charlemagne, the great conqueror and ruler. Through his own mother his roots are Scotch and English, Irish, Welsh, and French; his mother's forebears were among the first colonists to settle in Virginia and the Carolinas some three centuries ago.

When Douglas MacArthur discusses his immediate ancestors, especially his father and grandfather, it is almost as if they were contemporaries;

not infrequently he "reported" to his father (long since dead) when he felt he had done a job well and faithfully. Similarly, he is accustomed to refer to Washington and Lincoln as "my advisers," as if they were still living, and it may well be that this sense of being in communication with the past was one of the characteristics that made MacArthur sympathetic to Oriental peoples. In any case, it sharpened his own feeling for the historical import of everything he did; he saw himself as the latest in a long line of men who had answered the call of Army bugles. In reading the lives of his father and grandfather, it is easy to share MacArthur's own feeling that history really does repeat itself and 50 or 100 years ago is only yesterday; he frequently has been placed in almost the exact situations his forebears faced, and quite often he uses almost the exact language that they employed.

GRANDFATHER ARTHUR MAC ARTHUR

The first of the MacArthurs to come to America was Arthur, grandfather of Douglas, who arrived in eastern Massachusetts about 1830 and settled in Chicopee Falls, then part of Springfield, in 1842. He seems to have been as handsome, courtly, dignified, elegant in dress, intelligent, hard-working, and as poised as both his son and grandson—but distinctly less intense. He was a lawyer and literateur, a witty raconteur and famous conversationalist, popular and successful. He lived a good life, married three times and had two sons, was an associate of presidents and once very briefly of kings, was elected to public office, served 30 years as a judge. Being a MacArthur, he also got into a tremendous political controversy which stirred considerable commotion in its day.

Apparently the Widow Sarah MacArthur MacArthur (her maiden name and married name were the same) had been left some funds by her husband. Her son, born in Glasgow in 1815 and named Arthur for his father, went to study at Uxbridge and Wesleyan Academies and at Amherst University during the golden age of New England's cultural and literary renascence. The temper of the times was liberal and intellectual and there was "passionate interest in self-culture." Carried along in these currents, young MacArthur studied law in New York, was admitted to the bar, and practiced both there and in Springfield where he served as Judge Advocate of the Western Military District of Massachusetts—the closest he ever came to connection with the military. As an enterprising and promising young barrister he was on occasion associated with or opposed to Daniel Webster, Choate, and other great American lawyers. His first marriage was brief. His second wife was Aurelia Belcher, descendant of early New England settlers who were lawyers, soldiers and doctors.

Through her, Douglas MacArthur and Winston Churchill are related as eighth cousins, and MacArthur (like Churchill) was also a distant relative —sixth cousin, once removed—of Franklin D. Roosevelt. It was through

Aurelia Belcher also that Douglas MacArthur descended from Charlemagne.

The son of the Scots immigrant Arthur MacArthur and of Aurelia Belcher was born in Chicopee Falls in 1845 and four years later the lawyer—now 34—went west to Milwaukee. The eldest son was named Arthur, in accordance with a family tradition which dates back several hundred years. Another son, Frank, was a prominent attorney in the United States Patent Office and in private practice in New York. He died in his 30's and his branch of the family is represented by only one living descendant, Malcolm MacArthur, a retired broker and bachelor living in New York City. Malcolm and Douglas MacArthur—first cousins—never met until the latter's removal from command.

After moving to Wisconsin, Arthur MacArthur was elected lieutenant governor as a Democrat in the early 1850's. His own election was legal but that of the Democratic governor was manifestly fraudulent, and, in an effort to keep a Democrat in office, the disqualified governor appointed MacArthur to his post. An ugly situation developed and MacArthur was urged by his followers to use the armed force of the state militia to hold onto the office. This he refused to do, and after stalling for four days by a series of legalistic maneuvers he surrendered the post to the Republican candidate with the remark: "In this world there have never been but two kinds of government—a government of force without law, and a government of law without force." Thus ended the first dispute involving a MacArthur and the question of military as against civilian law.

Although this incident temporarily ruined the Democratic party in Wisconsin politics, MacArthur's personal popularity was not affected. He was elected and served for 13 years as judge of the important Second Judicial Circuit of Wisconsin and won the attention of Lincoln, who called him "a man to my liking." President Grant sent for him to come to Washington as associate federal judge of the District of Columbia and he remained for nearly 18 years, a leading judicial and social figure famous for his discourses on world affairs and for his interest in modern penological methods. He also served as president and chancellor of the board of regents of the National University School of Law, president of the Washington Humane Society, and president of the Associated Charities of the District of Columbia.

On his own 65th birthday, word was sent to the judge of the birth of his grandson Douglas. When he was 73, after 18 years on the federal bench, Judge MacArthur retired with full pay under the federal judicial retirement law; he is said to have given most of his pay to charitable and benevolent organizations. He returned to Milwaukee and spent the next nine years in what he called "the still air of delightful studies." He wrote many books, including a work on spiritualism; a defense of Mary, Queen of Scots; and *The Biography of the English Language*.

All in all he had enjoyed a delightful, full, and productive life when, at the age of 81, he went to Atlantic City on a visit; his son Arthur was a lieutenant colonel and a national hero; Arthur, Jr., Jr., had just graduated from Annapolis and young Douglas was being groomed for West Point. The state of his personal affairs being entirely in order, the old judge sat looking out across the Atlantic toward distant Scotland, closed his eyes, and very peacefully died. The date was August 27, 1896.

LIEUTENANT GENERAL ARTHUR MAC ARTHUR

Testimony in May, 1951, before Senatorial committees investigating the dismissal of General Douglas MacArthur:

General MacArthur: "My father was a man of great equanimity and modesty of character, rarely aroused, placid, congenial."

Senator Tobey: "General MacArthur, when you paid that fine tribute to your late father a few minutes ago—equanimity and poise, slow to anger, plentiful of mercy—I thought of saying, 'Like father, like son.' I pay you that tribute."

Douglas MacArthur: "Thank you, sir. There is no tribute you could pay me that I would appreciate quite that much."

. . . From his earliest boyhood, Douglas MacArthur resolved to follow the footsteps of his soldier-father, Arthur MacArthur; he began to think and speak of his father as "a noble man." When he was a cadet at West Point, he told friends, "I hope I can be as great a man as my father . . . and I will if hard work can make me so." He could not, of course, determine the inherent characteristics of his temperament such as "modesty of character"; he was as much his mother's son as his father's with results that we shall see later.

But in the actual physical details of his career, the younger MacArthur succeeded to an astonishing degree in realizing his ambition. His father was an officer for 46½ years, Douglas for 47½ years prior to his relief (plus four years at West Point). In the military phases of their lives there is not merely the similarity of events involving any soldiers and any battles but an almost exact duplication of actual events—the rallying of a broken line; a quick decision to lead troops beyond a given objective, the rescue of cutoff comrades. The citations recognizing the father's great courage and leadership in the Civil War could—with minor changes in place names and names of units—be interchanged with those won by the son in World War I in France. Forty-odd years apart the two men fought over exactly the same ground in the Philippines; the town that Arthur MacArthur last occupied in 1900 was the same one (Dagupan) where Douglas MacArthur first set up his headquarters in the liberation of Luzon in 1945.

In their respective careers, both men set many records of "youngests" and "firsts." Together they held the highest ranks ever attained in the American Army by members of the same family, and they are the only father-son combination ever to win our highest military award, the Congressional Medal of Honor. They served as a team in the Orient in the early part of the twentieth century; and each in his time was recognized as America's outstanding expert on Far Eastern affairs.

Each man was military governor of an Asiatic nation. Each became involved in a dispute with his superiors and appealed to the public over their heads. Each had a famous feud, Arthur with William Howard Taft and MacArthur against George Catlett Marshall. At the start, each of the MacArthurs had the commanding position, but in the end their antagonists had the upper hand.

The realization that Douglas MacArthur deliberately patterned his life on his father's makes more understandable the obvious anachronisms in his mode of expression and the Victorian quality of his speech. The father was a man of the nineteenth century and Douglas himself lived the first 20 formative years of his life in the nineteenth century; his impromptu writing style and his courtly manners are essentially Victorian, although —it is perhaps superfluous to point out—his devotion to the past extended only to basic ideals and concepts which are as valid in one century as in the next; in military matters MacArthur has never stopped learning and the most brilliant military maneuver of his career, the amphibious landing at Inchon, Korea, in 1950, was made in his 70th year.

THE BOY COLONEL OF THE WEST

Arthur MacArthur started his military career much younger than did his son; he was a veteran of two years of warfare and a brevet colonel at 20 while Douglas was still in his second year at West Point at that age. Young Arthur's boyhood in Milwaukee, where he studied with private tutors and in public schools, coincided with intensification of the political struggle that culminated in the Civil War. The boy idolized Lincoln, and in emulation of his hero he lay on the floor to read by firelight the same books Lincoln had read in his log cabin; history and biography, the Bible, *Pilgrim's Progress*, and others. He watched torchlight parades in the Lincoln-Douglas campaign, cheered when Lincoln was elected, and was reported (in Usher's *History of Wisconsin*) to have "witnessed the final scene in one episode of slave-running."

Even before the war started he begged his father to let him join the navy as midshipman. He was 16 when Lincoln called for volunteers, and he was so eager to enlist that his father had to hire a private guard-tutor to prevent his running away. For the year he was restrained at home, Arthur studied military tactics and strategy, and at 17 enlisted with his father's consent and was named (with his father's political influence) adjutant of the 24th Wisconsin Volunteers, the Milwaukee Chamber of Commerce regiment. He was undersized, slender, and weak, and when he attempted to shout his first order at drill, his voice cracked and squeaked so comically that 1,000 men roared with laughter; and the colonel threatened to write the governor and "demand a man instead of a boy for adjutant." Young MacArthur gritted his teeth and promised, "I know why I'm a soldier and when we get into action, I'll do my duty." No promise was ever better kept.

In the regiment's first battle at Chaplin Hills, Kentucky, in October, 1862, he was cited for his coolness and gallantry under fire; and in the battle of Stone River three months later, he established himself as the hero of the regiment.

He went on from battle to battle, sustaining several wounds from bullets and bayonets, and once his life was saved when a package of letters stopped a bullet aimed at his heart. At Missionary Ridge, after two flag bearers had been shot down, he seized the regimental colors and called on the troops to follow him. The 24th Wisconsin had been ordered to stop at the first line of Confederate trenches, but as young MacArthur urged them on, they followed him up the fire-swept slope. General Grant was watching the battle; and as he saw the line advance, he angrily demanded of an aide, "Why don't they stop at that position?"

"When those fellows get started, sir," someone replied, "all hell can't stop them."

"Well," said Grant, "it will be all right if it turns out all right."

The charge led by young Arthur MacArthur did turn out all right—far more so than a somewhat similar though broader-scale action in Korea in 1950 when Douglas MacArthur, without prior consultation of his superiors, urged his non-Korean troops on to the frontier of China. The results of that action are discussed later in this book.

At Missionary Ridge, the major commanding the 24th Wisconsin recommended the Medal of Honor for Arthur MacArthur. Shortly afterwards the major resigned, and with the consent of all the other regimental officers, MacArthur was jumped over their heads and made his successor. The Medal of Honor was finally awarded June 30, 1890—some 27 years after the action in which it was won.

At the close of the war, only 20 and still too young to vote, MacArthur was mustered out of service—he had been commissioned colonel, but there were not enough survivors in the regiment to warrant that rank. He spent a year in Washington at the home of his father, Judge MacArthur, studying history and beginning the study of law, and then went back into military service in 1866 as second lieutenant of infantry in the Regular Army. He was advanced to first lieutenant the same day and to captain four months later. After those meteoric promotions, the rate of advance slowed down drastically, and for the next 23 years he remained a captain. Most of those years were spent in the West and Southwest where he fought in the Indian wars against the Apache and Sioux. The Army throughout this period was at its lowest ebb, and for three months in 1869 there was no assignment for Captain MacArthur. During the whole period, when he was not fighting, he was studying. Tours of duty took him to Washington at various times and on June 8, 1889—when his son Douglas was nine years old and he himself 45—he won a Doctor of Laws degree from the National Law School in Washington, a remarkably ambitious achievement for a soldier who was largely self-taught; his determination to study and learn made him an extremely well-read and interesting man. He was also broad-minded, liberal, and forward-looking. He sponsored several Army innovations, notably the canteen and recreation rooms; he was a vigorous exponent of mental and physical stimulation for the soldiers, and his companies won several awards as the most efficient in the Army.

One of his tours of duty was in New Orleans, and at a Mardi Gras celebration during the winter of 1874-75 he met Mary Pinkney Hardy, a 22-year-old Virginia girl who had come down for the social season. The 30-year-old Union officer promptly "surrendered to the Confederacy" (as Douglas did in his second marriage), and a few months later Captain MacArthur and Miss Hardy were married at the bride's family home, "Riveredge," near Norfolk (since established as a state MacArthur memorial). The new Mrs. MacArthur was one of seven daughters and seven sons of Dr. Thomas Hardy and Elizabeth Margaret Pierce Hardy. From both her parents' families, the girl was descended from early settlers (pre-1700) of the southern colonies and from Revolutionary War soldiers. Her immediate background was one of huge plantation houses, crinolines, and wealth, though the wealth mostly disappeared after the Civil War. The men of the family were doctors, lawyers, soldiers, and merchants. Three of "Pinky's" (the family name for the bride) sisters had married Northerners they met in Massachusetts during summer vacations, and when Mary also chose a Northern war hero, four of her brothers who were Confederate veterans registered their disapproval by staying away from the wedding.

Mrs. MacArthur accompanied her husband back to his duties in the West, and three sons were born: Arthur on August 1, 1876; Malcolm (who died in infancy) a year later, and Douglas on January 26, 1880. Army records show that Captain MacArthur was transferred from Little Rock to Washington 18 months after Douglas' birth and remained for four years in the adjutant general's department, then returning to Western forts and outposts where young Douglas got his taste of frontier life.

When Douglas was entering his teens the father was stationed in Texas, where the boy studied at West Texas Military Academy and with tutors. Then in 1898 the now Colonel MacArthur sent his wife and Douglas to Milwaukee and took off again for the wars.

CHAPTER

3

The First MacArthur in the Philippines

AT THE TIME OF WORLD WAR II THERE WAS CONSIDerable confusion among the American public about the exact location of Manila and the Philippine Islands. In the minds of many, there was a vague historical relationship between Cuba and the Philippines. Cuba was known to be near Florida; the United States had gone to war with Spain over Cuba and as a result of that war had gotten the Philippines. Therefore it was frequently assumed that Manila (and the Philippines) must be somewhere near Cuba.

This confusion is nothing new. It was prevalent at the time of the fighting a half century ago when Arthur MacArthur—starting out from Wisconsin to fight against the Spaniards in Cuba—wound up fighting them 10,000 miles away in the Philippines.

Exactly how the United States got into war, first with Spain in Cuba, then with Spain in the Philippines, and finally with the Filipinos themselves is still difficult to understand even from the hindsight of fifty years.

One thing certain is that there was a small group of men strategically placed in America who believed "this country needs a war." Among them was the author of that statement, Theodore Roosevelt, then Assistant Secretary of the Navy, who was convinced that a country—like a man—should live "the strenuous life" and that the excitement and bloodshed of battle were "just bully." At the time, Hearst and Pulitzer were engaged in a newspaper circulation war and vied with each other in printing inflammatory accounts of the brutal mistreatment of the Cubans at the hands of their Spanish masters. Public excitement was so aroused and official Washington so excited that the battleship U.S.S. *Maine* was dispatched to Havana harbor to "protect American lives and property." Before long, the *Maine* was blown up in Havana harbor—allegedly by Spanish officers but quite possibly by an accidental internal explosion—and war to free the Cubans from Spanish rule inevitably followed. Simultaneously, the United States started a second war in the Philippines, 10,000 miles distant from Cuba and clear across the Pacific at the edge of the Asian continent.

The new war was a complete surprise to the people of America, having been secretly planned by Theodore Roosevelt in connivance with Senator Henry Cabot Lodge. Taking advantage of the absence of Navy Secretary Long from his office, Roosevelt, with the knowledge of Lodge—and even before the outbreak of war in Cuba—dispatched instructions to Admiral Dewey at Nagasaki. In what has been aptly described as "the most amazing conspiracy in American history," Roosevelt arrogated to himself the right of deciding his country's destiny and ordered Dewey "in the event of hostilities with Spain to capture or destroy" the Spanish fleet in Manila Bay. Dewey followed these orders to the letter, sailing undetected past the fortress of Corregidor to the Naval Station at Cavite where he bombarded and sank Admiral Montojo's fleet without the loss of a single American life. (In a strange historical repetition, Japanese airplanes in 1942 destroyed American power at Cavite without losing a man or plane.)

When news of this entirely unexpected victory reached America, the country immediately demanded that troops be sent to "support" Dewey; it was now that Arthur MacArthur was commissioned a brigadier general of volunteers and sailed from San Francisco with the third expedition, landing in Manila in July of 1898. MacArthur's troops and others being on hand (under the command of General Otis, whom MacArthur later succeeded), it then seemed entirely natural to drive the Spaniards entirely out of the Philippines, and with the assistance of Filipino patriots this was easily accomplished. Meanwhile the war in Cuba had been won with ease; the Spaniards in the Philippines were now defeated on both sea and land, and it was time for the American forces to go back to America. Instead, President McKinley, who had first attempted to check the wave of imperialistic fervor sweeping America, finally succumbed to it and concluded, "While we are fighting this war, we must take what we can get; afterwards we must keep what we can hold." The Hawaiian Islands—which had nothing to do with either Cuba or Spain—were immediately annexed with the consent of a revolutionary government which five years earlier had overcome the native monarchy. And now it was decided to keep the Philippines.

There was one important obstacle in realization of this aim: the Filipinos did not want their country to be kept by America. They had gone to war against the Spaniards to win their independence, and they objected vigorously to the substitution of American imperialism for Spanish. Feeling with considerable justification that they had been double-crossed by Dewey and his government, they rallied behind a fiery young independence leader, Emilio Aguinaldo, and after a period of uneasy truce, actual warfare started in the vicinity of Manila with a battle between General MacArthur's troops and Aguinaldo's forces. The warfare lasted three years and finally required more than 70,000 American troops.

At the start, the task assigned Arthur MacArthur was largely similar to the assignment given his son a half century later in Korea: both were given an all-out war to fight without adequate forces to fight it, under conditions that made "victory" impossible. Roughly speaking, both MacArthurs were in the similar position of being under superiors who could not make up their minds about how to cope with the situation confronting them. In the case of the older MacArthur, his commander at the beginning was General Otis, who is unanimously conceded by historians of the period to have set a record for inefficiency and indecision. Once MacArthur became so enraged at the bumbling Otis that he lost his usual self-control, slammed his hat on the ground and bellowed, "Otis is a locomotive bottom side up, with the wheels revolving at full speed."

Exactly as his son was to do later, the elder MacArthur protested with great vigor against the prospect of long drawn-out and costly fighting with no end in sight. He besieged General Otis with requests for additional troops and was turned down. The direct approach failing, he influenced the war correspondents in Manila to sign a message to their papers saying that "the only hope of an American victory is more men." Otis did not relieve MacArthur from command, but he did threateningly remind the reporters that they were under martial law and could be shot for their action. Eventually, however, the MacArthur policies prevailed, and the necessary reinforcements were sent.

The policy which the elder MacArthur was instructed to follow in the Philippines was one that had been "God-sent" to President McKinley. The president explained its origin to a group of Methodist missionaries visiting at the White House. "The truth is I didn't want the Philippines when they came to us as a gift from the gods; I did not know what to do with them . . . I sought counsel from all sides—Democrats as well as Republicans—but got little help. I thought first we would take only Manila, then Luzon, then other islands, perhaps also." He walked the floor of the White House night after night and then prayed on his knees for divine guidance.

"And one night late it came to me this way—I don't know how it was, but it came: . . . that there was nothing left for us to do but to take them all, and to educate the Filipines, and uplift and civilize and Christianize them, and by God's grace to do the very best we could by them, as our fellow men for whom Christ also died. And then I went to bed and slept soundly."

Here, for all its divine origin, was a policy of imperialism which shocked many Americans as greatly as did the later Korean "policy" of "killing Chinese." But after a great political debate that shook the nation, McKinley's policies were approved at the polls; he was reelected and the Philippines were kept—as Mr. Dooley put it, "We decided to give the Filipinos a measure iv freedom . . . whin they'll shtand still long enough to be measured."

Arthur MacArthur was apart from the controversy itself. His job was "to take them all" and, although only a small proportion of the Filipinos resisted, it was a long and disagreeable task which did little to glorify the history of American arms. In the heat of battle, the "God-damns" (American soldiers) and the "gugus" (compare this to the "Gook" of Korean times) very frequently ignored the rules of "civilized warfare." Both sides shot unarmed and helpless prisoners and practiced various methods of unrefined cruelty.

Douglas MacArthur later familiarized himself with all the details of this brutal war, and one incident in particular made a deep and lasting impression on him. This was the slaughter of some "poor naked Igorettes" whose spears and homemade shields were no defense against American bullets. More than 40 years later, a group of Igorots fought under Douglas MacArthur on Bataan and he singled them out for praise in the longest and one of the most flamboyant of all his wartime statements, which described in vivid prose the battle between the Igorots and the Japanese and ended in frequently quoted sentences: ". . . For sheer, breath-taking and heart-stopping desperation, I have never know the equal of those Igorots riding the tanks. Gentlemen, when you tell that story, stand in tribute to those gallant Igorots."

Back in 1901, the core of Filipino resistance centered in the elusive person of Emilio Aguinaldo, who was finally tracked down at his hideout in Northern Luzon and brought to Malacanan Palace, where Arthur MacArthur had his headquarters as military governor. MacArthur invited Aguinaldo to breakfast, sent for his family, and had him confined with every military courtesy—but nonetheless confined. The capture broke the heart of the resistance movement and many insurrectionists laid down their arms. From the Bataan peninsula, the local Filipino leader dispatched his aide, Major Manuel Quezon, to Manila under a flag of truce to determine whether Aguinaldo actually had been taken. Quezon asked this question of MacArthur, who pointed silently to a guarded room. Quezon looked, and his "whole world crumbled" when he saw Aguinaldo inside. Subsequently he gave up his own weapons, planning to resume his practice of law but, instead, he was thrown into a dungeon with 30 other men and held for four months under terrible conditions and with no charge against him. He never forgot this experience, which he said, "made me more anti-American than ever."

After Aguinaldo had been softened by his imprisonment, he issued a proclamation to his followers: "The time has come when the Filipinos find their path (to independence) impeded by an irresistible force. . . . Enough of blood, enough of tears and desolation!" He urged the Filipinos to "give up the struggle that has wrought such great harm to this country and accept the sovereignty of the United States." Forty-one years later, an old and embittered man who had been pushed aside after the insurrection and been thwarted (largely by Manuel Quezon) in his lifelong ambition for the presidency, Aguinaldo turned to the invading Japanese as a possible liberating force. In a broadcast from Japanese-held Manila he urged Douglas MacArthur on Corregidor, "Surrender your troops and give up the fight. Your continued resistance can do no good."

ARTHUR MAC ARTHUR AND WILLIAM HOWARD TAFT

Like his son later in Korea and Japan, Arthur MacArthur had a dual role in the Philippines. He was fighting the insurrectionists and at the same time acting as military governor over the friendly Filipinos; in this latter capacity he was a just and progressive administrator who extended, apparently on his own initiative, the right of *habeas corpus* to the Filipinos. With his extensive legal background and book-acquired knowledge of government, MacArthur might have gone much farther toward "uplifting and civilizing" the Filipinos, but he was military governor for only a year and two months and did not have the extensive opportunity his son later enjoyed in "democratizing" Japan. President McKinley did not consider that the U.S. Army—which had been widely criticized and officially investigated for its supposed mistreatment of the Filipinos—was the right medium for this effort and sent out William Howard Taft as head of a five-man commission to begin the establishment of civil government in September of 1900.

When Taft reached Manila in June of that year, MacArthur did not even meet the ship, sending instead an aide who introduced Taft to what he has called "the indescribable coldness of Army officers and Army men." Taft had expected a "welcoming populace" but there was none; and when he met MacArthur, the latter offered him a hand which "dripped icicles" in such quantities that Taft's perspiration stopped.

MacArthur had set up desks for the five commissioners and five secretaries in a room so small that the elephantine Taft could not squeeze past the furniture; and the general informed the commission he considered it an "injection into an otherwise normal situation." As his son was to do many times by his use of an unusual word, MacArthur sent the commissioners scurrying for their dictionaries by telling them he had already "mediatized" the volume of work flowing across his desk.

The two men clashed from the start. Taft proclaimed a policy of treating the Filipinos as "little brown brothers" to be won over by friendly talk. MacArthur, while he had no hatred for the Filipinos, knew that you couldn't stop to argue America's noble intentions when confronted by a tribesman shooting off a Mauser. MacArthur, Sr. (like his son), was faced with the actuality of growing casualties, destruction, and devastation —Aguinaldo was not captured until Taft had been there nine or ten months. MacArthur wanted enough troops to end the war decisively, and his soldiers sang,

"Oh, he may be a brother
Of William Howard Taft
But he ain't no brother of mine."

Taft came to despise MacArthur personally—though admitting he was a good soldier and personally friendly to the Filipinos—and his letters home and reports to Secretary of War Elihu Root were highly prejudiced expressions of this personal feeling. He wrote a description of his opponent which to some extent might also have been applied to Douglas MacArthur: "A very courtly, kindly man; lacking somewhat in a sense of humor; rather fond of generalizations on the psychological condition of the people; politely incredulous, and politely lacking in any great consideration for the view of anyone, as to the real situation, who is a civilian and who has been here only a comparatively short time, and firmly convinced of the necessity for maintaining military etiquette in civil matters and civil government." Taft also described MacArthur as lacking "any vigorous initiative . . . naturally timid and set in his opinion,"—the first parts of this, certainly, were not characteristics of Douglas MacArthur nor do they do justice to his father, whose whole life was the antithesis of this description.

Taft, who threatened more than once to resign unless backed by Washington, quoted MacArthur as saying, "The Filipinos need no civil government. They need military government pinned to their backs for 10 years with bayonets," and he also reported that the military commander looked at his job "as one of conquering 8,000,000 recalcitrant, treacherous and stubborn people . . . all his enemies."

Such controversial and partisan remarks by Taft have been magnified out of all proportions by opponents of the MacArthurs. It is assumed that the disagreements between Taft and MacArthur resulted from the latter's support of the broad principle that military rule should supersede civilian, at least in the Philippines, and that by inference he favored a form of colonialism enforced by military power. Taft's sympathetic biographers have quite naturally favored Taft, who pictured himself as a great humanitarian bestower of the blessings of civilization. In contrast, they have tended to portray MacArthur as a red-necked militarist insistent on destroying most of the Filipino people and ruling the survivors by armed force. This erroneous picture has been extended to include Douglas MacArthur, and to imply that—like father like son—he advocated subordination of civilian control to the military.

The fundamental assumption, however, is false and this fact deserves emphasis. Arthur MacArthur was a democrat and like his son believed democracy the greatest form of government yet devised. He was kindly and humanitarian, in practice as well as principle. His quarrel with Taft did not arise from any fundamental difference over military rule as opposed to civilian. His position was—as far as the immediate situation was concerned—that he was faced with the military actuality of a people who refused to accept peacefully the imposition of foreign rule. He had to deal with that situation by military means, and was under orders to do so.

Because of this, he did at first oppose the establishment of civil provincial governments, and he did this because he was apprehensive over military conditions. In his early opposition he was not only correct from the military standpoint but legalistically correct in blocking Taft's attempt to take over power before the date fixed by act of the American Congress. When the proper time came and both military and legal requirements were met, MacArthur withdrew his objections. Thereafter—as has been recorded by a member of Taft's commission who was somewhat more fair-minded than Taft himself—when the civil governments "were finally established, it was with his (MacArthur's) approval and, in many instances, upon his specific recommendation."

Ordinarily, the feud between Taft and MacArthur might have terminated on July 4, 1901, when at ceremonies in the Manila Cathedral Plaza the soldier turned over all authority to the Civil Governor and departed from the Philippines. A few years later, General MacArthur went to Manchuria with his young soldier son, Lieutenant Douglas MacArthur, as an observer of the Russo-Japanese War and then made a tour of the Orient before returning to California as commander of the Pacific department of the Army. As America's senior general—he had been made a lieutenant general by Congress before it abolished that rank (later restored)—MacArthur was the logical choice to become first chief of staff of the U.S. Army under the reorganization plan installed by Elihu Root. But Taft was now Secretary of War with considerable influence in this selection, and he saw to it that MacArthur was passed over in favor of General J. F. Bell.

Not long afterward, MacArthur was relieved of his command and—so the original published statement said—"ordered to take station in Milwaukee and perform such duties as may be assigned him by the war department." There was considerable public protest against a seeming slight; it was felt that MacArthur was being treated in cavalier fashion and should have been sent to Washington with the staff, aides and clerks needed in his work of completing a long report on his inspection of the Orient. The New York *Sun* raged, "Now MacArthur, divested of every legitimate privilege of his rank and record, vanishes into the boscage of disfavor and neglect."

MacArthur had spoken freely his views of the Far East in the period before his retirement. He frequently quoted Seward: "The Pacific coast, its shores, and the vast region beyond will become the chief theatre of events in the world's great hereafter." Having recently studied Japan at first hand, he added a warning of his own, "It will be impossible for America to keep the sea unless we meet quickly the desperate attack which Japan is now organizing against us." He had a brief brush with Theodore Roosevelt over the question of German Americans serving in the National Guard, and was sharply rebuked by the President, who remarked that an officer making the statement attributed to MacArthur "is unfit to hold a commission in the National Guard." However, basically Roosevelt and MacArthur were firm friends as well as being closely similar in appearance, and Roosevelt befriended Douglas MacArthur and made him a White House aide during his first assignment in Washington.

In fact, it appears that the supposed controversy leading to Arthur MacArthur's retirement was a minor matter. The situation was that, the Army having recently been reorganized, there was no position except that of chief of staff suited for an officer of his rank and experience. Therefore it was at his own request that he was transferred to Milwaukee, under an agreement to serve as "special presidential adviser" to his old and good friend, Theodore Roosevelt.

After two years of semiretirement, MacArthur formally retired in 1909 at the age of 64 and left it to his sons Arthur, by now well advanced in the Navy, and to Douglas, a lieutenant in the Army, to emulate his own long career. That Douglas did so is history; Arthur was also nearing the top in the Navy, having served with distinction in the Spanish-American War and World War I, when he died suddenly in 1923 at the age of 47, shortly before he would have become an admiral. One of his sons, Douglas MacArthur II, is in the State Department Foreign Service and at this writing is diplomatic adviser to General Eisenhower at European headquarters; his wife is the daughter of Alben Barkley. Another son, Bowman, is a lawyer in government service in Washington.

DEATH OF A SOLDIER

The manner of Lt. Gen. Arthur MacArthur's death was such as to contribute to the MacArthur legend. It came at a dramatic highlight of his life, on September 5, 1912, at a reunion of his old Civil War regiment and exactly 50 years to the day after that regiment had marched off to battle. Such curious coincidences are quite common in the MacArthur history; important things happen with frequency on family or national anniversaries or certain days of the months. Douglas MacArthur, as already noted, was born 65 years to the day after his grandfather's birth. His birthday is the twenty-sixth of the month and that day has always been an important one for him: he was recalled to active Army duty in Manila on July 26 (1941); his meeting with F.D.R. which decided the fate of the Philippines was likewise July 26, as was the first discussion of ousting the Washington bonus marchers, another highlight of his career. His orders to leave besieged Corregidor, probably the most important turning point of his life, were written on Washington's birthday. Further evidence of the neat way in which "destiny" rounds out events for him—his landing at Leyte, the famous "return" to liberate the Philippines, was made exactly 40 years to the day after he first arrived on that same island as a young soldier, and exactly eight years after that he landed at the captured North Korean capital of Pyongyang. Similarly, when he made his first visit to his wife's home town, it was on their fourteenth wedding anniversary.

The father's death occurred during an address to the Twenty-fourth Wisconsin Volunteers in the University Building, Milwaukee. He had been ill, but the governor and another scheduled speaker were unable to attend, so MacArthur ignored his physician's advice to remain at home. Shortly before, he had made two remarks which indicated he was thinking about his age and health. "When I die," he told his wife, "bury me in civilian attire. I have worn military clothes nearly all my life—let me rest in peace as an American citizen." And, "My country has bestowed upon me every honor except that of dying at the head of my troops."

Now as he stood facing his 100 old soldiers—once again "at the head of his troops"—suddenly younger and more animated, he began, "This may be the last opportunity I shall ever be offered to pay homage to you, my comrades." He recalled that of 1,150 men who had marched away with the regiment, less than 400 had come home to Wisconsin. He started to recall in humorous vein an incident of the march through Georgia: "It was during the campaign at Peach Tree Creek. . . . Your indomitable courage——," the voice faltered, and MacArthur put his hand over his heart. "Comrades," he began again, "I am too weak to go on." He sank into a chair, his eyes closed, and he was dead. Spontaneously, the old soldiers knelt down and recited the Lord's Prayer. Captain Edwin B. Parsons, toastmaster of the reunion, took an American flag from the wall and spread it over the body and then he too collapsed from a paralytic stroke and had to be taken home in an ambulance.

General Charles King took the news to Mrs. MacArthur at her home on Marshall Street. Apparently by premonition, she was waiting in the doorway. "He died the death of a soldier, madam, in the midst of his comrades." The widow collapsed and remained unconscious throughout the night. When she was revived, she said, "I must notify my sons," and telegrams were sent to Lieutenant Arthur MacArthur, U.S.N., and Captain Douglas MacArthur. After the funeral, Douglas MacArthur returned to duty and did not again see his "home town" of Milwaukee until 39 years later.

Among the hundreds of messages of condolence received by the family of Arthur MacArthur was one from William Howard Taft, who still disliked MacArthur but was mindful of the amenities. The death of the elder MacArthur and subsequently of the elder Taft did not end the curiously eventful relationship between the two families. It was the elder Taft who, as Theodore Roosevelt's secretary of war, carried out a diplomatic deal whereby the United States disgracefully agreed to let Japan have a free hand in Korea, thereby dooming that country to 35 years of brutal Japanese rule, in return for Japan's promise to keep hands off the Philippines. This deal, as John Gunther pointed out, was reminiscent of the Yalta agreement whereby the United States handed over portions of China to Soviet Russia. One of its ultimate results was that Douglas MacArthur was fighting in Korea in 1950-51. More recently, at this writing, General Douglas MacArthur and Senator Robert Taft, sons of the principals in this half-century-old feud, are on close terms of personal and political relationship. Whatever his personal views of the enmity between the elder Taft and his father, it is certain that Douglas MacArthur is intimately acquainted with every phase of it and every word that has been written about it. Since the foregoing sentence was written, it has become known that Douglas MacArthur will not let old feuds affect his association with the current generation of the Taft family. Being asked to comment on the circumstances of his father's retirement to Milwaukee, MacArthur ignored the opportunity to lambast the elder Taft. Instead he merely remarked diplomatically that the "post of chief of staff was already filled by another man" at the time of his father's transfer.

As to Lieutenant General Arthur MacArthur, one brief note should be added. As long as he is written about by historians, it seems certain that he (as well as his son) will be characterized in the words of General Enoch Crowder: "Arthur MacArthur was the most flamboyantly egotistic man I had ever seen—until I met his son." This is one of those pat and easily quotable descriptions that is repeated again and again, regardless of its accuracy. In its reference to Douglas MacArthur it is at least open to question. As to Arthur MacArthur, it seems definitely misleading and untrue. So far as can be judged from the recollections of people who knew him intimately, he was essentially a quiet and modest man, soft-spoken, whose flamboyance was limited to his heroic deeds as a young soldier. Douglas MacArthur also is essentially quiet; he very rarely raises his voice, and the flamboyant quality of his prose may well be a compensation for his underlying shyness.

CHAPTER

4

Douglas MacArthur, Soldier

LIKE HIS FATHER BEFORE HIM, DOUGLAS MAC ARTHUR had to wait for a year before beginning his military career. Parental objections based on his youth kept Arthur MacArthur from enlisting until he was 17 years old; with Douglas it was an unsuspected physical ailment that delayed his entrance to West Point. There had never been any question in his mind about becoming a soldier. His elder brother Arthur had wanted to go to West Point also, but an appointment to Annapolis opened; and when he passed the entrance examinations, he decided to go on with his naval career, even after learning that he still could be admitted to West Point.

Douglas MacArthur was 18 when in 1898 his mother took him to Milwaukee to take the West Point examinations for which he had already prepared at West Texas Military Academy and with private tutors. Any inclinations he might have had toward enlisting for the war in Cuba or going to the Philippines with his father were quickly diverted by his mother, who convinced him that he should get his military education first and do his fighting afterward. He took the examinations in May and passed them with ease; his grade of 93⅓ far excelled the 77.9 of his nearest competitor.

Mary MacArthur was completely devoted to her son, who already was beginning to shape up like his father and—whether or not she was aware of it—like herself. Because his father was frequently away from home during these years, it was the mother who guided young Douglas; it was she who sought to inspire him and instill him with ambition, and to convince him that he would reach great heights—that he was destined to do so. Both parents insisted on impeccable manners; for instance, Douglas was taught to salute his seniors, but the atmosphere in the home was not so much one of parental domination as of inspiration.

Like his father, Douglas in his late teens was already fair, just, broad-minded, given to juvenile philosophizing, poised, and a ready talker on any subject. The mother, while somewhat shy in personal contacts, was very strong-willed. She hated hard and loved hard; and once her mind was made up unfavorably about someone, she refused to listen to any arguments aimed at making her modify her opinion. Personally, she was beautiful in her younger years and extremely handsome as an older woman; she was feminine and loved feminine things, and was meticulous in her dress.

Some of his mother's characteristics were obviously either inherited by MacArthur or drilled into him by example. Like his mother, he is very strong-minded about people; they are either for him, or against him. But, again like his mother, if time proves him wrong, he will eventually manage to convey the sense of an apology without, perhaps, actually speaking it. In this connection, it is sometimes difficult for him to admit forthrightly that he has been wrong, although there are well-known exceptions to this generalization. A classic case was his realization that he had been mistaken in not fully accepting Billy Mitchell's then visionary doctrine of air power. More recently, as this is written, he has been "willing to concede" that the court martial sentences against green Negro troops in the early days of the Korean war were "excessive."

He was a stickler for accuracy, but apparently that tendency was not resented by his friends. He was so anxious to emulate his father in habits, dress, modes of speech, and general character that he also copied the older man's courtesy and, so far as inherently possible, his modesty. Then, as later, he was sure of himself, but this was something more than simple vanity. Having heard his father discourse on nearly every subject under the sun and having read avidly himself, he took a wide interest in the current affairs of the world. His sense of justice was stirred by the Dreyfus trial; he argued about military strategy in the current Ethiopian wars and "talked about famous men as if they were his friends."

Fully cured of his slight spinal ailment the 19-year-old MacArthur reported to West Point in June of 1899. Jaunty in his Western clothes and light-colored fedora, he wrote his biography in the register: "Born: Little Rock, Arkansas, Little Rock Barracks, Pulaski Co. Schools: 3 yrs. Public School; 2 yrs. private school; 4 yrs. normal school; 2 yrs. private study; 3 months special preparation for admission to West Point."

MacArthur's classmates describe him in terms that make him sound obnoxiously certain of himself, even though they state that this was not the case. His brilliance, style, and commanding good looks automatically made him outstanding; and he was respected for his quick and retentive mental powers, and personally admired by his contemporaries. "Brave as a lion and smart as hell," is one description, "a mind like a sponge." It also became quickly apparent to his classmates that he set high moral standards for himself and judged everything on the basis of whether it was morally right or wrong; for him there were no shadings or compromise. Once his mind was made up, he could have been, as a classmate said, "flogged alive without changing it."

Apart from his obvious qualities of leadership, two things distinguished the tall, tanned, dark-haired Westerner. His father was a famous general on the scene of the exciting events around Manila, and his mother came to live near him at the old Craney's Hotel in West Point, adjacent to the Academy. For Mary MacArthur this was a perfectly natural move. Her husband was on duty in Manila; her elder son Arthur (graduated from Annapolis in 1896) was at sea with the Navy, and there was no family home—she and Douglas had lived in the Plankinton House in Milwaukee. Later, MacArthur's classmates were to joke that among his imposing record of "firsts," he had been the "first cadet whose mother went through the Academy with him." There was a tendency at first to regard him as a "mother's boy," especially when he spent all his spare time with his mother and treated her with obvious devotion and respect, to the extent that when an upperclassman invited the young plebe to room with him, MacArthur went first to his mother to ask her approval. Then, as during the later years when she lived with him, MacArthur made daily reports to his mother on the details of army life, treating her as a contemporary and confidante. Before long the cadets came to accept the close mother-son relationship as nothing unusual, and Mrs. MacArthur became a welcome addition to West Point's somewhat sparse social life.

Mary MacArthur did not go to West Point, as later legend maintains, for the specific purpose of spurring her son on in rivalry against Ulysses S. Grant III, whose mother also lived in Craney's Hotel for a time. MacArthur himself always regarded Fiske as a greater rival for leading honors than Grant, who never attracted any special attention in the Army and who years later was described on his efficiency report as, "Suave, polite, courteous, indifferent to his duties as an officer, utterly worthless."

As an army "brat," MacArthur took to the West Point regime with an easy naturalness and pursued with direct, unwavering purpose his self-set goal of surpassing his classmates. Militarily he became corporal in his second year, First Sergeant of Company A in his third, and First Captain of the Corps as a first classman—the top honor. Academically he led the class in his first and second years, was fourth in 1902, and again leader in 1903. Grant pressed him only in their first year, finally finishing sixth in the class, and scored only one triumph in his entire four years—when he was chosen, instead of MacArthur, as model for a statue sculptured for the Academy. MacArthur's final four-year average for 16 subjects was 98.14, the highest in the first 100 years of West Point history; more recent comparisons are invalid because the curriculum has been drastically revised, in large part by MacArthur himself. It is interesting to note that he had perfect records in English, history, and law; excelled in mathematics, sciences, and civil and military engineering; and scored his lowest mark of 90.4 in drawing. He got the jump on his competitors in his plebe year by rooming with an upperclassman (later Dr. A. S. Hyde, a New York clergyman), who was privileged to keep his lights on for two extra hours of study at night.

In his four years, MacArthur was cited 42 times on "skin sheets" for infractions of military rules involving such minor offenses as lateness at breakfast, formation, and retreat, long hair at inspection, "swinging arms excessively while marching to the front at parade," and "trifling with drawn sabre in area." When questioned by senators investigating his dismissal from command after 52 years of service, MacArthur was asked whether he had always obeyed military orders. "Sir," he replied sternly, "there has never been a more subordinate officer in the United States Army." This pattern was established at West Point; records show he was never insubordinate or "obnoxious" and thus escaped being "called out" by upperclassmen for the brutal, bare-knuckle fights then sanctioned but soon outlawed. He was apparently subjected only to disagreeable but noninjurious forms of physical hazing, being forced to stand at attention for an hour and once made to do knee bends until he fainted. Repeatedly he was required to recite long passages from a speech of his father's or the latter's extensive military record—something that could not have pleased him more. He was not involved in a cadet rebellion against a dictatorial superintendent, whose wrath he once escaped during an unauthorized visit to his mother by hiding in the basement of Craney's Hotel and crawling out through a coal chute.

Instruction was by textbook, and each cadet was called on nearly every day in every class for oral recitation. In his nightly studies, MacArthur concentrated absolutely from the time he opened his books until lights out, never stopping to gossip or chat with George Cocheu of Brooklyn, who roomed with him in their final two years. Cocheu never saw MacArthur write or receive a love letter and never heard him discuss girls, though later report had him engaged simultaneously as a cadet to eight different girls. MacArthur himself seems to take pleasure in this gallant if fictitious record, and has neither affirmed nor denied it in an often-quoted response: "I do not remember being so heavily engaged by the enemy." At the Academy he was not a "hop fiend," though an adequate dancer, and his last social engagement at West Point was a Sunday dinner attended by the lady who later became the wife of Ulysses Grant.

World affairs were not discussed in or out of class; and MacArthur, accustomed to his father's stimulating conversations, was critical of the narrowness of the curriculum, which in later years he revised. In his cadet days he was not known as a "professional religionist—always rushing to the YMCA"; he was devout and never sacrilegious but felt no need to discuss his beliefs.

While he played football and other sports in Texas, he was only fairly proficient as an athlete. But one of the achievements necessary to a well-rounded cadet career was to play on a varsity team; and after a systematic analysis of his abilities and weaknesses, he chose baseball. He played first base and the outfield against the Naval Academy for two years, scoring one run in each game. The records also show one base on balls, one stolen base, no hits, no errors—to really live up to legend he should have hit a homer in the ninth with three on base, two out, and a count of three-and-two. Having won his "A" twice (during the war in France he still wore his monogrammed sweater), he gave up baseball and in his final year managed the football team, which was also a socially desirable position and entailed trips away from the Academy.

MacArthur graduated in June, 1903, and prepared to live—or to die—in upholding the oath—Duty, Honor, Country—whose swearing had been "the fulfillment of all my boyish hopes and dreams." The hopes and dreams, as he said in his famous address to Congress 48 years later, had "long since vanished" by the time he was removed from command, his long and brilliant military career abruptly terminated. But throughout his career he has retained a strong attachment to his class and has frequently said, "Of all the groups with which I have been identified, this is the one I most cherish."

THE YOUNG SOLDIER

After his graduation from West Point, MacArthur was immediately assigned to the Philippines, perhaps in response to his tremendous eagerness to visit the scene of his father's campaigns. As leader of his class, he had almost automatically gone into the then elite corps—the engineers—and much of his work in the Philippines was making military surveys. One of these was of the Bataan peninsula where he was to fight many years later. He also built a wharf, sea wall, and roads, and in the central Philippines came under fire for the first time. His surveying party was ambushed, and the man beside him fell from a shotgun blast fired at short range in the jungle. As MacArthur leaned over to catch him, a second blast blew his old-style campaign hat from his head. It was a narrow escape, and a hard-bitten old sergeant is quoted as having said, "If the Lieutenant will pardon me, I would like to remark that the rest of the Lieutenant's life is on velvet." MacArthur said later that he was pale and shaky, but quickly steadied as he watched the veterans around him. In this and other skirmishes he came to know the fighting qualities of the Filipino soldiers, whom his father had started to organize into an army force, and whom he was to lead years later.

Mrs. MacArthur had not been able to accompany her son on this assignment, but she did go along as far as Tokyo on the next, which took both General MacArthur and Douglas, now first lieutenant, to Manchuria as observers of the Russo-Japanese War. During this period the whole family was in the Orient; Lieutenant (j.g.) Arthur MacArthur had married Miss Mary Hendry McCalla (daughter of a well-known admiral, Bowman McCalla) and was stationed in Manila where his father and brother visited him, his wife and small son, a new Arthur, Jr.

Douglas MacArthur arrived in Manchuria too late to observe the fighting at first hand, but he did get a chance to study the Japanese army which had astounded the world by meeting and beating the Russians. Here was a startling development in world politics, the emergence of an oriental military power that could stand against a European nation; of equal significance was the fact that the Eurasian nation—Russia—had rekindled its interests in the Pacific after allowing it to lay dormant for some time. The full significance and the final results of this Russian thrust have not yet become apparent as this is written in 1951, after a year of bloody conflict between American and Russian power.

After their trip to Manchuria in 1905, the MacArthurs were dispatched on a confidential mission to Siam, Java, Malaya, Ceylon, and India and their impressions of affairs in Asia were incorporated in a long report written by General MacArthur with the collaboration of his son. General MacArthur was convinced that "the solution of problems in connection with the Pacific is perhaps to be the great work of the twentieth century." His son shared this conviction. It was on this trip, principally, that Douglas MacArthur formed the opinion that has been the guiding tenet of his view of world politics; he came to believe what he still believes: that the fate of the world for the next century or two revolves primarily around the need for raising the living standards of the great masses of Asia.

When Douglas MacArthur returned in 1906 from his trip to the East, he was assigned to Washington and in addition to other duties served as White House military aide to Teddy Roosevelt. Thereafter he attended and instructed at various schools, and in 1914 was assigned to the American forces sent to Vera Cruz. There he scouted behind the Mexican lines and with the help of Franz von Papen, then a young German diplomatic agent and later a notorious (but skillful) spy and diplomat in two wars, found and brought back to Vera Cruz three Mexican locomotives, which were needed because American locomotives were of the wrong gauge for Mexican tracks. When World War I started and America joined in 1917, MacArthur was a major on the War Department staff in Washington, in charge of censorship and public relations.

MAC ARTHUR IN WORLD WAR I

The legendary story of how the Rainbow Division of World War I was formed is probably true. It seems typical of MacArthur—of his legalistic ability to conform to the letter of orders while circumventing their spirit, of his insistence on following a course he believed right and nearly everyone else believed wrong, and of his flair.

Despite his junior rank as major, MacArthur vigorously and almost alone advocated a proposal to send National Guard units to France; most officers thought only the Regular Army could be trusted to face the Kaiser's veteran divisions. The debate became so warm that MacArthur's superiors lost their patience. One threatened him, "I can see, Major, that you are not interested in pursuing your military career much further," and he was ordered to refrain from any further discussion with his *immediate* superiors.

Though thus enjoined from following up the idea with ranking members of the general staff, MacArthur considered himself free—considered it his duty regardless of his own career—to carry the issue to Secretary of War Newton D. Baker, who took him to President Wilson. The president was won over by MacArthur's brilliant and vigorous arguments, which he based in large measure on the excellent record of National Guard units fighting under his own father in the Philippine insurrection. MacArthur pressed his advantage to urge creation of an elite division formed of crack units from as many states as possible, and declared enthusiastically, "It will spread over the whole country like a rainbow." Thus the Rainbow (42nd) Division was named, with General William A. Mann as its first commander, and MacArthur—promoted from major of engineers to lieutenant colonel and then colonel, National Army—as its chief of staff.

National Guard units from 26 states and the District of Columbia were selected (MacArthur saw that they included Iowa's 168th Infantry, formerly his father's 51st Iowa Volunteers) and ordered to report to Camp Albert Mills, hastily constructed at Garden City, Long Island; the first arrivals found only a railroad station and open fields. The division's first battle was strictly intramural, between New York's predominantly Irish 165th Infantry (formerly the 69th) and the 167th from Alabama; it was Catholic against Protestant, North against South, and city against country. The New Yorkers initiated the Alabamans by parading through their tent area to the tune of "Marching through Georgia." Peace was finally restored hours later, with considerable damage and a number of injuries. MacArthur reprimanded both regiments sharply, but there were no courts-martial; and he was heard to say, "Looks as if these boys will make darn good fighters when we get to the real enemy in France."

From the beginning, MacArthur was recognized as the dominant personality in the division. He hand-picked every member of his staff, choosing National Guard officers (many with legal experience) over Regular Army, and his selections were so excellent that Pershing later "raided" the Rainbow to obtain staff officers for his own GHQ. When there were vacancies in the division, MacArthur filled them from the National Guard, feeling that citizen-soldiers preferred citizen-officers to Regular Army, and being himself convinced that the enthusiasm and freshness of a National Guard officer was at times more valuable than the supposed experience of regular officers who had been "stagnating" for years while noncoms ran their outfits.

MacArthur took complete charge of organizing, evaluating, and training the division. General Mann was elderly and soon retired; and his successor, General Menoher, was an artillery expert who almost always deferred to his chief of staff's opinions. From Menoher, MacArthur learned the use of artillery; until then this was the greatest weakness in his military knowledge.

There was a race between the 26th and 42nd Divisions for the honor of being first in France, but the 42nd lost due to MacArthur's insistence that it be completely equipped down to the last pair of socks. There was a shortage of everything but MacArthur "was a real promoter—he could get short material like a Merlin." He frequently worked more than 24 hours without sleep, tightening up every detail of organization. When the division disembarked in France, it went into immediate intensive training throughout the bitterly cold winter, and in March of 1918 it was sent into the trenches for its baptism of fire.

MacArthur was already well known to the men of his division, for he deliberately followed the example of other commanders in adopting distinctive mannerisms and modes of dress. Recent commanders who have thus attracted attention to themselves were Montgomery with his beret, Patton with his pair of pearl-handled pistols and shiny helmet, Rommel with his famous slouch cap, and Ridgway with his grenade. In France, MacArthur achieved the unusual by taking the stiffening wire out of his garrison cap, which he wore at "just the tilt which permitted his personality to emerge, without violating Army regulations." He seldom carried any weapon except a riding crop, and wore high turtle-neck sweaters with a windbreaker, or a flowing muffler under a loose field jacket. Far from being unattractive, the total effect was one of elegance. Even when he tore his breeches on barbed wire, it was recorded, "The tear seemed either slyly or luckily contrived to expose one thigh and half a rump, rather than the whole of man's most ridiculous aspect." Incidentally, the mufflers MacArthur has worn all his life in raw weather are not so much an affectation as a necessity. He is very susceptible to quinsy sore throat.

Thus attired in this unorthodox but—for him—highly appropriate manner, conducting himself in a perfectly calm and easy way without showing pain or excitement even when a shell blew him off his feet or hot metal tore into his flesh; acting, in short, as if he had a personal guarantee of immortality from the recording angel, MacArthur set about making war on Germany.

The Rainbow went first into the line in the quiet Bacarrat sector, split into small groups attached to French units manning the trenches. To the horror of the French veterans who had been accustomed to washing their clothes in shell holes at certain hours and according the Germans the same privileges without a shot being exchanged, the green doughboys started firing at anything that moved and excited the whole sector. The first American raid was planned, and the apprehensive volunteers were amazed to see the divisional chief of staff climb out of the trenches and into No Man's Land with them. "I'm going on the picnic, too," MacArthur announced. For this feat the French gave him his first decoration, the Croix de Guerre, and the American Army the Distinguished Service Cross.

One French officer seeing him in action exclaimed, "My God, what a man!" Another said, "MacArthur prepares to attack with a smile, and smiling assaults the enemy." It must have taken a great deal of courage just to smile, because for much of the time he was in France MacArthur was ill with an infected throat which drained his strength; he was in intense pain and extremely thin. Nevertheless, despite illness and wounds, he kept going, was promoted to full colonel and finally brigadier general and "actually commanded," an official report said, "larger bodies of troops on the battle line than any other officer in our Army, with, in each instance, conspicuous success." Much of that success was due to his compliance with the three principles vital to an officer: know your troops, know your enemy, know the terrain. He gathered his experience at first hand, under fire in the trenches, in No Man's Land, and in attacks on German positions. Before an operation he always insisted on complete reconnaissance of a position and accurate and detailed information; frequently he went out to meet incoming reconnaissance patrols, and he himself did some scouting. War correspondents soon discovered him as "The d'Artagnan of the A.E.F." or "The Beau Brummel of the A.E.F."

MacArthur's coolness under fire became legendary; he seemed to regard death—if he thought of it at all—as "an experience as uneventful as taking a ride on the Fifth Avenue bus." Once a shell hit a farmhouse in which the staff were eating, and a new young officer dashed outside to a trench while even the veterans began looking for cover. MacArthur kept his place. "All Germany," he said placidly, "cannot fabricate the shell that will kill MacArthur. Sit down again, gentlemen, with me." (This, of course, is MacArthur's elegant paraphrase of the GI's: "They haven't got my number yet." During the heaviest Japanese raid on Corregidor, MacArthur was urged to hurry to a near-by shelter. Instead he said, "The Jap is not yet born who can make me hurry," and remained exposed during the entire raid.)

On one spur-of-the-moment inspection trip to the front trenches in the spring of 1918, MacArthur was caught in a mustard gas attack. The members of his party and doughboys quickly put on their masks, but MacArthur never carried a mask nor a weapon—he believed that it gave the soldiers courage to see him going about unarmed. He was almost totally blinded and for 10 days worked with a blindfold around his head, refusing to go to the hospital. Doctors feared he would lose his sight; but when the bandages were removed, it was completely restored. Even after that experience, he did not carry a mask. There was nothing heroic in MacArthur's being gassed. Indeed, it seems stupid for him to have refused to carry a gas mask, even though his avowed purpose was to inspire his troops by his courageous contempt of enemy weapons. Yet a soldier caught without a mask was disciplined, and if gassed, was not regarded as a hero, but as either unfortunate or careless.

The motto of the division, created by MacArthur, was "no alibis" and he made everyone, including himself, live up to it. The story is told of one sergeant saying—after hanging up a field phone in a front line dugout and acknowledging one of MacArthur's orders—"That son of a bitch Chief of Staff expects us all to be twelve-foot men."

Jake Lichter, who saw MacArthur first in Mexico and worked closely with him for 18 months as division supply clerk and officer, was asked about him 30 years later, at the time of his old chief's dismissal from command. "People," remarked Jake, "say he's a conceited damn fool who thinks he's God. I tell them I can't say anything except how he was with the Rainbow. With us he was a soldier's soldier. He talked beautiful then just like he did later, but there was no ego to him. He was natural and friendly, though he insisted on the attitude of a soldier from all of us. His first thought was always for the soldier, looking out for supplies, trying to check frozen feet and trench foot by getting them shoes and socks, getting hot food to them in the line and taking care of everything. When I got my commission, he personally came and invited me into the officers' mess; and you can imagine what that meant to me after eating with the fellows for so many months. I was near him a year and a half, and he never did anything wrong as a soldier."

It is difficult for later generations, accustomed to the supersonic speed of jet planes, to tanks, and swift, mechanized warfare to recapture the bitter flavor of that war in France. It was a war of trenches and dugouts, of mud, rain, and blizzards, gas attacks, bayonet and grenade fighting through artillery fire and against the deadly machine guns which had revolutionized warfare, driven the armies into holes like animals, and limited advances usually to hundreds of feet or yards of barren, shell-pocked, chewed-up ground won and lost and won again at the cost of much blood and heroism.

After its first engagements, the Rainbow went on to new and bigger battles, stopping the Prussian Guards in the Champagne-Marne defensive, then joining in the general Allied attacks of the Aisne-Marne campaign. "They crossed the Ourcq," General Peyton C. March reported lyrically, "in the face of the deadly machine-gun fire of the Germans. They had engaged and used up six enemy divisions.

"They had defeated and decimated the Kaiser's crack Prussian Guards, probably the finest troops the enemy has in his army. They had likewise defeated units of the Bavarian troops, which are among the best of the German Army. They had advanced irresistibly against the best the enemy could hurl against them, and at the end of the eight days the enemy had been forced to fall back . . . 10 miles."

MacArthur was in the division through all the fighting, winning so many decorations for gallantry that the citations alone would fill a booklet. Twice wounded and twice gassed, he refused to be sent to the hospital. He never took leave, never seemed tired, never forgot to write home to his mother, never got drunk on cognac (occasionally, when the water was bad, he drank wine), and never sang the bawdy A.E.F. songs. He never swore (though he did in later years), but once he lost his temper.

That was when by some error British uniforms were sent up for his men. They were packaged, and the supply sergeant unwittingly passed them out to a regiment—by chance to men of New York's Irish 69th

(165th) who shortly before had threatened to attack the British with bayonets if ever assigned to fight with them. MacArthur, not stooping to profanity, vigorously condemned everything from the King of England to General Pershing and immediately had the uniforms collected and shipped back, except for woolen socks which the men kept.

MacArthur had already tangled with Pershing over a proposal to split the Rainbow into a replacement division; and when the A.E.F. commander criticized him severely on another matter, MacArthur replied, "All that you say, General Pershing, is quite correct, except that the fault lies not in this Division. Rather, sir, it lies in orders as carried out by your staff." He went on, taking advantage of the opening given him by the mistake about the uniforms, protesting bitterly that in addition to being given British uniforms "even their very undergarments, such as sweaters knitted for the men by their mothers, wives, sweethearts, have been turned in for salvage along with the morale of these men."

"Young man," Pershing is quoted as replying, "I do not like your attitude." A dislike, as will be noted later, which continued throughout Pershing's life despite his admiration for the soldierly qualities of MacArthur, whom he personally decorated with the DSC and the DSM.

Being MacArthur, there were strong expressions of opinion when he thought something right or wrong. He refused flatly to accept a colonelcy in the infantry, instead of his own corps, the engineers. (Fifteen years later he had reversed this attitude; and when offered the post of chief of the engineers, replied shortly, "I'm a soldier, not an engineer.") He refused to wear a steel helmet, while insisting on them for his troops, and said, "I am setting a good example. I want my men to know that they come first." He refused promotion to command of the 1st Division, arguing that the 42nd Division had actually won the honor offered him and that as a reward General Menoher, the Rainbow commander, be given a corps. This was done, and for a brief time right after the Armistice, MacArthur commanded the 42nd. He disagreed with General Summerall, who wanted him to attack the Cote de Chatillon, one of the key hills in the Hindenburg line, by a frontal assault and after an artillery barrage; MacArthur, on advice from regimental commanders of the 84th Brigade which he commanded in the last part of the war, argued that the assault must be made by a surprise night bayonet attack, because of very strong flanking fire as well as direct fire from the heavily fortified hill.

Summerall, the I Corps commander, telephoned MacArthur's headquarters and ordered him to take the position by six o'clock the following evening. Apparently Summerall needed further reassurances that the attack would be made, for he visited MacArthur's headquarters that evening and repeated his orders. MacArthur replied, "General Summerall, this brigade assures you that it will capture Cote de Chatillon. If this brigade does not capture Chatillon, you can publish a casualty list of the entire brigade with the brigade commander's name at the top."

MacArthur ordered the bayonet attack and then called it off after discovering from an aerial reconnaissance map (which he had ordered to be made) that there was a gap at one point in the German barbed wire. He went over to discuss new plans with Colonel Walter E. Bare, 167th regimental commander, who later recalled, "Late that night . . . while we were talking, the Germans were constantly shelling the valley with gas shells, mostly mustard and tear gas. I remember well that both the General and I consumed so much of the gas that neither of us could hardly see or talk on account of the effect of the fumes." In the morning a force of 100 men slipped through the barbed wire while machine-gun and rifle fire pinned down the Germans. Taken from the flank by surprise, the Germans were driven from the position, a counterattack was beaten off, and the hill was taken in what Pershing called "an aggressive action against the most obstinate defense."

This action cracked the innermost defenses of the Kriemhilde Stellung, the last strong position in the Hindenburg line, and in the early days of November the Rainbow rolled on in a final attack until resistance lessened and the advance became almost a foot race between the American divisions, pressing wearily forward night and day in weather too cold for sleeping. At this time, due to a mix-up in orders relayed by Colonel George C. Marshall, practically the whole American First Army front became involved in fantastic confusion, and MacArthur himself was "captured" by a patrol of the American 1st Division.* A few days later, the war ended for MacArthur and the Rainbow Division on the heights overlooking Sedan, where they were ordered to stop just before the Armistice on November 11th to permit the French to occupy the historic city where Napoleon III had surrendered to Von Moltke in 1870.

After briefly commanding the division, MacArthur was replaced by General Flagler, whose demand for post-Armistice spit and polish was extremely annoying to the veterans of the Rainbow.

Following six months' occupation duty in the beautiful Rhine country near Remagen—later to become famous in American history as the scene of the first bridgehead captured in World War II—the Rainbow Division headed homeward. Its dead numbered 2,713 with 13,282 wounded. Most remarkable of all, of the 40,000 men who served at one time or another in the Rainbow, only 41 were listed as lost by having been taken prisoner. This is not only a testimonial to amazingly high morale and courage, but to the way the division fought. If a company or a battalion were cut off by the enemy, the nearest troops went immediately to their relief; MacArthur himself personally led a relief force that rescued a cutoff company from his father's old Iowa regiment. There were no "lost battalions" in the Rainbow; superior leadership and superb coordination prevented that.

In the spring of 1919, MacArthur, elegant in his raccoon coat and the

* This historic mess is described in detail in the first chapter of Part IV of this book, which deals with the Marshall-MacArthur feud. The confusion was so great that it requires some 50 pages to describe in the official history of the Rainbow, *Americans All*, by Brigadier General Henry J. Reilly (Columbus, Ohio, F. J. Heer, 1936).

flowing muffler that concealed a chest full of medals, sailed home from France. There was nothing in his face to show the terrible stresses, both mental and physical, that he had been under. He still had no romantic ties; his affections were reserved for his mother and others of his family.

He had left home as one of the Army's most brilliant and promising young officers. The promise had been fulfilled. He had shown himself not only a fighting man of great courage but a master of his profession. He had already received his next assignment, Superintendent of West Point, and his future was assured. He had proven the correctness of his contention that American citizen-soldiers could more than hold their own in battle. He had also offered his life not once but repeatedly for his country, and had proven himself fit to live by fulfilling his own dictum: "Only those are fit to live who are not afraid to die." Perhaps most important to him, he had done everything his idolized father could have asked of him.

MacArthur spent three years at West Point, winning a bitter fight against an economy-minded congress which sought first to abolish the Academy and then to reduce its term to two years. He also fought the entrenched and reactionary Academic Board (Faculty) and succeeded in liberalizing and modernizing the curriculum. He sponsored a broad sports program and when it came to the Honor System he was adamant in its enforcement; he flatly refused to reconsider the dismissal of a cadet who violated this honor code. During these years he also established a working schedule—starting at 11 A.M., with time out for an afternoon siesta. This left him ample time to watch daily athletic practice and to pursue his studies of history, literature, and military science. It also left him time to fall in love and marry, as will be recounted in a subsequent chapter.

II

Personal and Professional
1919-1951

CHAPTER

5

The Billy Mitchell Feud

ON COMPLETION OF HIS DUTY AT WEST POINT, MAC ARTHUR served two years in Manila, returned to command the III Corps Area in Baltimore, and in 1925 was chosen as a member of the court-martial that convicted Brigadier General William B. Mitchell of insubordination in one of the Army's most historic and sensational trials. Charges had been brought against Mitchell for continuing his heated crusade for the development of air power after his superiors had ordered him to remain silent.

As young men, Billy Mitchell and Douglas MacArthur were members of the same fashionable set in Milwaukee in which the MacArthurs were prominent although they had no family wealth; Douglas MacArthur inherited no money from either his father or mother and has never been particularly interested in acquiring it. In their teens, Mitchell, four years older, was something of an idol of the younger man. This friendship continued throughout Mitchell's life, despite the strain put upon it by the circumstances of the court-martial and by their strenuous disagreement over questions of military strategy and tactics.

Their disagreements were, in the final analysis, a matter of timing. In his concept of the uses of air power, Mitchell was some years ahead of MacArthur, as the latter readily admitted in later years, after having fought long and vigorously against proposals for creation of a separate Air Force. With startling accuracy, Mitchell pictured two decades beforehand the war that MacArthur fought in the Pacific from late 1942 until early 1945: "Any offensive to be pushed against Japan will have to be made under the cover of our own air power. . . . In the future, campaigns across the sea will be carried on from land base to land base under the protection of aircraft." MacArthur affirmed the correctness of these predictions after his return to the Philippines. "I couldn't have come here without the air," he said repeatedly. "The air brought me here."

Mitchell's courts-martial, deliberately provoked by him to bring his views before the public, attracted nationwide excitement similar to the controversy stirred up later by MacArthur's dismissal. Much public thought was in favor of Mitchell, and far ahead of the battleship-minded admirals and of generals who growled like Pershing, "No airplane has ever affected the course of a battle." Mitchell time after time challenged the admirals and generals, repeatedly defying orders to discontinue his public attacks, and his utterances became so open, critical, and frequent—and to much of the public, so sound and reasonable—that the Army responded by ordering a court-martial.

As he entered the courtroom in Washington, Mitchell had an especially warm "hello" and handshake for the impeccably uniformed MacArthur. Mitchell, combining a study of air power with a honeymoon with his second wife, had recently visited MacArthur and his own bride in Manila. This visit had cemented long-standing ties which had been further strengthened not long after the end of World War I when MacArthur invited Mitchell to speak at West Point.

In preparation for the trial, Mitchell and his attorney carefully scanned the list of prospective judges and privately expressed their satisfaction at the presence on the panel of MacArthur and of General Frank McCoy, both of them known as foresighted and liberal officers. But the defense challenged General Summerall (whose reputation was won as an artillery officer in France), as it did others reputed to be intolerant and strict disciplinarians.

At the court-martial MacArthur set one record: he remained silent for seven consecutive weeks while Mitchell, under the adroit legal guidance of his counsel, Representative Reid of Pennsylvania, turned the trial away from the question of his own insubordination into a presentation of the case for air power. For all his deserved fame as a great talker, MacArthur is likewise a good listener; and he listened attentively to a parade of witnesses—Spaatz, Arnold, and others later to become famous names—who defended and amplified Mitchell's views. MacArthur was greatly impressed by their statements, though not thoroughly convinced that air power could yet do all the things they claimed for it.

Except for his debonair appearance, the fact that his wife attended all the court sessions, and his unaccustomed silence, attention was centered on MacArthur only once during the long trial. Representative Fiorello LaGuardia, asked to confirm his statement that Mitchell was not being tried by a jury of his peers but by officers already decided on his guilt, replied smilingly, "I did not know that General Douglas MacArthur was on the court when I made that statement."

It was a dramatic moment when the ballots of the judges were handed in, the verdict of "guilty" announced, and eventually a punishment decided upon of suspension of Mitchell from rank, command, and duty for five years. MacArthur, his face tense and drawn, seemed to take the result harder than Mitchell did, and the latter remarked to his secretary, "MacArthur looks as if he had been drawn through a knothole."

Soon rumors began to circulate that MacArthur had not only successfully opposed a longer sentence but had in fact voted "not guilty." It was subsequently learned that a search had been made of the courtroom wastebasket, and that a comparison of handwriting showed that MacArthur had cast that lone ballot of "not guilty." In accordance with protocol, MacArthur himself did not discuss the case when a friend telephoned that night to congratulate him on the finding. "So you think it was a good verdict," he commented noncommittally. More than 20 years later, however, MacArthur wrote Senator Wiley in Washington, confirming his vote of innocence and adding, "It was fully known to (Mitchell) and he never ceased to express his gratitude for my attitude. . . . I was one of Billy Mitchell's most intimate and devoted friends from the beginning to the end. Our families came from the same place, Milwaukee, and enjoyed the most cordial intimacy for many decades."

This revelation (which both Mitchell and MacArthur tried to keep quiet at the time) did not become generally known until the time of MacArthur's dismissal. Its result was to destroy many carefully constructed theories which had sought over the years to prove that MacArthur, "having convicted Billy Mitchell," was a backward and reactionary officer. With that contention destroyed, anti-MacArthur writers have eagerly sought some other way to damage MacArthur's reputation in connection with the trial, but the best they have been able to do so far is to repeat Billy Mitchell's description of MacArthur sitting in the court with "his features as cold as carved stone."

When MacArthur was made Army Chief of Staff in 1930, Mitchell wrote his congratulations and MacArthur replied, "When I become stabilized in my new office I shall be delighted to foregather with you all and do a little shooting, if such things really exist any more. I am afraid you will have to tie the ducks down and mark them with my name, but I will certainly enjoy it." Obviously, the two men were on terms of intimate friendship.

It is true that in his last years Mitchell did become embittered about his trial. But, as his sisters and other intimates have assured the writer, he repeatedly expressed his gratitude for MacArthur's friendship and his vote. "Douglas MacArthur," he said on many occasions, "is the best military man we had in the war in France and is the greatest strategist in the U.S. Army."

However, the fact that MacArthur voted for Mitchell's acquittal cannot possibly be cited as evidence that he was as far-sighted as his friend with regard to the future of air power. But once he did become convinced of its effectiveness—and his conviction dates from about the time of the German blitzkrieg—not even Mitchell himself could have been a more enthusiastic user and supporter of air power.

At the trial itself the issue to be voted on was not air power but insubordination, and MacArthur's vote is ample affirmation of his contention that he has always upheld the right of officers to express their opinions freely and publicly, even if opposed by their superiors. Or, as he himself put it during hearings after his own dismissal, "I do not believe . . . that any segment of American society [meaning the military] shall be so gagged that the truth and the full truth shall not be brought out. I believe it is in the public interest that diverse opinions on any controversial issue shall be fully aired. . . . Otherwise you do not get what is the foundation of the very liberty that we breathe, that the people are entitled to have the facts, that the judgment of the Government itself is subject to their opinion and to their control. . . ."

THE MITCHELLS AND THE MAC ARTHURS

The somewhat similar termination of the careers of the two men gives interest to a brief report on their family relationship which has existed for a century. One phase of it, in fact, is still a point of considerable controversy today.

The grandfathers of Billy Mitchell (Alexander) and of Douglas MacArthur (Arthur) were bosom friends in Milwaukee 100 years ago. When the Civil War came, their sons hurried away with their regiments. In the 1890's Billy and Douglas were frequent companions; they played the usual boyhood pranks, climbed and jumped off roofs and got into the customary scrapes. Douglas was especially fond of Mrs. Mitchell because she frequently intervened to save him from disciplinary action at the hands of his own mother. When the Spanish-American War started, Billy, a young lieutenant, served on General Arthur MacArthur's staff in the Philippines.

Douglas MacArthur lived only a year and some months in Milwaukee; but he always considered it home, "as it was my father's home, and his father's before him, and it was from its public schools that I left for West Point to pursue a military career." He was nominated for the presidency from Wisconsin in 1948 and he frequently spoke in later years of retiring to Milwaukee. There were plans sponsored by the Alonzo Cudworth Post of the American Legion to purchase his old home on Marshall Street (named for a distant relative of MacArthur's prime antagonist, George Marshall), restore it, and present it to him as a gift. These plans were at least temporarily shelved as a result of some poor staff planning when MacArthur finally did visit Milwaukee—for the first time since 1912—after his dismissal in 1951. Members of the post were lined up at a point along the parade route, and MacArthur was expected to stop, greet them, and receive some gifts. However, he knew nothing of the arrangements. His car continued past without pausing (it was even asserted that he signaled the driver to go on, although this is incredible), and afterward a disgusted officer of the post was quoted as saying, "We wouldn't buy him a nickle cigar—let alone a house."

The latest MacArthur-Mitchell reunion occurred during this visit when Janet Mitchell Mackie (Billy's sister) went to see him at the Plankinton

House where he had lived with his mother more than 50 years before while preparing for West Point. Nearly 40 years had elapsed since their last meeting; and Mrs. Mackie commented, "I don't know whether to call you Douglas, or General." "It's Douglas," the General ordered. "If you ever call me 'general,' I'll throw you right out that door."

Their conversation turned to earlier days when, after his graduation from West Point and first foreign duty in the Philippines and Manchuria, MacArthur often visited his parents in Milwaukee. Echoes of those days are still heard. On one such visit, the handsome (but somewhat shy, the girls complained) young lieutenant wrote his only publicized bit of romantic poetry on the back of a place card:

"Fair Western girl with life awhirl
Of love and fancy free,
'Tis thee I love
All things above
Why wilt thou not love me?"

Isaac Don Levine says in his biography of Billy Mitchell that this poem was addressed to sister Janet. Janet—now Mrs. Mitchell Mackie—agrees that it was written to her. But her sister Harriet—now Mrs. Martin Fladoes—says it was written to *her*. The respective friends of the two now elderly ladies are divided into two camps on the subject. In Harriet's copy of the Levine book and those of her friends, the name "Janet" is crossed out and "Harriet" written in.

MacArthur's popularity as a young man made him a controversial figure in Milwaukee society. The girls liked him, and the men regarded him as a dangerous rival. Mrs. George B. Miller, then Inez Fuller and a next-door neighbor of the MacArthur family, recalled recently, "The men in Milwaukee were always glad that Douglas was in the Army and away from home most of the time . . . they never said the same things about him that the girls did. All the girls thought he was so handsome and such a dashing young man." She recalled that her late husband, then courting her, was highly annoyed when MacArthur came home for his visits. "Inez," he once said jealously, "don't tell me that you, too, are swept away by those brass buttons of Douglas MacArthur's."

In one historic matter MacArthur is still remembered affectionately by the grandfathers and great-grandfathers who were youthful gallants in those days. He attended a meeting of the Loyal Legion—sons and grandsons of Union officers—of which his father was president. At the time cigarette smoking was banned at the meetings. Not aware of this, Douglas lit a cigarette and soon everyone was smoking—the ancient taboo was destroyed. It is interesting to note that, perhaps as an aftermath of this incident, one of MacArthur's first actions as superintendent of West Point in later years was to abolish an ancient ban on cigarette smoking.

CHAPTER

6

MacArthur's First Marriage

MAC ARTHUR WAS 42 YEARS OLD AND SUPERINTENDENT at West Point when, so far as official records go, he fell in love for the first time. In doing so he violated one of the rules usually observed by men eager to get ahead in their business or profession: don't get involved with the boss's lady friends. Mrs. Henrietta Louise Cromwell Brooks, Jr., a 26-year-old socialite and heiress presumptive who had obtained a recent Paris divorce, was understood to be unofficially engaged to General John J. Pershing at the time MacArthur—the Army's youngest brigadier—met and fell in love with her. It was love at first sight; the General proposed the first night of their acquaintance at a West Point ball in 1920, and Mrs. Brooks said afterward that if he hadn't spoken, she would have.

Mrs. Brooks, the daughter of Mrs. Oliver Cromwell (later Stotesbury), was fully as eligible matrimonially as the handsome General. Her father had left the family a handsome legacy, and her banker stepfather was said to have a fortune of $150,000,000. There had also been a substantial financial settlement from Walter D. Brooks, Jr., a prominent and well-liked Baltimore society man whom she divorced in France after six years of marriage and two children. In Paris she and her brother, Jimmy Cromwell (later the first husband of tobacco heiress Doris Duke), were frequent guests at the mansion which the Ogden Reids had loaned to General "Black Jack" Pershing and where the A.E.F. commander entertained the great and near-great of postwar diplomatic, military, and social circles. When Pershing returned to Washington, Mrs. Brooks returned also and became his official hostess. Despite the difference in their ages (Pershing was 30-odd years older), they were rumored to be contemplating early marriage. One of Pershing's colonels was also courting the wealthy and lively divorcée. Then MacArthur came along.

The future Mrs. MacArthur confided her news to General of the Armies Pershing at a dinner party one night. Other guests reported this colloquy:

"Jack, I am going to marry Douglas."

Pershing—after a surprised pause: "Young lady, you better look out or you will find yourself in the Philippines." Which, very shortly, she did.

The wedding was high-society with all the trimmings. MacArthur had requested on January 14th and been granted a two-months' leave of absence to go to Europe, but instead he went to Palm Beach to "El Mirasol," the villa owned by the bride's mother. From there he wrote to Walter B. Wolf of Chicago, his former operations officer in France, regretting that Wolf had been unable to accept his request to serve as best man, ". . . you have been at my right hand so often when Tragedy ruled, that I have a sense of loss that you will not be by my side when Fortune deals more gently with me. . . ." MacArthur and his wife had their first quarrel the day of the wedding—St. Valentine's Day, 1922—when he came to the villa at four o'clock and found her still gaily decorating a room with the ceremony only a half hour away. Peace was restored and the wedding procession marched through a pathway outlined with red, white, and blue ribbons to an altar decked with palms and flowers and the flags of the Rainbow Division and West Point. The bride wore a diamond necklace given her by the groom, an apricot chiffon gown, and carried a white prayer book. MacArthur wore his dress uniform and all the decorations he had won for courage and professional skill. Chaplain Wheat of the Army officiated. At a reception for 200 people, Mayor Cooper C. Lightbow presented the groom with a large (10-inch) silver key to the city of Palm Beach.

They honeymooned in Florida and then took up residence in the superintendent's quarters at West Point where MacArthur presented the cadets to his bride in groups of 50, and gave his favorites among the future officers a piece of wedding cake. Three months after the wedding MacArthur completed his tour at West Point and his orders for reassignment came through, and as predicted they were for the Philippines. Gossip became so widespread as to the reasons for this transfer that Pershing was finally forced to take note of rumors that he had "exiled" his younger and successful rival. "That," growled the Army's top general, "is a lot of damned poppycock." Nevertheless, the bride and many of her friends preferred to believe that the story of romantic revenge was true. "Jack wanted me to marry him," the new Mrs. MacArthur said. "When I wouldn't, he wanted me to marry one of his colonels. I wouldn't do that—so here I am packing my trunks."

MacArthur and his wife were very much in love, and the new groom was devoted to his stepchildren; but before long the first strains in the marriage became apparent. Mrs. MacArthur wrote home that Manila life was "dull" compared to the Scott Fitzgerald whirl she had enjoyed in Paris; to pass the slow hours she became a part-time Manila policewoman. MacArthur would not dance; he preferred studying professional subjects to partying, and he seems to have refused to compromise between his wife's desire for gay activity and his own unswerving devotion to his career.

MacArthur's wife was as ambitious as he himself to help him further that career. In this regard, she was almost as helpful as his mother, of whom MacArthur is accustomed to say, "She made my father a lieutenant general, and she made me a four-star general." Perhaps MacArthur himself has never heard the story of how his first wife had a great deal to do with the timing of the acquisition of the second of those stars.

The second star—the Army's highest rank of major general—still seemed some years ahead when he and Mrs. MacArthur returned on leave to visit his mother who was ill in the Wardman Park Hotel in Washington. MacArthur's old Chief Army Clerk, Manning Marcus of the Rainbow Division, came to visit them; MacArthur introduced him fondly to his wife and then went into his mother's sick room. Mrs. MacArthur seized this opportunity. "Mr. Marcus," she said, "Douglas has always spoken highly of you and his friends in the Rainbow Division. I know you are a lawyer here in Washington and that the Division Veterans' Association is powerful politically. I wish you would get busy and get his promotion—he's been a brigadier general for six years now. And he foolishly insists we live on his army pay." *

She mentioned that she had considerable money of her own from the divorce settlement, and went on, "I don't care what it costs. Just go ahead and send the bill to me personally. Don't tell Douglas."

Marcus, then and now a Washington lawyer, was not interested in the money; but he agreed to undertake the mission. With two Rainbow colonels (Ross and Anderson), both famous fighting leaders and holders of the Distinguished Service Cross, Marcus called on Secretary of War Weeks and presented the case for the promotion of MacArthur on the basis of his distinguished war record. Weeks, who obviously anticipated the purpose of their visit, remarked cryptically, "Kissing goes by favors," and reached into a drawer for a large folder containing the names and records of a number of brigadier generals, all older and longer in the service than MacArthur. "MacArthur has plenty of time," Weeks pointed out. "He is certain to get to the top. He's too young now."

The delegation reported to MacArthur their action in his behalf, without disclosing that it had been initiated by his wife. He heard them silently, neither urging them to continue their efforts nor instructing them to discontinue them, until they quoted Weeks' last remark. Then MacArthur protested, "Too young! Why Genghis Khan commanded the union of his clans at 13 and at 48 commanded the largest army in the world. Napoleon was only 28 when he was the world's most celebrated military leader. Mustafa Kemal Pasha was 38 when he commanded his country's armies!"

Repulsed in her direct attack on the Secretary of War, Mrs. MacArthur tried again on another front. Jimmy Cromwell arranged an interview for Manning Marcus with George Wharton Pepper, who left the Senate floor to receive a document setting forth MacArthur's many qualifications for

* $536 monthly.

promotion. Pepper promised to do what he could. On his return to Manila, MacArthur wrote a friend in Washington, "Have you heard anything about my second star?" The friend went to the War Department and was shown documents drawn that same day promoting MacArthur to major general, the youngest in the Army at 45. This was in January of 1925 and that same month he was transferred to Atlanta and then to command of the III Corps Area in Baltimore.

Louise MacArthur was overjoyed at the termination of their Manila exile, and she eagerly reopened her extensive estate, "Rainbow Hill," in Green Spring Valley near Baltimore. Here the MacArthurs entertained many of America's political and business leaders; and if MacArthur had been less devoted to his career, he might have been tempted to leave the Army and take one of the many business positions he was offered. Many other officers were doing so, but each defection only made MacArthur more certain that he must remain and do everything possible to rebuild the Army from the ineffectual skeleton force into which it had crumbled as a result of a national attitude of neglect and disrespect toward our armed services. Consequently, he ignored numerous pointed suggestions from his wife that a corporation vice president earned more money than even a major general.

In 1928 MacArthur was ordered back to Manila to command the Philippines department, and the marriage came to an end. He agreed to a divorce "on any grounds that will not compromise my honor." With this understanding, Mrs. MacArthur headed for Reno and filed suit for divorce from "Donald MacArthur" on the grounds of failure to "provide me with the common needs of life." The mistake in names obviated any publicity prior to her appearance in court. No case was entered by MacArthur's lawyer, who held a power-of-attorney sent by the General from Manila. Just before Mrs. MacArthur took the stand, the error in names was rectified with permission of the judge, the divorce was promptly granted, and the divorcée uttered to reporters the traditionally gallant farewell to arms. "We were wholly incompatible. I have the greatest respect and admiration for him and we part as friends." She waived all claims to alimony.

The marriage ended with no regrets apparent on either side, and only a few bons mots from each of the divorced pair to mark its somewhat stormy passage. When Manila editors offered to keep news of the divorce out of the papers to avoid "embarrassing" him, MacArthur instructed, "Put it on the front page if you want to." He was far too polite to add, "I want the whole world to know it." For her part, the former Mrs. MacArthur was quoted as remarking, "Sir Galahad carried on his courtship as if he were reviewing a division of troops." She subsequently married Lionel Atwill and was asked how life with an actor compared to being married to MacArthur. "No difference," was her reply. When MacArthur became a hero for his defense of Bataan and was promoted to a full general, she said, "It looks like I traded four stars for one (Atwill)." At that time, hysterical women wrote her threatening letters for having divorced him and even suggested—since MacArthur was obviously destined to be president and tradition would not accept a president with two living wives—that it would be patriotic and proper of her to discontinue living.

Reporters pestered her for years whenever MacArthur was in the spotlight. At the time of his dramatic return to the United States in 1951, Mrs. Brooks-MacArthur-Atwill-Heiberg (her fourth husband is a retired colonel, and they live in Washington), turned away would-be interviewers with the statement, "I don't talk to anybody at any time about anything concerning General MacArthur. . . . Ask his secretary. He has a large staff of people to take care of things like that." It is noticeable that pictures of MacArthur with his first wife show him looking grim and occasionally glum (so do the early pictures with Jean MacArthur), but perhaps his most telling comment on his first marriage is that he makes no mention of it in Who's Who.

Published accounts, which MacArthur never bothered to deny, credit his former stepfather-in-law, E. T. Stotesbury, with helping him to land the top Army post of Chief of Staff in 1930. Stotesbury, a prominent Republican and heavy contributor to President Hoover's 1928 campaign, was said to have brought personal pressure on cabinet members to push MacArthur for the job against a number of candidates including General Hansen Ely, General Fox Conner, General W. D. Connor, and General George Van Horn Moseley. Patrick J. Hurley, the colorful Oklahoma oil millionaire who was Hoover's Secretary of War, was said to be opposed to MacArthur because he was divorced: "In Oklahoma, any man who cain't hold his woman isn't considered worth much." But Hurley lined up behind MacArthur and urged Hoover to appoint him.

Normally, as the country's only four-star general, though retired, General Pershing would have had a very strong influence in making this selection—and Pershing was known to favor General Fox Conner and to be opposed to MacArthur. But Pershing was in Europe, and Hurley took advantage of his absence to back MacArthur. When Pershing returned, he voiced his objections to Hoover; and the President summoned Hurley to an unscheduled late evening White House conference. Hurley argued that MacArthur was thoroughly experienced, young, vigorous, brilliant, brave, and the best-equipped officer for the post. When he finished, Pershing said, "I know all that. But I still don't want him."

Hurley carried his point by stressing that when he served under Pershing in France, the A.E.F. commander never permitted subordinates to make any important decisions for him; the roles now being reversed with Hurley heading the country's entire military establishment, he would now insist on the same right. Pershing gave up. He slapped Hurley on the back and said to Hoover, "Damn it, he's right! He was one of my boys. Let him go ahead and make his own mistakes."

Four years later Pershing was gracious enough to say, "I have only praise for General MacArthur as Chief of Staff. He thoroughly comprehends the requirements necessary to develop . . . a unified fighting force for the national defense. He is progressive without being radical. His courageous presentation to high authority of his sound views has been admirable. By wise administration of his office, he has won the entire confidence of the Army and the country."

Pershing was exaggerating somewhat when he included the entire country as sharing his estimate. Actually, in the aftermath of one explosive event during MacArthur's administration—the Bonus March—the country had heaped abuse and ridicule on him in bitter measure.

CHAPTER

7

The Bonus March

MAC ARTHUR HAS HEARD THE VOICE OF THE PEOPLE on numerous occasions in his life. He heard it raised in tumultuous acclaim in Melbourne, Manila, Tokyo, San Francisco, Washington, and New York. He heard it in the derisive "boos" of college students who shouted him down as a warmonger in 1935 because he urged national preparedness. He heard its call—a very faint call—when he permitted his name to be advanced as a presidential candidate in 1948. He heard it shouted in scorn and hatred in 1932 after he drove the Bonus Marchers out of Washington. And he has, of course, learned from these experiences.

"You know," he said to friends after his spectacular homecoming receptions in 1951, "I'm enjoying all of this, of course, but don't think it is going to my head. I know the sentiment of the people can change overnight. I've been pretty popular several times before, but in 1932 you couldn't have sold me for 10 cents on the dollar. That can happen again; and if it does, it won't bother me a bit, not for a minute."

Anyone less thick-skinned than a rhinoceros would have been bothered by the barrage of abuse, ridicule, and hate of which MacArthur became the target in 1932, and MacArthur is a sensitive individual. Nearly 20 years later, his actions in dispersing the Bonus Marchers are still a subject of controversy and a source of much misunderstanding. A completely false myth has been perpetuated that President Hoover, acting out of fear and terror, called out the Army, that MacArthur ordered the soldiers to shoot helpless and unarmed veterans, and that several were shot. Mrs. Eleanor Roosevelt, perhaps unwittingly, gave wide publication to one version of this myth as recently as 1949. The only truth in the story is that the Army was called out and did disperse the Bonus Marchers. Judged from any angle, this was the correct thing to do in the situation and in a similar situation it should and would be done again. No orders were given to the Army to shoot, and nobody was shot by the Army.

The Bonus March in 1932 was nothing new in our history; there were others in the 1780's and after the War of 1812, the Mexican War, the Civil War, and the Spanish-American War—indeed, the establishment in 1790 of the District of Columbia as a site for our national capital was a direct result of the first bonus march which had driven Congress from hide-out to hide-out in several states to escape the threatening demands of mutinous ex-soldiers.

In the spring of 1932, with millions unemployed, the country was in the grip of despair and hopelessness. President Hoover and Congress could find no answer to the depression, and Washington society could discover no better way of hiding its fears than to continue the social merry-go-round in an "eat, drink, and be merry" frame of mind. The Army Chief of Staff is usually a prominent figure in Washington society; but MacArthur—living with his mother in quarters at Fort Myer and following his lifelong program of austerity and study—took little part in the forced gaiety of the unhappy period.

National dissatisfaction with the administration culminated in the Bonus March on Washington and produced a riotous climax. Starting from Oregon where Walter Waters, an unemployed cannery superintendent, began a much publicized hitchhiking trip to the national capital, the Bonus March gathered 20,000 unemployed followers who besieged Congress for immediate adjustment of bonus payments to World War I veterans. The men—many accompanied by women and children—camped out on the Anacostia mud flats, slept in empty federal buildings, pitched tents and shanties, and lived on handouts. At first MacArthur fed some of them from Army rolling kitchens, but this was ordered discontinued. Many of the demonstrators visited his office, and those identifying themselves as veterans of the Rainbow Division were always admitted and given money (usually $5.00) from his own pocket.

As more and more supposed veterans jammed into the city, the administration charged that Communists had taken over the movement and were seeking to overthrow the government. These allegations were discounted by many people who realized that then, as now, it was common practice to tag any dissenting person or group as Communist. But time—and the confessions of former Communist leaders—have shown that the administration was absolutely correct.

Benjamin Gitlow, a former Communist, has revealed that under orders of the Comintern the party laid plans "to bring about in Washington a massacre of the hunger marchers as a result of provoked, violent clashes with the authorities." This was confirmed by two other former Communist officials, John T. Pace and Joseph Kornfeder, who disclosed that the party had sent 100 skilled agitators to mingle with the veterans and provoke disorders. "Our purpose," Pace said, "was to use the bonus demand to build a revolutionary force and to gain followers for the cause of the revolution. We wanted to turn the veterans into haters of the government, to stir them up to direct action. We sought to provoke a conflict between veterans and the law-enforcing agencies."

This they succeeded in doing after a comparatively quiet period of demonstrations before the White House and at the Capitol, where the Senate refused to act on the bonus plea, although public sentiment was on the side of the ragged, sometimes shoeless ex-soldiers who squatted at night beside their camp fires in "Camp Marx" and "Communist Camp," and washed and drank from the filthy Potomac.

Tempers grew tense, anger mounted, and after numerous clashes between the demonstrators and district police, two former soldiers were shot and killed. The district commissioners appealed to Hoover for immediate aid, reporting they were unable to maintain order, and Hoover on July 28th sent for War Secretary Hurley. Hurley and MacArthur had already talked over their course of action if the Army were called on, and Hurley accordingly prepared (at MacArthur's insistence) written orders: "The President has just informed me that the civil government of the District of Columbia has reported that it is unable to maintain law and order. . . . You will have United States troops proceed immediately to the scene of disorder. Cooperate fully with the District of Columbia police force which is now in charge. Surround the affected area and clear it without delay. Turn over all prisoners to the civil authorities. In your orders insist that any women and children who may be in the affected area be accorded every consideration and kindness. Use all humanity consistent with the due execution of this order."

For many days MacArthur had watched the growing tension that finally erupted into bloodshed and killing. He had discussed the situation not only with his official associates but—as was his custom throughout her life—with his aging mother. MacArthur hoped that the District of Columbia police could handle the demonstrators short of killing them; but he told his mother, "If the President gives me orders to go the limit, I will take charge myself."

Several days before the Army was called out, MacArthur told a fellow Rainbow Division officer, "If the President gives me orders to act, I would not give this distasteful and disagreeable job to any other officer of the United States Army. If anything should go wrong, it will be the kiss of death for that officer's future." From the personal viewpoint, his own career could not be hurt; he was already at the top. From the standpoint of the quickest and most humane way of handling the situation, he was convinced that with his own knowledge of dealing with soldiers, his prestige as a battlefield leader and now as Chief of Staff, he could prevent further bloodshed and killing.

When the order came from the President, MacArthur still could have turned to the nearest second lieutenant, or more specifically to the commander of the military district of Washington, passed the instructions along to him, and washed his hands of all further responsibility. Instead he assumed full personal responsibility. One retired brigadier general (Pelham Glassford of the Washington police) had already failed, and the temper of the Bonus Marchers was such that any indecision—or on the other hand, any senseless provocation—could easily have caused a riotous explosion. The situation called for steady nerves, a sure hand, and a firm display of authority.

MacArthur was wearing a white linen suit when Hurley handed him the fateful order, and he immediately dispatched an aide to his home at Fort Myer for a uniform. The Filipino orderly answered the bell, and Mrs. MacArthur directed him which uniform to take. The jacket of the one that was delivered to MacArthur was loaded with ribbons and his prized sharpshooter medal.* In his office MacArthur donned this uniform, mounted a horse, and with his staff aide, Major Dwight D. Eisenhower, went out to observe the actions of a hurriedly assembled force of cavalry, tanks, and infantry to whose command he had assigned Brigadier General Perry L. Miles.

Using tear gas and the flat side of sabers, the troops drove the Bonus Marchers before them, and within a few days all had retired from Washington. MacArthur himself was gassed as he stood talking to several men he recognized as former Rainbow Division soldiers; he remarked, "I wish you were on my side in this one." The shanties and tents of the demonstrators were burned, but MacArthur denied this was done by his soldiers; "There were no such orders, and in this army nobody does anything without orders." He congratulated the troop commander, Brigadier General Perry Miles, for carrying out his assignment "without firing a shot and without serious injury to either soldiers or civilians."

Overnight, MacArthur became the most hated man in America, or, at least, second only to Hoover in this respect. The din did not decrease, even though most of the nation's press was solidly behind the action and said it should have been taken sooner. A dissent to this general press support was expressed by the Baltimore *Sun:* ". . . may we suggest that somebody, somewhere in Washington clap an official hand over the mouth of . . . MacArthur. That gentleman who sent all the way to Fort Myer for a uniform so that he could be properly garbed for a military operation which could have been carried out by a colonel and a few men armed with tear bombs, is unburdening himself of military romanticism undefiled, bare of the tiniest alloy of common sense. . . ."

The Democrats vociferously took up this refrain as propaganda material for their campaign to elect Roosevelt for his first term as president, and MacArthur was damned and blasted from one end of the country to the other. The storm increased when Hurley, apparently attempting to express satisfaction over the lack of serious casualties, was quoted as saying, "It was a great victory. MacArthur is the man of the hour." Hurley quickly

* In recounting these circumstances, there is no intention of suggesting that MacArthur would have removed the ribbons even if he had foreseen the storm that his wearing them created. They were part of the uniform brought to him; he was proud of the uniform and of the decorations. But it is an interesting fact that far fewer pictures of MacArthur with his medals have been taken since the Bonus March than before it.

repudiated the quotation and explained, "There is no glory in this terrible episode—no hero."

MacArthur's supporters declared that it had been an act of rare moral courage for him personally to take an assignment he could easily have given a subordinate. But MacArthur himself never apologized; indeed, he reaffirmed his belief in the course that was followed. He believed the Communist-led mob was "animated by the essence of revolution," that many—as was confirmed by investigation—were not veterans, and that any further delay would have "threatened the institution of our government."

He was proud of the way his troops maintained discipline and withheld their fire in the face of flying brickbats and clubs. He formally reported to Hurley, "They had neither suffered nor inflicted a serious casualty. They had not fired a shot, and had actually employed no more dangerous weapons than harmless tear-gas bombs. . . . Any contention that injury to individuals was caused by them is entirely without foundation." (Not long afterward, the Roosevelt administration was confronted with a similar situation and avoided a showdown by shipping the veterans to Florida, where they were caught in a sudden tropical storm and many died.)

As to the fact that he had worn his medals—for which he was criticized with special venom—MacArthur contented himself with saying, "Should I be ashamed of them? I earned each one in action." Friends said he had worn them to impress ex-soldiers, who themselves were wearing decorations on their shabby civilian clothes.

Isolated from the passions of the time and the natural pity that was aroused by the presence of women and children among the Bonus Marchers, it is difficult to find anything to criticize about MacArthur's action. The only thing left to criticize therefore, is the language he used on this occasion, referring to the demonstrators as "the enemy," and declaring his belief that the situation, if not dealt with immediately, would have "threatened the institution of our government." The reader is free to decide for himself whether these terms were necessary and justified, or ridiculously exaggerated.

In 1932 MacArthur tried to ignore the clamor against him, but finally his nerves cracked under the incessant, stinging attacks of columnist Drew Pearson (then in partnership with Robert Allen), whose expert needling prompted one American president to call him a "liar" and another to call him a "S.O.B." MacArthur filed a $1,750,000 libel suit, asserting that the Pearson-Allen stories had accused him of "conduct unbecoming an officer [and of being] dictatorial, insubordinate, and disrespectful toward his superior officers."

After some parleying with lawyers for the newspapermen, MacArthur withdrew his suit; and he admitted later that he had made a mistake in taking notice of the columnists. He kept silent when Pearson goadingly exulted over his "victory," but he never forgot the original insult. Upon his return from Tokyo nearly twenty years later, a friend mentioned something Pearson had written; and MacArthur snapped, "I don't read him."

CHIEF OF STAFF— FIELD MARSHAL OF THE PHILIPPINES

Most of MacArthur's term as Chief of Staff—from 1930 to 1935—was spent in trying to make Congress understand that the United States could not afford to strip itself completely of military power. Those were years of the depression; the national watchwords were economy and pacifism. Some congressmen were in a mood to abolish the Army altogether, and it was only due to MacArthur's own efforts, and to the backing given him by President Roosevelt, that he was able to salvage some semblance of an armed force. At the lowest point in those years, the Army had been pared to only 60,000 combat soldiers, and there were barely sufficient funds to maintain them.

Because he was pointing out the obvious and the obvious was unpopular, MacArthur was denounced by members of Congress as "a thief . . . a warmonger . . . an insatiable pillager of the public purse." One of the less acrimonious terms applied to him was "a polished popinjay." University of Pittsburgh students paraded in protest when he was invited to address them, and greeted him in stony silence when he warned, "We should at all times be prepared to defend ourselves."

MacArthur's military record as Chief of Staff is only slightly less controversial than other aspects of his career. His detractors have attempted to show from bits and pieces of his statements that he was reactionary, blind and unaware of the uses and implications of modern weapons. His non-critical admirers, on the other hand, credit him with having foreseen and prepared for World War II exactly as it happened and exactly as it was fought.

What is correct is that he did foresee the nature of the war. That is proven by such statements as: "Tanks—planes—submarines will be the decisive weapons in the next war. Mass movements of airplanes and huge concentrations of tanks will win the battles." No reasonable person can quarrel with the accuracy of this statement, both as to land battles and submarines. However, it is stretching truth to say that MacArthur did set up the exact organization in the U.S. Army, and provide the exact weapons, to win that war. No one could have done that against the parsimonious and pacifistic currents of the time; and the wonder is not that MacArthur did not do more, but that he accomplished as much as he did.

Back in 1933 when Hitler came to power, MacArthur made a remarkable prophecy which revealed his deep insight into the working of historical forces. At a time when the whole world was speculating fearfully on the menace of Nazi Germany, MacArthur said, "In the final analysis, the issue is Moscow. Without Moscow's workings in the nations of Europe there would be no Hitler, and if Hitler takes Germany into war again, it will be the result of Russian intrigue and planning. He is Russia's creation and he will be Russia's unwitting instrument."

His accomplishments, as set forth by one of his admirers in the introduction to a book by MacArthur (*MacArthur on War*, ed. Frank C. Waldrop [New York, Duell, Sloane and Pearce, 1942]), may be summarized as follows: he foresaw modern "total war" (using that phrase) of massive striking power, lightning movement, many machines. He urged the Garand rifle, the armored corps, air power, the four-army plan, a mobile striking force, industrial mobilization. He worked to develop the Industrial Mobilization Plan of 1931 which served as a basis for mobilization in 1941 and afterward, and his plan for the general mobilization of manpower was essentially used 10 years later.

In the opinion of other officers, MacArthur's most important reforms were the four-army plan, the GHQ air force, and the tank school. The four-army plan, while it proved insufficient for the needs of global war as it developed after 1941, was an important advance in providing defense zones for a mobilization and command basis for future emergencies. The GHQ air force idea, which MacArthur sponsored and put into effect as far as funds permitted, called for an independent striking force of 1,000 planes which could be quickly mobilized for the defense of any threatened region of our country. While it likewise proved unsuitable for the needs of a war which covered much of the globe, it was a definite contribution to our air defenses. The Army tank school at Fort Knox became the foundation on which our mighty armored force was eventually built.

In addition, MacArthur pioneered the reorganization of divisions to their present triangular form of three regiments, and initiated "a comprehensive program of modernization in the Army's tactics, equipments, training . . ." To the everlasting gratitude of soldiers and officers, he sponsored a new uniform with open jacket and soft collar; also he fought for a more liberal system of promotion.

One of his chief battles was to get funds to put the Army on wheels, increase its mobility and striking power. "I have humiliated myself," he said in this connection. "I have almost licked the boots of some gentlemen to get funds for the motorization and mechanization of the Army." The refusal of Congress to give those funds resulted in one of our good tanks—the Christie—being sold to Russia rather than to the United States Army.

Whatever he did achieve was accomplished after innumerable congressional fights, one of which became so heated that MacArthur gathered up his papers and walked out of the hearing with the remark, "Gentlemen, you have insulted me. I in my profession am as high as you in your profession. When you are ready to apologize, I shall return." (In another connection, these last three words were to become famous bits of MacArthuriana.)

At the unprecedented request of President Roosevelt, MacArthur continued as Chief of Staff after the expiration of his four-year term. The understanding was that he would remain "pending the appointment of a successor," and after he had stayed nearly a year, F.D.R. offered to appoint him as his own successor. Prior to this offer, MacArthur had for some time been giving deep thought to the problem of what to do next.

At 55 he had risen to the top of his profession so rapidly that there was nowhere for him to go except downward in responsibilities and scope of authority. A corps commandership was the highest job open in the Army, and he wrote friends at Governor's Island in New York to supply him with plans of the commanding general's house so that he could check the arrangements and comforts for his mother, whose ability to move around was limited. For a time, he considered studying law (as his father had done while still in the Army) but he rejected the idea.

A solution to his problems came when Manuel Quezon, soon to be elected President of the Philippines Commonwealth, walked into MacArthur's office one day and asked his old friend for a frank answer to the question, "Can the Philippine Islands be defended?" Legend has it that MacArthur snapped back a single word, "Yes!" But actually his answer was, "I don't think so . . . but . . . they can be protected . . . if you have the necessary money . . . $5,000,000 yearly for the next 10 years." The American government was in the process of approving the law to grant complete Philippines independence, but no one had given any thought to defense, even though Japan had already embarked on its campaign of Asiatic expansion.

MacArthur did so now, swiftly outlining plans to build up a defense force based on a small regular army and a large reserve of trained citizens. "Then," he told Quezon, "no nation will care to attack you, for the cost of conquest will be more than the expected profits."

Quezon asked if he would care to go to the Philippines and put into execution the ideas he had expressed. MacArthur, quickly warming to the idea, seeing an answer to the problem of a future career, replied, "Manuel, I have done all that I can as a soldier in the service of my country. Unless there is another war, I do not see any prospect of further constructive work that I can do for the government and people of the United States. The Philippines is my second country, and there is nothing I would like more than to undertake the task you are proposing. America has a great responsibility for the future safety of the Filipino people. We cannot just turn around and leave you alone. All these many years we have helped you in education, sanitation, road building, and even in the practice of self-government.

"But we have done nothing in the way of preparing you to defend yourself against a foreign foe. We have trained a few officers and a few thousand Philippine Scouts and you have created your own constabulary, but this force is more of a national police force than an army. This is the time—if it is not too late—to help you organize your own defense. If you can secure the consent of the Secretary of War and the President of the United States for me to go to Manila as Military Adviser to the Philippines Commonwealth, I shall consider the assignment as a fitting end to my military career."

The consent was given, a law then before Congress was amended to permit MacArthur to take the assignment. He then stood by for word from Quezon, which came as soon as the latter had won the presidency of the new Commonwealth. Before accepting, MacArthur had made one final consultation. The 55-year-old soldier asked his 82-year-old mother, "Shall I go? Shall I take the post?" Mrs. MacArthur was enthusiastic. "I want you to do it, Doug-y," she urged. "I feel it is ordained that you go, and that it will lead you to an even greater role." She insisted on accompanying him, even though she was bedridden most of the time. She told friends that she realized the end of her life was nearing, and if "my son leaves without me, I will never see him again." MacArthur honored his mother's wish, and he was at her side when she died a few weeks after their arrival in Manila in the fall of 1935.

Working on the ship with his staff, which included Major Dwight D. Eisenhower, MacArthur drafted a national defense act, later passed as "Law No. 1" of the Philippines Commonwealth. He was well aware that he was starting from scratch in an unarmed, nonindustrial country, but he was not too pleased when this fact was emphasized in a bit of byplay at a dinner given in his honor by the Manila Gridiron Club. Arriving, he was greeted by two ragged figures carrying popguns. The host performed the introductions, "General MacArthur, I want you to meet the Philippines Army."

"Thanks," MacArthur replied a bit shortly. "I didn't know I had even two soldiers to start with."

Two years later he retired from the United States Army "in order to accelerate the promotion of junior officers," and accepted from Quezon the gold baton of Field Marshal of the still inconsequential Philippines forces, and a salary of $16,500 yearly plus a penthouse apartment. This appeared to most Americans to be an extremely grandiose title and MacArthur was ridiculed as "the Napoleon of Luzon." The Filipinos, however, were inspired to patriotic fervor by the thought of having a Field Marshal at the head of their army.

To MacArthur the title made no difference; he continued to live quietly and unostentatiously even though the whole meaning and center of his life had now been shifted as a result of his second marriage. This is the proper time, perhaps, to tell the story of his new wife and of his son, who were to remain with him from these Manila days until his final dramatic homecoming in 1951. The account of his controversial professional career in the Philippines belongs in the final section of this book, and it is given there.

C H A P T E R

8

MacArthur's Family

SOME OF MAC ARTHUR'S CRITICS, WHO ATTEMPT TO attribute to him dictatorial ambitions which in fact he does not possess, professed to believe that when he descended from the airplane Bataan in San Francisco, he would be followed down the ramp by a white horse. He would then—so the joke went—mount the horse (named Corregidor) and ride through the streets of America to rally the people behind him.

Instead, there stepped from the plane behind him in San Francisco and at all their subsequent stops, his tiny (five feet, two inches), smiling, somewhat self-conscious, and obviously devoted wife, and their bewildered but essentially poised young son, now seeing his home country for the first time.

In the tumultuous welcomes that followed their return and in their subsequent travels, millions of Americans have gotten a glimpse of Mrs. MacArthur and of 13-year-old Arthur. The boy, with his Air Force jacket and peaked cap, set a short-lived style craze for young Americans entering their teens. His mother, whose tastes run to beanie-type hats and smart but simple dresses, has created no revolution in fashion, but the sight of mother and son have tended to humanize the figure of MacArthur.

Arthur, a gentle and intelligent boy whose adolescent inclinations are more artistic than military, has had a dazzling introduction to his home country. In a few brief weeks of his 13th year were crowded more experiences than are even dreamed of by the average boy—box seats at the Yankee Stadium and the Polo Grounds, gifts from baseball heroes and from the mayors of great cities, lunch at the Stork Club, the sound of millions and millions of voices raised in tribute, a front row seat in Congress during his father's moving and historic homecoming address.

Arthur's early life had somewhat conditioned him to these things; from the time he was old enough to appreciate his surroundings he must have felt that his father was top man, the boss and commander. For years his mother and father talked of home, trying to tell him what America was like. But when the reality came, it was overwhelming. "America," he said shyly, "is much more than I thought."

Neither Arthur nor his mother seems to have any of the General's oratorical gifts. The boy has inherent poise, and eventually attained the point where he could say two words, "Thank you," over the radio microphones instead of his first half-audible "Hello." His mother has mastered two sentences, which by repetition have become familiar to radio audiences as her customary acknowledgment of the introduction that follows her husband's sonorous speeches. "I have never made a speech in my life," she says breathlessly. "I always leave that to the General." But for all of her life, Jean MacArthur has been listening to speeches—not as polished, perhaps, nor as oratorically perfect as those of her husband, but around similar themes—war, devotion to duty, heroism, love of country. That background is part of the story of the woman who, in her 38th year and his 57th, became Douglas MacArthur's second wife—"My beloved wife," as he calls her, "and my finest soldier."

One day toward the end of April, 1937, Miss Jean Marie Faircloth, then 38 years old, walked out of her home in Murfreesboro, Tennessee, "to spend a few days" with an aunt in Louisville. Except for her immediate family, no one paid any special attention to her departure; she was always coming and going on trips. Fourteen years later Mrs. Jean Faircloth MacArthur returned to her home town with a handsome young son and with her husband, for the time-being the most spotlighted man in the world. Some 200 reporters, cameramen, and radio broadcasters recorded the joyful welcome given them by the whole town of Murfreesboro and the whole section of Tennessee.

If Douglas MacArthur was born to be a soldier, Jean Faircloth was certainly born to be a general's wife—though she nearly didn't make it; it must have been the sometimes overworked MacArthur "destiny" that kept her from marrying another of her suitors. Just as young Douglas MacArthur drew himself erect and saluted the nearest flag when his mother told him he might some day see the Statue of Liberty, so Jean Faircloth was known as the "salutingest" little girl in Murfreesboro. From her earliest years she was excited by the sight of a uniform, thrilled by a band, and when she grew up she was active in the Daughters of the Confederacy and Daughters of the American Revolution, and took charge of the Fourth of July programs and other patriotic celebrations in Murfreesboro, at which her grandfather was frequently an orator before his death.

She was born December 28, 1898, in near-by Nashville, the daughter of Edward C. Faircloth and Sallie Beard Faircloth, who later divorced her husband and became Mrs. Frederick Smith. There were two brothers and a half-brother and half-sister in the family which—during Jean's early years and the time between her mother's marriages—centered around the home of Jean's grandfather, Captain Richard Beard. Captain Beard of the Confederate Army and young Arthur MacArthur of the 24th Wisconsin Regiment—whose grandchildren were to marry 75 years later—fought against each other in the battles of Missionary Ridge and Stones River. Family reunions were always the occasion for refighting old campaigns. A colored family servant, Mammy Dromgoole helped raise Jean as a youngster, and Jean went to private school in Murfreesboro and then to fashionable Ward-Belmont College in Nashville for a single year.

This brief outline of Jean's early years indicates a pleasant, conventional and sheltered young life high-lighted only by parades and celebrations at which an energetic and somewhat inane girl waved flags and shouted hurrahs. Only part of the picture is true. Jean's parents were unorthodox and somewhat Bohemian. Her father, a Canadian by birth, is now remembered as a prosperous banker and miller, and so he was in his later years. As a young father he was restless and improvident, the family was far from rich, and there were infrequent occasions when Jean as a youngster had no shoes or went to school with cardboard tucked over thin soles. After the divorce her father changed his ways, earned a sizable fortune, and made up for his early neglect by generously providing funds for Jean's education and travel.

Jean's mother, still well-loved in Murfreesboro and remembered as "Miss Sallie," was a dramatic, generous, and impulsive woman, truly liberal in human relationships not only for the South and for her times, but for any region and any age. During the summers she operated a resort hotel, which had been her father's summer home, in the mountains south of Murfreesboro, and it was there that Jean fished, swam (in dresses—for this was before modern bathing suits), danced and flirted when she was in her teens.

One year (when Jean was 12) Miss Sallie left the children with Grandfather Beard and went to New York to play leading roles in a stock company under the stage name of Peggy Castleman, and after her return she organized and directed local theatrical organizations and for a brief time was on the road with a dramatic troupe. After divorcing Faircloth in 1907, Miss Sallie married Frederick Smith who—so local gossip reported—had been an early suitor and who left town in disappointment when she married for the first time. In the true tradition of broken-hearted lovers, Smith wandered to far distant lands. He roamed through South Africa, South America and Europe, working sometimes as a newspaper correspondent, and eventually returned home with an attractive if slight British accent and a famous red vest which he wore on festive occasions when the family gathered for sessions of song-singing, recitations, and "play acting."

Jean not only succeeded her mother as the youthful heroine of school plays and as the girl who presented bouquets to the orators on patriotic occasions, but became her mother's errand girl. Miss Sallie had a large number of Negro families who were her friends and to whose homes Jean was frequently sent with friendly and neighborly gifts—not alms—of food and clothing. When her mother died in 1934, there were as many Negroes as whites at the church services.

Because of her mother's example, Jean Faircloth grew up without racial prejudice—or as nearly so as it is possible for any human being—and it may well be that this was one of the qualities that attracted MacArthur to her. In any case, it is certain that her feelings in this matter made her sympathetic to the peoples of the Orient, among whom she lived for 14 years after her marriage. It is equally certain that the complete absence of any trace of racial prejudice in MacArthur was very largely responsible for his great success in Asia; it is difficult in this regard to think of any other American who could have won the deathless loyalty of the Filipinos and the deep respect of the Japanese as MacArthur did. Therefore, MacArthur was probably entirely correct in his sweeping statement: "Far from being an advocate of white supremacy, I know and understand the needs of the colored peoples throughout the world . . . perhaps better than any other American." There was nothing theoretical behind this claim. MacArthur spent 24 years among Asiatic peoples; and when he and Jean Faircloth chose godparents for their son, they selected the late President and Mrs. Manuel Quezon, each of them descended from several races. The respect that Oriental peoples feel for MacArthur is partly due to his style and commanding presence, but far deeper than that it is a response to the sincerity of his inner affection for them. This was a deep and genuine thing, both in himself and in his wife.

From her mother, too, Jean MacArthur learned or inherited compassion and friendliness. She is a woman completely without pretense or affectation. A typical gesture occurred during the tremendous welcoming parade in Washington when, surrounded as she was by dignitaries, she spotted an A.P. photographer who had served in Tokyo and called out, "Hello, Charley. How are your wife and babies? Come and see us whenever you can." On her return to Murfreesboro, she showed that she had not forgotten a name or a face in the 14 years of her absence.

Jean Marie was 19 when World War I came, and she did war work at home. When a number of army trainees fell ill in the influenza epidemic, she volunteered her services in the local hospital as a nursing assistant—one of the few local girls to risk her own health in this way.

Her father died in 1929 and left her a legacy of $200,000, which enabled her to realize all her generous dreams. She had her mother's house painted and remodeled, gave money to scores of relatives and friends, some of whom she still helps when a family crisis arises; she sent Christmas and birthday gifts to many at home during all the years of her absence. Among the Negroes she assisted was Mary Ellen Vaughn, a household servant of her early years. Miss Vaughn won a degree at Fiske College in Nashville and now publishes a weekly Murfreesboro newspaper.

With the money she inherited, Jean went on several ocean trips, having developed a love for travel on voyages to the Pacific coast and to Europe with her father, and by visits to Army friends in Texas and the Philippines. She financed singing lessons for her half-sister Angelina Smith, and in 1931 treated her to a trip to South America on which Angelina met her future husband. But though Jean continued traveling, taking her half-brother, Harvard Smith, on a round-the-world cruise in 1933, she herself did not become engaged. There was a time when half of Murfreesboro believed she was engaged, and apparently she thought so, too. There had been a number of suitors, several of them Army officers. (The saying was, "If you want to win Jean Marie, you better get a uniform.") But this one was a civilian businessman. Even three years after his firm transferred him to Texas, Jean was still wearing a bracelet which may—or may not—have been intended as an engagement token. She finally decided to find out whether it was or not, and started out on another trip, intending to visit an English family in Shanghai. En route she stopped over between trains in Houston and lunched with her former suitor. They parted friends—and unengaged. Now in her 37th year, she sailed from San Francisco in October, 1935, on the S.S. *President Hoover*, which also had as passengers a large number of Washington officials en route to the inauguration of the Philippines Commonwealth, and General Douglas MacArthur, military adviser to the new government.

At a cocktail party given by the Alfred Ehrmans the night before the ship reached Honolulu, Miss Faircloth and MacArthur were introduced. From that moment she called him "General" or "the General" and later "my General" or "the boss." He was—as she learned—accompanied by his 82-year-old mother, confined to her cabin by illness, and by his widowed sister-in-law, Mrs. Mary MacArthur. They chatted briefly at the cocktail party and at the captain's dinner that night; and Jean Faircloth was delighted when she found her cabin packed with flowers as the ship left Honolulu, a gift from the General. The friendship progressed swiftly, and instead of debarking in Shanghai as she had planned, Jean went on to Manila.

It is a pity to spoil the legend that MacArthur's mother, knowing herself near death, hand-picked his future wife and said at their first meeting, "My dear, my son will love you very much." In fact, Mrs. MacArthur came on deck only once during the voyage and she did not then or later meet Miss Faircloth, but it is reasonable to assume that she would wholeheartedly have approved her son's choice.

In the Manila Hotel, MacArthur took connecting suites for his mother and Mary MacArthur, and himself. In accordance with his custom of many years, MacArthur "reported" to his bedridden mother each evening and recounted the day's activities. Because of her illness and because of her concern over the failure of his previous marriage, he did not tell her of his new romance with Jean Faircloth, with whom he had frequent social engagements. Mrs. MacArthur's condition soon worsened; medicine sent out by Clipper arrived too late, and she died on December 3, 1935, only a few weeks after they reached Manila. She was mourned by the Manila press as "el primero soldado"—the first to die for the new Commonwealth. The loss was a grave one for MacArthur; his mother, father, and brothers were now all dead, and he was the last survivor of his immediate family. For more than a half century he and his mother had been extraordinarily close; she was companion, confidante, colleague, adviser, disciplinarian, friend, and beloved mother. Except for his absences on duty abroad and the years of his first marriage, she had made her home with him much of the time. Now her body was sent home to be buried beside her husband in Arlington National Cemetery.

MacArthur pursued his courtship quietly, not hastening matters because of his mourning. After 15 months in Manila, MacArthur departed by Canadian liner, while Jean Faircloth flew to Honolulu where they joined one another aboard the *Lurline* for the voyage to San Francisco. He went to Washington, she to Murfreesboro, keeping their plans secret. She shopped unobtrusively in Nashville for her trousseau and had things packed or shipped to Manila—it was only when her half-sister, Donna Angelina Smith, saw her writing "Manila Hotel" labels that Jean admitted that she "might" marry General MacArthur. (Incidentally, she is still remembered by storekeepers in Nashville who sold her her trousseau. They say she is extremely easy to please. Unlike many women shoppers who try on a dozen models, she spots something she likes, asks for it in a size to fit her chic 100-pound figure, and takes it with her.) One night at a dinner party during this period, someone spoke lightly of MacArthur; and Jean replied with some warmth, "I'll have you know that General MacArthur has a most enviable military reputation." The other diners regarded her with interest, but agreed among themselves that her remark was not an indication of a new romance, since she had the reputation of always finding something good to say about anyone: "He may be a philanderer, but he has such nice manners," or, "She's very extravagant, perhaps, but she does have such lovely taste."

The day before she was to meet her fiance in New York, Jean flew into Louisville and confided her plans to her astonished Aunt Marie. "My lands," her aunt commented, "the people of America will certainly be surprised when they know you are marrying General MacArthur." "Well," Jean called back as she flew out the door, "the people in Manila won't!"

For his part, MacArthur had been equally secretive; and his first disclosure was to his former aide, Colonel T. J. Davis: "I'm going to be married, T.J., and I'd like you to be my best man." In contrast to the champagne-and-society atmosphere of his first wedding, a private ceremony was held in the chapel of the Municipal Building in New York with a deputy clerk officiating. The bride wore brown, and MacArthur a brown civilian suit. Afterward they went to MacArthur's suite at the Astor for a wedding breakfast of ham and eggs. Recognized by a reporter who spotted the newlyweds strolling on Park Avenue, the General commented briefly, "This is going to last a long time."

Back in Manila the MacArthurs lived in an air-conditioned penthouse atop the five-story Manila Hotel, its wide windows looking out over the bay to the distant fortress of Corregidor. Mrs. MacArthur, who always has loved to chatter and still does, quickly got used to a new and quieter way of life.

In the evenings, except for occasional small dinners for a few Filipino or American friends, the General read from his 7,000-volume library and she too became a regular reader. He rarely took her out except to the movies and never danced with her; in fact the closest she ever came to a night on the town in 14 years was after the General's dismissal in 1951 and their return to New York, where they quietly entered an upstairs box in the Waldorf-Astoria ballroom one evening and watched the performers at a Jewish theatrical benefit. Afterward they started going to ball games and plays.

In Manila they walked frequently (MacArthur also did daily calisthenics in those days) and sometimes swam in the outdoor pool of the hotel, MacArthur looking anything but a forbidding military figure in the bathing suit which emphasized his thin, expressive hands and the sensitive, intellectual cast of his head. Jean MacArthur would not have changed a minute of her life. She was very sure that her husband was the greatest man in the world and was completely happy from the day of their marriage. She found it enchanting to be in close touch with military life and to hear her husband discuss his problems in attempting to build up the Philippines army. She read military histories, as well as lighter literature, and on birthdays and Christmas gave him presents of biographies of Confederate generals. She began to think and sometimes to talk in a new way; words like "duty, honor, country," which had always been thrilling abstractions, took on a new meaning when MacArthur uttered them. She clipped from a Manila paper and sent home one of his statements: "This is the call of duty; I cannot fail." Many times he told her, "Jean, destiny sent me here to defend the Philippines." She began to attend his church, the Episcopalian, although she had been and still is a Presbyterian church member in Murfreesboro.

When her baby was on the way, she prayed for a boy "to carry on the MacArthur military tradition," and the boy's first gift was a life of Robert E. Lee. As was traditional in the MacArthur family, the boy was named Arthur. After his birth in the hotel apartment on February 21, 1938—only a month after his father's 58th birthday—she engaged a Chinese woman servant named Ah Chuh as amah (nurse). A Filipino soldier took charge of the household and kitchen; another Filipino soldier drove the limousine which the Commonwealth government supplied for its Field Marshal.

MacArthur worshiped the young son who had come along in what—already in the late 1930's—he had begun to call his "old age." The boy was one more link binding the family to the city of Manila, where MacArthur's father had governed and his mother had died.

Late in 1940 and again in 1941, the American government began suggesting—and then ordering—that official dependents return from the Orient, but there was never any thought in the MacArthur family that Jean and her son would leave the Philippines. MacArthur was still employed by the Philippines government when the first orders came, and they did not apply to his family; later, after he was recalled to active service in the United States Army in July of 1941, his wife still would not consider leaving him. It is an unfortunate fact—though in no possible sense any fault of hers—that many families of American businessmen also stayed on in Manila because she stayed; they believed that although Japanese-American tension was obviously growing, they would be safe in ignoring evacuation suggestions. "When Mrs. MacArthur goes," many wives told their husbands, "we will go." Consequently, they stayed too long and were interned.

At 4 A.M. on December 8, 1941, MacArthur was advised by a telephone call of the Japanese attack on Pearl Harbor, and it is a matter of record that before going to his headquarters, he took the Bible from his bedside table, read for a while, and then prayed. For the next 16 days, Mrs. MacArthur with the boy and amah spent most of the time at the apartment, from which she saw Japanese planes bomb and sink ships in the harbor, so close that the hotel shook with the concussion; she saw them smash the naval base at Cavite—nine miles distant across Manila Bay. But the most difficult part of these days for her were not the sights and sounds of war, but the concern she felt for her Filipino and American friends. Many of the latter telephoned her frantically: "What shall we do, Jean? How about my children, what will happen to them?" They knew she was in a privileged position, that she would get out—if anybody could—before the Japanese came, and they begged her to help. But she was powerless to do anything.

On Christmas Eve, MacArthur declared Manila an open city, and it became obvious to everyone that it would soon fall to the Japanese. MacArthur had reached this decision after long soul searching and after realistic appraisal of the military situation. It was obvious that his forces could not hold, and to attempt to defend Manila would simply provoke needless slaughter of civilians. Therefore, he proclaimed the city open in the hope that the Japanese would discontinue their air attacks, and that when they entered, they would come in a quiet and disciplined manner.

On Christmas Eve, Jean took a last look at the tree she decorated for her son, whose fourth birthday was now only five weeks away. Except for the MacArthur family silverware, which was removed and hidden by Filipino friends, she never again saw anything in the apartment; those belongings that weren't plundered by the Japanese were destroyed when the hotel was burned in the liberation of Manila three years later. The MacArthurs crossed Manila Bay by night to the fortress island of Corregidor where, with the amah, they took up residence in an officers' home on Topside—the high, flat portion of the island which guards the entrance to Manila Bay. Four days later Japanese planes made their first attack on Corregidor. The MacArthurs were in their house when the sirens sounded, and the women and baby were rushed to nearby shelter. But MacArthur refused to take shelter, and remained outside for two hours while the enemy planes bombed and strafed until Topside was a wrecked and flaming ruin. His small Filipino orderly, Sergeant Domingo Adversario, stood in front of him, holding his helmet "one half front my face, one half in front General's face" while they leaned against an embankment. One bomb blew down most of the house with a near hit, and a steel splinter wounded Adversario in the hand that was holding the helmet. After the planes finally went away, MacArthur went for his family and explained to his wife, "Sometimes I have to expose myself to set an example for the troops."

It is a pity that this heroic and Wagnerian scene was not photographed or painted—MacArthur standing there calmly challenging death, with the faithful Filipino standing by him amid the crashing thunder of the bombs, the roar of the flames and the explosive crack of 20-mm. shells fired by the diving Zeros. A day or two later Sergeant Adversario told me, "I feel General's knees shaking."

The MacArthurs found another small house back toward the eastern end of the island, formerly a lieutenant's or second lieutenant's quarters in the days when Corregidor had been a peaceful garrison. Most of the time MacArthur worked at the house, going to his office in Malinta tunnel only to study maps and send or receive messages. When air-raid sirens sounded, Mrs. MacArthur would take her son and the amah and be driven a half mile to the tunnel, and sometimes during the hours when raids were to be expected, she sat outside with her husband at a mess tent, or with the nurses or the few other women on the Rock, knitting and chatting. She wore simple cotton dresses and crocheted turbans; and Arthur, a pallid, placid child, too young to realize his surroundings, strutted around playing soldier in an oversized overseas cap. Jean MacArthur acted as if living in the midst of battle were an old story. She was always as calm and as confident as her husband, always encouraging when she visited the hospital tunnels which soon began to overflow with wounded as the severity of the bombing and artillery attacks increased. The MacArthurs ate at a mess table outside the tunnel (later inside, when the tempo of shelling increased); and they shared the same rations as everyone else on the Rock, mostly canned salmon and rice. Their only extra food was some fruit juices for the baby; but there were, however, small cakes for MacArthur on his 62nd birthday, January 26, and for the boy, who was four years old on February 21, 1942.

It would seem only natural that MacArthur must have discussed with his wife the possibility of getting her out of the surrounded and besieged battle zone; but if in fact he did so, she gave no indication of it. When President Quezon agreed to leave in mid-February after repeated urging from Washington, his wife urged Jean MacArthur to accompany them. "No," Mrs. MacArthur said, "I will stay with the General."

"But what will happen to the boy?" Mrs. Quezon asked.

"We three are one," Jean answered, in a thought she must have learned from her husband. "We drink of the same cup."

On February 23, secret orders were delivered to MacArthur at the small house on Corregidor. President Roosevelt directed him to proceed to Australia to take command of the "Southwest Pacific Area," traveling by way of Mindanao with a delay not to exceed one week. MacArthur, who had hoped until that moment that the Philippines would be relieved, was stunned by the order; and Jean was no less perturbed. She had heard the nurses say frequently, "As long as Junior (their name for little Arthur) is here, we will be all right," and she knew that if the MacArthurs left, it would be a stunning blow to morale of the besieged American and Filipino forces.

For hours the MacArthurs sat on the darkened porch of the little house, and at times the General wept openly. Finally he spoke, "Jean, I am American-Army born and bred and accustomed by a lifetime of discipline to the obedience of superior orders. But this order I must disobey." But eventually he agreed to leave, and took with him 14 of his staff in addition to his family.

Jean MacArthur shared her husband's tendency to claustrophobia, and they decided not to travel by the safer means, a submarine, but by PT boat. If they were going to die, they would do it above the water and not under it. The date was fixed for March 11, 1942, and in the late afternoon of that day—after the planes had gone and during a lull in the shelling—Mrs. MacArthur went from the tunnel to her house to pack. It took only a few minutes to put in some shirts and underclothes for MacArthur (he reached Melbourne wearing civilian socks), a dress and underclothes for herself, and food and medicines for Arthur. At 7:30 MacArthur came to the house.

"Well, Jean," he said, "it's time to mount up." At the dock, bearded Lieutenant Bulkeley, the skipper of PT 4L came out of the shadows and put the MacArthurs' two suitcases and the amah's small bundle aboard. One of the suitcases bore a prophetic label: "New Grand Hotel—*Yokohama*," where the MacArthurs had stopped over on their honeymoon voyage from San Francisco to Manila. Aboard the PT boat, they were heading in the opposite direction from Yokohama, and the chances of their ever getting there couldn't have been rated much higher than one in 100,000. But three years and six months, 10,000 miles, and many battles later, MacArthur spent his first night in defeated Japan at the New Grand Hotel.

No Japanese ships or planes sighted the little armada of PT boats during the two-night journey to Mindanao (they anchored in obscure coves by daylight), but the trip was a very severe experience for the MacArthur family. From the minute they crept through the mine fields off the black hulk of Corregidor and opened up their throttles, the boats began to pitch heavily, and both Arthur and his father were very sick. Jean watched over them as best she could in the cramped below-decks sleeping quarters. For hours she rubbed her husband's hands to restore circulation. She has never discussed the General's illness; but a staff officer said, "It was almost paralysis, a stiffness, rigidity of the limbs that made it practically impossible for him to move. It must have been a nervous reaction. We were afraid for a time that he was going to die, and we thought of transferring him to a submarine. But he rallied and decided to finish the trip by boat."

The party got through just in time. As they reached Mindanao, Japanese warships were closing in along the route they had followed, and aerial patrols were increasing. Very shortly all the small interisland shipping was sunk and one of the PT boats destroyed by planes.

Young Arthur and the Chinese amah now had their first airplane ride, a seven-hour flight from Mindanao to Darwin, stretched out on a mattress under the waist gunner's position with Mrs. MacArthur. MacArthur, who had not flown for some years, was up in the radio operator's seat while Generals Sutherland and George were jammed together in the bombardier's compartment in the nose.

The MacArthurs went on south to Melbourne, where the General set up headquarters in Menzies Hotel and Jean bought clothes more suitable for the approaching Australian winter. She was safe, her husband and son were safe, but she was terribly sad at the thought of those who had been left behind to death or capture. MacArthur, shocked at the discovery that there were no forces available or in prospect for the relief of the Philippines, was a heartsick, badly shaken man; and he leaned heavily on his wife in this period of bitterness and loneliness. He had known criticism and adversity before, but these had been mere challenges to retort and to fresh action. Now he was helpless, unable to send the help he had promised to Bataan.

"This month," Mrs. MacArthur said later, "was the most difficult one of our lives." In gratitude for the strength and love she showed him in this trying period, her husband purchased a wrist watch for her and had it inscribed: "To My Finest Soldier—MacArthur."

For two years, while her husband was fighting in New Guinea and on back to the Philippines, Mrs. MacArthur and her son lived in Lennon's Hotel in Brisbane. When MacArthur was with them, she personally cooked all his meals, and—far more important—she never attempted to discourage him from doing what he felt he had to do as a soldier, going ashore on beachheads under fire and deliberately exposing himself to danger when it was necessary to inspire his troops.

Arthur, growing up among Australians, picked up a slight accent. His mother taught him to read and write, but she had difficulty explaining the meaning of the word "home" about which she talked so much. There was home—the United States, a homeland he had never seen—and a home, a house, where they would live and his father would come every evening.

When Manila was recaptured early in 1945, Mrs. MacArthur boarded a refrigerator ship and took her seven-year-old son back to the city of his birth. The Manila Hotel was in ruins from shells and flames, and the family found a fairly large, undamaged house outside of the terribly devastated downtown district. There was still fighting in the hills around the city, and the first night Arthur tossed restlessly in his bed. "Are those guns ours?" he finally asked his mother.

"Yes, dear, those are ours."

"That's all I wanted to know," Arthur said. In a few minutes he was asleep, completely relaxed.

MacArthur went ahead to Japan, and for the final part of his signature to the surrender documents he used an inexpensive pen which belonged to his wife. The family set up their home in the former American embassy, a huge, walled-in establishment built under President Hoover—it was called "Hoover's folly" by his critics—and designed to impress the Japanese with the wealth and power of America. Seeing the barren rooms, Arthur asked, "Do we have to live here, Mother? Will it be a home?"

"It will be a home," she reassured him. The General put in, "Arthur, brace up. Your mother will take care of us."

He told Jean, "We'll do simply here . . . no splendor. Do what you can to fix it up." She improvised for curtains and decorations, using colorful Japanese materials, and fixed up a round table in front of a fireplace for Arthur's toys and collection of miniatures, and his wood-carving set. Mrs. MacArthur kept the household accounts and did the banking, and a staff of servants who had been in the embassy in prewar days ran the house smoothly and efficiently.

For nearly five years (broken only by brief visits to Manila and Seoul for the inauguration of those republics), MacArthur followed an unchanging routine which took him to headquarters in the Dai Ichi Building every day, including week ends and holidays, from 10:30 or 11 until 2, and from 5 P.M to 8:30 or 9. He never went out in the evening, not even to attend the annual reunion dinners of those who escaped from Corregidor with him by PT boat. His wife acted as his official representative at parties or receptions, visited hospitals and Army posts, and occasionally found time for brief trips to Japan's beautiful mountain or sea resorts. She was highly popular, both with occupation personnel and the Japanese, whom she came to admire and like. She never insisted on personal privileges as wife of the supreme commander; instead she stood in line at the PX and Eighth Army store, and once when she forgot her PX card, she insisted on going home for it. Another day she stood quietly in an expectant crowd outside the PX. Finally she heard a woman say, "They're waiting to see Mrs. MacArthur." Not wanting to disappoint them, Jean MacArthur slipped back into the store by a side entrance, sent for her car and then emerged smiling and waving.

The MacArthurs did their only entertaining at lunch, which began sometime after 2:00 and lasted until 3:30, or sometimes later. Two or three guests—and sometimes as many as 40—ate the simple but solid food and listened spellbound as the General launched into one of his vivid historical and philosophical monologues. When smaller groups were present, Mrs. MacArthur guided the conversation; and with larger ones she chatted easily with the guests at her end of the long I-shaped table, finding something equally interesting to say to Cardinal Spellman or Leo Durocher. Always, eagerly, she pressed visitors for news of home.

Her dresses (size 10) were sent by friends at home. Once she attempted to make a hat for herself. MacArthur inspected it and inquired, "Jean, is that a hat?"

"Yes, General, it's a hat."

"Well," said MacArthur, after further inspection, "it's becoming."

The principal concern of both parents was Arthur's education and their desire to get him to the country he had never seen, but they would not leave until MacArthur had finished his work. After the outbreak of the war in Korea, Jean MacArthur told Nora Waln, "The General and I are looking forward to rediscovering America and to showing Arthur his country. Our son has never been home. We've been away too long to go home for a visit. We've been too close, through too many things, for any of us to go alone. I couldn't send Arthur. I couldn't go without him or the General. When we go, we must go together. We three are one. This September we start our sixth year in Japan, my thirteenth in the Pacific."

When he was younger, Arthur once asked, "Have I got enough points to go home?" He had heard GI's discuss the point system under which individual soldiers were rotated home after certain periods of service.

Meanwhile, his mother did what was possible to raise him as an American boy in an alien conquered country ruled by his father. "I want him to grow up a normal boy, better than average, but not a genius," she once said, "because I know a genius is a lonely man." There were no suitable schools in Tokyo, so Arthur studied with his private tutor, Mrs. Phyllis Gibbons, a 50-year-old Englishwoman who described him as "quite intelligent . . . but a poor speller like any other American boy."

Mrs. Gibbons, who has since come to the United States, has a musical background; and she discovered that Arthur has talent. When he was 11, he composed two piano pieces; and when given a zither for his 13th birthday, he immediately picked out the "Third Man Theme." He has his father's independence; and once Mrs. Gibbons scolded, "Arthur, I wish you would play Chopin with both hands. Not Chopin with the left and MacArthur with the right." In Tokyo, the boy romped each morning with his four dogs and his father, saw a movie on Sunday nights, went to the PX on Saturdays, for B-29burgers and sodas, and to church with his mother on Sundays. He belonged to a Cub Scout pack, read Joe Palooka, and thought he would like to play second base. He also rode horseback, skated (taking in stride a broken arm from a skating fall, while MacArthur worried himself sick about it), carved book ends for "papa," swam, learned tennis from a Japanese Davis Cup player, saw some baseball games and had a pal his own age—the son of his father's physician, Colonel Canada, and was photographed with young Crown Prince Akahito.

News of the Korean war came to the MacArthurs at 4 A.M. on June 25, 1950; and once again Jean knew the loneliness of waiting while her husband went to the battlefields. She shared with him the exultation of victory at Inchon, and the despair and confusion that followed the Red Chinese attack. As the war dragged on in a bloody, seemingly endless stalemate, home seemed farther and farther away. Then on April 12th of 1951, while the MacArthurs were entertaining two American senators at lunch, Jean was called away from the table by a phone call from Mrs. Sidney Huff, the wife of her husband's old friend and aide. Listening to an Armed Services Radio broadcast, Mrs. Huff had heard the news of MacArthur's relief from command. The news was shocking, but for Jean MacArthur the blow was tempered by the realization that suddenly the 14-year exile was ended, and the family was going home.

Their departure from Tokyo was painful and emotional for the MacArthurs, for other Americans, and above all for the Japanese. The wife of an American correspondent described the final hours in a tearful letter home: "I was completely dazed and had the stunned feeling one has when confronted with the death of a relative." Crowds began to gather at 4 A.M. at Haneda airport, Japanese mingling with American soldiers, sailors, and marines. "It was a silver gray, chilly, but clear morning," wrote Mrs. Walter Simmons, "and just after we arrived at the field, the sun came up." As the MacArthurs arrived, after driving through streets lined by perhaps 250,000 Japanese, saluting guns were fired and jets flew over the airport. The MacArthurs' house servants, both Filipinos and Japanese, stood weeping by the plane; and there were even tears among the unusually nonemotional Japanese officials as MacArthur gripped their hands by turn. His face ashen, MacArthur slowly looked over the whole scene from the plane steps, saluted, and went inside. When the plane took off, handkerchiefs fluttered from the hands of Japanese men and women, several of them weeping openly. "This is Japan's saddest day," said a young Japanese. "It is sadder than Hiroshima."

Even after a gigantic reception in Honolulu, the MacArthurs still did not realize the welcome that awaited them in American mainland cities. Flying toward San Francisco, the General made plans to "drive quietly into town by a back way." Those plans disappeared in a surging, tumultuous demonstration that was repeated in the now historic series of welcomes across the country. At these receptions the MacArthurs openly showed their affection for each other, as if they were young lovers, and the General always introduced Jean to the crowds as "my finest soldier." Their reception in Murfreesboro was "Miss Jean's Day," and MacArthur took a back seat while she was presented with six stars (capping his five) by her hometown friends.

They had talked of home and dreamed of home so long, that it was little wonder that in the first few weeks Jean MacArthur went overboard in her eagerness to show Arthur the great sights of America. The two of them were like a pair of youngsters who had saved up for weeks for sodas, and then gulped them in one swallow. For a brief period, she rushed him around as if she were afraid that being home wouldn't last, and they would wake up to find themselves in Tokyo again for another 14 years. The quiet ball games they had planned were turned into productions, every sightseeing trip and shopping tour was reported in detail in the papers. Then Jean MacArthur whisked her son out of the spotlight. If she has her way, there will be no further public attention focused on him as he goes through the years of his adolescence.

At this writing the MacArthurs have settled down in the Waldorf Towers in New York presumably permanently, in a $133-a-day suite which they are rumored to have gotten on a year's lease at a bargain rate of about $450.00 monthly. "Here's where we lighted," MacArthur said of the hotel, "and here's where we'll stay." The MacArthurs' belongings, shipped after them from Tokyo, had grown considerably from the two small suitcases they took out of Corregidor in 1942. The shipment totaled 49 tons of furniture, 43 pieces of baggage, and three private automobiles. None of the latter belonged to MacArthur (though he has been presented with two Cadillacs since his return), and only a portion of the furniture was theirs. The remainder belonged to the six families of aides who accompanied them from Tokyo.

The suite at the Waldorf is not the little white house in the South that Jean MacArthur dreamed of for so long, nor is it the large White House in Washington that the General dreamed for a time of occupying. But it is close to shops, theaters, ball parks, Arthur's school, and the General's office, and handy for the politicians who may want to come calling. Most important, the General comes home every evening; and as long as he does that, it doesn't matter too much to Jean MacArthur where she lives, so long as it is on American soil.

III

Sidelights and Highlights

CHAPTER

9

The MacArthur Stories

MANY PEOPLE ARE WILLING TO CONCEDE THAT MacArthur is a pretty fair general, a good administrator, religious, a kindly father, and has other more or less fine traits. "But," they say, "he took his personal furniture on the PT boats out of Corregidor, leaving the nurses behind, and I can't place any faith in a man like that." Or they say—most ridiculous of all accusations—he is not a brave man. Or he is "venal," or "luxury-loving." Then they cite a story to support the accusations.

There are basically 10 or a dozen of these stories which have been widely circulated, in many cases with malice aforethought, which, if true, would discredit MacArthur. None of them is true. In themselves they are mainly petty and unimportant, but they do have an importance far beyond their content because they have influenced uncounted numbers of people in their basic judgment of MacArthur and have created a state of misunderstanding and prejudice which makes impossible any attempt to see his work and his life in true perspective.

Denying a falsehood is at best a negative and unsatisfactory procedure; but in the case of MacArthur it has to be done, and the best way is through examination of some of the specific stories that are still told about him and will no doubt persist in some histories as long as he is mentioned.

To get down to specific cases about MacArthur. It is said, for instance, that he "cowered in a dugout in Tacloban" after setting up headquarters in that Leyte town a few days after the D-Day landing in October, 1944. What are the facts? MacArthur took over the home of an American named Price for his GHQ. The house was one of the largest buildings (nearest to GHQ and officers' billets) in the town, and consequently a conspicuous possible target for Japanese bombers which were overhead every night and sometimes by day. Noticing a mound of earth in the yard, MacArthur asked, "What's that?" He was told that it was an air-raid shelter 20 feet underground, well furnished, lighted, and ventilated. He ordered it filled in by bulldozers and the mound leveled off. This act of dispensing with a possible life-saving shelter might seem reckless and ridiculous, but as any experienced soldier knows, once the commander of an army (or a division or lesser force) goes underground, his army goes underground also. A psychology is built up of seeking shelter at the slightest threat, and before long the whole army is dug in and stalled.

But the stories that came out of Leyte in 1944 completely reversed the facts, and had MacArthur not covering the dugout, but cowering in it. It was one of the many stories which, either completely distorted or magnified and exaggerated, were brought back from the Pacific by sailors, marines, and others and which are still widely believed in the United States. I had personal experience in the way some of these stories started. I was told "on the best authority of eyewitnesses" that when MacArthur left the "open city" of Manila with his family in December, 1941, for the comparative safety of Corregidor, he took along not only his wife, child, and Chinese amah, but also whiskey, silverware, furniture, a grand piano, dozens of trunks, and—crowning blow—a near life-sized fire engine which amused little Arthur. These stories were told by Americans who had ignored earlier State Department warnings to leave Manila and suddenly found themselves trapped. Feeling somewhat left behind myself at that moment, I was more than ready to believe them. However, on reaching Corregidor, I found that in truth the MacArthurs had taken only a small supply of clothing and that Arthur's fire engine was a wooden toy six inches long. Nor were the tunnels such subterranean luxuries as we had imagined. On the basis of the original story, I had built up a complete and entirely erroneous mental picture of MacArthur, and many others have done the same. But the story was not true.

Similarly, it is categorically not true:

1. That MacArthur built himself a "million-dollar palace at Hollandia." (See picture section.) The implication of this and numerous similar stories was that MacArthur loved luxurious living. Actually, nothing could be further from the truth. Even in luxurious surroundings as in the embassy in Tokyo or the Waldorf Towers in New York, his personal tastes are simple, his demands small.

2. That he ever made heavy real estate investments in the Philippines. He did take some flyers in gold-mining shares, as he had every right to do. Quite possibly some of these investments (or speculations) turned out satisfactorily and gave him a profit which, added to considerable savings from his pay as a Philippines and American Army officer, left him comfortably well off. The stories of his large land holdings probably grew from the fact that two of his staff did have considerable Philippines investments. Colonel Andres Soriano, his military secretary, a wartime officer, was and is a big businessman in the islands. Also, Courtney Whitney, the Manila lawyer who later joined MacArthur's staff and became his spokesman when they returned to America, was connected with various gold-mining promotions and other corporations.

3. That MacArthur took great loads of furniture, whiskey, silverware, etc. on the PT boats which took his party from Corregidor en route to Mindanao in the journey described in the previous chapter. Lieutenant John D. Bulkeley, U.S.N., skipper of the boat which carried the MacArthurs and now a commander and attached to the Atomic Energy Commission, has made a special statement for these pages about that journey. "You can put my name to this," Bulkeley writes. "The General and his party—meaning General MacArthur, wife, boy, and amah—carried between them two suitcases, both together not weighing more than 35 pounds. In them were some clothes, but mostly food, for I had stated to the General that I could not provide rations for the party. Their rations were about as poor as ours, and on arrival we ate what was left (of theirs), and there were only a few cans of salmon and one small child's can of orange juice. There was absolutely no piano, furniture, family portraits, or any other piece of furniture or personal equipment. Mrs. MacArthur had only one dress and one slack suit . . . the slack suit was beyond repair by the time the trip was over . . . The child had no toys that I knew of . . . the amah had her stuff in a small handkerchief not over 12 inches in diameter . . . I personally carried the luggage aboard and made only one trip." Bulkeley has been telling the truth about this journey for years but still receives many inquiries about it from admirals, generals, and others.

It is likewise untrue that MacArthur ever referred *in communiques* to "My Navy" or "My Marines." His communiques did mention "naval forces attached to this command" or similar phrases, but the communiques were always in the third person and thus could not have used "my." He did, of course, use "I" in discussing outside of communiques the actions of forces under his command. That is SOP (Standing Operating Procedure) for generals.

Parenthetically, the writer has been unable to ascertain the truth of reports that American Marines being trained to distinguish between a gun—meaning a pistol or revolver—and a rifle, were taught to point to the respective weapons and roar in cadence: "This is my gun—This is my rifle—MacArthur's a bastard!" These stories about MacArthur versus the Navy and Marines are long out of date; peace has long since been established among them. But even in World War II when the bitterness was most intense, MacArthur never ceased to use—and to praise in his communiques—whatever Navy or Marine elements he could get and which fought the way he thought they should fight. For example, in his drive from Lingayen gulf to Manila in 1945, he employed Grumman (Navy) planes and Marine pilots in support of ground troops, because they were best at this work. In the past, however, he did share the old doughboy conviction that the Marines were publicized out of all proportion to their numbers in World War I.

As an example of another MacArthur story, it is untrue that he hid constantly (or even occasionally) in Malinta Tunnel on Corregidor during the siege, a veritable "Dugout Doug" too timid to emerge. Stories questioning MacArthur's courage are so absurd that it is useless to deny them. As to the tunnel, his office was there, but he lived in a house a half mile or so distant. (Having been his neighbor in a house 50 feet distant, the writer claims competence to testify on this point.)

A final untrue accusation is that MacArthur waded ashore on well-guarded islands at which posed photographs were taken, false captions then being written to make it seem he had actually landed on invasion beaches. The fact is that the pictures in this book of MacArthur at Leyte were taken by Captain Henschel on D-Day. One of Henschel's good friends, Captain Francis Wai of Honolulu, was killed a few yards from the spot. Mortars were still falling and bullets flying when MacArthur came ashore but he paid no attention to them.

To give some little satisfaction to those who persist in thinking that some of those stories *must* be true, and who finally find their accusations reduced to the relatively mild charge that he always poses for pictures, it can be stated that there is some truth in this. MacArthur almost never—perhaps a dozen times in 50 years—made an appointment to pose for a picture; he would not even do this for news photographers in Tokyo when he was a presidential candidate in 1948, although he did agree to "walk slowly" while they were focusing. But while not actually sitting for pictures, MacArthur does pose in the sense that when he sees cameramen approaching, he is acutely aware of them and strikes a characteristic attitude. In fact, the chief difficulty in getting pictures for this book was in trying to find some that were candid. Almost none existed; since the age of three MacArthur has been conscious of the camera.

THE LEGENDS OF MAC ARTHUR

A good many of the incorrect stories about MacArthur are not uncomplimentary, but rather of a legendary nature. His personality, combined with the long and imposing record of his achievements, creates such an impact that people tend to borrow from MacArthur's own vocabulary to find words to describe him. He is "MacArthur, Man of Destiny," "MacArthur the Magnificent." Or, as General "Wild Bill" Donovan summed it up in a broadcast during the dark days of Bataan, "General MacArthur—a symbol for our nation—outnumbered—outgunned—with the seas around him and the skies above controlled by the enemy—fighting for Freedom."

It is easy to personify MacArthur as the All-Time, All-American Hero, and as a result many feats actually performed by others have been attributed to him and he is made the center of tales summarizing and dramatizing in a single episode the whole essence of a battle or campaign. A picture has been created of MacArthur personally steering PT boats in wild torpedo attacks, running to shoot antiaircraft guns, hoisting flags right and left with his own hands, charging enemy trenches with a pistol in one hand and a prayerbook in the other, appearing in so many spots at so many times that even two Paul Bunyans would have been kept busy.

As an example, it was discovered through a series of battle experiences that the .38-caliber pistol used by American officers in the Philippines at the turn of the century did not have sufficient punch to stop the Moro "juramentados." These warlike zealots swore on the Koran to kill at least one of their infidel enemies, bandaged themselves tightly from head to foot to stop bleeding, hopped themselves up on dogma and dope, and then charged an American position. Though hit many times, they kept coming, and as a result the American Army adopted the hard-hitting .45 automatic.

MacArthur, however, is credited with making this discovery all by himself in a single dramatic encounter when he calmly placed six bullets in a crazed Moro's heart—all within a hand's span—only to have his attacker keep charging until he finally collapsed at the young lieutenant's feet. MacArthur himself has no recollection of this incident. Nor (it must be confessed) does he remember the details of the first time he came under fire in the Philippines.

What is certain is that MacArthur did not (as the story goes) shoot it out hand to hand with a Japanese colonel in his ruined Manila penthouse during the liberation of that city. Nor did General Homma, who lost the first round of the battle of Bataan to MacArthur, commit suicide in that same penthouse. Homma, it will be recalled, turned up alive to refute that story, but got little satisfaction from it as he was shortly executed for war crimes.

A story typifying the dangers of frontier life in the 1880's pictures the four-year-old MacArthur narrowly missing death from an Indian arrow. A calmer version is that he was playing outside a stockade one day when there was an alarm of approaching Indians, and his mother and a sergeant ran to carry him inside the walls. The attack did not materialize. Anyway, MacArthur lived in Washington between the ages of eighteen months and five years.

Another wonderful MacArthur story, which takes pages of type in various books, tells how as a young lieutenant he watched the Japanese charge up a steep hill at Mukden in the face of devastating Russian fire, and then joined them for the seventh charge which swept the Czar's troops out of their trenches. Alas, again, MacArthur wasn't there; he did not reach the Far East in 1905 until the Russo-Japanese fighting had ended.

A widely circulated West Point story credits MacArthur with openly defying convention, courtesies, and military procedure to demonstrate his filial devotion. In presenting diplomas to the class of 1903, William H. Taft is said to have expressed his lingering dislike of the then Major General Arthur MacArthur by deliberately ignoring the custom of handing the sheepskin to the Army father of a cadet who then had the honor and satisfaction of giving it to his own son. Highly angered, Cadet MacArthur took the diploma, ignored Taft's outstretched hand, walked over and presented the diploma to his father and sat down at his feet. It would be difficult to imagine MacArthur doing anything so unmilitary, but outside of that there are two fatal defects in this story; the diplomas were not presented that day by Taft, but by War Secretary Elihu Root. Major General Arthur MacArthur was in San Francisco.

MAC ARTHUR AND DESTINY

MacArthur's contempt of death and coolness under fire have been observed and noted by thousands of individuals. One example: In World War I he called for an artillery mission on the German trenches in preparation for a local attack. He then went forward to the American trenches, climbed out of them only 150 yards from the Germans, and with two highly unhappy artillery officers watched the effect of the shells that were whistling only a dozen feet over his head. On another occasion in France he led American troops forward to seize German positions which were still under American artillery fire.

Many attempts have been made to explain his conduct in battle. It is said that he is fatalistic; that he is certain that "destiny" will take care of him. This is probably correct to a point, but there is far more to it than that. Man is born with a natural fear of loud noises and the instinct of self-preservation. Any soldier must learn to overcome these instincts to the extent of being able to go on with his job under fire, no matter how badly his nerves are jangling. MacArthur not only had perfect nervous and muscular control, but he did not even sweat under fire, sweating being a common fear reaction when life is endangered. This was partly due to the fact that (like Joe Louis and others) he has a very low pulse rate, but in greater measure it was due to superb mental control. Unlike a soldier busy throwing a grenade or firing a gun, or a man like Patton who would jump up and down and swear, MacArthur had no physical release to lessen the mental pressure, yet he was able to ignore danger completely. It is my conviction that he had absolutely convinced himself that "only a man is fit to live who is not afraid to die." Having done this, he lost all fear of death.

As for his actions in deliberately exposing himself, he himself gave a readily understandable and nonfatalistic explanation when his wife once remonstrated with him for seemingly needlessly exposing himself during a Japanese air attack on Corregidor when there was a shelter only a short distance away. "I have no right to gamble my life," he said, ". . . but it is absolutely necessary at the right time because of the effect all down the line. The soldiers say, 'I guess if the old man can take it, I can take it too.' "

It has been especially noticeable in the past 10 years that—for all his undoubted faith in his destiny—MacArthur has seemingly used timing and a sense of drama in choosing the places to "gamble his life." He did not, for instance, frequent the front line during the losing battle of Bataan. He did not personally plod through sniper-infested jungles in the dark days of New Guinea. But when he was engaged in a successful, bold stroke of great importance, as at Hollandia and Leyte and later at Inchon in Korea, he insisted on going onto the beaches while they were still under rifle and machine-gun fire. Some of the men closest to him got the impression he almost expected and anticipated death at these historic high-points—a dramatic death at such a moment would be in consonance with the whole pattern of his life and moreover would be a climax which not even his soldier-father had achieved.

Nevertheless, even if MacArthur did choose to gamble with destiny mostly at dramatic moments and not push fate too hard at obscure ones, it is highly certain that he did have a strong sense of a mission in life which he was destined to fulfill. One word most frequently used about him is "destiny." "MacArthur has a date with destiny." "He has the strongest sense of his own destiny of any man I know." "His faith in his destiny is monumental." He himself often employed the word, which was a common one in his family. As was noted earlier, his mother, in urging "Doug-y" (her lifelong pet name) to go to the Philippines in 1935, said she felt it "ordained" that he should build up the Commonwealth defenses. After his arrival, MacArthur said repeatedly, "By God, it was destiny that sent me here."

After the first shock of his unexpected dismissal by President Truman, he soon recovered by convincing himself, "Destiny is sending me home to tell the people the truth." At one time, however, his faith was badly shaken. When his first offensive in New Guinea was getting off to a slow and uncertain start, he would inquire dramatically and rhetorically, "Am I destined always to be the leader of a lost cause?"

Whatever the part of destiny in his life, MacArthur deserves at least an assist in the box score for shaping his own career. His faith in the future did make it relatively easy for him to face danger; but it was sheer will power, devotion to duty, and magnificent powers of physical endurance that made it possible for him to work and fight tirelessly throughout two world wars, to put in day after day and year after year at his desk in Japan, to visit Korean battlefields 14 times in the eighth decade of his life, and at the age of 71 to amaze the Senatorial investigating committee with his "iron-man" staying powers and intellectual alertness during three days of intensive questioning.

MacArthur has not expected destiny to pull him through life in a silken carriage; he worked—he has been probably one of the hardest working men who ever lived—to make things happen. This quality is well illustrated by a story which seems to be a classic in the Army, as it has been told numerous times about various people. As condensed from MacArthur's own version, a young officer (in this case himself) is given a theoretical problem of defending a port from an approaching invasion force and asked what he would do.

"I would send out my fleet to intercept the enemy," MacArthur replies.

"Your fleet is destroyed, your land forces are short of supplies, some of the men you counted on have been taken away. Now what would you do?"

"Well, sir," MacArthur answers, "first of all I'd round up a sign painter. I'd have hundreds of signs prepared saying, 'These waters are mined,' and I'd float them in the harbor. Then I would get down on my knees and pray hard. Then I'd go out and fight like hell."

An interesting sidelight on this supposedly theoretical problem is that it became a reality when Japan attacked the Philippines and MacArthur followed his own plan: Use all the psychological advantages, pray hard, fight hard.

CHAPTER

10

The MacArthur Speeches

MACARTHUR'S HIGHLY CONTROVERSIAL "I HAVE RE-turned" speech had its origin in Australia in March of 1942. The General, obeying presidential orders to leave Corregidor and take command of Allied forces he believed to be in Australia, boarded a train in Alice Springs after a long trip south by PT boat and airplane. His long-time friend and former secretary of war, Major General Pat Hurley, met MacArthur there and conferred with him aboard the plane. In an impassioned monologue stressing his unfaltering purpose to relieve the Philippines, MacArthur several times made the emphatic promise, "I shall return." Hurley passed this word on to newspapermen, and MacArthur formalized it with a message written on the back of an envelope—words that would live in history:

"The President of the United States ordered me to break through the Japanese lines and proceed from Corregidor to Australia, for the purpose, as I understand it, of organizing the American offensive against Japan. A primary purpose of this is the relief of the Philippine Islands. I came through, and I shall return."

The slogan, "I shall return," became the battle cry for the Philippines. It was printed on millions of gum wrappers and cigarettes brought in by submarine to unoccupied areas of the Islands. Chalked on sidewalks and walls, whispered by Filipinos, it became a rallying cry for them equal to the "V . . . —" of the French resistance movement, and a bugaboo to the Japanese.

So when MacArthur spoke into a portable microphone on October 20, 1944—D-Day, four hours after H-Hour—while the Leyte beachhead was still under Japanese fire, it was completely understandable that he should say, "I have returned." Later in the speech he said, "Rally to me," and because many people cite these sentences as "sacrilegious," in bad taste, and generally offensive, it is widely supposed that the whole speech was in a similar first-person-singular vein.

The whole speech is too long to reproduce, but the first paragraph and the key portions follow: "To the People of the Philippines: I have returned. By the grace of Almighty God our forces stand again on Philippine soil—soil consecrated in the blood of our two peoples. We have come, dedicated and committed, to the task of destroying every vestige of enemy control over your daily lives, and of restoring . . . the liberties of your people.

"At my side is your President, Sergio Osmena. . . . The seat of your government is now therefore firmly reestablished on Philippine soil. . . .

"Rally to me. Let the indomitable spirit of Bataan and Corregidor lead on. As the lines of battle roll forward . . . rise and strike. . . . For your homes and hearths, strike! . . . In the name of your sacred dead, strike! Let no heart be faint. Let every arm be steeled. The guidance of divine God points the way. Follow in His Name to the Holy Grail of righteous victory!"

After reading this speech many times, I still fail to see anything sacrilegious or in bad taste. MacArthur has seen no need to defend or explain it; but, by way of information, it was not intended for publication in the United States (being released by a well-intentioned press officer), but was directed to the Filipino people. It was one of a trio of speeches carefully prepared at the suggestion of Colonel Carlos Romulo (later President of the United Nations General Assembly), a skilled and experienced Filipino newspaperman and wartime propagandist who had operated the Voice of Freedom Radio on Corregidor during the siege. Romulo followed it with his own speech, couched in terms similar to MacArthur's, which sound strange to an American ear but were astutely calculated to stir up Filipino resistance. President Osmena made a third and similar speech.

It was the first broadcast word spoken on Philippines soil by MacArthur since his promise from Corregidor, "We shall arise in the name of Freedom, and the East shall be alight with the glory of our liberation." The Filipinos who heard MacArthur on his return to Leyte understood his language; they heard—and struck. Their resistance saved uncounted American lives. So the speech accomplished its all-important purpose, which is all that can be asked of any speech.

Further—and this is more fact than argument—if any person ever had the right to use "I," it was MacArthur on Leyte. *He* was returning, the American forces were coming for the first time; later in this book there is a discussion of the difficulties he faced in doing this. Except for MacArthur, those American forces might have "returned" to Formosa, or France, or Okinawa, or Timbuctoo, but never to the Philippines. It was only his burning insistence on liberation of the Philippines that modified grand strategy for the Pacific; no one else alive could have done it because nobody felt about the Philippines as he did.

It is also an indisputable fact that he was to the Filipinos the human symbol of everything America stood for. It is quite true that he insisted on "I shall return" in place of "we" in this slogan. He was the general and leader; he had made the original promise. To use "we" in place of "I" would not only have been inaccurate but would have confused the Filipinos and detracted from the strength and punch of the propaganda.

By comparison, General Eisenhower's broadcast on his own historic D-Day in France omitted all reference to God but contained far more "I's" than did MacArthur's. Addressing the people of Western Europe, Eisenhower said among other things, "*I* have this message for all of you . . . *I* say . . . *I* say . . . until *I* give you . . . when *I* shall need . . . *I* call on you . . . *I* am proud . . . *I* repeat to you."

The respective communiques are also interesting. Eisenhower's began, "Under the command of General Eisenhower, Allied naval forces . . . began landing Allied armies this morning on the northern coast of France."

MacArthur's started: "In a major amphibious operation we have seized the eastern coast of Leyte Island in the Philippines. . . ." and continued with a strictly military report.

SOME OTHER FAMOUS SPEECHES

The speech of MacArthur's that will probably live longest is the one delivered to Congress in April, 1951, after his dismissal from the Far East. He worked long and hard drafting it, writing and revising up until he left the Statler Hotel to go to the Capitol. None of the millions who saw him on television or heard him on the radio is likely to forget the tremendous emotional impact of his closing lines:

"When I joined the Army, even before the turn of the century, it was the fulfillment of all my boyish hopes and dreams. The world has turned over many times since I took the oath at West Point, and the hopes and dreams have all since vanished, but I still remember the refrain of one of the most popular barracks ballads of that day which proclaimed most proudly that old soldiers never die; they just fade away. And like the old soldier of that ballad, I now close my military career and . . . just fade away, an old soldier who tried to do his duty as God gave him the light to see that duty . . . Goodbye."

At least two other MacArthur speeches were brilliant oratorical performances. The first—delivered on the U.S.S. *Missouri* in Tokyo Bay after he had received Japan's surrender—was written. The other was not, being delivered without script or notes at the annual reunion of the Rainbow Division Veterans Association in Washington, July 14, 1935. Speaking without notes, MacArthur delivered an outstanding oration. Scores of laudatory letters were received afterwards from many parts of the world asking for copies, which were printed from a transcription and mailed to listeners. The writer's impression is that MacArthur had memorized the speech; in any case, he used parts of it verbatim on numerous other occasions, including the ceremony when he became Field Marshal of the Philippines.

A tremendous demonstration of purely extemporaneous thinking, of slightly different nature, was his testimony for three solid days before the Senate committee investigating his removal. Testifying without notes or documents, MacArthur rarely hesitated for a fact or a word, giving the senators a vivid display of his historical knowledge, culture, passionate sincerity, vision, and cogency. Scarcely less remarkable from a physical standpoint was his sitting for nine hours without a recess, which caused one restless Democratic Senator to grumble, "I don't believe MacArthur is 71 years old. Why, he must have the bladder of a college boy!"

Still another historic MacArthur tour de force was his three-hour talk (or lecture) to Roosevelt at Pearl Harbor which convinced the President to change the whole strategy of the Pacific war. Even if this result had not been achieved, the feat of making Roosevelt listen for three hours was in itself historic.

After listening to MacArthur for all this time, Roosevelt remarked, "Douglas, you have taught me more about the Pacific than I had learned in all my life." But when he was alone with his physician, the President said, "Cary (Admiral Grayson), give me an aspirin before I go to bed. In fact, give me another aspirin to take in the morning. In all my life *nobody* has ever talked to me the way MacArthur did."

MAC ARTHUR AND THE ENGLISH LANGUAGE

MacArthur is at his articulate best in carefully prepared speeches, in the give-and-take of testimony, in conversation, and in informal comment. He seldom speaks extemporaneously, although he has produced several highly quotable efforts of this nature. When he attempts to dash off some written sentiment, he frequently trips over his pen and falls flat on his syntax. A number of his brief expressions are notable. "I shall return" took its place as a military slogan with "England expects every man to do his duty," and "They shall not pass!"

To a reporter who inquired the "formula for defensive warfare," MacArthur snapped, "Defeat!" Asked his strategy for winning in the Pacific, he answered, "Kill Japs." After Japanese bombs had blown up his house on Corregidor and nearly killed him, the General remarked calmly, "Look what they've done to my garden."

"It was not the sombrero that made the West," he told an appreciative women's audience in Iowa, "it was the sunbonnet." The manager of the U.S. Olympic boxing team at Amsterdam, seeking to withdraw in protest against partisan decisions, received an icy MacArthur glare and the warning, "Americans don't quit." The General terminated a discussion among his officers with the succinct order, "Let's get on with the war."

He could have fun with words, as in reporting to Calvin Coolidge on his leadership of that victorious Olympic team. Instead of a matter-of-fact record, he displayed his classical knowledge in a vivid and humorous paraphrase of Homer which started:

"In undertaking the difficult task, I recall the passage in Plutarch wherein Themistocles, being asked whether he would rather be Achilles or Homer, replied, 'Which would you rather be, a conqueror in the Olympic Games or the crier who proclaims who are conquerors?' And indeed to portray adequately the vividness and brilliance of that great spectacle would be worthy even of the pen of Homer himself. . . ."

Pat Hurley, Secretary of War when MacArthur was Chief of Staff, once remarked to Major Warren Clear, who did the research for War Department speeches, "Mac seems to get the Glory of God into all his speeches; all I ask is some anemones and forget-me-nots."

MacArthur at his least lucid emerges when he attempts some special effect involving abstract words like "glory, honor, valor, courage." At this time his hurriedly written prose blossoms into full flower; some critics feel that it has been ripening for a half century and indeed its aroma is Victorian. Like everyone else, he has acquired over the years a number of phrases and expressions which he considers perfectly suited to certain occasions and instead of paraphrasing, he quotes himself nearly verbatim time after time.

Some of his thoughts do double duty, like the following example: "The athletic code, therefore, has come down to us from even before the age of chivalry and knighthood. It embraces the highest moral laws and will stand the test of any ethics or philosophies ever promulgated for the uplift of man. Its requirements are for the things that are right and its restraints are from the things that are wrong. Its observance will uplift everyone who comes under its influence."—*Maj. Gen. Douglas MacArthur, report as Chairman of American Olympic Team, 1929*

> "The military code . . . comes down to us from even before the age of chivalry and knighthood. It embraces the highest moral laws and will stand the test of any ethics or philosophies ever promulgated for the uplift of mankind. Its requirements are for the things that are right and its restraints are from the things that are wrong. Its observance will uplift everyone who comes under its influence."—*Gen. Douglas MacArthur, speech to the Rainbow Division Veterans Association, 1935*

When he made his sensational return to the United States after 14 years in the Orient, he had been absent so long that his American audiences were unaware he was using stock expressions and they found them a refreshing novelty from current slang. When he told senators, "This is a very compendious list," it was a charming bit of pure Dickens. Americans who had thought his communiques stilted, archaic, and conceited get a completely different impression when he uses those same words in his speeches; the words suit the personality of the man.

Over the years, these are some other of the pure MacArthurisms he has found useful:

"I do not know the dignity of their birth, but I do know the glory of their death." Used in speech to the Rainbow Division Reunion in 1935; in decorating posthumously Captain Colin Kelly in 1941; at Punchbowl National Memorial Cemetery, Honolulu, while returning to Washington in 1951. And on uncounted other occasions. The words are engraved on a battle memorial in his wife's home town, Murfreesboro, Tennessee.

"From the Far East I send you one single thought, one sole idea—written in red on every beachhead from Australia to Tokyo—there is *no* substitute for victory!" Message to West Point cheer leader, September, 1949, for Army-Navy football rally.

"In war, there is not substitute for victory." Speech to Congress, April, 1951. Also letter to Congressman Martin which was alleged to be one of the reasons for MacArthur's dismissal. It is obvious that MacArthur had little patience with a loser, whether in war or a football game.

The "twilight" of MacArthur's life has lasted for many long and eventful years which included not only two wars and his rulership of Japan but the most dramatic homecoming of an American general in our history. As far back as September 8, 1941, MacArthur wrote in a private letter, "My little boy is nearly four years old now—the complete center of my thoughts and affections. I am fortunate in having him in the twilight period of my life."

To Congress nearly 10 years later he said, "I address you with neither rancor nor bitterness in the fading twilight of my life."

"I shall keep the soldier's faith," ended both his report as Chief of Staff in 1934 and his first speech to the Australian press in 1942. He felt able to report on numerous other occasions, "I have kept the soldier's faith."

Many times he used the cheering expression, "Old soldiers never die," in messages to ill or wounded contemporaries.

The peroration of his address to Congress, reproduced at the beginning of this section, was a well-edited variation of the thought he expressed in a message to the 1947 West Point graduating class: "Nearly 48 years have gone since I joined the long gray line. As an Army 'brat' it was the fulfillment of all my boyish dreams. The world has turned over many times since that day, but through the grim murk of it all the pride and thrill of being a West Pointer has never dimmed. And as I near the end of the road, what I felt when I was sworn in on the Plain so long ago I can still say—'that is my greatest honor.'" This sentiment was dashed off on the bottom of a letter to him, his customary method of replying. In editing his Congressional message, he wisely eliminated the phrase, "grim murk of it all," along with other changes.

A public figure called on for so many speeches, letters, and messages as MacArthur could certainly be forgiven for these repetitions and even for some variation in ideas regarding his greatest honor. Thus, he momentarily demoted West Point from this high place in his Chicago speech of April, 1951, and said, ". . . I still possess that to me the greatest of all honors and distinctions. I am an American."

MAC ARTHUR'S MEMORY

MacArthur was born with brains and spent a lifetime of study developing them. The fact that he was more intelligent, better informed, more skilled in his profession than most of those he dealt with on his own level of rank was a source of more than a little friction. He has practiced his profession of engineering—built roads and bridges—and has a better than layman's knowledge of medicine, chemistry, and law and is, of course, a fine executive.

His feats of memory are so phenomenal that many associates have felt called on to challenge them. Seeing him skim through a page in an extremely brief time, observers have not believed he could absorb the printed words and have questioned him weeks later about the book or magazine item, only to find that he remembered it perfectly.

Because of his memory for faces, it is sometimes believed that he keeps a private file in his office of everyone he has ever met or is likely to, and that he is briefed before seeing visitors. This is not the case; he does not need reminders. I have watched several times when he was confronted unexpectedly by persons he had not seen for 20 years. One was a Filipino scout corporal, who gave his name and said, "I had the honor to serve under the General at McKinley." MacArthur seemed to be groping, apparently having no recollection whatsoever of the individual. "Oh, yes," he began, "that was in 1924. Sergeant Calugas had the desk near the door. We went on maneuvers in September," and so on with generalities which (I thought) would give the impression of being remembered to this wholly unremembered man. Then he said, "Yes, and one day my chauffeur was sick and you drove my car." He does this frequently with others, recalling a conversation that took place years previously. The effect, of course, is highly flattering to each visitor.

In later years, MacArthur left most of the detail to his staff officers but whenever important decisions arose he reverted to the working habits of his younger days and himself studied plans and proposals from all possible angles. As a fairly young officer learning his trade in battle, he was meticulous in organization and planning. In France during World War I he would spend as much as three or four hours planning flank patrols to be carried out by a few men, making notes on a card, numbering items in order of importance, then discussing all points with his staff, getting their full opinions, and finally making complete handwritten notes to be turned into a field order.

It is well known that once he forms an opinion, he takes a long time to change. Pat Hurley, then his superior as Secretary of War, once said,

"Thank God the General is right most of the time. It's hell to convince him of it when he's wrong. Takes all night and all the next day and sometimes a month or two, to bring him around." This was true because, before making a final decision, MacArthur always canvassed all possible opinions, and consulted his advisers and the authorities. Thus he was thoroughly able to defend a position once he had taken it.

THE CONVERSATIONALIST

MacArthur is such a vital, and magnetic individual that people meeting him for the first time are often "stunned . . . overwhelmed . . . hypnotized" by his personality, the sweep of his ideas, his astonishing memory, and his conversational versatility. Even professional reporters, accustomed to meeting scores of national and international figures, are frequently highly impressed.

George Johnston, the Australian journalist, was awed by MacArthur's performance at a press conference, and recorded that each answer to a question was not only "utterly complete but a polished essay on military lore." In conversation, Johnston reported, MacArthur could talk continuously for two hours and never grope for a word. He would quote, always aptly, from Napoleon, a line or two from a melodrama seen a quarter of a century before, or a speech by Lincoln, a statement by Plato, a passage from Scripture. There were deep piety, swift epigram, and vivid description in his words.

An interviewer of many famous persons, John Gunther, said in *The Riddle of MacArthur* (New York, Harper, 1951), "I have seldom met anybody who gives such a sense of the richness and flexibility of the English language; he draws out of it . . . as out of some inexhaustible reservoir. . . . He never stops; he is an old-fashioned monologist par excellence. . . . Sometimes he is so bewitched by his own eloquence that he forgets what he has just said."

Frank Kelley and Cornelius Ryan wrote in *MacArthur: Man of Action* (New York, Doubleday, 1950): "The very brilliance of his conversation gives the impression of greatness. Perhaps this is because MacArthur *acts out* every part." Senators who heard him testify after his dismissal were equally impressed by his talking and acting, and on several occasions they spontaneously praised him for "great statements."

A word about MacArthur's "acting." His ability to express himself is consummate. When he is "bitter" about something, he spits out the word as if it had a bad taste. He uses his hands, face, eyes, voice, and his pipe to emphasize a point or underscore a mood. What makes this not simple acting but something more is that his feelings are genuine and sincere—he emphasizes and underlines those feelings. Thus he is not acting in the stage sense of feigning an emotion.

Even as a young man, MacArthur lived to the hilt any role he was called on to carry out; the point is, he did not act it—he lived it. As first sergeant of his class at West Point, he was the ideal first sergeant down to each gesture, intonation, and order. When he accepted Japan's surrender, he was the ideal commander of the forces of victory triumphant over evil. When he "faded away" in his speech to Congress, his critics thought he was "hamming," but in truth he was simply using the legitimate postures of oratory to express what he himself felt—the old soldier saying farewell after 52 years of serving his country. I did, however, detect one note in that speech which—while no doubt justifiable within the latitude allowed an orator pleading a cause—sounded slightly false to one who has known MacArthur. He recounted that the last thing his Korean soldiers said to him before his homecoming was, "Don't scuttle the Pacific!" It is somehow difficult to imagine a Korean infantryman coming up to him hissing this difficult English sentence. Furthermore, the expression is an old favorite of the General's.

MacArthur has always drawn a strict line between himself as an individual and as an officer or official. Knowing this, friends enjoyed watching him at parties during his term in Washington as Chief of Staff. If he were acquainted with everyone present on more or less intimate terms, he was easy, relaxed, and friendly—though rarely informal—and thoroughly enjoyed the attention which he always attracted. But if a diplomat (say the Brazilian ambassador) came into the room, he instantly became a different person. He was now General Douglas MacArthur, Chief of Staff of the United States Army, and he comported himself with the "dignity inherent" in that position.

While on official visits abroad, he raised a commotion in one of the Balkan countries by insisting through the American ambassador that he be provided with a private railway car. "Douglas," a friend commented, "would just as soon have traveled on roller skates if he had been there as a private citizen. But the dignity of the American nation required that the Chief of Staff travel in a private car. So Douglas hollered until he got it —not for himself personally but for the American Chief of Staff."

CHAPTER

11

MacArthur and Politics

AS THIS IS WRITTEN, THERE IS EVERY REASON TO BElieve that MacArthur will certainly be a leading figure—and possibly even the decisive influence—in the 1952 presidential nominations and elections. Before explaining why this is so, it might be well to point out that prophecies of a political nature are risky enough even in a newspaper, where they can be modified from day to day as dictated by death, withdrawals of candidates, or other quick changes. They are doubly risky in a book to be published approximately a year before the elections. But barring any changes in the vital statistics of the leading figures, these things are likely to happen:

MacArthur, a lifelong Republican, is not and will not be an active candidate for the Republican presidential nomination. Nevertheless he will take an extremely active part in the maneuvers prior to the Republican convention and will do everything in his power to keep General Dwight D. Eisenhower from getting the nomination. Present indications are that MacArthur may use his influence to support Senator Robert A. Taft, the son of his father's old rival in their historic feud of a half century ago. But if Taft cannot get the nomination, there may be other Republicans equally acceptable to him as a candidate.

The battle for the nomination and the subsequent presidential campaigns will offer MacArthur an opportunity to carry on the most vigorous —and to him the most important—fight of his long career. All the guns of his eloquent oratory will be turned on the administration in a battle to vindicate his position in Korea, to prove that his dismissal from command was unjust, and to demonstrate that he is right—and his opponents wrong—in his views of foreign policy.

From the tone of his addresses up to the time this book was published, it is logical to assume that MacArthur will avoid any rough and tumble, dirty politicking. But it would still be possible for him to get over telling attacks on a high level, and even if no names are mentioned the public will be able to make the missing identification when MacArthur squares off against his old aide, General Eisenhower—should Eisenhower decide to run. A few anecdotes illustrate the feelings of the two men for each other.

MacArthur has been heard to refer to Eisenhower as "the best clerk who ever served under me." When Ike was mentioned for the presidency in 1948, MacArthur was quoted as saying, "I don't think he's got the guts to tackle the job."

For his part, Ike, the returned hero of European victory, was once approached by a gushing woman—it happened at a reception in Denver. "General Eisenhower," she said, "you've done a simply wonderful job, but I must tell you that my real idol is Douglas MacArthur. Have you met him?"

"Not only have I met him, madam," Eisenhower replied, "but I studied dramatics under him for five years in Washington and four in the Philippines."

Eisenhower—although this has not previously been known publicly—did not favor getting MacArthur out of the Philippines in 1942 to command the forces which were to sweep all the way from Australia to Tokyo. In February, 1942, when there was a great public demand that MacArthur be gotten out of besieged Bataan and when his appointment to Supreme Allied Command of the Southwest Pacific was under consideration by Roosevelt and his top advisers, Eisenhower recorded his personal opinion to this effect: I think we are being too much influenced by newspaper editorials about MacArthur, in what should be a purely military decision. Pa Watson (White House aide) says MacArthur is worth five Army corps and must be gotten out of Bataan. I disagree. He is in exactly the right place on Bataan.

Any slim chance that might have existed for a personal reconciliation between the two men disappeared as a result of Eisenhower's remarks at the time of MacArthur's removal from command. His face a study of puzzled surprise, Ike said, "I hope he will not return to the United States and become a controversial figure. I wouldn't like it to lead to acrimony." He added, "When you put on a uniform, there are certain inhibitions you accept." The first remark may possibly become the one that will endure longest as a result of the still continuing controversy stirred up by the firing of MacArthur. Ike's second comment, which can only be construed as a rebuke, was offensive and unacceptable to MacArthur.

MacArthur will certainly not resort to personalities in any formal campaign oratory but it has already become evident in his speeches that he holds the Europe-first generals, and especially Eisenhower, primarily responsible for breaking up the American Army after World War II. It annoys him considerably that Eisenhower—who was hailed as a hero for getting our troops back home in 1946—should be again hailed as a hero for sending them abroad once more in 1951, only five years later. At the end of the war, when Eisenhower became Chief of Staff, the generals were in practical command in Washington; and the administration would have followed their advice about the future of our armed forces. But, under Eisenhower, our army crumbled to a few training divisions, plus the occupation forces in Europe and Japan.

MacArthur is said to feel that the point system, which made soldiers eligible for discharge as individuals upon the acquisition of so many points for length of service and battle experience, was the most ridiculous idea ever contrived. The troops should have been brought home by units, he contends, which would have maintained both morale and organizational cohesion. MacArthur is believed to be still indignant over Ike's visit to the Far Eastern theater: "He came out there and told the soldiers he would get them home to mother, and they gave him, 'Three cheers and a Tiger. Hip, hip, hooray.' So, our army dissolved."

If Eisenhower is a candidate, his record in Europe will also certainly be given deep and critical study, no doubt with especial reference to his 1942 deal with Darlan and other French fascists in North Africa, and his later decision to stop the Allied armies at the Elbe and permit the Russians to take Berlin. All sorts of nefarious motives, which never entered Ike's head at the time when he was an admitted babe in the woods in European politics, will be attributed to him.

Even if Eisenhower is removed from the political picture through refusal to run or failure to win the nomination, MacArthur will still carry on his war against the Europe-first generals: George Marshall, Omar Bradley, Eisenhower, and their supporters. His attack would aim at the highly vulnerable record since 1941 of the Democratic administrations, which, however high-minded their intentions, have suffered subsequent disastrous reverses in the diplomatic-military field to outweigh purely military victories.

If he does this, MacArthur could reveal that early in the war with Japan he strongly urged that all possible pressure be brought on Russia to go to war with the Japanese and open a second front in Manchuria. It was his argument that it was a manifest absurdity for Russia to be on peaceful and friendly relations with Japan while every other allied nation was at war with *all* the axis powers. He contended that his proposition was militarily feasible, that Russia had already absorbed the great shock of the German attack and had begun her own counterattack. The Russians would certainly have lost Vladivostock, and the Japanese might have plunged a few hundred miles into the vast wastes of Siberia, but that would not have affected the Soviet's main war effort against Germany, nor would they have been expected to divert any strength from Europe. But at the same time it would have completely changed the Pacific war situation, forced the Japanese to retract from the south, relieved the pressure on China, and given the United States Siberian bases for air attacks on Japan itself.

MacArthur's suggestion was coldly and totally ignored, he may point out, and his message not even answered.

But two years later, with the war in the Pacific already militarily decided and Japan on the point of extending feelers toward surrender, the same men who had ignored MacArthur's earlier suggestion went to Yalta and begged Russia to come into the war, paying a price whose final cost is not yet reckoned. MacArthur, who as our leading Asiatic student and strategist was not even consulted about Yalta nor informed of it officially afterward, is said to feel profoundly and profanely about this disastrous agreement.

MacArthur could prove that he is not second-guessing or being wise in the aftermath. If challenged, he could demonstrate that—while not in a position as Southwest Pacific Theater Commander to make any overt attempts to influence Washington decisions as to European strategy—he did time and again express his concern over the postwar situation in Europe. "I hope," he was accustomed to say, "that they are making the wise political decisions in respect to Europe. The Russian should not be allowed in Western Europe; he does not belong there; and if he is even allowed to take and keep Poland, there will certainly be another war."

He could also prove that months before Yalta, he told President Roosevelt—in their conference at Pearl Harbor in July, 1944—that once the Philippines were taken, Japan could be beaten into surrender by the use of air and sea power alone, without the necessity for an invasion. Admiral Nimitz shared this view, and so informed the President. By the time Roosevelt, with General Marshall, went to Yalta, MacArthur was already firmly established in the Philippines, yet the concessions—at China's expense—were made to get Russia into a war in which she fought exactly six days.

The official justification for Yalta is that it promised to save a million American lives by making unnecessary an invasion of Japan; but MacArthur in his political speeches could attempt to demolish this argument by proving that Roosevelt had already been informed by his top Pacific commanders—MacArthur and Nimitz—that this invasion would not be necessary, that Japan would surrender. In fact, Japan did soon seek to surrender; but in accordance with the pattern in those days, MacArthur was not even informed of that fact.

In his speeches, MacArthur may blame the Europe-first, or administration, generals for the Yalta disaster, and repeat his strong attacks on General Marshall for implementing the China policy which helped deliver that country to the Reds in what MacArthur has called the greatest disaster in our history. He will also review again his version of the events in Korea leading to his dismissal, and blame the Marshall-Bradley-Collins-Vandenberg group and Truman himself for failing—even after Congress appropriated many billions—to put our country into a position of preparedness against attack.

The General's attacks on foreign and military policy of the past decade may carry considerable weight with the voters, especially if he documents them with evidence of the sometimes shabby, sometimes misleading, and frequently indecisive manner in which he was dealt with by Washington between 1941 and 1951.

Of course, if Eisenhower should win the nomination despite MacArthur's opposition, that would leave MacArthur with pretty much nothing to do except really "fade away," unless he chose to attack both Eisenhower and the Democratic nominee with "a plague on both your houses." But if another Republican than Eisenhower wins the nomination and the presidency, MacArthur would probably serve as his adviser on diplomatic and military affairs in the capacity of elder statesman. The General has frequently referred to "elder statesmen" since his dismissal; and while the references were not directly to himself, it is evident that he is thinking along those lines.

As a noncandidate but active participant in the campaigning, MacArthur would enjoy several advantages—that of hindsight in some matters, though he can demonstrate in others that he was foresighted as well. He would offer a diversionary threat his opponents would be forced to counter, even though it would do those opponents little good to run down or discredit his political views.

In speeches since his homecoming, his political views have gradually emerged. On the main issues of the day, they may be summarized as follows:

The state of the nation:

"Much that I have seen since my return to my native land . . . has filled me with immeasurable satisfaction and pride. Our material progress has been little short of phenomenal. . . . Talk of imminent threat to our national security through the application of external force is pure nonsense. It is not of any external threat that I concern myself but rather of insidious forces working from within which have already so drastically altered the character of our free institutions. . . . Foremost of these forces is . . . Communism. It has infiltrated into positions of public trust and responsibility. . . . There can be no compromise with atheistic Communism—no half-way in the preservation of freedom and religion. It must be all or nothing. . . ."

Free enterprise and taxation

"It was the adventurous spirit of America which . . . carved a great nation . . . which raised the living standard of the American people beyond that ever before known . . . and which elevated the laborer, the farmer and the tradesman to their rightful station of dignity and relative prosperity. This adventurous spirit is now threatened . . . by an unconscionable burden of taxation. . . . More and more we work not for ourselves but for the state. . . ."

On foreign aid

"We should do all in our power to alleviate the suffering and hardship of other peoples, and to support their own maximum effort to preserve their freedom from the assaults of Communist imperialism. But when this effort is carried beyond the ability to pay . . . it ceases to be altruism and becomes reckless imprudence."

On political control of the Armed Services

". . . I find in existence a new and heretofore unknown and dangerous concept that the members of our armed forces owe primary allegiance and loyalty to those who temporarily exercise the authority of the executive branch of the government, rather than to the country and its Constitution which they are sworn to defend. No proposition could be more dangerous."

On foreign policy

". . . Is there any wonder that Soviet propaganda so completely dominates American foreign policy? And indeed, what is our foreign policy? . . . The sorry truth is that we have no foreign policy. Expediencies as variable and shifting as the exigencies of the moment seem to be the only guide. Yesterday we disarmed, today we arm, and what of tomorrow? We have been told of the war in Korea that it was the wrong war, with the wrong enemy, at the wrong time and in the wrong place.

"Does this mean that they intend and indeed plan what they would call a right war, with a right enemy, at a right time and in a right place? If successful in mounting the North Atlantic Pact . . . do we mean to throw down a gage of battle?"

The Korean war

". . . In Korea, the result has been indecisive. . . . The high moral purpose . . . yielded to the timidity and fear of our leaders as, after defeating our original enemy, a new one entered the field which they dared not fight to a decision. Appeasement thereafter became the policy . . . on the battlefield. . . . Now that the fighting has temporarily abated the outstanding impression which emerges . . . is the utter uselessness of the enormous sacrifice . . . a million soldiers, a like number of civilians, a nation gutted. The threat of aggression . . . has not diminished. Indeed, nothing has been settled. No issue has been decided."

On world peace

". . . We must finally come to realize that war is outmoded as an instrument of political policy, that it provides no solution for international problems; that it but threatens the participants with mutual national suicide. . . . Mounting cost of preparation for war is in many ways as materially destructive as war itself. . . . While we must be prepared to meet the trial of war if war comes . . . we must lead the world down the road to the abolition of war from the face of the earth. Such is the role as I see it for which this great nation of ours is now cast. In this we follow the Cross. If we meet the challenge we cannot fail."

Despite his lifetime Republican leanings, MacArthur has been a political asset to two Democratic presidents at times of election. Roosevelt, as is detailed in the next section of this book, was able to make potent political capital of the General's return to the Philippines in 1944. Similarly, Truman's dramatic and much publicized flight to Wake Island to meet MacArthur just before the 1950 state and Congressional election was primarily political in purpose. Nothing was discussed there of such urgent nature as to require a face-to-face meeting. But MacArthur was at the height of his popularity following the successful Inchon landings, while Truman was in the public doghouse for his slanderous attack on the Marine Corps. By his trip, Truman once again reminded the people that the war in Korea was his—and not MacArthur's—and associated himself in the public mind with the victory that then seemed sure.

In his previous long-distance and brief flirtations with politics, American public opinion has been sharply divided about MacArthur. He attracted the support of the reactionary elements of the right, and of the lunatic fringe of America-Firsters and their ilk. He was bitterly disliked by large segments of labor, by many former GI's, sailors, and marines, by liberals and pseudoliberals, and, of course, by the Communists. The anti-MacArthur view at present is summed up by the New York *Post*, whose self-conscious liberalism is tinged by thinly concealed circulation appeals to racial and religious minorities. The *Post*, with its customary liberal tolerance, called him "a desperate, demagogic Republican politician fighting a dirty political war."

From his record, however, MacArthur does not clearly belong in any easily defined group. In his recent speeches, his remarks about "free enterprise" have been orthodox, right-wing Republican in tone. But his liberal record in Japan, plus his attacks on colonialism in Asia, show he feels no special kinship with or respect for the captains of international commerce. He is completely liberal in racial relations. By no stretch of the imagination can he be considered an isolationist, with regard to either Europe or Asia, where he has strongly urged realistic planning to meet the needs of the vast masses for food, clothing, and shelter, and their determination to be rid of colonialism and to achieve "heretofore unfelt dignity, and the self-respect of political freedom." He sharply refused to associate himself with the proposals of Taft and ex-President Hoover that all our forces be brought back to American soil.

Also from his record, MacArthur should have little difficulty in disposing of the Democratic allegation that he challenged the supremacy of civilian authority over the military. He never for a moment questioned Truman's right to remove him. His rule in Japan was the least militaristic of any armed occupation in history. Returning to the Philippines, he insisted on being accompanied by President Osmena as head of the civil government in exile and sent all the way to Washington for him. There was no military government organization whatever attached to MacArthur's armies in the Philippines; and he was so eager to restore civilian authority that he did so even before the last shots were fired in the devastated ruins of Manila and while the southern islands were still in Japanese hands.

Summing up, MacArthur has been in more or less close association with five presidents. Teddy Roosevelt made him a White House aide; Woodrow Wilson approved his crusade for the use of citizen-soldier divisions in World War I; Hoover made him Chief of Staff; F. D. Roosevelt kept him in that office, recalled him to active service in 1941, promoted him and approved his campaign to liberate the Philippines. Truman fired him. Of the five, the two Roosevelts—Republican and Democrat—obviously had the greatest influence on his political thinking, as became evident in his rule of Japan. MacArthur took on the gigantic Japanese trust—the Zaibatsu—with a whoop and holler that would have delighted the original trust-busting Teddy Roosevelt. It was not a simple task because the Zaibatsu was no ordinary trust as America knows the word, but a nation-wide monopoly controlling 80 percent of all Japan's business and so intertwined with the government that it was difficult to separate them. MacArthur tackled the job with enthusiasm, until finally halted by Washington. Also, some of his labor reforms and other social legislation in Japan out-New Dealed Franklin Roosevelt.

MacArthur's previous political experiences have not been too happy. He got one vote for the presidency in 1944 which prevented Dewey's nomination from being unanimous. He did not seek the nomination in that year, but he did in 1948; and a measure of his isolation from public opinion at home was his conviction that he had a chance of success. Of course, he never did. One reason was that he never made any sort of campaign from Tokyo, being prevented (if not by his own wishes) by a 1944 Army-Navy agreement banning political activity for servicemen and officers on active duty. He did manage to write a few letters to supporters in Wisconsin, including a formal statement: "I do not actively seek or covet any office (but) I would be recreant to all my good concepts of good citizenship were I to shrink because of the hazards and responsibilities involved from accepting any public duty to which I might be called by the American people."

Senator Joe McCarthy, later to become one of his strong supporters, waged an all-out fight for Harold Stassen, the other candidate in the Wisconsin Republican primaries. McCarthy compared the General to two "physically weak presidents," Roosevelt and Wilson, and appealed to Catholic voters by repeated references to MacArthur's two marriages. MacArthur's opponents also stirred up the old Billy Mitchell courts-martial, asserting that MacArthur had voted to convict the airman, who is a local Wisconsin hero.

MacArthur's supporters were chiefly those who had opposed Roosevelt, and who had accused the President of depriving the General of supplies —allegedly for political reasons—during the Pacific war. In his efforts to force Washington to pay more attention to the Pacific, MacArthur had *seemingly* welcomed the assistance of any person, newspaper, or faction that supported his views, regardless of the fact that many of these supporters stood for things in domestic politics which MacArthur normally would have opposed. I have underlined "seemingly," because I do not think the story is generally known of how MacArthur lost the support of Col. Robert R. McCormick's Chicago *Tribune*, a very strong factor in Wisconsin politics. On a visit to Tokyo prior to the 1948 primaries, McCormick expressed to MacArthur his concern over the "socialistic economic policies" he was implementing in Japan. MacArthur replied to this effect: "This is not socialism. But it would be better for Japan to have real socialism, than the socialism of the monopolies." A day or two later McCormick announced that his newspapers would back for the presidency not MacArthur, but Robert A. Taft.

In 1948 MacArthur won only eight delegates of twenty-seven in Wisconsin, and the final denouement of his inactive trans-Pacific candidacy held overtones of pathos. He was no threat to any of the leaders, who easily could have allowed his name to receive an ovation at the convention as a tribute for his services to the nation. Instead, the GOP leaders went out of their way to show disrespect for him. His supporters went to Philadelphia with millions of petitions, mostly obtained through publication of daily coupons in the Hearst press. General Wainwright, still sick and weak from the ordeal of imprisonment after his capture at Corregidor, was waiting in a hotel room to second the nominating speech of Harlan Kelley, a blind war veteran and attorney of Wisconsin.

It was planned to precede these speeches with a parade of Philadelphia *Inquirer* newsboys carrying baskets full of petitions, down all the aisles. The party leaders, however, kept sidetracking the nomination for hour after hour, and finally the impatient newsboys demanded their $5 pay and went home. Other boys were rounded up at $5 a head, but finally the money gave out and the supply of boys became exhausted.

Senator Vandenberg was nominated at 3:10 A.M and a half hour later, with the convention hall practically deserted, the MacArthur managers were told they would be recognized. Wainwright was awakened and rushed to the stage. There were few newsboys and fewer delegates to hear Kelley assert, "We average American citizens are horribly confused. We do not know whether we have just finished a war, whether we are engaged in a war, hot or cold, or whether we are about to plunge into a war. . . . We need a leader in fact, as well as in name. . . . A man who in his dealings with Russia will make us proud instead of apologetic or ashamed. . . ." Wainwright followed with a weak-voiced speech to the empty chairs. On the first ballot MacArthur got eleven votes, and on the second, seven. Dewey was unanimously chosen on the third.

When General Whitney took the news to MacArthur in Tokyo, he "hung his head in deep emotional stress"—but whether at the failure of his effort or at the thought of Wainwright talking to the empty spaces of the convention hall, nobody knows. The defeat was something of a shock also to the Japanese people, who could not understand how America could turn its back on this great leader.

To summarize MacArthur's present political position: it is certain—at least at this writing—that he will not be an active candidate for the GOP nomination; if he had plans to the contrary, he would not have taken up residence in the Waldorf Towers, which is hardly a suitable address for a grass-roots candidate. Ever since his return from the Far East, his friends have been urging him to think first of his health—which is excellent—and have told him "to coast from here on in."

Although he does nothing on his own behalf and instead actively backs some other candidate, this will not be sufficient to discourage his perennial admirers from placing his name on primary ballots in several states where he has strong, if poorly organized, support. There will certainly be undiminished efforts in his behalf by such indefatigable gentlemen as one Erwin Hohensee, who at his own expense has maintained "MacArthur for President" offices in Washington since 1948. But these uncertain and sporadic gestures could not by any stretch of the imagination add up to the nomination.

However, once a man has desired the presidency, he never seems entirely to give up hope; and MacArthur in this respect is no different than any other man. If the voice of the people called loudly enough, MacArthur would not be so "recreant to his duty" as a citizen as to ignore it. But, as this is written, there is no such prospect.

IV

Some Recent Controversies

A Prefatory Note on Global Strategy

IN DISCUSSING HIS STORMY 10 YEARS IN THE PACIFIC from 1941 through his dismissal in 1951, Douglas MacArthur has been heard to say, "I have always felt that my real enemy was behind me—in Washington—not in front of me."

If anyone man fits the description of what MacArthur regards as his "real enemy," that man is General George Catlett Marshall. Yet MacArthur has made it clear that he himself, at least, does not believe that Marshall acted as he did because of his well-known and long-standing feud with MacArthur. Rather he regards Marshall as the acknowledged leader and symbol of the "Europe-first" global strategy. He believes that strategy to be blind and disastrous. He believes that because of it the "Europe-first" generals—Marshall, Eisenhower, Bradley, and their followers—were prepared to "scuttle the Pacific" during the war against Japan in 1941-45, and were equally prepared to "scuttle the Pacific" when our armed adventure in Korea turned into a real war.

He believes that the men who look first to Europe are "infatuated" with that area, and this is true to a large extent because of personal interests: that their careers have been connected with Europe, their interests lie there, it is for them the best and most attractive place to fight "the right war, in the right place, at the right time, against the right enemy." The plans they pursue, in MacArthur's opinion, are not global strategy but a form of thinking which would regard one bomb on Belgrade or Brussels as sufficient provocation for World War III but which considered the Korean war as a "skirmish."

The words "global strategy" have a scientific sound, as if it were something worked out with slide rule and calculating machine, and based on cold figures of ammunition production, factory capacity, and shipping tonnages. Actually, this is only part of the story. The final application of grand strategy in World War II depended on such human factors as the state of Churchill's hangover, Harry Hopkins' ulcers, George Marshall's patience, and Douglas MacArthur's eloquence. Similarly today, such factors as morale, friendship, tradition, and the personal interests of the men involved affect decisions of world policy and strategy as much as any coldly calculated facts and figures.

To understand this, it is only necessary to review what *almost* happened to change American grand strategy in 1942. Long before we got into war through Japan's attack in 1941, it had been decided—supposedly immutably on a basis of cold calculation of all the factors—that our main front lay in Europe. Through the early months of the war, while nearly all America clamored for action against Japan, the planners in Washington clung to the "main topic of the war against Germany." They resolutely refused to waver, even when the British themselves (probably looking to the postwar future and the position of Russia in Europe) urged additional action against the Japanese.

The concept behind this grand strategy, as it was set forth in a letter from President Roosevelt to Harry Hopkins, General Marshall, and Admiral King in July, 1942, was this: "I am opposed to an American all-out effort in the Pacific against Japan with the view to her defeat as quickly as possible. It is of the utmost importance that we appreciate that defeat of Japan does not defeat Germany and that American concentration against Japan this year or in 1943 increases the chance of complete German domination of Europe and Africa. On the other hand, it is obvious that the defeat of Germany, or the holding of Germany in 1942 or in 1943, means probably, eventual defeat of Germany in the European and African theaters and in the Near East. *Defeat of Germany means the defeat of Japan, probably without firing a shot or losing a life.*" *

These views supposedly were law, infallible and unalterable. Yet at this same time, General Marshall, Secretary of War Stimson, and Admiral Ernest King became incensed with the British because they were suggesting other means of attacking Germany than the cross-channel invasion of France which Marshall, especially, believed absolutely essential to defeat Germany and save Russia from collapse. The United States at this time apparently was close to "turn(ing) our backs (on the British) and tak(ing) up the war with Japan"—as Stimson put it. Marshall, King, and General Arnold prepared a memorandum for Roosevelt proposing this drastic action.

Afterward, Secretary Stimson described these maneuvers as a bluff (which was partially successful) to force the British to agree with American plans. Roosevelt described them as a "red herring," and chided his military leaders for proposing to "take up their dishes and go away," or—

* This sentence, which I have italicized, surely makes strange reading in the light of Yalta. If Roosevelt believed this in 1942, if he was given similar assurances, as he was, by MacArthur and Nimitz in 1944 that no invasion of Japan would be necessary, it becomes increasingly impossible to understand the Yalta concessions in 1945, at a time when Japan was already strategically on the ropes.

as it has been put in another way—"to take their landing craft to the Pacific and go make war there." But Robert E. Sherwood says (in *Roosevelt and Hopkins* [New York, Harper, 1950]) that "there is . . . considerable difference of opinion" as to whether the threat was real or a bluff. He adds, ". . . it is my impression that the plan was far more than a bluff in General Marshall's mind and certainly in Admiral King's. Indeed, the first step in it—the assault on Guadalcanal, was approved. . . ." It is also true that until the time of the North Africa invasion, larger numbers of troops were sent to the Pacific (though not to MacArthur) than to any other war theater.

Sherwood further says, "Disagreement at this stage gave evidence of becoming so acute that the U.S. Chiefs of Staff seriously considered radical revision of the long-determined grand strategy of Germany first." However, the matter was settled, and the Germany-first strategy was—as everyone knows—followed.

So far as this book is concerned, the point is that there is nothing inexorably final about "global strategy"—which is the reason our generals are so divided about it. In World War II it was debatable at times even to the men who decided it, although General Eisenhower has written that so far as he knows, "the wisdom of the plan to turn the weight of our power against the European enemy before attempting an all-out campaign against Japan has never been questioned by any real student of strategy." Eisenhower wrote that sentence on page 28 of his war history, *Crusade in Europe* (New York, Doubleday, 1948), but only six pages earlier he had reported how vigorously he had fought to give priority to the Far East early in 1942, and had described as annoying "side shows" the various plans then contemplated for attacking Germany. Whether, six years after his book was written, Eisenhower would still consider the Germany-first strategy as above question is not for discussion here. Suffice it to say that the strategy our planners followed did defeat Germany and Japan, that it left Russia in control of much of Europe and most of Asia, and that (thanks to Stalin) its results have not been world peace but war, and the threat of more wars. Whether the way MacArthur proposed to fight would have produced better results offers an interesting field for speculation, but no proof is possible.

To MacArthur (though Eisenhower would not rank him a "real student of strategy"), the strategy of beat Germany first was anything but final and perfect. A former Chief of Staff, with more battlefield experience and a knowledge of history at least equal to (and in most cases far surpassing) that of the men who made the decisions in Washington, he did not agree that the war with Japan could be let slide until Germany was defeated. Never a man to conceal his opinions, he sought to keep some of America's attention focused on the Pacific and Asia, with whose future he believes the future of America is bound for the next century.

Similarly, when war came in Korea, he pushed his views as to the prime importance of Asia, and pushed them to the point where they became unacceptable to the other generals.

In this writer's understanding, the conflict between the generals is to a large extent one of timing. The Marshall-Bradley-Eisenhower group believe that for *the immediate future,* our interests in Europe are paramount, and those in Asia are decidedly secondary. MacArthur believes that the line must be held everywhere against Communism, that what happens in Asia is just as important as developments in Europe. In the not distant future he foresees the rise of the great masses of Asia and their industrialization. If they become and remain our friends, we will be able to survive against their great numerical superiority. If they are our enemies, we will perish. The fight for Asia—*and it is predominantly a fight to assist, not to conquer,* the great multitudes of those still economically backward nations—is going on now. Except for Japan and a few outlying areas, the great bulk of Asia is under Russian domination and has turned to Communism in its hope for economic advancement. In MacArthur's view, the results of the last war created a delicate situation for Russia in the Far East, especially since Japan has been won over to our side. Russia has recognized this and has moved in on the Far East. To Russia, the Far East is its area of predominant importance. Consequently it must also be our own area of predominant importance.

This fundamental difference of opinion as to whether Europe is the main theater of our national interests, or whether the Pacific and Asia are at least equally important, is the main fact underlying the controversies in which MacArthur has been involved from 1941-1951 and which finally led to his relief from command. Those controversies, together with some others of a strictly military nature and a background of the feud between Douglas MacArthur and George Marshall,* are discussed in the following pages of this book.

* When this book was written General Marshall had not yet resigned from his post as Secretary of Defense.

CHAPTER

12

The Marshall-MacArthur Feud

WHEN DOUGLAS MACARTHUR WAS SUMMARILY DISmissed from his commands in the Far East, he did not need two guesses as to who was primarily responsible for the insulting manner in which his relief was carried out. "The President," he was quoted as saying, "'let George do it.' Whoever was on the firing squad, it was George Marshall who pulled the trigger."

MacArthur thus interpreted the rude manner of his dismissal as Marshall's climactic act of vengeance against him in a feud which has been going on behind the scenes for some 30 years and has—at least in the opinion of many of the men around MacArthur—been a contributing factor in influencing all-important decisions on American strategy and policy.

It would, of course, be oversimplification to attempt to attribute the tremendously important Asia-versus-Europe priority disputes to a personal fight between MacArthur and Marshall for power and supremacy. MacArthur himself says there is nothing in this theory, that the disagreements between the two men have involved purely matters of policy, and that there is no question of jealousy or rivalry in their conflicting views.

But it is at the same time an indisputable fact that the two men have personified the opposing viewpoints on world strategy and diplomacy. It is also true that they are completely different in character and experience, and that they heartily dislike each other. Those things being true, both men must be slightly above other humans in understanding and forbearance, if they have in fact risen above personal feelings and refused to be influenced by them in their actions vis-à-vis one another at crucial moments in our history.

The full impact of their bitter disagreement was lost to the public when—testifying on separate days in the investigation of MacArthur's dismissal—the two five-star generals accused each other of virtual treason in impersonally phrased but deeply felt language. MacArthur charged that the China policy which was supported and implemented by Marshall and which contributed to the conquest of that country by the Communists was "the greatest political mistake we made in a hundred years . . . we will pay for it, for a century." Marshall countered with the terrible accusation that MacArthur had by various statements seriously damaged the morale of American soldiers engaged in battle; that he lacked foresight and balance, and that, given his way, he would "wreck" and ruin about every important policy of the United States.

Senators, well aware of the explosive potentialities of the enmity between the two men, tip-toed lightly around it to avoid stumbling into a trip wire which might touch off further point-blank blasts. On the first day of the hearings, MacArthur was asked his opinion of the Joint Chiefs of Staff—Collins, Vandenberg, Sherman, and Bradley—and gave assurances that he held them in the greatest esteem. The omission of General George Marshall's name was so obvious, inasmuch as he was a leading actor (possibly the leading actor) in the firing of MacArthur, that an administration senator hastened next day to correct it.

"You have a high opinion of . . . the present Secretary of Defense?" Senator McMahon asked.

"I have," answered MacArthur, who is a gentleman as well as a soldier.

When Marshall had his turn on the stand, he made a perfunctory gesture of courtesy toward MacArthur as ". . . a brother Army officer . . . for whom I have tremendous respect as to his military capabilities and military performances, and from all I can learn, as to his administration of Japan." The amenities thus observed, Marshall launched into a devastating, week-long attack on his brother officer.

The writer approaches cautiously the subject of this historic feud. I have discussed it with neither Marshall nor MacArthur; and while it is evident in the closing chapter of this book that I felt Marshall acted unfairly in handling his antagonist's dismissal, I shall try to be impartial here. One thing I have discovered and which seems to me highly amazing is that these two unusually brainy and articulate men have the greatest difficulty in communicating with each other. Marshall says one thing, MacArthur understands another. In two cases—two of the most fateful in our recent history since they involved the Pearl Harbor attack and the method of MacArthur's dismissal from command—there were actual physical failures in radio facilities. When Marshall has been involved in important actions which also even indirectly involved MacArthur, the result has frequently been confusion and several times disaster on the scale of actual loss of lives and surrender of divisions.

To explain the background of their conflict: Marshall was born in the same year, 1880, 11 months later than MacArthur. The son of a prosperous coal and wood dealer of Pennsylvania, Marshall was unable to obtain an appointment to West Point and entered Virginia Military Institute, graduating as first captain of his class (the same honor MacArthur won at West Point) and all-South football tackle, but 15th in the academic standings in comparison to MacArthur's all-time high marks. That Marshall eventually rose to top commands despite his non-West Point background is a tribute to his ability, but he was always an Army "outsider." Once, while Chief of Staff of the Army, he expressed his views to a civilian seeking a commission: "At West Point officers get a four-year indoctrination which makes them 'West Point officers' and it takes me longer than that to shake it all out of them." Yet it is a curious fact that leaders of the Marshall clique in the Army are all West Pointers, while MacArthur, without doubt influenced by the fact that his father was not a West Pointer and also by his father's Spanish-American war experiences with the citizen-soldiers, has always favored non-West Pointers and has been the stanchest regular Army supporter of the National Guard and of citizen-soldiers and officers. Of the five Army men closest to him today, none is a West Pointer. MacArthur's World War II Chief of Staff, Sutherland, was a VMI graduate, as was Almond, his Chief of Staff in Japan.

Marshall began his Army career in 1901 and climbed slowly up the promotional ladder through service at home and in the Philippines, developing an ability for planning which marked him for staff work for the rest of his life. MacArthur, graduating two years later, fought and observed war in the Philippines, Manchuria, and Mexico. In World War I, MacArthur was the hero, a dashing, much decorated leader of troops and a brilliant combat commander. Marshall was an efficient but relatively obscure planner and staff officer. But he won the friendship and backing of General Pershing, who called him the finest officer of the war. In contrast, War Secretary Baker publicly hailed MacArthur as "our greatest front-line commander."

It was in the final days of this war in France that the paths of Marshall (a colonel) and MacArthur (brigadier general) crossed for the first time; and even though their connection was remote, the result was chaotic. General Pershing expressed to Marshall—then operations officer of the First U.S. Army—his wish that the army make all haste to capture the historic city of Sedan. To make this possible, Pershing intended that the boundary lines between MacArthur's Rainbow Division (in which he commanded a brigade) and the French Army on its left should be temporarily disregarded. As expressed by Pershing, it was his wish that "the I Corps assisted on its right by the V Corps, will enable him to realize this desire." At First Army headquarters in Soully, General Connor and Colonel Marshall drew up an order to effect this plan. Later, Brigadier General Hugh Drum and Marshall modified the order and inserted the words, "For this purpose boundaries will not be considered as binding."

As finally issued, the historic order said:

"*Memorandum for Commanding Generals, I Corps, V Corps.*

"Subject: Message from the Commander in Chief

"1. General Pershing desires that the honor of entering Sedan should fall to the First American Army. He has every confidence that the troops of the I Corps, assisted on their right by the V Corps, will enable him to realize this desire.

"2. In transmitting the foregoing message, your attention is invited to the favorable opportunity now existing, for pressing our advantage throughout the night. Boundaries will not be considered binding.

"By command of Lieutenant General (Hunter) Liggett."

At the time this order was issued, the I Corps—which included MacArthur's Rainbow Division—was headed straight for Sedan. Off to its right was the V Corps, which included the American 1st Division. It was Pershing's intention that the V Corps should "assist" the I Corps by continuing its attack on its *own* front.

However, when the order reached the American 1st Division, its instructions to disregard boundaries were understood to mean that all boundary lines within the U.S. First Army should be disregarded, and all troops attack at once toward Sedan. The division was exhausted by days of fighting and was preparing to dig in at the close of day, but the orders it received had instructed it to keep going throughout the night. Consequently officers of the 1st Division routed out their weary doughboys and started them on what Pershing, in a masterpiece of understatement, later called "this unnecessary forced march."

The division completely changed the axis of its advance and headed over muddy roads and through bitter cold directly toward Sedan. Its troops cut into, through, in front of, and behind the American 77th and Rainbow Divisions, halting their progress and causing a colossal and historic mix-up, a true masterpiece of unmilitary confusion. In this confusion two companies of the 168th Iowa Regiment (attached to MacArthur's 84th Brigade of the Rainbow) became involved in combat the night of November 5-6, 1918, with elements of the American 1st Division and traded shells and fire for some time in and around the town of Haracourt. MacArthur and his Chief of Staff, Lieutenant Colonel Walter B. Wolfe, made a dangerous personal reconnaissance to locate and separate the contending American units; and as they returned in the early morning from accomplishing this task, MacArthur was covered and captured by a 1st Division patrol, whose soldiers mistook him for a German officer because of his unusual headgear. They refrained from shooting him from a distance only because they believed valuable information might be obtained by taking him alive.

Had the Germans attacked during these hours of unutterable confusion, there is little doubt that the result would have been disastrous. Possibly it was simply an inexplicable lapse in military common sense that caused the wording of this order, but the men of the Rainbow Division have always been convinced otherwise. It is their conviction that the First Army planners (Marshall, Drum) were so anxious to have Sedan taken by a regular Army division—the 1st—that they deliberately ordered it to cut through the adjacent National Guard divisions. The state of mind of the 1st Division was illustrated by the remarks of one of its regimental commanders, Colonel Theodore Roosevelt, Jr. Roosevelt led his men all the way through the 77th and Rainbow Divisions until he came into contact with the French. He told their protesting commander, "My orders are to march on Sedan. I am prepared to do so!" Eventually the French took the city, however.

After the war, Marshall hitched his wagon to Pershing's star, became his aide-de-camp for five years and then undertook a series of routine assignments at staff schools, as instructor, and in China—serving three years at Tientsin in 1924-27. It was in this period that Chinese Communists, under the direction of Soviet military and political leaders, began the efforts which two decades later gave them control of all China, this final result being, if not helped, then certainly not hindered by the policies put into effect by Marshall as envoy to China and as Secretary of State.

Meanwhile, MacArthur had managed to keep his rank as brigadier general after World War I, this being made possible through friends in Congress who tacked onto a military bill the so-called "MacArthur amendment" enabling his temporary rank to be made permanent; this accounted in part for the fact that until World War II he was always so much higher in rank than Marshall. By 1930 MacArthur had climbed to Chief of Staff despite the strong opposition of Pershing, and despite his supposed "exiling" by Pershing to the Philippines in 1922 as a result of a romantic rivalry.

Two years after MacArthur had been made Chief of Staff, Pershing telephoned to ask him a favor. He requested the promotion of George Marshall, by now a colonel, to brigadier general. MacArthur promised to study the request; and when he went home that night to his quarters at Fort Myer, he told his mother (whom he always kept informed of the day's doings) of the matter. "I would like to do it," he said, "but George has no experience commanding troops. I will have to refer it to a board." He made similar remarks to others, and it was reported back to Marshall that MacArthur had called him a "desk soldier." From that day on—so it is believed by many of MacArthur's intimate friends—"George Marshall has hated MacArthur," or, as MacArthur himself puts it, "My worst enemy has always been behind me." This writer, however, is unaware of any definite, impartial evidence to show that Marshall ever acted in a spirit of revenge; not, at least, until he wrote the final order for MacArthur's summary removal from command in the Far East.

The board agreed with MacArthur that Marshall lacked command experience, and he was assigned as commander of the 8th Infantry Regiment. A year later official Army records showed that the regiment had dropped far down in efficiency ratings. Marshall hoped to stay on with troops, fearing that it would be fatal to his career if he were given another staff or teaching post. But at this time, in 1933, there was an opening in the post of senior instructor in the Illinois National Guard. Civilian officers of the Guard, many of them prominent businessmen who had become intimately friendly with MacArthur in the Rainbow Division, wrote to the

Chief of Staff asking the appointment of a certain officer as instructor. MacArthur replied that the officer, being due shortly for promotion, was not available, but that he would send instead "one of the best officers in the American Army." That officer was Marshall, who obviously was *not* due for promotion in MacArthur's Army.

To Marshall, news of the transfer came as "a savage blow," as his biographer (William Frye, *Marshall, Citizen Soldier* [New York, Bobbs-Merrill, 1947]) has recorded. It was equally devastating to the second Mrs. Marshall, who had just finished hanging 325 yards of curtains on the 42 French doors in their attractive quarters at Fort Moultrie, North Carolina. Prodded by his wife and by his own natural concern for his career, Marshall wrote to the adjutant general of the Army and to MacArthur protesting against the assignment. When he received MacArthur's reply—so Mrs. Marshall has written in her biography, *Together* (Atlanta, Tupper and Love, 1946)—"George had a gray, drawn look which I had never seen before," and "One week later we were on the way to Chicago."

Marshall has not disclosed the contents of the letter from MacArthur, but it is known that in reply he stated that "under the circumstances" he would be glad to accept the assignment in Chicago—the "circumstances" obviously being a promise of a better job later on. The incident did not end there. When General Charles C. Dawes, former vice-president, heard of the assignment, he protested vigorously and profanely, "What! He can't do that. Hell, no! Not George Marshall. He's too big a man for this job. In fact he's the best goddamned officer in the U.S. Army." To this and other protests MacArthur replied, "Don't worry about Marshall. We have one of the best jobs in the Army picked out for him. He's never going to be a brigadier general. He's going to be the next chief of infantry." However, as Marshall wryly pointed out when this statement was reported to him, the post of Chief of Infantry was already filled for three years to come.

Pershing, offended at this treatment of his protégé, later slapped back at MacArthur by refusing to approve plans of the Rainbow Division Veterans Association to establish a memorial military cemetery of its own in Ohio. It was planned to inaugurate the cemetery with the return from France of the body of Private Dyer Bird of Ohio, the first combat casualty of the division in World War I. Private Bird's father was brought to Washington, where Chief of Staff MacArthur promised the War Department's cooperation in returning the body ceremoniously. Pershing expressed his sympathy and indicated he would approve. Heartened by his attitude, the Rainbow representatives remarked enthusiastically that they had already consulted MacArthur and obtained his assistance. Immediately, Pershing's attitude changed, and he turned thumbs down on the project. When informed by the delegation of the way they had handled the proposal, MacArthur commented, "That's where you made your big mistake, boys. You should have kept my name out of it."

With MacArthur subsequently out of the way in the Philippines, where he became Field Marshal of the Commonwealth Army, Pershing renewed the campaign for his protégé. Marshall, promoted to brigadier general, established a friendship with Harry Hopkins which proved invaluable to his ambitions. With Hopkins and Pershing both pushing his case, Roosevelt appointed Marshall Chief of Staff of the Army with the all-important job of getting the United States prepared for war. In doing this, the President jumped Marshall over 20 senior major generals and 14 senior brigadier generals. Among those by-passed was General Hugh Drum, who was generally regarded as the best-qualified candidate but who lacked political influence and who was also opposed, from within the Army itself, because of his religion. (Note: This anti-Catholic prejudice was first overcome with the appointment of General J. Lawton Collins, current Chief of Staff.)

The previous roles of the two men were now reversed; Marshall became the commander and MacArthur the subordinate. Marshall had a strong voice in shaping plans and policies which directed major attention toward Europe, and he controlled supply sources which as Pacific tension increased in the fall of 1941 began to deliver small numbers of men, planes, and equipment to MacArthur in the Philippines.

An unintentional newspaper error—now explained here for the first time—did nothing to improve Marshall-MacArthur relations. With the United States practically at war in the Atlantic and with storm flags flying in the Pacific, a seemingly gratuitous insult was offered Marshall by a Washington newspaper. A reporter for the paper, doing research for some material on MacArthur, came across a resolution requesting the President to rename MacArthur as Chief of Staff. The resolution was signed by every chapter of the Rainbow Division Veterans Association throughout the country. The reporter noticed that the resolution was addressed to Roosevelt as President, but failed to take note of the date, down in a corner of the page. The date was 1935, and the resolution had been passed at that time when MacArthur's extra year as Chief of Staff was about to expire. Among other things, the resolution said of MacArthur that he had "high courage, extraordinary efficiency, superior mentality, boundless energy, and power of effective decision."

The reporter wrote and the paper printed the story as a current action inspired by MacArthur's recall to active duty in the Philippines on July 26, 1941.* As reported, the action seemed a deliberate attack on Marshall, and made it appear that the Rainbow Division was seeking his replacement by MacArthur. Although the paper discovered its error, no retraction was printed. While not blaming MacArthur, Marshall naturally resented the seeming insult, and some traces of this resentment may have lingered

* MacArthur appears to have gone over Marshall's head to maneuver his own recall and appointment as over-all commander in the Philippines at this time. Marshall was considering such action, but MacArthur seems to have forced his hand. This intimation is given in the War Department volume, *Chief of Staff: Prewar Plans and Preparations*, by Mark S. Watson, which also tells the full story of planning for the Philippines defense in 1940-41.

even after Walker Colston, then president of the Rainbow Veterans, wrote Marshall a note explaining the mix-up.

Beginning from mid-November, 1941, it was obvious—or should have been obvious—that Japan and America were going to war; neither side could afford to back down from the position it took. Roosevelt's critics have accused him of provoking the Japanese to war, but this is true only in the sense that he refused to yield to them, and that the terms he offered were completely unacceptable to Japan, being no better than those that would be offered a defeated nation. It is also true that Roosevelt and his advisers recognized the likelihood that Japan could not accept these terms and would respond to their ultimatum by military action, for which Japan was obviously prepared, and the American leaders were determined to have Japan strike the first blow. But—failing correctly to assess the intelligence available to them—they expected the blow to fall against Thailand (Siam) or the Netherlands East Indies and consequently were lax in putting American forces in Pearl Harbor on the alert. Marshall, in these crucial days, signed only one warning message sent out of Washington to Pearl Harbor and to MacArthur in Manila. This was a "final alert" on November 27; after that date and until December 7, Marshall appears to have let matters be handled by those subordinates who subsequently took the blame for what was obviously a command failure at the very top, and which made possible the complete success of the Japanese attack on Pearl Harbor.

As far as MacArthur is concerned, as a result of the November 27 message from Marshall and subsequent War Department warnings in early December, his forces had already been on the alert for some days when on the evening of December 6 a Japanese message was intercepted in Washington and slowly decoded and translated. The message was in 13 parts, with a 14th to follow; Roosevelt, reading the first sections, recognized the imminent danger of war. The 14th section came in early Sunday morning, accompanied by two additional messages, one instructing the Japanese embassy to destroy its coding machines and secret documents, and the other instructing that the 14-part message be delivered at 1 P.M. that day. This clearly indicated overt Japanese action could be expected at that hour. Marshall had not been available the previous evening (he testified he "could not remember" where he was), but he was finally found on the bridle path and reached his office at about 11:15 A.M., some 14 hours after the first message was handed to the President.

Marshall immediately recognized that the message was a war warning, and he wrote out dispatches directed to MacArthur in Manila (where Washington expected the Japanese blow to fall if against any American territory), to the Panama Canal Zone, the Pacific Coast commander, and to Pearl Harbor. Although the indicated time of threatened Japanese action was only two hours away, Marshall did not use the telephone on his desk which would have put him in instant communication with the commanders in Pearl Harbor. He testified that he had not done this because the Japanese might have listened to the radiophone conversation, and have construed as a hostile act any orders alerting the garrisons in Hawaii. As a matter of fact, although Marshall probably was not aware of it at the time he testified, the radiophone from San Francisco to Honolulu was "scrambled" (and had been for years), so that if the Japanese had listened in, they would have heard only unintelligible gibberish.

Even though the phone was not used, the messages would, if transmitted immediately by radio, have given two hours' warning of the impending attack on Pearl Harbor and both the Army and Navy commanders in Hawaii testified they would immediately have gone on full war footing. However, at this exact fateful moment in our history when Marshall's message was handed to the operator, the Army radio transmitter was *temporarily out of communication* with Hawaii. Marshall left the office without waiting to ascertain if his message had actually been sent. Marshall, though sufficiently concerned about the message to inquire three times about transmission time, turned down a Navy offer to transmit it by their radio. A colonel to whom he handed it dispatched it by Western Union and it was delivered by a bicycle messenger in Hawaii hours after the Japanese planes had swarmed over Pearl Harbor and the nearby air fields. The message to MacArthur himself had gone through without difficulty; but as a consequence of the attack on Hawaii, no effort could be (or, at least was) made to relieve his beleaguered forces in the Philippines.*

The board which investigated the Pearl Harbor disaster absolved Marshall of any responsibility for the failure to follow up his message, although holding "in retrospect" that he could have used the trans-Pacific telephone or several other means of communication.

Once the American-Filipino forces were driven into Bataan, MacArthur sent a steaming series of messages to Washington asking help for the Philippines. The records show that Marshall, through Eisenhower, worked indefatigably to cope with this problem, *in his own way*. He repeatedly promised that help was on the way; F.D.R. made the same promise. But what Marshall meant by "help" and what MacArthur understood him to mean were two entirely different things. Marshall was referring to a small number of blockade runners—not one of which ever reached Corregidor—and of submarines which brought in a dribble of supplies; enough to keep the doomed army going for a few days. But MacArthur (and President Manuel Quezon) believed for a long time that a determined, major effort would be attempted actually to land large, decisive forces in the Philippines. MacArthur's wishful thinking rather than any misinformation from Marshall was largely responsible for this belief, even though at least one message from Roosevelt to Quezon would make

* It has always seemed to me that there has been a tendency to overestimate the importance of our *ship* losses at Pearl Harbor. Perhaps more important was the fact that the Japanese—who had expected to lose two carriers—escaped without damage due to the destruction of our unalerted planes on their fields before they had a chance to search out and attack the enemy task force. Thus the Japanese were left free to pursue with full strength and in full confidence their drives into the Southwest Pacific.

it appear that it was justified. "Although I cannot at this time *state the day* (italics mine) that help will arrive in the Philippines," the U.S. President said, "I can assure you that every vessel available is bearing to the Southwest Pacific the strength that will eventually crush the enemy and liberate your native land." This, to put it mildly, was a totally misleading message. Similarly, the fact seems to be that while Marshall repeatedly assured MacArthur that every effort was being made to send help, he did not at any time *specifically* state that this would be limited to blockade-running efforts and a few submarines.

Because of the attempt to send in the blockade runners, it is technically true that Marshall did everything in his power to relieve MacArthur's forces, and there can be no doubt that Marshall (with Eisenhower actually doing the work) as well as Stimson and Roosevelt were entirely sincere in their efforts to "help" Bataan. "We sweat blood," as Eisenhower has said. But any realistic appraisal would show that this help was in the nature of giving a dying man drugs to prolong his breathing for a few days. Marshall wanted to keep MacArthur fighting as long as "humanly possible"—and gave him orders to that effect—but there was never any serious consideration in Washington at this time of reversing the long-standing decision to make all other objectives secondary to the defeat of Hitler. It is also incontrovertibly true that insofar as official messages went during World War II, official reports, the matters of promotions, and other Army business, Marshall was always fair to MacArthur. But personal likes and dislikes, human feelings, do not appear on official records, and for his part MacArthur has always been convinced that his opinions and views would have had more sympathetic consideration in Washington if almost anyone except Marshall had been in charge. Perhaps he is wrong in that conviction.

The first time that MacArthur realized—and he did not believe it even then—that the Philippines would not be relieved was when he received a message written by Marshall and signed by Roosevelt directing him to leave Corregidor and proceed to Australia. While he was traveling south pursuant to these orders, a new and disastrous misunderstanding occurred involving him and Marshall.

Before leaving Corregidor, MacArthur had made arrangements to cover the time of his expected absence. Marshall had given him absolutely no indication that he would not continue to command the Philippines in addition to the Southwest Pacific Command he was ordered to take over; it was not until after he reached Australia that Marshall explained to him that by agreement with our allies, no Theater commander could also hold a subordinate command. Thus when he left Corregidor, MacArthur—not knowing this—assumed he was merely transferring his command post temporarily from the Philippines to Australia. He put this in writing in a letter to President Quezon: "I retain full command here in the Philippines and have left part of my staff at Corregidor, pending my return there. . . . All communications for me go there just as before." Prior to leaving, he had given various orders to Generals Wainwright and Moore designed to make food supplies last for 20,000 men until July 1, expecting that Corregidor would hold until that time and he would be able to lead back a relief expedition. He also maintained his subcommand in these parts—the Luzon force under Wainwright; Corregidor under General George Moore; the Visayas and Mindanao (central and southern Philippines) under Generals Chynoweth and Sharp, and as MacArthur's own deputy, Brigadier General Beebe.

The intent behind this organization was far-sighted; if one sector of the Philippines were overwhelmed and forced to surrender, the others could fight on. There is no record that MacArthur informed the War Department of the details of these divisions; they represented no change in the setup and he has said that he saw no reason for him to make any report, inasmuch as he never dreamed that he was about to be replaced in his command. When he left Corregidor and was en route to Melbourne by PT boat, bomber, and train, messages from F.D.R. and Marshall addressed to "The Commanding General" and obviously intended for Wainwright, continued to reach Beebe who, in accordance with MacArthur's orders, forwarded them to Melbourne. Finally a message directed to Wainwright by name as "Commanding General, Philippines" came from Washington, promoting him to lieutenant general, and Beebe capitulated and recognized that Marshall had replaced MacArthur with Wainwright.

It has since become known that Marshall—lacking direct information from MacArthur and completely failing to comprehend the latter's ideas about the command setup—became thoroughly angry when he learned that Wainwright had been given command of one sector only, and promptly gave him over-all command. Similarly, Marshall was "astonished" that MacArthur took some of his key staff men to Australia with him. From MacArthur's point of view this was a perfectly normal and necessary move; he believed large forces awaited him in Australia and he needed a staff to help lead them back to the Philippines. Marshall, knowing the Philippines to be doomed but being unable or unwilling to inform MacArthur of this in so many words, thought the staff should have been left behind to assist in carrying on Wainwright's hopeless battle.

In explanation of Marshall's action in placing Wainwright in MacArthur's former command, it has been said that the Chief of Staff felt that it was impossible to carry on the fight in the Philippines under the situation as set up by MacArthur—that of local tactical control in the various sectors without a single commander. Marshall believed that MacArthur would be too far away in Australia to control the battle, and therefore appointed Wainwright to command.

MacArthur's first intimation of this shift was a message signed by Wainwright as Commanding General, Philippines. He immediately demanded to know "by virtue of what authority" Wainwright had assumed that position. The latter cited his authority from Washington. In an effort to counteract the potentially disastrous effects of this action, MacArthur had statements issued both by Beebe and Major Carlos Romulo making it clear that he still commanded the Philippines; Romulo's message was directed to Filipinos whose morale had been shaken by the indication that MacArthur—the center and symbol of their resistance—had been separated from command over them.

However, it was too late; and when Wainwright finally surrendered, the Japanese commander, Homma, forced him to broadcast orders to the 25,000 Filipino troops on Mindanao and 20,000 in the Visayan Islands to lay down their arms. Wainwright contended he commanded only the Harbor Defense of Luzon—that is, Corregidor and the satellite islands in Manila bay. But Homma angrily produced a captured copy of Wainwright's own general order assuming command of all the Philippine forces. Confronted by this proof, Wainwright had no choice but to yield to Homma's threats and to obey the Japanese general's orders. As a result the Japanese gained control of the Visayas and Southern Philippines with very little fighting; and 45,000 Filipino soldiers (members of the American Army) were compelled to lay down their arms at a single stroke. This was a neat coup for the Japanese. Even though the Filipinos might have offered only guerilla resistance, the existence of a force of this size would have given the Japanese considerable trouble.

Here was another prime example of the inability of Marshall and MacArthur to understand each other, regardless of which of them was at fault. The possibility suggests itself that Beebe, as MacArthur's deputy, might similarly have been forced to surrender; but that is a matter of speculation, and all that is known is that Wainwright in fact *was* compelled to yield to the Japanese demands.

Another point of basic disagreement between the two men was emphasized at the Senate hearings investigating MacArthur's dismissal. Secretary of State Dean Acheson, who proved himself far more adroit at defending unsuccessful and disastrous foreign policies than in carrying out successful ones in the Orient, made a feeble attempt to blame MacArthur for originating the course of action that contributed to the loss of China to the Communists.

Acheson produced a telegram of December 7, 1945, signed by Generals MacArthur and Wedemeyer and Admiral Spruance, which listed assistance to be given to Nationalist China and suggested that the assistance "be made available as a basis for negotiation by the American Ambassador to bring together and effect a compromise between the major opposing groups in order to promote a unified democratic China." The implication made by Acheson was that MacArthur favored a coalition of the Chinese Nationalists and Chinese Communists. General Wedemeyer, questioned subsequently at the investigation, conceded that this sentence —lifted out of context—would appear to have that meaning, but he vigorously denied that such was his intention or that of MacArthur. Spruance made a similar denial.

MacArthur refused to hold still for Acheson's accusation. He roared back with a telegram declaring that Acheson was guilty of "a prevarication without color of factual support" in suggesting that MacArthur would ever favor "a political coalition of such diametrically opposed and irreconcilable forces. . . ."

Acheson had further made the astonishing implication that our whole disastrous policy in China had been suggested by MacArthur, and that soon after his telegram, George Marshall had been sent out to China to implement this policy. As a matter of fact, while on his way out to China in late 1945, Marshall visited MacArthur in Tokyo. MacArthur asked something like, "Where are you going, George?" Marshall replied to the effect, "Up to Nanking, Douglas."

Beyond some such desultory exchange, the two men held *no formal or informal discussion whatsoever* on a course of action whose final outcome was to contribute to the loss of all China, a loss as important as any in our recent history. Marshall asked no advice or comment from MacArthur, who probably had more experience in the Orient than any other American. Nor did MacArthur, who, as governor of 80,000,000 Japanese was vitally affected by any decision in regard to China, ask any questions.

MacArthur made this clear in his reply to Acheson, stating that his telegram to Washington was not "discussed, or even alluded to in any way, shape, or manner by General Marshall when he visited my Tokyo headquarters en route to China. It is fantastic to believe that had he been en route to implement a recommendation of mine, he would have failed even to mention it to me." He went on to declare that the course Marshall followed was to "employ the potential of American assistance as a weapon to force the existing government into a political alliance with the Communists. This was the exact opposite of the intent of (my) message."

MacArthur concluded with a terrible indictment of Marshall as a diplomat, accusing him in effect of responsibility for the later bloodshed in Korea. The effect of Marshall's policy, he stated, "could have been foreseen. It at once weakened the government and materially strengthened the Communist minority. It was one of the greatest blunders in American diplomatic history for which the free world is now paying in blood and disaster and will in all probability continue to do so indefinitely."

In a year in Nanking, Marshall failed to effect the coalition he sought between the Chinese Nationalists and Communists. Back in Washington as Secretary of State, he continued to use various forms of pressure against the Nationalists, but his interest in the Orient was only secondary. He sponsored the Marshall plan of recovery which worked in Europe, and which was later extended on a smaller scale to some countries of Asia. He suppressed the Wedemeyer report, which was critical of his China policy, and for a time discontinued aid to Chiang Kai-shek because of the corruption and inefficiency in his government and army. MacArthur, on the other hand, believed that we should have accepted Chiang Kai-shek "horns, cloven hoofs, and all" in preference to letting China fall to the Communists.

It was against this background that MacArthur felt he must protest against the more recent Korean policies—or, in his mind, lack of policies—supported by Marshall. MacArthur's public statements resulted in the decision to dismiss him, as is told in the last chapters of this book. The manner of the dismissal was left to Marshall, who ordered that a radiogram be sent to Secretary of War Frank Pace in Korea, instructing him to make personal delivery to MacArthur of the order for his relief. However, at this moment, exactly as at the time of Pearl Harbor, there came *another mechanical communications failure* involving Marshall and MacArthur. "Due to a breakdown in a power unit in Pusan," Marshall testified, the instructions never reached Pace; and MacArthur received the news at third hand from a radio broadcast, a manner of notification which shocked and offended the American people and greatly contributed to their excitement over the firing.

As of this writing, Marshall has had the upper hand in this long feud—he is still in office, MacArthur is out. But MacArthur may yet have the last word in his memoirs. For his part, Marshall has decided not to write his memoirs because, "To be of any historic importance they have got to be accurate . . . [but] if you do put it all in, you may do irreparable harm. You almost ruin a man . . ." Friends say that Marshall was referring to MacArthur who might easily have been (but was not) "almost ruined" when Marshall pulled the trigger to remove him from command, even as Marshall's own career was almost ruined 20 years earlier when MacArthur refused to sponsor his promotion.

The inner feelings that animate MacArthur and Marshall in their contest with each other may eventually be explained by themselves. Meanwhile, some characteristic differences are of record. Marshall holds that the "people" are to blame for the world's troubles; MacArthur blames their leaders. "The basic error," Marshall said in discussing the war in Korea, "has always been with the American people." On the other hand, MacArthur has repeatedly said, "Ninety-nine per cent of the people want peace. It is the leaders who are responsible for war." He pointedly added in testifying in Washington after his dismissal that the American people have the right to change their leadership every four years.

In this writer's opinion, many of the basic differences between the two men come down to this: MacArthur is a combat soldier; Marshall is—like Eisenhower—a military executive and diplomat, rather than a field soldier. It is an unpleasant but incontrovertible fact that all the business of war resolves itself in the end to one thing: killing. Unless an officer has seen and participated in killing, unless he has exposed himself repeatedly to it, there is a gap in his professional knowledge, the ultimate aim of his business is a mystery to him. Marshall revealed his awe of the combat soldier when he reported how Generals Vandenberg and Collins had gone to the front in Korea; his naive account of that visit, given in testimony in the MacArthur hearings, was strictly that of a GHQ officer, and a GHQ officer has a different view from a combat officer.

MacArthur has had extensive battlefield experience in three wars; Marshall—although he sometimes went to the front in World War I in France—has not; his lone combat decoration is the Silver Star with this citation: "By his superior professional attainments, his tactical skill, his sound judgment, and his courageous conduct in obtaining information through personal visits to the most exposed lines, he contributed in a determined manner to the training, morale and operations of the division in the Toul sector, the Cantigny sector, and the movement for the offensive at Soissons." In addition to his other and higher medals, MacArthur has seven Silver Stars, none of them won for contributing to "training, morale, and operations."

These records are cited with no intention of being derogatory to Marshall, but to emphasize the difference in the Army experience of the two men. MacArthur planned the invasions of Leyte and the amphibious operation at Inchon (among many others) and went along to see how they worked; he personally came under the same fire that was killing his troops. Marshall helped plan the D-Day invasion of Normandy from his desk in Washington and read reports of its progress at that desk, to which he was practically chained by orders of Roosevelt, and from which he broke away wherever possible to tour the war zones; he went to Normandy, for instance, as soon as he could after D-Day. Marshall's greatest ambition had been to command the field armies in Europe; but after much deliberation Roosevelt decided on Eisenhower because, "I could not sleep at nights without George in the United States." General Pershing, who had personally sponsored Marshall's career and who disliked MacArthur personally, summed up in this way his professional opinion of the two men: "Marshall is a great chief of staff . . . MacArthur knows his troops. . . . He's a fighter—a fighter—a fighter."

On the subject of "knowing troops," General Bradley has written (*A Soldier's Story* [New York, Henry Holt, 1951]): "No commander can become a strategist until first he knows his men. Far from being a handicap to command, compassion is the measure of it. For unless one values the lives of his soldiers and is tormented by their ordeals, he is unfit to command. He is unfit to appraise the cost of an objective in terms of human life." Bradley wrote this, of course, as a generalization and certainly not with respect to Marshall, whom he ranks as our greatest military executive. However, if it is true as a generalization, it may also be true in this comparison of MacArthur and Marshall, the former compassionate to emotional extremes, the latter having had little opportunity in his military career to get to know troops, having commanded them for only a year.

The differences in thinking that result from the different careers of the two men were strikingly evident throughout all their testimony at the MacArthur hearings. Marshall was unable to answer a question as to how many American soldiers were in Korea. He explained, "I think [not of individuals] . . . of divisions." MacArthur, thinking of the individuals he had seen die in what was obviously even then a stalemated war in which no military decision was possible, repeatedly and emotionally voiced his deep concern over "this . . . unconscionable slaughter . . . this dreadful killing."

Marshall bitterly denounced MacArthur for expressing this concern for his troops, declaring, "I am disturbed . . . at the effect that will sweep through that force [in Korea] . . . [because] their commander has stated his views which accentuate the casualties that they are suffering and in effect that it is without justified purpose." The soldiers themselves, however, were well aware of the casualties they were suffering and that the campaign had become a stalemate; it is difficult to believe that their morale would be lowered by the knowledge that their commander was worried over their casualties. On the other hand, it should be emphasized that the "justified purpose" of Marshall—in which he was supported by all the Joint Chiefs of Staff—was his belief that it was better to continue the "accordion war" in Korea than to risk extending the struggle to the whole world.

Quite possibly it is fortunate for the country that we have in Marshall a man who can overlook immediate bloodshed and formulate a long-range policy in which he has such confidence that he is able to justify the present losses. After the Chinese attack in Korea, the administration entered upon a policy of "buying time" in Korea while hoping to end the war by "killing Chinese." In countering MacArthur's repeated attacks on this policy, Marshall did not specify what had become a further fact: that months before the truce our military leaders had come to look upon the war as having some fairly desirable aspects in that—while causing only "acceptable losses"—it was giving our soldiers, marines, sailors, and airmen actual combat training, and at the same time arousing the nation to the need for preparedness. President Truman underlined that view by his hot-headed comparison of battle deaths in Korea to the nation's annual traffic losses.

MacArthur was outraged at the concept of buying time at the expense of lives, of letting the Korean nation pay for the time we thus supposedly bought, and of paying for it ourselves in the blood of our young men rather than using our technological and scientific superiority to fight for us. "It is a fact," he declared, "you have lost a million men now. . . . The war in Korea has already almost destroyed that nation of 20 million people . . . I have seen, I guess, as much blood and disaster as any living man, and it just curdled my stomach, the last time I was there . . . I vomited. Now are you going to let that go on, by any sophistry of reasoning, or possibilities?"

Yes, Marshall answered, we could not take the risk that we would lose our Allies and that Russia would go to war with us and extend, rather than end, the bloodshed.

MacArthur answered: The chance of war with Russia "may be there, but this in Korea is a certainty. What are you going to do? Once more, I repeat the question, 'What is the policy in Korea?' "

Marshall waited only a reasonable length of time after MacArthur was fired before hurrying out to Tokyo and Korea, a trip he had never made while MacArthur was in command. The trip was in connection with the rotation plan, and hence the morale of the troops, about whom MacArthur had been so concerned. And with MacArthur out of the way, Marshall jumped at the Russian proposal for truce talks, a proposal he had found completely unacceptable when it was advanced by MacArthur. Why couldn't Marshall have done these things while MacArthur was in command? Some part of the answer is, perhaps, contained in this chapter. The final answer will certainly be part of the military and political history of our times.

CHAPTER

13

World War II—Clark Field

MACARTHUR'S PART IN WORLD WAR II SHOULD BE BRIEFly summarized as a prelude to this and the two following chapters. From 1935 through 1941 he worked to build up the defenses of the Philippines. His efforts have been criticized as less than completely successful, but without them—and without the weight that his word carried in Washington after he was recalled to active service in the American Army in mid-1941—there is no doubt that the Philippines would have been less prepared than they actually were when the Japanese attacked in early December 1941. After destroying half of the small U.S. air force and causing the U.S. Asiatic fleet to retire to the south, the Japanese brought ashore land forces on the island of Luzon.

MacArthur's forces executed a planned and fighting withdrawal into the Bataan Peninsula, with their backs to Corregidor and other island fortresses. Numerically, the Bataan-Corregidor defense was largely a Filipino fight. The Filipinos numbered about 60,000 unseasoned soldiers, who had been given 5 and one-half months training. There were 12,000 crack Filipino scouts, and the Philippine Division—American Army regulars—plus about 12,000 Americans, of whom only 7,000 were combat troops and of that number less than 3,000 infantry—only one regiment. MacArthur was ordered to Australia by President Roosevelt prior to the surrender of Bataan and Corregidor. He fought his way back to the Philippines in a series of brilliantly executed amphibious operations requiring two years, liberated the islands, and went on to accept Japan's surrender in Tokyo Bay on September 2, 1945, and became Supreme Commander over defeated Japan.

Paradoxically, MacArthur won his greatest fame for a losing battle—Bataan; he was one of those rare generals who is capable of rising above defeat. Even his most persistent critics, who go over and over his record with a fine-tooth comb in a search for errors that would prove him a bad or incompetent general, have been forced to agree that his campaigns from New Guinea through the Philippines were daring in concept and brilliant in execution. Even so, controversy and dispute surround nearly everything he did in these war years. Each time those years are reviewed, the question finally comes up—as it did during the Senate investigation of his removal from command—what about Clark Field? Well, what about it?

Time and again it has been shown that MacArthur was not responsible for the loss of about half the U.S. air strength in the Philippines as a result of a Japanese attack on Clark Field on the first day of the war—which was December 8, Manila time. Repeated efforts to saddle him with blame have always failed for the simple reason that there is no case against him beyond the general over-all responsibility of a commander for whatever happens in his area. Even so, his critics always renew their attacks. John Gunther, that able and fair reporter, assumed there is "a conspiracy of silence . . . to protect" MacArthur. And recently the historians, Richard H. Rovere and Arthur M. Schlesinger, Jr., have made the strange assertion that he was unprepared for the Japanese attack on the Philippines although in fact he spent six years preparing for it; the Bataan withdrawal, for instance, was practical in two separate and extensive maneuvers.

Actually, the ascertainable facts of Clark Field are well known, and there is no conspiracy of silence. A recent volume by Walter D. Edmonds, *They Fought with What They Had* (Boston, Little, Brown, 1951), gives all the details. The story of Clark Field began, really, when MacArthur went to the Philippines in 1935 to attempt to build up a defense force.

In the six years between 1935 and 1941 he made many arresting, optimistic statements: "By 1946 I will make of the islands a Pacific Switzerland that would cost any invader 500,000 men, three years, and more than $5,000,000,000 to conquer . . . In all history there is no example of this kind of attack being attempted on a comparable scale since invasion of Greece by the Persians in the fifth century, B.C. Those invasions resulted in complete failure."

"These Islands must and will be defended. I am here by the Grace of God. This is my destiny."

"The inescapable price of Liberty is an ability to preserve it from destruction."

"I wish to reiterate my fixed opinion that when the Philippine Islands defense plan reaches fruition, the people of these Islands will be in a favorable position of defensive security. . . . I am certain that no Chancellery in the world, if it accepts the opinions of its military and naval staffs, will ever willingly make an effort to wilfully attack the Philippines after the present development has been completed."

But, as he emphasized to reporters, the defense of the islands could be accomplished only "with the help of God and the U.S.A."

Because the Japanese did succeed in landing in the Philippines, forcing surrender of our forces and occupying the principal cities, it is generally assumed that MacArthur's predictions were 100 per cent wrong.

Yet it is a fact that the Japanese lost close to 300,000 men in the Philippines, that they never conquered or subdued more than small portions of the Islands in nearly three years of fighting, and that the defense of Bataan fatally delayed their timetable. Similarly, MacArthur's predictions can be fairly used to judge him as a military prophet only if it is taken into consideration that they were based on completion of a 10-year plan (he actually had only six years) and on the reasonable assumption that the U.S. Navy would be the deciding factor in any defense of the Philippines, with the British also joining in to protect Hongkong and Singapore. "The help of God"—as he said—"and the U.S.A." Even after 1940—when the American Congress climaxed 10 years of blind isolationism by refusing to appropriate $5,000,000 for fortification of Guam—the Navy was still charged with the mission of defeating the Japanese fleet and relieving the Philippines in the event of an attack.

MacArthur's plan was to train 40,000 reservists yearly to support a force of 10,000 regulars and 7,000 constabulary. The Commonwealth could not afford a real navy, so there were plans for a small fleet of fast torpedo boats (there were four when the war started) and a fleet of fast medium bombers and fighters (but by the spring of 1941 there were only 50 to 60 Philippines Army planes, mostly trainers). The plan started off well in 1936; conscripts from all sectors of society were called up for training and paid five centavos daily. Military drill was interspersed with instruction in reading and writing, American and Philippines history, and teaching of respect for government and democracy. The Filipinos were proud of their new army, and for his part MacArthur had always had great faith in the Filipino as a soldier; well-trained he is as good as any in the world.

MacArthur went ahead with his plans even after President Manuel Quezon seemed to tire of the whole defense program. Quezon was a mercurial and unpredictable man, with a strong sense of justice and a desire to help the underprivileged (though he himself lived like a potentate), but with a deep split in his personality stemming from the fact that he never got over the original injustice of America seizing the Philippines at the time of the Spanish-American War. At one moment Quezon fiercely resented any suggestion that the Filipinos were not ready for full self-government and not fully able to take care of themselves under the leadership of Field Marshal MacArthur. At the next he was inclined to wash his hands of the whole problem and argue fiercely that America had taken the islands over the dead bodies of the patriots who fought at his side in 1900. Having taken them (albeit with a conscience-salving payment of $18,000,000 to their former Spanish masters), it was up to America to defend them. In 1940 and 1941 he occasionally urged the development of "moral strength" to resist another 300 years of foreign occupation, in place of armed strength to defeat or at least seriously oppose a foreign invasion. He publicly stated that the Philippines could not be defended. But MacArthur countered, "The Filipinos can defend themselves if they want to."

In mid-1941 Japan took control of most of French Indo-China and established her forces firmly on Hainan Island, next door to the Philippines. At long last, the United States awakened to the obvious and began to prepare for war in the Pacific. Dutch and British forces were strengthened in their colonies and possessions, and on July 26 Roosevelt called MacArthur to active duty as a lieutenant general in command of United States Army Forces in the Far East (USAFFE).

MacArthur responded to his recall to active service by declaring, "I am glad to be able to serve my country at this crucial time. The action of the American Government in establishing this new command (USAFFE) can only mean that it intends to maintain at any cost its full rights in the Far East. It is quite evident that its full determination is immutable, its will indomitable. To this end American and Filipino soldiers can be expected to give their utmost." In a letter home he wrote, "I have been recalled . . . to defend the Philippines if war comes. I propose to do so . . . and believe . . . the Army of the Far East will be heard from."

In his messages to the War Department, MacArthur optimistically declared that given sufficient air strength, it would be possible to meet and defeat the Japanese invaders on the beaches. Attacking over water from Formosa, their invasion fleets could be cut up by air bombardment; and if he were supplied an air force capable of maintaining air control, the Japanese could be beaten and repelled. General George Marshall, then Chief of Staff, and most of the top planners in Washington likewise believed the Philippines could be held. They agreed that the long-range bomber, the B-17, had altered the defensive picture in the Philippines and that its defense was now a possibility.

As a result, modifications were made in War Plan Rainbow, the basic American military plan for war with the Axis. This plan—ironically enough given the same name as that of MacArthur's World War I division—set forth the basic premise that, in the event of war with both Germany and Japan, the main American effort would be made in the Atlantic with a holding war in the Pacific. In August of 1941, not long after his recall to active service, MacArthur wrote Marshall suggesting that the mission of the forces in the Philippines under War Plan Rainbow be changed from that of holding only the harbor defenses of Manila—meaning Bataan, Corregidor and the satellite islands—to include "defense of the entire Philippines archipelago." This change was approved, and in the early fall of 1941 Washington initiated a plan of building up American forces in the Philippines. The small American garrisons around Manila began to be augmented by additional small antiaircraft and light tank units; new ships were sent to strengthen the Asiatic fleet and a program of plane reinforcement—intended to be completed by April, 1942—was begun. This was a serious effort; for instance more B-17's—35 in number—were sent to the Philippines than to Hawaii. Major General (later Lieutenant General) Lewis H. Brereton was sent out to command the air forces and arrived early in November. He brought with him a message from General Marshall telling of the War Department's plans for additional reinforcement.

When MacArthur read this, he exclaimed exultantly, "They are going to give us everything we asked for!" Marshall had also emphasized to Brereton that he recognized a "calculated risk" was being taken in sending the B-17's to the Philippines in advance of building up a strong pursuit and interceptor force, and installing an adequate warning system.

Meanwhile, beginning in the summer of 1941, MacArthur had made a number of predictions—one set for public consumption and another to military associates. The former are frequently cited today as definite proof that he did not expect any attack, but it is naive to accept at face value such statements by any government leaders in a time of crisis. What is always done at such times—and MacArthur does it also—is to talk strongly in the hope of discouraging the prospective enemy.

For instance, he told John Hersey in an interview for publication that Japan would not attack the Philippines, that she was tired after four years of war in China, that the Allied forces in Southeast Asia could handle a threat to British or Dutch territory.

But to a general staff officer passing through from Washington, he used other words, "The Philippines are not the door to the western Pacific and its littoral, nor even the lock, but they are the key that unlocks the door. The Jap cannot ignore the Philippines in his southward move. He will have to strike here." In other words, MacArthur fully expected the attack. What he said otherwise for public consumption was just that—for public consumption and for consideration by the Japanese. To another officer he privately deplored the weakness of his forces and dearth of material. "But," he added, "I will fight as long as I have a man to fire a gun."

He told Colonel Warren Clear, en route to Singapore on an intelligence mission, "Tell Brooke-Popham (British air marshal and commander at Singapore) that you are bringing him a gift from me of one million rounds of .50-caliber ammunition. . . . It is necessary to our position here that the British hang on as long as possible. The Japanese probably *will hit them the same day they hit us.*" This was in June of 1941.

As a matter of hindsight, MacArthur's certainty of a southward Japanese attack was premature. The final Japanese decision to go south—rather than to attack Russia—was not reached until late September or early October; until then their admirals (who wanted to go south) and their generals (who favored attacking Russia) waged a long and bitter dispute which finally terminated in the decision to fight the United States and Great Britain provided no diplomatic settlement could be reached.

By early November, MacArthur was firmly convinced that the Japanese were coming south, and that they would hit the Philippines. Yet it is a fact that he did not think they would strike until the spring of 1942, probably in April. He occasionally wavered in this opinion and predicted an earlier attack as when, on November 10, he told Brereton that Ambassador Kurusu—then en route to Washington in a supposed attempt to reach a last-minute agreement by negotiation—was "being used as a stooge" and that the war would start "sooner than April."

But aside from this statement to Brereton, all of his predictions that this writer has been able to trace—including an off-the-record prediction to newsmen—fixed the date of the expected attack as "sometime in April." This is interesting, and it would be important and even evidence of a major and costly failure on MacArthur's part, if he had allowed this belief to lull him into a sense of temporary security, if it had caused him to slack his preparations, or had resulted in his ignoring any orders or alerts from Washington or from his own intelligence. But the fact is—as will be shown later—that his forces were on *full war alert* several days before Pearl Harbor.

Why did MacArthur think the Japanese would attack in April? The background is interesting. He knew that at the rate of buildup of men and planes from America, the Philippines would by April, 1942, be as ready as they ever would to meet the invasion. Therefore, he *hoped* the attack would not come until then, and with his customary optimism nearly convinced himself that it would not.

His intelligence chief, Colonel (later Major General) Charles A. Willoughby, fixed June, 1942, as the likely date of the attack, although he predicted "it might come sooner." It is quite possible—though it cannot be proven—that Willoughby adjusted his own predictions to his knowledge that MacArthur *did not want* the Japanese to move until he was ready. Otherwise, as a product of "sound military deduction and reasoning"—as it has been described in the aftermath by other intelligence officers—Willoughby predicted with great accuracy the Japanese strategy and tactics for the invasion.

On the other hand, an intelligence network set up in Southeastern Asia by Colonel Clear—using Chinese, Japanese Communist exiles, Thais (Siamese), White Russians, Indo-Chinese, and others as agents—passed along information indicating that the attack might start as early as January. MacArthur seems to have preferred not to believe this.

But no one—with the probable exception of Moscow, which did not furnish any information to its British allies or American friends—guessed accurately or obtained accurate information as to the magnitude and timing of Japanese plans for simultaneous assaults on Pearl Harbor, the Philippines, Malaya, Hongkong, Thailand, and other areas. No one learned that if the so-called peace negotiations in Washington failed, the Japanese would strike immediately. For the nations attacked, this was one of the major intelligence failures in history; for the Japanese, a triumph in maintaining military secrecy. General Marshall's biographer (William Frye) has said that all the information was available in Washington, but that the military there failed to collect it in one place and assess it—and thus failed to see that the proper precautions were taken at Pearl Harbor.

But in the Philippines the danger of a Japanese attack was well recognized. As early as November 27, General Marshall notified MacArthur of the likely collapse of negotiations with Japan. Marshall also warned, "Japanese future action unpredictable but hostile action possible at any moment.

If hostilities *cannot* be avoided, the United States desires that Japan commit the first overt act." In reply, MacArthur advised Washington, ". . . air reconnaissance has been extended and intensified in conjunction with the Navy. Ground security measures have been taken. Within the limitations imposed by the present state of development . . . everything is in readiness for the conduct of a successful defense. Immediate liaison and cooperation and cordial relations exist between Army and Navy." On December 6 (Manila time), MacArthur further reported: "all air corps stations here on alert status." A day later, he addressed a message to Marshall, advising him "complete coordination and cooperation most satisfactorily accomplished" as a result of conferences with British and Dutch military leaders.

In fact, beginning December 2, unidentified (later known to be Japanese) planes began to fly over the Philippines and for *five nights thereafter* American planes flew search missions to locate the intruders; they were given permission by MacArthur to take offensive action if the planes came close enough to violate the territorial integrity of the Philippines, but to avoid offensive action otherwise. In other words, for six nights before the war started, American radar (there was only one set in commission) was functioning on full alert; Japanese planes were picked up and American planes sought (unsuccessfully) to locate them. On the morning war started, news of the Pearl Harbor attack was flashed to the Philippines and relayed to the air commanders (who had been partying at the Manila Hotel until 2 A.M.) shortly after four o'clock in the morning. From that time on, the tactical handling of the planes was entirely out of MacArthur's hands and in those of General Brereton. There is no dispute about that; what is disputed is the question of a supposed strategic decision, as will be told shortly.

Shortly after noon that day—some eight hours after it was known that a state of war existed between Japan and the United States—Japanese Navy medium bombers followed by strafing fighters struck a devastating blow at Clark Field. Seventeen (out of nineteen) B-17 bombers caught on the ground were destroyed, and about 40 pursuits at Clark and near-by fields—representing approximately one half of the total American air strength that had been sent to the Philippines up to that time.

The bombers had been ordered aloft at eight o'clock in the morning, cruising around to escape being attacked at their base while awaiting orders for a mission against Formosa. The bombers and fighters both came down while the pilots went to lunch and the planes were being gassed and armed in preparation for this mission. There was nearly an hour's warning of the approach of a large formation of Japanese planes, but only four American P-40's—which proved no match for the enemy Zero—were able to get into the air from Clark Field. The Japanese bombers and fighters completed their attack with a minimum of interference.*

* The interested reader is again referred to Walter D. Edmonds' book, giving a complete account of the movement of every American airplane during these fateful hours.

Ever since, the surviving air officers have maintained that MacArthur was responsible for destruction of the bombers because he had refused to grant permission, when it was requested early in the morning, for an attack on Formosa. General Brereton set forth the accusations against MacArthur in his war diaries, stating that at 5 A.M. he conferred with MacArthur's chief of staff, General Richard Sutherland, who told him to prepare the bombers for action but to await orders before undertaking offensive action. Brereton says that these orders were not issued until some time after 10 A.M., supposedly having been delayed on the grounds that there had been no declaration of war as yet, and that the recent War Department directive had forbidden any "offensive action." Sutherland's account is almost exactly the opposite.

According to Sutherland's statement—not previously published—Brereton said to him, "I am going to attack Formosa."

"All right," Sutherland replied. "What are you going to attack? What's up there?"

Brereton admitted that he had no information, and agreed that a reconnaissance mission was necessary to locate worthwhile targets. Permission was given for this mission and three planes eventually took the air, none of them reaching Formosa. At 10 o'clock or shortly afterward, it was decided to carry out the bombing mission but *Brereton himself* decided to time it for the last daylight hours. This would have meant a mid-afternoon take-off, so that in any case—regardless of any supposed delay by MacArthur's headquarters in approving the mission—the bombers would have still been held at Clark Field by Brereton until long after the hour at which the Japanese attacked. It is largely for this reason that Sutherland insists that Brereton alone was responsible for the bombers being on the ground; Brereton had complete tactical command and had been given permission for the Formosa raid. He did not move the bombers even though some of his air officers were begging that this be done.

Until Brereton's diaries were published, MacArthur had ignored the controversy and refused to place any blame for the loss of the planes, and, in the interest of amity, had even swallowed his own inclinations and publicly defended Brereton, though he privately characterized him and others of his command as "bumbling nincompoops." However, when provoked into a statement on September 27, 1946, MacArthur in Tokyo flatly denied Brereton's version and gave a roundup of the whole air picture in the Philippines at the time the Japanese attacked.

"In order that there may be no mistake as to all the facts in the case," MacArthur said, "I wish to state that General Brereton never recommended an attack on Formosa to me and that I knew nothing of such a recommendation having been made, that my first knowledge of it was contained in yesterday's press statement.

"That such a proposal, intended seriously, should have been made to me in person by him; that he has never spoken of the matter to me either before or after the Clark Field attack.

"That an attack on Formosa with its heavy air concentration by his small bomber force without fighter support, which because of the great distance involved, was impossible, would have had no chance of success. . . . In the short interval of time involved it is doubtful if an attack could have been set up and mounted before the enemy arrived.*

"That the enemy's bombers from Formosa had fighter protection available in their attacks on Clark Field from their air carriers, an entirely different condition from our own.

"That I had *given orders* several days before *to withdraw the heavy bombers* from Clark Field to Mindanao, several hundred miles to the south, to get them out of range of enemy land-based air. . . . Half the bombers, 18, had already been so withdrawn when war broke.

"That General Brereton was fully alerted on the morning of December 8 and his fighters took to the air to protect Clark Field but failed to intercept the enemy . . . Tactical handling of his air force, including all measures for its protection against air attack of his planes on the ground, was entirely in his own hands.

"That the over-all strategic mission of the Philippines command was to defend the Philippines, not to initiate outside attack.

"Our air forces in the Philippines, containing many antiquated models, were hardly more than a token force with insufficient equipment, incompleted fields, and inadequate maintenance. They were hopelessly outnumbered and never had a chance of winning. They were completely overwhelmed by the enemy's superior forces. They did everything possible within their limited forces.

"I attach no blame to General Brereton or other members of the command for the incidents of battle. Nothing could have saved the day for them. They lost, but with no discredit. The date of April 1, 1942, to which General Brereton refers was the earliest possible date for the arrival of the reinforcements which would make a successful defense of the Philippines possible. It was not merely an anticipated date of enemy attack." The reference to the date was in connection with Brereton's allegation that MacArthur had told him no Japanese attack was expected before April.

As stated in his reply to Brereton, MacArthur had given orders "several days before" the attack for the bombers to be dispersed to Mindanao. The air commanders, preferring Clark Field both because of its superior facilities and its proximity to the comforts of Manila (where their party was scheduled for the night of December 7th) had stalled and temporized before a second peremptory order from Sutherland caused them to send

* Two comments seem pertinent on MacArthur's statement. It seems unusual that he did not personally confer with his air commander that morning, though there may be an explanation involving the hurried movements of the two men. Further, although MacArthur deprecates (and I think correctly) the chances of a successful raid on Formosa, it is a fact that later in the day, *after* the Clark Field attack, he notified the War Department of his plans to bomb Formosa. Here again, the explanation may be that he did not at the time have details of the damage done at Clark Field.

part of the planes southward. Excuses were given for delaying the departure of the others, but it was promised to send them shortly.

All of the Clark Field discussion remains in a sense academic because, as MacArthur has clearly and fairly stated, the fact is that even if the planes had not been caught on the ground, they could not have lasted long against Japanese air superiority. But since the airmen have chosen to make the specific point of their attack the allegation, or inference, that they might have destroyed the Japanese planes on Formosa before those planes destroyed them, here is an interesting fact: the fields which Brereton says he intended to attack *were not the fields* from which the Japanese bombers took off. This is known through postwar interrogation of Japanese air personnel who did participate in the attack. The Japanese, temporarily fogbound on Formosa, feared that the B-17's might catch them on the ground. But they had no reason to worry; our air force did not know the location of those fields; in fact, our charts and maps of enemy installations were extremely sketchy, this being due mainly to the restrictions from Washington against any provocative act, such as reconnaissance over Formosa.

As to the tactical handling of the planes, both bombers and pursuit, it is a matter of fact that MacArthur was not in the remotest way responsible for the tactical movements of each individual plane at fields 90 miles or more distant. The air officers *were* responsible, and—especially after a large enemy flight was detected approaching Luzon at 11:30 A.M.—it was their duty to provide fighter cover for the helpless bombers at Clark Field. But due to confusion and inexperience, this was not done. Air force officers like Brereton have always stressed the loss of the bombers, as if to divert attention from the fact that the fighters—which would *not* have gone along on any raid on Formosa and hence were in no way affected by any supposed failure on MacArthur's part—were likewise caught on the ground.

Walter D. Edmonds, after long and exhaustive study, concludes that it is pointless to place the blame for the disasters of that day on "failures in judgment of any one or more of our Commanding Officers." He also states that the key to handling of the bomber force "lies in Brereton's first conference with Sutherland, of which there are two fundamentally opposed accounts." Which means, in the final analysis, that final judgment depends on whether Brereton or MacArthur (and Sutherland) gave an accurate version of the day's happening. Since this is so, it might be apropos to mention briefly some of the other war mishaps in which Brereton was intimately involved. It is, of course, an old legal maneuver to divert attention from the substance of an accusation to the personality of the accuser. But when in a case like this, the personal integrity and professional competency of both accused and accuser are involved, it is certainly relevant and imperative to examine the record. General Omar Bradley tells of several incidents in the European war in which Brereton's role ranges from disastrous to bullheaded; in fact, Bradley, who is extremely fair-minded, mentions Brereton time after time in his war memoirs without finding a single complimentary thing to say about the air officer.

The first mishap involved the failure of an air mission arranged by Brereton—then 9th Tactical Air Force Commander—to provide support for a pre-D-Day maneuver off the English coast. The planes never showed up, and Bradley reports Brereton was not only "strangely unconcerned" over this failure but gave the "brush off" to arrangements for air-ground support training. Far more deadly was Brereton's last-minute change in carefully worked out plans for air bombing to precede the American breakout from the Normandy beachhead. Bradley's whole use of the bombers was predicated on their coming in on a course parallel to our front lines, but the airmen on their own initiative and without consulting Bradley changed this plan; Brereton asserted—a very close parallel to his alleged Formosa plan—that Bradley *was* informed in advance, but Bradley says this is simply not true.

In his war history, *A Soldier's Story*, Bradley says, "In a press conference two days later Brereton was to declare that it (the breakout) owed its slow start to the sluggish getaway of our troops on the ground. He neglected to add that the delay had been caused by the removal of those American dead and wounded air had strewn in our way." Thus, if the words of Bradley and MacArthur can be accepted, Brereton bungled in separate instances thousands of miles apart in different hemispheres of war, and in each case tried to escape responsibility.

To return to Clark Field, the report of General Marshall absolved MacArthur, stating "the destruction . . . [was] due to the limited dispersal fields and lack of sufficient radar warning." While Marshall fails to point it out, a very large factor was inexperience on the part of individually competent but not yet war-trained air corps officers, pilots, antiaircraft, and radar crews and all others concerned. I recall one sunny day on Saipan nearly three years later when $100,000,000-plus worth of B-29's were standing on the fields after our first raid on Tokyo. No air cover was around—the commanders thought the Japanese were too far away to cause trouble—and suddenly a half-dozen or so Zeros began cavorting overhead and setting fire to several of the Super-Forts. If such things were happening after three years of war, it is easy to understand how the Clark Field disaster occurred after only a few hours of war.

Two weeks after the attack on Clark Field, Brereton reported to MacArthur that the situation was "untenable from the air standpoint" and took off for Java and other southerly points. As MacArthur has justly stated, the remainder of the air force did the best it could. General George and a handful of pursuits remained to fight it out from improvised fields on Bataan, but these planes soon wore out or were shot down; and MacArthur said to George, "Just three planes. I'm begging them (Washington) for just three planes. Without them I am blind, and you can't fight blind."

MacArthur's non-military critics appear to have overlooked one matter in the early days of the war which has been the subject of some professional comment. It was not until December 23, a day after the principal Japanese landing in Lingayen gulf, that he ordered his field commanders to put into effect War Plan Orange II—the withdrawal into Bataan. This gave his quartermasters only one week's time to move food and ammunition into the peninsula where his troops were soon under siege. In addition, the number of men that crowded into Bataan was nearer 100,000 than the 42,000 for whom the original defense plans had called. Thus food and supplies soon gave out, and these—not men—were the principal shortages on Bataan.

Some of MacArthur's subordinate generals believe that he should have realized that as soon as his air force was destroyed, he had lost strategic command and would have to abandon any idea of holding the shoreline of Luzon and should have started the withdrawal immediately. MacArthur's reply would probably be that he could not have withdrawn until the Japanese had actually committed themselves and breached his shore defenses; as long as there was even a slim chance of repelling their landings that chance had to be taken. The question is a speculative one of timing and judgment, and is not categorically answerable.

CHAPTER

14

World War II—Bataan to Australia

MAC ARTHUR'S CONCERN FOR THE FUTURE OF AMERICA in Asia is based in large measure on happenings behind the scene during the Battle of Bataan. During that battle, our physical and spiritual ties with the Philippines—then as now of prime importance to our whole position in the Pacific and the Orient—were perilously close to snapping.

It was this fact that led him to take one of the most criticized actions of his career—forwarding to Washington, in the middle of the Bataan battle, a proposal by President Quezon for "neutralization" of the Philippines and withdrawal of all Japanese and American forces. MacArthur is well aware of these criticisms. "The historians are jumping on me," he was quoted as saying recently. "They are twisting that matter every possible way. But they don't know what was behind it. They don't know the facts, or the background." Here is the background, and the facts.

To MacArthur, it was no new experience when he found himself fighting in Korea to see American ships, planes, and men being sent—not to Korea—but to Europe, in the opposite direction, or kept at home in America. The same thing had happened in the Philippines in 1941-42 when he watched his forces slowly go under and saw how near to being lost were all the fruits of 40 years of American effort in the Philippines. For a time, it was touch and go.

In War Plan Orange—the Philippines defense plan which had existed for many years—the estimate was that when the Japanese attacked the islands, the fortress area at the entrance to Manila Bay could hold out for six months, by which time the U.S. Navy would defeat the Japanese Navy or drive it back to home waters. Then the Philippines would be relieved. In shifting over from War Plan Orange to War Plan Rainbow, it seems to be a strange and inexplicable fact that this plan for relief by the Navy was dropped and no substitute plan set up for relieving the Philippines.

But, so far as the forces defending Bataan and Corregidor were concerned, they believed that if they held out for three or four, or possibly even as long as six months, the American Navy would fight its way through to them and they would be relieved. This was a complete illusion but it was an illusion which kept the fight going in Bataan. MacArthur himself shared it. Looking back recently at those days, he was heard to say thoughtfully, "Perhaps—I deluded myself." His troops, certainly, were deluded right until the final shot was fired.

The Filipinos, and the Americans who led them and stood beside them in the Battle of Bataan, fought because they believed the reinforcements —"help," they called it—would reach them from the United States before they went under. Until he was finally given indications—though never direct word—to the contrary, MacArthur himself believed that help was coming. These men on Bataan were not "global-minded." They believed that the Philippines were just as much a part of America as the state of California, and that the United States would do everything in their power to give them assistance. They simply could not conceive of any "sophistry of reasoning"—as MacArthur used the term in connection with Korea —whereby, a portion of American soil having come under occupation by the Japanese enemy, the United States would first rush troops to Europe.

This was not alone the viewpoint of the troops; I heard MacArthur discuss it many times: "This is the only place where American land forces are fighting. American prestige in Asia is forever at stake. Surely the United States will do everything possible to send additional supplies and planes to us." Certainly, he agreed, the Japanese were strong and there was danger. But he still held a chain of air bases through the Philippines down to Australia—a route for the bombers, while fighters could be launched from carriers and land on Mindanao. There would be losses, but that was a part of war. Convoys were still going into Murmansk despite 80 per cent losses, streams of American bombers were pouring across the Atlantic to Europe, troops were arriving in Ireland and England. But here Americans were fighting in territory under the American flag; the government could not and would not let them down.

From Washington the problem looked different. American policy then as now had as its rightful and principal object the protection of American cities from destruction and of continental American soil from occupation. The fact that the Philippines would fall to Japan was considered lamentable (as is the recent destruction of Korea) but "acceptable" from the Washington viewpoint. The fight in Bataan "bought time" for the build-up in Europe. Being only one aspect of the whole global problem that confronted the planners in Washington, the fate of the Philippines was of second- or third-rate importance. Much of the fleet had been sunk at Pearl Harbor, the Japanese were far stronger than had been expected, and the Philippines simply could not be relieved as planned, even though it went against the grain of every American not partisan to the Germany-first program to watch apparently idly while a gallant army went to its doom.

But, though convinced their Germany-first strategy was right, there was a moral commitment, too, in regard to the Philippines which was clearly recognized by President Roosevelt and Secretary of War Stimson. Exactly how General Marshall felt about this angle is unclear. General Eisenhower (then an unknown brigadier general) was summoned to Washington by Marshall and told to handle the problem of what to do about the Philippines. Eisenhower himself felt that "a great nation such as ours, no matter how unprepared for war, could not afford cold-bloodedly to turn its back upon our Filipino wards and the many thousand Americans, troops and civilians, in the archipelago." Eisenhower has recorded that in their first discussion of the problem, Marshall "significantly and characteristically . . . did not even hint at one of the most important factors . . . the psychological effects of the Philippines battle upon people in the United States and throughout the Pacific." It was Eisenhower's impression that, "Clearly he [Marshall] felt that anyone stupid enough to overlook this consideration had no business wearing the star of a brigadier general." On the other hand, William Frye has stated in his biography of the wartime Chief of Staff, that ". . . there is evidence that Marshall lacked a complete understanding of the manifold political and social implications of the war until some time had elapsed after Pearl Harbor. . . ."

Whatever the truth of this angle, Eisenhower and his associates strove mightily to get what they called "help" to the Philippines.* The President, in a message late in December, 1941—the siege of Bataan started January 1—promised the Filipinos their "freedom would be redeemed and their independence established and protected." Read literally, this was a grim warning that their freedom would be first lost and later redeemed. But so great was the faith of the Filipinos in the United States that their president, Manuel Quezon, could not believe the meaning of the word "redeemed." He conferred about it with MacArthur, who suggested the possibility that the word had been garbled in transmission, and Quezon preferred to believe that this was so. In a message spurring on the Filipino troops, he changed the word and told his forces that Roosevelt had solemnly pledged, "the freedom of our country will be preserved. . . ."

Meanwhile, on December 30, Roosevelt told the War Plans Division in Washington "to explore every possible means of relieving the Philippines. . . . I realize great risks are involved but the objective is important." The planners reported after an intensive study that any major relief expedition would require nearly all of our war strength and "starve" Europe. The Navy—which had a post-Pearl Harbor complex that the Japanese were supermen—would not risk its few carriers to provide escorting air cover for a major expeditionary force, or even to ferry airplanes to MacArthur. Consequently, the planners decided, no real relief was possible without changing the entire grand strategy of the war.

Even in the face of the planners' report, Roosevelt decided that some-

* Eisenhower tells the story of these efforts in *Crusade in Europe*. He believes that although "in the final result our efforts proved feeble enough," everything humanly possible was done.

thing must be done for the Philippines and he adopted MacArthur's suggestion for running in supplies from Australia by individual surface ships, and from Pearl Harbor by submarines. On the basis of these efforts, the President and General Marshall reported to MacArthur and to Quezon that "help was on the way."

This, however, was not "help" in the way that the troops understood the meaning of that word. The trickle of supplies that actually reached the fighting men—a relative handful of ammunition and fuses brought by submarine—could only help them fight a few days longer until more of them were killed in a hopeless battle. They did not expect anyone else to take their places in the line and do the fighting for them; but they did expect airplanes, food, medicines, ammunition.

MacArthur believed this "help" would be ample, and on January 15 of 1942 he issued a "proclamation" which all unit commanders were ordered to read to their troops. This statement—as I have recently found out—was not based on any specific secret radiogram from Washington to MacArthur informing him of the departure of a convoy. Rather it was a compilation of all the repeated assurances that had been given by Washington since the outbreak of war: Roosevelt's broadcasts, an official announcement that the U.S. Navy was taking action which "will result in positive assistance to the defense of the Philippines," Marshall's repeated promises that "every effort was being made to help," a broadcast by Elizalde—the Filipino representative in Washington—assuring that "help will be forthcoming."

If there was any truth in these and other statements—and MacArthur never for a minute doubted there was—they could mean only one thing: a major effort was being made to relieve the Philippines. Until recently, the writer of this book had always believed that MacArthur's statement was based on a definite message. When I learned that this was not so, I was inclined to feel that MacArthur had, without justification, lied to his troops. However, I am assured by many people who have read all the pertinent messages that this is not the case; that in fact MacArthur was fully justified in what he stated even though there was no single, definite message that prompted his statement.

His historic message, which in an hour turned the Battle of Bataan from near defeat into a determination to hold until help arrived, read as follows:

"Help is on the way from the United States. Thousands of troops and hundreds of planes are being dispatched. The exact time of arrival of reinforcements is unknown, as they will have to fight their way through Japanese attempts against them. It is imperative that our troops hold until these reinforcements arrive.

"No further retreat is possible. We have more troops in Bataan than the Japanese have thrown against us; our supplies are ample; a determined defense will defeat the enemy's attack.

"It is a question now of courage and determination. Men who run will merely be destroyed, but men who fight will save themselves and their country.

"I call upon every soldier in Bataan to fight in his assigned position, resisting every attack. This is the only road to salvation. If we fight, we will win; if we retreat, we shall be destroyed."

MacArthur spoke of this message with officers on Corregidor, saying he had sent it "because the line on Bataan is liable to go at any moment. Morale is desperately low." Colonel Warren Clear of the general staff, who had been trapped in the Philippines by the outbreak of war, had been in Washington not long before and had pleaded with Harry Hopkins (who sometimes had the last word in military matters) for modern 90-mm. A-A guns for the Philippines to replace the antiquated three-inchers whose shell fuses had to be cut individually by hand before each round. Hopkins had replied that none was available; everything was going to Britain. On the basis of this and other information, Clear ventured to tell the general that in his opinion the messages from Washington were not true, and that no ships, troops, or planes were actually being sent to the Philippines.

"If you are correct," MacArthur said after a long pause, "then never in history was so large and gallant an army written off so callously!"

The Bataan army, already on half rations and suffering from disease and exhaustion, responded magnificently to MacArthur's promise. They held, then counterattacked, and by the last part of January the tables had been turned. General Homma's army (and this is fully confirmed by postwar interrogation of survivors) was beaten, crushed, incapable of further attacks without reinforcements. The Filipinos and Americans, despite their shortage of food and ammunition, were now toughened, battle-wise, confident they could hold until the arrival of the promised reinforcements. They expected the first convoy daily and the rumors spread: "A general order was issued in San Francisco yesterday forbidding the overloading of supply ships for the purpose of keeping flags from dragging in the water. . . . Ten thousand troops have landed in the south and started toward Manila. . . . A Negro parachute division has landed behind the Japanese. . . . A thousand bombers have reached Australia."

But as day after day passed with no sign of the convoy or of airplanes, reaction set in. President Quezon had not wanted to leave Manila in the first place. He felt it his duty to remain in the captured capital and do what he could to soften the occupation, and had gone to Corregidor only on the insistence of MacArthur who got him there by some high-pressure methods that had him on his way across Manila Bay almost before he knew what was happening. Quezon was in terrible pain from tuberculosis and on most days unable to walk, but he attempted to persuade MacArthur to let him return to Manila. In Quezon's mind, the war was an American war; the Filipinos were fighting at his insistence by the side of the Americans, but there was a limit to the sacrifices he could expect his people to make for the protection of distant America and still more distant Europe. He became increasingly impatient about the situation, and in late January began to protest vigorously in order to make his position known to Roosevelt.

"We have decided to fight by your side," he said in part of one lengthy message addressed to MacArthur but intended for the President, "and we have done the best we could. . . . But how long are we going to be left alone? Has it already been decided in Washington that the Philippine front is of no importance as far as the final result of the war is concerned and that, therefore, no help can be expected here in the immediate future, or at least before the power of resistance is exhausted?"

I do not know whether Marshall, Hopkins, Stimson, or someone else wrote Roosevelt's reply. Whoever it was managed to convey a meaning which—at least to Quezon and MacArthur—was completely misleading on first reading. The first part of this reply (quoted earlier in these pages) said, "Although I cannot at this time *state the day* (italics mine) that help will arrive in the Philippines, I can assure you that every vessel available is bearing to the Southwest Pacific the strength that will eventually crush the enemy and liberate your native land."

The President went on, "Vessels in that vicinity have been filled with cargo of necessary supplies and have been dispatched to Manila. Our arms, together with those of our allies, have dealt heavy blows to enemy transports and naval vessels and are most certainly retarding his movement to the south . . . our heavy bombers are each day joining General Wavell's command. A continuous stream of fighter and pursuit planes is traversing the Pacific; already 10 squadrons of the foregoing type are ready for combat in the South Pacific area. Extensive arrivals of troops are being guarded by adequate protective elements of our Navy. The heroes of Bataan are effectively assisting by gaining invaluable time, and time is the vital factor in reenforcing our military strength in this theater of war." In other portions of the message, Roosevelt made further general references to "future victory," which tended to lessen the force of his direct statement that the arrival of help was a day-to-day matter. In fact, no single vessel he mentioned ever reached Manila, not one of the "continuous stream of fighter and pursuit planes" got there, nor a single soldier from the "extensive arrival of troops."

MacArthur had his hands full. Quezon was always at him, importuning him to know when help would arrive, and refusing to be silenced by the General's repeated assurances, "Manuel, I will bring you in triumph on the points of my bayonets to Manila!" The war was such a small one in area that MacArthur also was able to keep touch with detailed tactical matters; he knew where every platoon was, and the movements of each of the four or five patched-together airplanes that occasionally managed to sneak off a dusty field on Bataan for a reconnaissance mission, or even an improvised attack. But for the most part, MacArthur fought the battle of Bataan with radio messages to Washington; his real fight was to try to get reinforcements, and he bombarded the War Department with message after message explaining the condition of his command and promising victory if he could be given some assistance.

War correspondents on Bataan were permitted—and indeed urged—by the censors to back up these official messages with dispatches reflecting the desperate needs of the fighting forces. "Dear Mr. President," read one mythical but widely publicized radiogram to Roosevelt, "our P-40 is full of holes. Please send us a new one." Another dispatch reported a subscription fund among the fighting men to "purchase a bomber for Bataan," and promised a bonus to the crew that flew it out. MacArthur's chief of staff, General Richard Sutherland, contributed a bon mot usually credited to his superior. When a Japanese submarine shelled Santa Barbara, Sutherland cracked, "Tell them to hold out for 30 days, and we will bring them help." Through press messages, America became aware that MacArthur's fighting men were calling themselves: "The Battling Bastards of Bataan—No poppa, no momma, no Uncle Sam."

Quezon, especially, was depressed and shaken by the continuing shedding of his country's best blood in what seemed a needless sacrifice if America had already written off the Philippines. The Japanese, holding Manila, had made a public promise to grant "independence" to the Philippines, and while Quezon was doubtful of Japanese intentions, he saw in this offer an opportunity at once to end the "possibly useless sacrifice" of the Philippines Army and the American forces. Quezon was incensed, and incredulous, when he learned American troops were being sent to Europe.

One day early in February, Quezon had his wheel chair pushed into MacArthur's office in Malinta tunnel on Corregidor. Immediately he launched into a bitter tirade, and ended by announcing that he would have himself carried into Manila under a white flag, confer with the Japanese, and accept their offer of independence. MacArthur soothed him with an eloquent plea, and with a warning, "Instead of putting you in your palace, Manuel, the Japs will more likely slit your throat. What you propose is ridiculous. You are deluding yourself if you think the Japs mean what they say."

Quezon, of course, was not the only one deluding himself at this moment of history. The whole matter of the Philippines, both on the scene and in Washington, was being treated in a completely illusory manner. Let us look at this complicated situation:

In Washington, there was a refusal to recognize the realities of the situation on Bataan, both military and political. Morally, no one would face the fact that there must be a limit to the length of time when less than 70,000 exhausted Bataan defenders could be expected to carry on, almost single-handedly, America's war against the Axis. To avoid facing this moral fact, the Washington planners permitted themselves to be deluded into believing that through some miracle the military realities would be changed if they succeeded in smuggling a few boxes of ammunition and some food into Bataan. As Quezon had suggested in his January message, Washington had to all practical purposes "decided that the Philippine front is of no importance as far as the final result of the war is concerned. . . ." But instead of answering that message truthfully, the reply had mentioned "every available ship . . . supplies . . . dispatched to Manila . . . a continuous stream of fighter and pursuits. . . ." No one in Washington had the courage to tell MacArthur (or Quezon), in answer to his storm of messages, that, finally and absolutely, no major reinforcements were being sent, that this was not even contemplated.

On Bataan and Corregidor, MacArthur was deluding himself into believing such major help was coming; his men believed it absolutely; Quezon had convinced or nearly convinced himself that he could expect reasonable treatment from the Japanese. Quezon, too, as it fortunately turned out, deluded himself into underestimating the courage and endurance of his countrymen and the loyalty to America that they displayed so gallantly during the long years of Japanese occupation. MacArthur was asked recently if he *really* had believed help was coming, or whether he had completely misled his men and himself. "By God, I did believe it!" he declared. Had he been informed, in definite messages from Washington, that a major relief effort was being made? "No," he answered. "I went over those messages since to see how I could have gotten that impression. And, do you know—those messages didn't say yes, but they didn't say no. They are full of meanings which could be interpreted two ways. I see now that I may have deluded myself."

A few days after MacArthur had apparently convinced Quezon that it would be futile to think of dealing with the Japanese, the president came to see him again, this time at the General's house outside of Malinta tunnel. He had not abandoned his idea of seeking an understanding with Japan, Quezon stated, but he now had a new proposal, which had been approved by his cabinet at an emergency meeting in the bomb tunnels of Corregidor on February 8, 1942—a month after the Bataan siege started.

The proposal was that the Philippines be given full and immediate independence from the United States and be neutralized by agreement between America and Japan, which would immediately withdraw all their troops. The U.S. High Commissioner, Francis B. Sayre, also on Corregidor, had added a statement of his own saying that unless American reinforcements were actually coming, he would approve Quezon's proposal. During a discussion that lasted many hours, MacArthur attempted to convince the president that his proposal was not a wise one, that it would be taken as a sign of weakness, that the Japanese could not be trusted. But Quezon was adamant; it was either that, or he would go to the Japanese. The Filipinos, he argued in effect, had "bought all the time" they could afford to pay for, for the United States. There was no further point or sense in their sacrifice, which was simply slaughter with no hope of victory.

After long consideration, MacArthur decided to forward Quezon's message to Roosevelt, and he added one of his own which discussed the purely military phases of the proposal. "You must determine," MacArthur told F.D.R., "whether the mission of delay would be better furthered by the temporizing plan of Quezon or by my continued battle effort. The temper of the Filipinos is one of almost violent resentment against the United States. Every one of them expected help and when it has not been forthcoming, they believe they have been betrayed in favor of others. . . ."

MacArthur was asked, nearly 10 years later, why he had not refused to relay this message and why he had seemingly endorsed the Quezon plan —actions for which he has been accused of everything from cowardice to virtual treason.

"It was a compromise," he stated, "and it was the only way I saw of keeping Quezon from carrying out his threat to negotiate with the Japanese. For this reason alone I would have transmitted it. Further, I could not have stopped it if I had wanted to—I had no authority to prevent the President of the Philippines from transmitting any message he wished to have sent. For my part, I did not endorse the idea. I discussed the purely military aspects. What I was really doing was trying to bring pressure on Washington to send me reinforcements. That was it—pressure!"

It might be added that, short of killing Quezon, there was no way that MacArthur could have prevented him from passing on any word or order that he wished to the Filipino soldiers and people. Even this would not have been sufficient; the whole cabinet would have had to be throttled, and no such mass action could have been kept secret on Corregidor. This is no joke; some long-distance superheroes have gone so far in their criticism as to suggest that MacArthur should have silenced Quezon "at all costs." I think it should be made clear that MacArthur fully understood how Quezon felt, he sympathized with him, and he still understands and sympathizes with his position 10 years later.

In Washington, the Quezon proposal was regarded as shockingly "unrealistic." Indeed, any American living in the safety of continental America would undoubtedly agree with that evaluation. But there comes a time in the fate of every nation under invasion or under attack when it must be decided whether it is better to die rather than compromise with superior force, or surrender, and go on living. So far in history, no nation and no army has yet decided to die to the last man. France, Germany, Russia have all surrendered in the past. As this is written in 1951, General Eisenhower is having difficulty forming European armies to implement the Atlantic Alliance, because of a feeling in many European countries that it would be better to be overrun by Russian armies than to become a battleground for war with Russia and America as the principal opponents. So, in February of 1942, Quezon faced the reality of what was happening to his people and had to consider whether further sacrifice was worthless.

Eisenhower has described the message from Quezon as "a bombshell," and for all its "unrealism," it did succeed in awakening Washington from the unrealistic daydreaming which had guided its own wishful-thinking attitude toward the Philippines. The accounts of the men in Washington who dealt with the matter at the time (Secretary Stimson's is the most sympathetic) do not, of course, recognize the fact which I have stated in the preceding sentence. But I think it is a fair conclusion to say that Washington suddenly realized that the great and powerful American nation was depending almost entirely on an army of mostly untrained Filipinos—led and supported by smaller numbers of isolated Americans—to fight its global war, and that it was making only back-handed efforts to assist them. Nowhere else, in Europe or the Pacific, were Americans at grips with the enemy—it would not be until October, after interminable bickering back and forth with the British—that the first American soldier confronted the first German soldier in Africa. The messages that went back to Corregidor indicate that it was finally realized in Washington that if the Filipinos surrendered or compromised, they would eventually be liberated in any case when America finally defeated Japan, and that, as Quezon had argued to MacArthur, "there must be a limit to the sacrifices they could be called on to make in the name of 'buying time' for the purposes of global strategy."

The proposal for "neutralization" of the Philippines by Japanese-American agreement was never for a moment considered, but General Marshall did draw up a message for the President which authorized MacArthur to allow the Filipino troops in his command to surrender. At the same time, Marshall ordered MacArthur to have the Americans continue fighting as long "as humanly possible" and with "full understanding of the desperate situation to which you may shortly be reduced." The message also suggested the evacuation of Quezon, Sayre, and of MacArthur's wife and son.

In a reply to Quezon, Roosevelt reaffirmed America's determination to defeat Japan and declared unequivocally, "those Americans who are fighting now will continue to fight until the bitter end . . . to the death." He explained the military steps being taken to build up strength in the Southwest Pacific which would eventually become sufficient "to meet and overthrow the widely extended and arrogant attempts of the Japanese." But, he pointed out, "military and naval operations call for recognition of realities. What we are doing there constitutes the best and surest help that we can render to the Philippines at the present time."

For his autobiography, the late Manuel Quezon concocted a fanciful version of how Roosevelt's message (which had been written by Secretary of War Stimson) had an "overwhelming" effect on him, causing him to discard all thought of accepting independence at the hands of the Japanese, to decide to leave Corregidor, and "as long as I lived to stand by America regardless of the consequences to my people and to myself." Stimson, of course, was delighted with this fairy-tale and proudly reprinted it in his own autobiography. The fact, however, is that Quezon was furious about the message, and even went to the extent of writing out his resignation as president, intending to hand it to MacArthur and thereafter to seek independence at the hands of the Japanese. However, members of his cabinet talked him out of this, and before long he was taken out of the battle zone by submarine.

For his part, MacArthur was incensed by Marshall's "totally unrealistic" message—he has called it a "terrible message." (Marshall, it has been said by another officer who is partisan to neither of them, "has always been willing to fight to MacArthur's last soldier.") How in heaven's name could a few thousand Americans continue to fight if the Filipinos—the great bulk of his forces—were permitted to surrender? There weren't even enough Americans to hold a line one fourth of the way across Bataan Peninsula; even movement to Corregidor would be impossible without the Filipinos. How long is "humanly possible," what is meant by "fighting to the last man"? Is it really to the last man in each platoon, or is it to the last six, five, four, two, one? Those were some of the questions raised by the orders from Washington. However, MacArthur controlled his anger and contented himself with replying to Roosevelt that he would not surrender the Filipino elements under his command and that he counted on them "to hold fast to the end." This they bravely did.

This exchange of messages seemingly—at least in hindsight—made it clear that no immediate relief of the Philippines was possible, and that the Bataan force was doomed. Yet, in his usual optimistic way, MacArthur continued to believe that a major relief expedition was coming, his hopes bolstered by assurances that "help" (meaning submarines and blockade runners) was on the way. He is still convinced 10 years later that a convoy could have come straight west from Honolulu to the Philippines; the battles that were later fought in the Coral Sea and at Midway might have been fought en route, but—he believes—help could have been sent; the Philippines could have been held. (This writer, not a military strategist, disagrees; but that is MacArthur's belief.)

MacArthur, while never told definitely that this major help was coming, was never told that it was not. Why wasn't he given this information? I suppose the answer is that, in the eyes of the men then in command in Washington, it would have been improper to tell a commander that his force was being written off; you just hint at it, while at the same time telling him "everything possible is being done to help." He is supposed to be sufficiently wise to know that these messages don't actually mean what they promise, but at the same time he is expected to "delude himself" sufficiently so that he can make false promises to his troops and keep them fighting. That, at least, is what happened in the case of MacArthur at Corregidor.

Had MacArthur been told the score in plain words he might have fought differently. He might have sent out specialists while small boats were still available; he might (in fact, it is certain he would) have attempted a breakout to the mountains for large scale guerrilla fighting. I believe his soldiers, knowing the truth, would have fought just as well as they did fighting for a lie.

In any case, the double talk was still going on long after MacArthur himself left Corregidor. Late in March, a desperate plea for help from Wainwright was sent to General Marshall, who promised that "immediate attention" would be given to his requests for supplies. On April 17, only hours before the end in Bataan, Wainwright reported to Washington that the food situation was desperate. Eisenhower (as he recounts in *Crusade in Europe*) replied that "some supplies" were en route by submarine—as if its arrival could change the picture. Indeed, it was not until the Japanese had already broken the Bataan line that Wainwright was given permission by Roosevelt to use his own judgment about prolonging the futile fight.

CORREGIDOR TO AUSTRALIA

"Tell the president I will never surrender. Tell him I will stay here with my men till we rot. Tell him that!"—Douglas MacArthur, in mid-December, 1941, to an officer under orders to escape from the Philippines and return to Washington.

On Washington's Birthday, 1942, the decision to get MacArthur out of the Philippines (if possible) was made by President Roosevelt; his intimates have called it an "indescribably difficult" decision. In a large sense the decision was not based on the immediate interests of the people of the Philippines, nor of MacArthur himself, nor was it made with the idea of speeding up the defeat of Japan; it was a decision which reflected the "Germany-first" grand strategy. The background was that relations between the Australian Commonwealth and Great Britain were badly strained. The Australians, seeing the Japanese hordes pouring down from the north, had decided (very much like Quezon) that the time had come when the interests of their own country superseded the demands of global strategy. They were threatening to withdraw their divisions from the Middle East to defend their own homeland, and it was very largely to bolster the morale of the Australian and New Zealand people—while still keeping the Australian troops in Egypt—that Roosevelt ordered MacArthur to proceed to Australia and take command there, promising to send American troops also.

Ironically enough, it was on the same Washington's Birthday (actually 24 hours earlier, because of the international date line) that MacArthur's hopes had soared to their highest point. On the morning of that day he received word of arrival at Mindanao, 350 miles south of besieged Corregidor, of the S.S. *Coast Farmer* with a cargo of food and ammunition. In a jubilant radio to Washington, MacArthur declared that the "so-called blockade" of the Philippines did not exist and went on, "She had no difficulty getting through. The thinness of the enemy's coverage is such that it can readily be pierced along many routes including direct westward passage from Honolulu. I have secure bases for reception in Mindanao and the Visayas." He reported his troops on Bataan had fought the Japanese to a standstill: "With his present forces the enemy appears to be unable to make the attack required to destroy me." He promised that he himself would attack—and he did push out patrols which encountered few of the enemy; at this time, in fact, the Japanese had only three battalions in the line in Bataan.

But in the early morning hours of the 23rd (Manila time), a top secret message was delivered to MacArthur at his home on Corregidor. The message was an order: MacArthur was told to leave the Philippines and proceed to Australia to take command of the "Southwest Pacific Area," traveling by way of Mindanao with a delay not to exceed one week. This message, written by Eisenhower, also told him to "ensure a prolonged defense of Mindanao"— although just how it would have been possible for him to do this is difficult to imagine.

At first, the stunned MacArthur could see only one meaning in the order: the Philippines could not, or would not, be reinforced. After many hours of consideration he told his staff that he could not obey the order; he would not leave his men. But meanwhile—as soon as they learned of the message—members of the staff had begun preparations for his possible departure. Two submarines had already come in from Pearl Harbor and others were due, and one of them could, if necessary, be used for the journey. There were also the PT boats, and their commander was summoned to headquarters and told to conserve his remaining fuel in readiness for a possible secret mission.

MacArthur called the senior members of his staff into consultation * and showed them a message of blunt refusal which he had prepared for transmission to the President; he expected them to support his stand, but the officers unanimously disagreed with him. For hours, while the flashes of Bataan's big guns lit the night horizon, the argument continued in a scene which would have been completely unreal in any other than this grim setting. I will not go, MacArthur insisted. "Not going" meant disobedience to orders, relief from command, court-martial, certain imprisonment or death for himself and his family. You must go, his staff replied. "Going" meant personal escape from a seemingly hopeless situation. It meant life and freedom for the members of his small group, but it also meant leaving the American and Filipino fighting men to almost certain doom. MacArthur contended that to desert the Filipinos in this hour of crisis would harm the United States forever in Asia. It would crush the morale of the troops and of Corregidor's nurses, who regarded the movements of the MacArthur family as a barometer of their own fate.

His officers pointed out another possible interpretation—which they insisted was the most reasonable—of the order: that a relief expedition was waiting in Australia for MacArthur to lead it back by the month of June, before all food and ammunition were gone. A review of their messages and of official statements from Washington from the beginning of the war strengthened this view.

The reader will have noted the inconsistencies in this discussion. If MacArthur really believed that large forces were in or en route to Australia—and from his Washington dispatches he had reason to assume this was the case—it would seem illogical that he hesitate to seize the chance

* General Sutherland has no recollection of these conferences.

to lead such forces. On the other hand, if he failed to return in time to save the Philippines, his men would certainly charge him with deserting them to save himself, his family, and staff. This was a terrible problem, and it would show complete ignorance of MacArthur's tremendous moral courage (and contempt for death) to believe that in reaching a decision he was influenced by thoughts of personal safety. However, that he recognized the likelihood that such beliefs would be held by others was shown by his later reaction, his refusal to allow it to be said that he "escaped" from Bataan. A highly colorful account of the subsequent journey, obviously written or dictated with MacArthur's approval, compares it with a rescue expedition dashing from a beleaguered garrison to "bring up the cavalry," and quotes the General as saying, "We will go with the fall of the moon; we will go during the Ides of March." It adds, "The General did not escape from Bataan. He came through to a greater task."

(As a personal observation on the seemingly false histrionics of his debate with his staff, I caught a glimpse of MacArthur the morning after his order came and was shocked at the change in his appearance. He looked years older, drained of the confidence he had always shown, desperately ill. He had obviously suffered a terrible blow. Staff officers would tell me only that "a message has come from Washington." A few hours later, MacArthur had regained his composure but was still obviously perturbed when he gave permission to another correspondent and myself to try to get through to Australia by blockade runner: "Go ahead," he said, "and even if you don't make it, even if you are drowning at sea or being machine-gunned in a lifeboat, or starving on a raft, don't regret having tried, for if we don't get reinforcements, the end here will be brutal and bloody." Until then, at least, he certainly believed help was coming.)

After long discussions with his staff, MacArthur reconsidered his stand, tore up his first reply to the President, and on February 24 radioed, demurring at any too sudden and abrupt departure for reasons which he stated (this message is still classed "top secret" years later) and which involved commitments to his present command. He requested that he be permitted to determine the time of his actual movement. Roosevelt replied the following day, leaving to MacArthur the full decision as to his timing and method. No further messages were exchanged on the subject, although the impression was subsequently created by MacArthur himself and by his staff that he engaged in heated radio discussion with Roosevelt before receiving a final, peremptory order on March 10: "Leave immediately."

Wainwright, summoned from Bataan, remembered later that MacArthur had told him, "Jonathan, I want you to understand my position very plainly. I am leaving for Australia pursuant to repeated orders of the President. Things have gotten to such a point that I must comply or get out of the Army. I want you to make it known to all elements of your command that I am leaving over my repeated protests. . . . If I get through to Australia, you know I will come back as soon as I can with as much as I can." But Wainwright did not delude himself. He believed that this meant the end; and when he gave the news to his generals on Bataan, their troops already riddled by death, wounds, dysentery, and malaria, eating about one quarter of normal daily rations, "They knew the score as well as I."

Reaching Mindanao after a rough trip by PT boat, MacArthur was perturbed to learn that Manuel Quezon was stranded in the nearby island of Negros after a small interisland ship had been sunk by Japanese planes while the President and his party were ashore. MacArthur promptly dispatched an envoy by small plane with a letter urging Quezon to join him in Australia not "merely for the sake of security" but to be with him "in the great drive for victory in the Philippines." He was extremely anxious to have the ill and depressed Filipino leader with him.

This letter of MacArthur's emphasizes his basic conviction that he could relieve the Philippines but it also contains several puzzles. Inasmuch as the official files in Washington disclose only the two messages already mentioned on the subject of MacArthur's orders to leave, it is difficult to understand his implication that he had engaged in a radio debate with the President, quite possibly he wished to impress Quezon with the importance of joining him. MacArthur wrote in part:

"The United States is moving its forces into the South Pacific Area in what is destined to be a great offensive against Japan. The troops are being concentrated in Australia which will be used as the base for the offensive drive to the Philippines. President Roosevelt has designated me to command this offensive and has directed me to proceed to Australia for that purpose. He believed this is the best way to insure the success of the movement. I was naturally loath to leave Corregidor, but the Washington authorities insisted, implying that if I did not personally assume the command, the effort could not be made. As a matter of fact, I had no choice in the matter, being peremptorily ordered by President Roosevelt himself. I understand the forces are rapidly being accumulated and hope that the drive can be undertaken before the Bataan-Corregidor situation reaches a climax. . . . I want you and your family to join me . . ." Quezon flew to Australia and then to Washington to set up his government in exile, and died there of tuberculosis before MacArthur's return to the Philippines.

On his safe arrival at Mindanao, MacArthur congratulated the PT boat commander, Lieutenant John Bulkeley, and awarded the boat's crews the Silver Star "for gallantry and fortitude in the face of heavy odds." Later in Australia there would be another rash of medals. Some of MacArthur's staff were given the DSC for "breaking through the Japanese lines." As a matter of accuracy, no gallantry whatsoever was required on the part of the staff to leave Bataan or Corregidor; anyone who was there would eagerly have seized even the slimmest chance of escape in preference to the grim alternative of remaining behind. MacArthur, of course, was highly intelligent in thus publicizing the trip as a gallant exploit rather than an "escape." By treating it as he did, he made the Japanese look ridiculous, gave dash and élan to the feat; and it was hailed all over the free world with an exultation which drowned out Japanese cries of "deserter," Mussolini's taunt of "coward," and Hitler's pun about "fleeing generals."

MacArthur's already low opinion of the "nincompoop" airmen in the Philippines was not improved during this journey. From Corregidor he had radioed Lieutenant General George Brett in Australia to "detail the most experienced pilots and the best available planes in top condition" to pick him up at Mindanao. But he found no planes at all at Del Monte air field. Brett had dispatched four "beat-up" Flying Fortresses (the best he had available, he has recorded), of which two turned back and the third crashed off the island. General Sharp, MacArthur's commander for the southern Philippines, considered the fourth so rickety that he returned it immediately; and now MacArthur sent Brett a testy message: "Only one of four planes arrived and that with an inexperienced pilot comma no brakes and supercharger not repeat not functioning." He again demanded the best planes and pilots: "This trip is most important and desperate and must be set up with the greatest of care lest it end in disaster." Brett thereupon managed to borrow four new Forts from Admiral Leahy, who had refused them previously, and on March 16 the immediate MacArthur party flew on to Darwin. The General sat in the radio operator's seat, Generals Sutherland and George were jammed together in the nose, while Mrs. MacArthur, Arthur and the amah, Ah Chuh, lay on mattresses under the waist gunner's position.

Seven hours later they reached Darwin, where MacArthur called over an American officer and asked about "the United States forces assembled in Australia for the Philippines rescue force." The officer replied in bewilderment, "So far as I know, sir, there are very few troops here." MacArthur turned to Sutherland and commented, "Surely he is wrong." Within the next few hours, however, he was to learn how small a part was planned for the Southwest Pacific in Washington's grand strategy of "Germany first."

CHAPTER

15

World War II—The Comeback

"IT WAS THE GREATEST SHOCK AND SURPRISE OF THE whole damn war."—Douglas MacArthur, commenting on his reaction when he reached Australia in March, 1942, and found that instead of vast American forces having been assembled for the relief of the Philippines, Australia itself was threatened with "another Bataan."

From the moment he decided to obey orders and leave Corregidor, MacArthur convinced himself—even more thoroughly than he had convinced himself that the Philippines would be relieved—that the vast rescue force awaited his command. So great was his faith that it was not shaken by the first disturbing intimation he had received on the air field at Darwin.

When he reached Darwin, he was near exhaustion from the journey by PT boat and bomber, and after flying down to Alice Springs in North Central Australia, he could go no farther by air. He boarded a jerkwater train in the desert town after dispatching his deputy chief of staff, Brigadier General Dick Marshall, to Melbourne to determine the strength and whereabouts of the American forces. Pat Hurley, the former war secretary who had been recalled to service and was now a brigadier general, joined MacArthur at Alice Springs and told him what a wonderful morale stimulant the Battle of Bataan had been to the entire Allied world.

"Mac," Hurley said, "the American people have always had a hero. In our lifetime there have been Dewey, Pershing—whether you like it or not —and then Lindbergh. Now they have taken you to their hearts. You are the hero."

MacArthur showed no interest in the subject. He could talk of only one thing: finding the American forces, getting them organized and moving back to the Philippines before it was too late. Repeatedly he declared, "I shall return."

Dick Marshall reboarded the train at Adelaide with devastating news. There were exactly 25,364 American Army personnel in Australia, including a small number of partially trained combat troops. There were 260 planes, some in flying condition. No naval forces of any consequence. Nobody knew anything about the Philippines relief expedition; instead the Australians—who had sent most of their front-line fighting men to help England—were in a state of near panic and planning to withdraw to the "Brisbane line," leaving all the northern ports open to the Japanese.

There was also a message from George Marshall, giving a more complete picture than he had been given earlier. Marshall's message completely crushed his hopes. It said in rough paraphrase: that owing to serious shipping shortages and commitments for other areas in the global war, there would be definite limits on what the Southwest Pacific Area would get. No troops were promised beyond the two divisions in or en route to Australia, but it was promised to bring the existing air units to full strength. (At almost the same time, however, Marshall was continuing his encouraging messages to Wainwright, promising to help him with supplies.)

This news literally stunned MacArthur. He turned deathly white, his knees buckled, his lips twitched. An officer who had known him for 20 years said later, "I have never seen him so affected. He was . . . heartbroken." After a long silence, MacArthur whispered miserably, "God have mercy on us." Unable to sleep, he spent the whole night pacing in the train. Two factors made the blow almost insupportable; his conviction that to let the Philippines go was terribly wrong both morally and strategically, and his own personal position—his promise to the men of Bataan that he would be back very soon with food and ammunition and reinforcements.

When MacArthur reached Melbourne next morning, he had recovered sufficiently to make a brief speech to cheering crowds, "I have every confidence in the ultimate success of our joint cause; but success in modern war requires something more than courage and willingness to die, it requires careful preparation . . . sufficient troops . . . sufficient materials. . . . No general can make something out of nothing. My success or failure will depend primarily upon the resources which our respective governments place at my disposal. My faith in them is complete. In any event I shall do my best. I shall keep the soldier's faith." Later he told Parliament, "We shall win, or we shall die."

Meanwhile, all of MacArthur's thoughts were directed at helping the men he had left behind in the Philippines where the Japanese were swiftly building up with reinforcements from Singapore for what obviously would be a decisive drive. Angered at the way he had been "deceived," MacArthur even made an attempt to return personally to the Philippines. The Japanese drive there began on April 1 and by April 8 our lines were giving way everywhere on Bataan. In the hope of saving some of the Bataan force from imprisonment or death, MacArthur had worked out a desperate plan for a breakout straight north to the port of Olangapo. He radioed the War Department telling of this plan, and offering to return and lead the attack in person, "if in your opinion my presence would help."

No approval was given, and MacArthur wired Wainwright to attempt the breakout, having already ordered him, "When the supply situation becomes impossible, there must be no thought of surrender. You must attack."

Wainwright, being a soldier, relayed the orders to General King on Bataan: "Tell King that he will not surrender. Tell him he will attack. Those are my orders." MacArthur and Wainwright could not have failed to know that somewhere along the chain of command these orders could not be followed. When they reached King (who was a soldier, too), he was face to face with the realities: his outnumbered men, many ill or wounded, were existing on 14 ounces of food daily, and one commander reported, "Even if my troops were unopposed, they couldn't crawl forward on their hands and knees." There was no longer any semblance of organized resistance, further struggle was simply slaughter, and on April 9 emissaries from King went forward under a white flag. MacArthur voiced his sorrow in a heartfelt communique: "The Bataan force went out as it wished—fighting to the end of its flickering, forlorn hope. No army has ever done so much with so little. Nothing became it like its last hour of trial and agony."

A few planes, three B-17's and ten B-25's, had been scraped together at MacArthur's orders and these flew up to Mindanao and then bombed Manila air fields. This was all he could find of the huge forces he had believed were in Australia for this purpose. Beyond giving Corregidor's defenders a brief hope that help had at last arrived, the raid accomplished nothing. But it did prove MacArthur's contention that the air lanes to the Philippines were open; help could have been flown in earlier, though it is problematical whether in sufficient force to hold the Islands.

Roosevelt (i.e., Marshall) hoped Wainwright would hold Corregidor indefinitely, but later he modified his orders of "no surrender" to leave the eventual decision to Wainwright. On May 5, after a month of pounding from the air and by direct artillery fire, Japanese assault troops won a toe hold on the island of Corregidor and began fighting toward Malinta tunnel which was being shaken by 400 artillery shells a minute. Inside the tunnel, hospital corpsmen working without rest to save the wounded, believed that the intensified fire was a prelude to MacArthur's return. They even knew the hour: "MacArthur will arrive at 6 A.M. from Australia. The Yanks and tanks and MacArthur are on their way." But at 11 A.M. on the sixth the commanding doctor told the nurses and corpsmen: "Girls and boys, Old Glory is coming down, and a bed sheet is going up."

Wainwright, fearing that Japanese tanks would break into the tunnel and slaughter the wounded and nurses, knowing that further resistance was pointless, had made the bitter decision that he must surrender. He sent a last message to Roosevelt from Corregidor: "We have done our best, both here and on Bataan, and although beaten, we are still unashamed."

Meanwhile MacArthur had been bombarding Washington with messages, and a day after Corregidor finally went down, F.D.R. made an attempt (at Marshall's request) to stem the torrent. In a personal letter, Roosevelt declared that the armies of the Soviets were killing more Germans and tying up more Axis personnel than any other Allies; therefore America's immediate aim must be to help the Russians keep fighting. This, of course, was no news to MacArthur. In February, on request from Washington, he had dictated from Corregidor a message to the Soviet Red Army to be used on its anniversary, February 23. As quoted by Robert Sherwood, the message said:

"The world situation at the present time indicates that the hopes of civilization rest on the worthy banners of the courageous Russian army. . . . I have participated in a number of wars and have witnessed others, as well as studying in great detail the campaigns . . . of the past. In none have I observed such effective resistance . . . followed by a smashing counterattack. . . . The scale and grandeur of this effort marks it as the greatest military achievement in all history."

Sherwood has recorded that this single message noticeably changed the entire Russian propaganda attitude toward America; it became friendly overnight.

It was at this time that MacArthur made his proposal that Russia be urged to open a second front against Japan; he believed that since they were doing so well militarily and since they had priority on American supplies, they should reciprocate in this fashion. As already noted in this book, he received no answer to his suggestion. His other proposals, strictly military in nature and designed to start the counteroffensive moving against Japan, customarily met opposition and rebuff from Washington, although it is not true—as was widely rumored at the time—that Marshall had finally lost his patience and sent MacArthur one message reading: "Shut up!"

MacArthur soon became convinced that he was opposed by a powerful group of enemies in Washington whose considerations of both world strategy and Pacific strategy were influenced by their hatred of him. To intimates he named names. "George Marshall, who hates me . . . a Navy cabal . . . a New Deal cabal." He despised Harry Hopkins; had the utmost contempt for the British military leader in Washington, Sir John Dill, and wavered between including or excluding Roosevelt in his group of supposed enemies. What was the truth? There is no possibility of doubt that a group of admirals in Washington did everything in their power—which was considerable—to block MacArthur and limit his share of the war. Secretary Stimson said of this bloc, "The Navy's astonishing bitterness against him seemed childish."

As to MacArthur's other "enemies," it is also certain that many Democratic politicians were suspicious and frightened of him after the anti-New

Deal press suggested him for the presidency, even though he promptly declared he did not "covet the nomination . . . and would not accept." There is no doubt that these politicians did everything they could to lessen MacArthur's popularity; they were among the most eager spreaders of stories minimizing MacArthur's fight in Bataan, asserting he had run out on his troops, and depicting him as a coward. As to George Marshall, the official records show that within the limits of over-all strategy, he did in fact attach great importance to MacArthur's area and did oppose the Navy's increasing efforts to limit Southwest Pacific Area forces, although he was in agreement with the Navy on the fundamental premise that the Marianas (Saipan, Guam), rather than the Philippines, were the key to Pacific victory. For their part, the men in Washington regarded MacArthur as a nuisance, petulant, unable to see beyond his own theater, incapable of understanding "global strategy." They resented the tone of his messages and press releases, and heartily wished he would shut up and let them get on with the war as they wanted it to be fought.

The following were, approximately, the reasons for MacArthur feeling at the time that his worst enemies were "not in front, but behind me, in Washington;" as already noted, he has since somewhat modified his views:

He had been misled about "help" for the Philippines.

On the basis of those distorted promises, he had been led to make untrue statements to his troops, and had been handicapped in his tactics.

He had never been told the real intentions regarding the Southwest Pacific until he had been "tricked" into proceeding to Australia in the belief that large forces were being assembled there for an immediate relief expedition.

While traveling to Australia, out of contact with either Washington or the Philippines, he had been replaced in his command by Wainwright, and as a result of this action Washington not only turned over a force of 45,000 men to the Japanese but deprived him of the bases he had planned to use for future action.

He had been "led to believe" he would command the whole Pacific and instead was given the Southwest Pacific Area. Only after arriving in Australia was he told to what extent commitments "elsewhere" would "definitely limit" the forces sent to him.

While to him every minute was precious if anything were to be done to hold the Philippines, there had been a month's delay in furnishing him a directive due to necessity for working out details with the Australian and Dutch governments. When his orders were received, they made only passing, unrealistic mention of the Philippines and directed him to "place Australia in a posture of secure defense."

His area of control included Guadalcanal, but when the first offensive action was ordered by Washington to take that island, command of the operation was not given to him but to the Navy.

In sum, MacArthur saw himself shoved off into a distant corner of the

Pacific, isolated by enemies at home as anxious to destroy him as they were to fight Japan. Beyond any personal considerations, he was fearful of disastrous future consequences that might result from letting the Japs dig in both militarily and in a propaganda sense in the Philippines and Southeast Asia. By waiting too long, by showing obvious disinterest in Asia, the United States might lose the benefits of 40 years of work in the Philippines and might eventually find all Asia lined up in solid opposition. Many of these fears have, 10 years later, become realities or near realities.

MacArthur reacted vigorously to what he regarded as the mistaken policy. He fought against it with every possible weapon, following a course of action which approached, but did not go as far as, his future campaign of appealing for public support against the Korean policies which he believed indecisive and unrealistic. Even Roosevelt's personal letter and the special emissaries sent to make further explanations could not silence MacArthur. Several times he quickly won these emissaries over to his side and dispatched them back to Washington to plead his cause.

MacArthur's first direct approaches to Washington having failed, he attempted a quintuple squeeze play through Prime Minister Curtin of Australia, to whom he expressed himself as "utterly disappointed" with the immediate assistance promised. At MacArthur's insistence, Curtin asked Churchill for troops (and a single British Navy aircraft carrier); but Churchill replied that the main effort was being made elsewhere, that he had no troops available, he saw no immediate threat to Australia, but, if necessary, would divert to that area troops then en route to India. MacArthur counterattacked with a new message: Curtin to Churchill to Sir John Dill (member of the combined chiefs of staff in Washington) to Roosevelt to Marshall, who turned thumbs down with the comment that what MacArthur proposed would be a good plan if Japan alone were the enemy, but otherwise it was worthless. Marshall had already reported to the President that to meet MacArthur's requests would slow down preparations for "Bolero"—the planned transchannel invasion which was not carried out— and Roosevelt ruled that this should not be allowed to happen. MacArthur then asked for a U.S. aircraft carrier, but was again turned down. He protested to Marshall that the troops sent him were insufficiently trained, and by this and other protests made life miserable for the men in Washington by refusing to sit back and fight the little sideshow war they had planned for him.

MacArthur in person was hard to get along with in those early Australia days. Congress had voted him the Medal of Honor for his defense of Bataan, fulfilling his old desire to follow his father in winning this highest and most coveted of American decorations, but he took no time out to celebrate. "Let's get on with the war," he told his officers. He was short, sharp, and frequently insulting to those he felt had failed him in the Philippines, showing especially his contempt for the Navy and Air Force. Lieutenant General George Brett bore the brunt of those attacks on the airmen. Brett, who was senior U.S. commander there when MacArthur arrived to take over, found himself shunned and pushed aside, treated in what he considered rude and cavalier fashion, and he described the Bataan commander as "suffering a feeling of guilt in having left his men at the most critical moment of their hopeless fight." He was angered when MacArthur criticized the air leaders as "lacking discipline, organization, and purposeful intent."

If MacArthur was troublesome, his staff was worse. Some of them acted like men who had personally lifted him down from the cross after he had been crucified by Marshall-Admiral King-Harry Hopkins, and they determined that nothing again should ever hurt him. To them everyone in the world was either for MacArthur, 100 per cent in favor of everything, or against him, an enemy. They moved in an atmosphere of unreality. The world centered around MacArthur; nothing else was important. They interpreted and magnified everything MacArthur said or felt—or that they imagined he felt. For example, if MacArthur said, "I wish I'd been able to help Jonathan (Wainwright) hold out a little longer," this remark passed from man to man of the staff and came out, "Wainwright shouldn't have surrendered. MacArthur never would have surrendered." *

These 14 officers who had come out of Corregidor with MacArthur were known as "the Bataan staff" or the "Bataan gang," a name that stuck to their survivors for 10 years. They formed an exclusive group that resented and suspected "outsiders," one of whom commented, "The defense of Bataan seemed to have an extraordinary effect on them. They wore an air of superiority that was most irritating to men who had endured the hardships and perils of other fronts." Actually the name "Bataan staff" was a misnomer; these were not front-line Bataan officers but men whose jobs had centered chiefly around headquarters in Malinta tunnel. In fairness, all of the staff (with the possible exception of the "publicity man" whose censorship was aimed at "protecting . . . and glorifying . . . the General") did important war work. Major General Willoughby was, for all his eccentricities, a good intelligence officer. Major General Dick Sutherland (later Lieutenant General) was a sound, productive chief of staff who carried most of the load for MacArthur at many times, although personally he was brusque, short-tempered, autocratic, and of a generally antagonizing nature.

* Correspondent friends have told me that they personally heard MacArthur speak insultingly of Wainwright. I am also told that at the time Bataan surrendered, MacArthur sent a bitter message to the War Department in which he suggested that Wainwright had temporarily lost his sense of judgment. For my part, I have heard him say only that Wainwright made an error in judgment in placing King, an artilleryman, in command of infantry on Bataan. MacArthur added that if Wainwright had kept personal command, the "outcome would have been different." I assumed him to mean that some of the Bataan force might have broken out to the north to continue fighting as guerrillas; if he means that Wainwright could have *won* the battle, the statement is obviously absurd.

BREAKING OUT OF AUSTRALIA

MacArthur soon realized that if he waited for the American admirals to send him ships to move back to the Philippines, he would be a very old man (and the Filipinos would all be speaking Japanese) by the time he arrived. He did manage to get rid of his "bumbling" air commanders and in their place arrived a short, bristly haired, pugilistic-looking but friendly major general named George H. Kenney. MacArthur's restoration to full health and activity might well be dated from the day that Kenney walked into his headquarters in Brisbane, sat quietly through a long tongue-lashing on the subject of airplanes and pilots, gave an unusual promise of "personal loyalty" which MacArthur demanded from all "outsiders" in those days, and set about helping his new commander win the war. The importance of Kenney to MacArthur in the following three years cannot be overestimated.

The Japanese were making threatening gestures against Australia from both the eastern and western ends of New Guinea and the only way for MacArthur to force them to commit themselves was to go up to New Guinea and confront them in the area of his own choosing. But he had no ships for such a move. Kenney freed him from this inhibition.

"Give me five days to prepare," Kenney promised, "and I'll shift the whole goddam United States Army to New Guinea by air." He did shift a whole division and MacArthur thus started the offensive which by spring of 1944 carried him to Hollandia in one of the "bold massive strokes" he had promised for liberating the Philippines. These campaigns were carried out with the imagination, flexibility, versatility, and boldness that stamp MacArthur as one of history's great military commanders. They were fought with what MacArthur called "a new concept of war." He cut off, isolated, and left to die a succession of Japanese strong points. Above all he put America's technical and industrial superiority to work to save American lives—this was always his one primary purpose—and his vast gains were made with a minimum of losses.*

Perhaps the foregoing section of this book has placed too much emphasis on the "wounded warrior" aspect of MacArthur's period in Australia. What has been said is true, but I think he deserves the greatest credit for his personal triumph over the defeat and despondency that would have crushed a man of less moral stamina, courage, faith, and abiding determination to serve not only his own ends but what he regarded as interests of primary importance to his country.

* Kenney has told the airman's story of these brilliant campaigns in two books, the most recent, *The MacArthur I Know* (New York, Duell, Sloan and Pearce, 1951). General Eichelberger's *Our Jungle Road to Tokyo* (New York, Viking, 1950) is the infantry commander's story of this cruel struggle.

MAC ARTHUR AND ROOSEVELT AND THE U.S. NAVY

No account of MacArthur's controversies during World War II would be complete without a brief story of his two-year battle with the United States Navy, and of his one historic meeting with President Roosevelt at Pearl Harbor.

Both were highlighted by the situation which arose after MacArthur, early in 1944, took the key base of Hollandia in New Guinea. The question now was: Where to go next?

The Joint Chiefs of Staff had agreed in March on an invasion of Mindanao—largest and most southerly of the Philippines—in the fall of 1944, and while the Washington admirals accepted this decision, they were still not wholly in favor of it, were in fact sniping away at it, and were insisting that after Mindanao the next jump should ignore Japanese control of the rest of the Philippines and go clear north to Formosa and on to China. This opinion was in direct contradiction to everything MacArthur believed in strategically and morally, and his insistence on the original plan terminated in a new round in his battle with the Navy.

The first round had been prolonged for many months, but it was mainly shadowboxing. In the first few days of Japanese air attacks on the Philippines in December, 1941, Admiral Hart dispatched part of the Asiatic fleet out of Manila Bay, and when the Japanese pounded Cavite naval station (in that bay) into near uselessness on December 10, the remaining submarines and surface ships followed. It is a surprising thing, inasmuch as submarines were to play such a large and important part later in the war, that the submarines in the Philippines accomplished almost nothing even though there were 29 of them there (the bulk of the Navy's submarine forces) when hostilities started. The small remaining forces included a half-dozen PT boats which did their job excellently, some flying boats that operated until shot down or destroyed on the water, a few auxiliary vessels and gunboats, and a Cavite staff which transferred to Corregidor and handled much of MacArthur's communications. Stranded sailors also fought in the front lines on Bataan and Corregidor, and the Fourth Marine Regiment fought gallantly in the best marine tradition.

In naval circles, Admiral Hart's departure to the south—which was fully authorized by his superiors—is described as a successful maneuver which saved the Asiatic fleet from destruction in Manila Bay; it is an ironic commentary on the turns and twists of history that an American admiral should be praised for "escaping" from the very bay into which Admiral Dewey had sailed so boldly 43 years earlier to destroy the Spanish fleet; of course, our Navy sailed right back in again in 1945, after air power had cleared the way.

Hart's ships went on down to Java to join up with the Dutch naval forces in accordance with plan, but the destruction of Britain's *Prince of Wales* and *Repulse* off Malaya by Japanese planes had taken the backbone out of this proposed combined Allied fleet (which would have been helpless anyway without air cover), and the ships were either picked off piecemeal by Jap bombers, destroyed in surface engagements, or were successful in escaping to less dangerous waters farther from the enemy.

Without the fleet, which, as MacArthur saw it, had been formed and maintained for years for the sole mission of protecting the Philippines and now had departed south without firing more than one or two torpedoes in defense of this American territory under the American flag, and without the planes; the Islands were left completely naked of any outer defenses. The enemy invasion fleets could and did land their forces without danger of being intercepted while afloat and vulnerable to surface, submarine or air attack.

MacArthur, who had counted on the fleet to intercept the Japanese convoys before they landed their troops or to attack them while they were doing so, was furious. He repeatedly denounced Hart for "running out on me with the Asiatic fleet" and formed an opinion of the admirals as low as that he held toward the airmen who had lost their planes on the ground. Poor Admiral Hart—who looked tough, and wasn't—has already been belabored so much in other books that there is no desire to repeat the accusations here. Suffice it to say that he seems to belong in that group of admirals and generals described by Harry Hopkins as "thinking only about retiring to farms somewhere and won't take great and bold risks. . . . Roosevelt has got a whole hatful of them in the Army and Navy that will have to be liquidated before we really get on with our fighting." MacArthur was completely contemptuous of Hart.

In reporting this opinion of MacArthur's, the writer wishes to make clear that he does not subscribe to any implication of general timidity on the part of the Navy—nor did MacArthur himself ever make such blanket charges. But that there *was* a lack of boldness verging on defeatism in the days after Pearl Harbor cannot be doubted; the failure to relieve the Marines on Wake Island was disgraceful, for example. Henry L. Stimson recorded in his autobiography (with McGeorge Bundy, *On Active Service in Peace and War* [New York, Harper, 1948]) that what he and Roosevelt feared was "the Navy's apparent lack of aggressive spirit. Frank Knox (Navy Secretary) was a fighter, and his spirit was not broken by the disaster at Pearl Harbor, but the Naval high command as a whole was shaken and nervous." The Washington admirals wanted to write off the whole Philippines and Southeast Asia Area.

After the Asiatic fleet disappeared, MacArthur took a none-too-subtle dig at the Navy. He requested Roosevelt to take some action to combat Japanese propaganda, which was claiming the whole American fleet had been destroyed at Pearl Harbor, and was repeatedly asking the taunting question, "Where is the U.S. Navy?" In reporting this to Roosevelt, MacArthur added tellingly, "I am not in a position here to combat" this propaganda. In response to this, Washington asserted in a communiqué that the Navy was engaged in activities which would result in positive assistance to the defense of the Philippines—which, of course, never happened.

It should be stressed that MacArthur never shared the West Pointer's juvenile dislike for all things naval; he had no time for such jealousies. On the contrary he respected a fighter, whatever his service, and his contempt was reserved for those he considered guilty of cowardice or timidity. However, his low opinion of Hart, reported and amplified by his staff, provoked a natural, violent and aggressive reaction among naval men which lasted throughout the war and took the form of counteraccusations like those implied in the name "Dugout Doug," first invented by young sailors and officers left behind on Corregidor. The antagonism was widened and deepened by the attitude of MacArthur and his staff in Australia, and began to disappear only after the General came in contact with naval officers and sailors fully as aggressive as himself—Admiral Halsey, Dan "The Amphibious Man" Barbey, and others.

Almost without exception, the strategic proposals that MacArthur made were blocked or modified in Washington. MacArthur did not attend any of the meetings which decided strategy, although once he was represented by his Chief of Staff. On this occasion, as on all previous ones, the decision was against him and in favor of the Navy.

MacArthur's first chance to argue his own case in person came when he was summoned from Hollandia to Hawaii by a somewhat cryptic message from General Marshall in July of 1944 and found President Roosevelt waiting to discuss Pacific strategy with him. MacArthur, who had come without aides or statistics to support his position, believed the President had already made up his mind on future moves when he pointed at the map of Mindanao and asked, "Where do we go from here, Douglas?"

There are several versions of just what was said at the opening of this conference. As MacArthur recalls it, the President reopened the entire question of whether the Philippines or Formosa should be attacked next —this question having apparently already been settled months before by a decision to attack Mindanao in the Philippines, despite the Navy's preference for Formosa. However, Roosevelt's question would indicate that he accepted the Mindanao decision as final, and that the discussion thereafter was whether to continue to liberate the entire Philippines, or to jump from Mindanao all the way to Formosa. MacArthur, of course, favored clearing up the Philippines, while Nimitz wanted to go on to Formosa and then to the coast of China.

The ensuing debate between Admiral Nimitz and MacArthur was carried out on a high level of decorum, as reported by Admiral Leahy: "After much loose talk in Washington, where the name MacArthur seemed to generate more heat than light, it was both pleasant and very imperative to have two men who had been pictured as antagonists calmly present their differing views to the Commander in Chief."

MacArthur, finding the President apparently already decided in favor of Formosa, made a moving and convincing extemporaneous argument. He pointed out proudly that in two years of fighting in his area, fewer

Americans had been killed than in the single battle of Anzio. He insisted the Philippines were the key to the stolen conquered Japanese empire and that the Japanese would "shoot the works" to hold on there. Once defeated, they would soon be forced to surrender without the necessity of an invasion by land forces; air and naval power alone would bring her to her knees. Reviewing America's moral commitments to the Islands and his own promise to return, he told the President the moving story of Filipino guerrilla resistance and of the effective information network that was operating under the noses of the Japanese.

In the end, MacArthur's eloquent persuasiveness—backed by facts and figures of shipping requirements and a brilliantly complete, though impromptu, battle plan—won out over Nimitz's thorough but less passionate presentation.* F.D.R. finally said, "You win, Douglas," and in the most cooperative spirit Nimitz and MacArthur set about making plans; the two men displayed absolutely no animosity toward each other and were in agreement on most important points of grand strategy, especially that Japan would be forced to surrender without invasion of the homeland. The target date of November 15 for Mindanao was confirmed, and with Roosevelt's subsequent advocacy, the Joint Chiefs of Staff approved the plan to retake all of the Philippines as the next major campaign.

MacArthur takes delight in telling the story of this conference. In 1951 he explained to the Senate committees investigating his dismissal why the defense of Formosa—which he was now urging vehemently after his dispute with President Truman—was so important now, when in 1944 it had been more important to take the Philippines than Formosa. He stated that the objectives were different in 1944: "To stop and . . . blockade . . . the flow of materials . . . from the South Pacific, and that we could do . . . more readily and easily from the Philippines than we could from Formosa. Moreover, in landing in the Philippines we had a friendly population to support us . . . and . . . certain moral reasons for liberating that Christian nation that had been our ally." He added, "As a matter of fact, the Navy wanted to go into Formosa rather than the Philippines, and it was largely a moral question that decided the issue."

As an important sidelight on this decision, it is certain that Roosevelt was considering a political question also. As Robert Sherwood has said in *Roosevelt and Hopkins*, the Philippines "were more attractive politically" than Formosa. When MacArthur landed in Leyte—that central island having been finally chosen instead of Mindanao at the timely and aggressive suggestion of Admiral Halsey and the landing date advanced to October 20—Roosevelt was able to say in a speech a week before the presidential elections of 1944: "And speaking of the glorious operations in the Philippines—I wonder—whatever became of the suggestion made a few weeks ago that I failed for political reasons to send enough forces or supplies to General MacArthur?"

* A dramatic series of hitherto unpublished photographs in the picture section show the conflicting emotions of the two men as the debate swung from Nimitz to MacArthur.

This was an extremely telling point which enabled Roosevelt to counter one of the strongest charges made against him by supporters of Dewey. (Roosevelt had told MacArthur at Pearl Harbor, "I'll lick that son-of-a-bitch up in Albany if it's the last thing I do.")

MacArthur repaid the President for approving the Philippines campaign by issuing what can only be considered a series of "political" announcements which enabled Roosevelt to deal effectively with allegations that he had slighted MacArthur because he feared him as a possible rival. The two men exchanged "magnificent messages" of mutual congratulation on the landing, and MacArthur's pre-election communiques and statements gave every indication—at least to the voting public—that Leyte would be a swift and practically costless campaign. His most extreme statement declared on October 30—10 days after the landing and shortly before the election—that two thirds of Leyte were effectively under American control, enemy resistance had collapsed in many areas, the Japanese were trying to evacuate, and the Americans held an unbroken coastline of 212 miles.

Read carefully, each of these statements could be justified, but the net effect was so misleading that war correspondents protested vigorously. MacArthur's press officer then let the cat out of the bag: "The elections are coming up in a few days," he said, "and the Philippines *must* be kept on the front pages back home." MacArthur knew he would be criticized for the seemingly flagrant misappraisal of military intelligence implied in his communiqués (he calls them "communeeks"), and he was. But unlike some other generals in history, he did not alter his campaign to make it fit his claims. When the Japanese (far from evacuating) rushed in all possible reinforcements, MacArthur did not push ahead with costly attacks but fought with his usual skilled and versatile—but not reckless, life-expending—campaigns. Under pressure by the war correspondents, Carlos Romulo asked MacArthur, "What shall I tell the press by way of explanation of the slowness in taking Leyte?" "Tell them," MacArthur instructed, "that if I like I can finish Leyte in two weeks. But I won't! I have too great a responsibility to the mothers and wives in America. I will not take by sacrifice what I can achieve by strategy." He added, in words he frequently uses, "I have seen too many lives wasted unnecessarily in battle."

As a matter of fact, the "fighting was still indecisive," as General Eichelberger said, a month after MacArthur pronounced it in the mopping-up stage, and final organized resistance was not crushed until late in December.

Against this apparent failure as a military prophet, MacArthur was completely correct in his prediction that Japan would shoot the works in the Philippines; the naval battles there were decisive. He also predicted—more than eight months before the fact, the surrender of Japan. Had his opinion been asked and taken into consideration, the costly concessions made to Russia at Yalta would never have been made.

Impatient to press on to Luzon after the Leyte battle, MacArthur engaged in another bitter fight with the Navy. Once more the question that had seemingly been permanently settled at the Pearl Harbor conference arose—whether to continue with the liberation of all the Philippines or go on to Formosa? But meantime all members of the Joint Chiefs of Staff, except Admiral King, had begun to reconsider the Formosa plan which they originally favored and all gradually turned to MacArthur's views. Admiral Nimitz refused flatly to take his fleet past Luzon to Formosa unless Japanese air strength on Luzon were first neutralized. George Marshall was won over, after arguing that we should be made first to go to Formosa and then return to free Luzon. King, determined to defeat the Luzon plan, argued that its operation would tie up the Navy's heavy carriers longer than practicable; but MacArthur quickly countered that he could get along with light carriers and the island of Mindoro, using land-based planes from there to cover the Luzon landings.

Planning for Mindoro, which lies just south of Luzon, MacArthur set a target date for December 5, but again encountered Navy opposition—this time nearly unanimous. Admiral Kinkaid strongly objected to taking the landing force and escort vessels into the narrow waters between Leyte and Mindoro unless supported by land-based air from Leyte and was backed by both Nimitz and Halsey. In the face of Japanese suicide-plane attacks which had recently made a terrifying and damaging appearance in Philippines water (in all 279 ships were to be sunk or damaged in the Philippines), Kinkaid thought the passage would be "unduly hazardous" and ought to be canceled at least temporarily. MacArthur, fuming about "court-martialing admirals," finally agreed to a postponement to December 20. Thereafter the Mindoro landings and subsequent Lingayen (Luzon) landings went off on schedule, even though one admiral, under heavy kamikaze attacks, urged that the latter be called off after the convoys were already nearing their objectives.

A postscript must be added to this section to report a happy ending. MacArthur's World War II disputes with the Navy involved questions of strategy, tactics, timing, use of weapons, rather than petty personalities. During the five years he ruled Japan he established friendly personal relationships not only with the admirals under his command but with the air generals, and was universally admired by them. Under his command in Korea the first real, perfect "unification" of the armed services was effected in battle, and the admirals were breathless in admiration for his brilliant amphibious operation at Inchon.

MacArthur has said of this campaign, "The integration of the three fighting services has been as complete as I could possibly imagine. . . . I would rate it as 100 per cent and the only reason I do not rate it higher is because I believe the mathematicians say 100 per cent is all there is."

After Inchon, navy men were actually calling him, with respect and admiration, "Admiral MacArthur." Anyone in the Navy who had suggested such a possibility back in the contentious days of 1941-45 would have been confined to the nearest brig for mental examination.

Time also caused MacArthur to revise some of his views. During World War II his staff bitterly blasted Admiral King for supposedly keeping supplies from MacArthur's SWPA command. Consequently it was a sensational surprise to hear MacArthur say in 1951, "Good old Ernie King. . . . If it hadn't been for good old Ernie, they would have scuttled the Pacific and let Japanese Fascism take over. He kept battling George Marshall, and wouldn't let anything go to Europe until Marshall agreed to let 10 per cent go to the Pacific. Old Ernie saved the Pacific."

I think the point is this: during the war, MacArthur was resentful because only a small percentage of the supplies for the Pacific trickled through the Navy at Pearl Harbor into his own area—and he was completely convinced that the strategic road to Japan lay through New Guinea and the Philippines. In retrospect, he is able to be grateful to King for keeping attention focused on the Pacific as a whole; his perspective has broadened with the passage of the years.

REUNION AT GUIMBA

The greatest test of MacArthur's standing with his men came when he was reunited with some of the survivors of Bataan and Corregidor. He met them at the town of Guimba on Luzon in late January of 1945 after 510 of them had been snatched from a Japanese prison camp at Cabanatuan by a daring Ranger raid. If MacArthur felt any apprehension as he went among these men he had left behind, if he feared they would curse him, there was no sign of it in his compassionate, tear-stained face. He greeted many of the frail, emaciated prisoners by name, told them to eat all they could and get well, and promised them the American flag would fly again soon over Manila and Corregidor.

During the three long years of their captivity, they had called MacArthur a traitor and a coward. They wrote of him:

"Our leader has vanished like last summer's rose 5 ems
'Gone to get Help' he would have us suppose . . .

"Let him go, let him go, we are the braver,
Stain his hands with our blood, dye them forever.
Recall, oh ye kinsmen! how he left us to die,
Starved and insulted by his infamous lie."

And of the Filipinos:

"Who fought and died as the white man planned
And never quite learned to understand . . .
Lied to, cheated and sent to die
For a foreign flag in their native sky!"

And of an American platoon, retreating into Bataan:

"Their first engagement, well-fought behind,
And MacArthur's promise in every mind.
'The time is secret but I can say
That swift relief ships are on the way . . .
With decorations and honors too.'
MacArthur said it, it must be true."

As MacArthur greeted these men, all their bitterness was suddenly gone. They seemed to realize that only his burning insistence on returning to the Philippines had spared their lives. And seeing the new equipment, trucks, helmets, guns, airplanes, uniforms—all strange to them—they realized the job that America had faced. Some resentment has remained, especially among the 200 or so survivors of 1,600 men whose prison ship was bombed and sunk by American Navy planes at the start of a long, ghastly journey to Japan. Some books have been published by them which picture MacArthur as a traitor and a coward. But with the passing of time most of them have come to realize what the defense of Bataan meant to the Allied world. MacArthur himself refuses to hear it said that Bataan was a "defeat."

After his troops took back Bataan and Corregidor in daring and brief actions in February, 1945, he declared, "Bataan with Corregidor . . . made possible all that has happened since. History, I am sure, will record it as one of the decisive battles of the world. Its long protracted struggle enabled the United Nations to gather strength to resist in the Pacific. . . .

"Our triumphs of today belong equally to that dead army. Its heroism and sacrifice have been fully acclaimed but the great strategic results of that mighty defense are only now becoming fully apparent. The Bataan garrison was destroyed due to its dreadful handicaps but no army in history more thoroughly accomplished its mission. Let no man henceforth speak of it other than as of a magnificent victory."

CHAPTER

16

Some Brief Notes on MacArthur's Japan

SINCE MACARTHUR'S RELIEF FROM COMMAND IN THE Far East, the center of interest in his administration of Japan has shifted from the question of "What did he do?" to, "How long will it last?" Inasmuch as one of these questions lies in the past and the answer to the other is in the future, this book will attempt only a brief discussion, and the reader who is especially interested in the Japanese phase of MacArthur's career is referred to volumes by John Gunther, Edwin O. Reischauer, Russell Brines, Richard Lauterbach, Robert B. Testor, and many others. There is also, for vivid reading, MacArthur's own report in his testimony to Congress.

As to what MacArthur did, there is almost unanimous agreement—even among his enemies—that the occupation was a formidable accomplishment. In September 1945 MacArthur went unarmed into a country of some 78,000,000 supposed fanatics, whose soldiers had fought to the death on distant battlefields rather than surrender, whose homeland was bombed, shell-shocked, smashed, disorganized, defeated for the first time in its history, stripped of its empire and of its deepest convictions. Five and a half years later, dismissed by his own government, he departed—followed by the tears and cheers of some 82,000,000 new won friends of whom he could report, "They responded to the good deeds that we have given them . . . they are in our camp strategically, economically, financially, and to some extent spiritually." He left behind him a rebuilt and revitalized nation. By his work he had shown the rest of Asia that America's aims were idealistic and benevolent, and not imperialistic, and he demonstrated that economic progress and improvement can be achieved in Asia without surrender to the tyranny and false promises of communism.

Although the pressure of outside forces has already sharply altered the original direction of MacArthur's reforms, and the Japanese themselves will certainly make further changes, it is his firm conviction that the spirit will remain. What took place, he has said, "does not mean that the Japanese character has undergone a great moral reformation. It means that a very isolated and backward nation has had a chance to taste of, and enjoy and practice . . . freedom (which) it will not willingly give up."

Ironically enough, the American leaders who did not have sufficient faith in MacArthur to let him finish his job in Japan are gambling America's future in Asia on their faith that he worked well, and that he has succeeded in turning Japan from militarism and steering it away from communism. That is the meaning of the peace treaty, recently made public at this writing, whose spirit and intent were largely inspired by MacArthur. The treaty is more like a pact between friendly nations than between victors and vanquished. Under its generous terms, the Japanese will pay no reparations or damages, they will be free to recapture their old markets, the United States will help them by purchasing their products, thus adding to the billions it has already poured into Japan to help its recovery.

What we are gambling on is that reforms supervised by MacArthur have gone deep enough, in a practical sense, to prevent rebirth of the old conditions of highly centralized control of the national economy, of the police, politics, and other elements which proved fertile ground for the "military caste so long to control the destinies of the Japanese people and to prove a menace to the welfare of other people." We are gambling that the land reform, women's suffrage, strengthening of the labor movement, and other revolutionary changes have eliminated conditions which might have led the Japanese toward communism. We are counting on the economic relationship to prove so profitable to the Japanese that, as a practical matter, they will remain in the Western-United Nations camp. Above all, we are gambling that after 2,000 years of isolation and fanaticism, the Japanese have been so impressed by democracy that they will continue to practice it.

MacArthur believes they will.

His views in this connection, as the architect of the occupation, are interesting. The Japanese, he said, "watched us carefully, they were struck enormously by the spirituality of the American home. When our men . . . came in with their self-reliance, their assurance, their reasonable self-restraint, when they saw those men, the first thing they did was to build their chapels, even before we built our hospitals, and it made an enormous impression on them.

"The more they became acquainted with the American way of life, the more that they understood what that way of life meant to them—they got more fun out of life, they got more return for what they put into life. They began to realize that the liberty of an individual, the dignity of man, were not merely flamboyant expressions of rhetoric, but were real methods by which we tried, at least, to regulate our methods of living. They have absorbed them to an astonishing degree."

If MacArthur is wrong, if Japan turns back to the old paths, the experiment will have been a costly and tragic failure, despite all its nobility of purpose and the generally clean, idealistic, and high-minded way in which the occupation was administered. What happens in the future is to a large extent dependent on how deeply "democratization" penetrated the Japanese mind. There are many who think that MacArthur is wrong, that everything in Japan has changed except the Japanese themselves.

A typical expression of this point of view comes from Alan Raymond, a veteran correspondent who would certainly be classified as "a cynical debunker" by MacArthur. It is Raymond's opinion that after the occupation Japan will be pretty much the "same old Japan run by very much the same people who ran it before the war, with the old family and religious traditions unaltered except for a few surface legal reforms which can be swept away at any time." He thinks Emperor Hirohito has a deeper hold than ever on the people "as the one great national symbol that survived the defeat," that the nationalistic Shinto religion is as strong as ever despite its official separation from the state, and that little permanent or lasting good will come from the occupation.

Many observers have commented on the sure-handed way in which MacArthur took over in Japan, seeming to know exactly how to handle the defeated nation, when to be strong and when to yield, how to deal with the touchy question of the Emperor; he knew exactly where he was going even though he had never lived in Japan except for a very brief period in 1905 and had only visited there on ships that stopped to coal en route to or from the Philippines. Somewhere along the long road from Australia back to the Philippines he had turned his attention to Japan and had worked out a complete plan for a social revolution. The challenge and opportunity of reforming a feudalistic and backward nation—"something out of the pages of mythology," in MacArthur's words—was handmade for MacArthur. Long before victory was assured, he had laid his plans, and he was so determined not to let the opportunity elude him that he made a bid for the post in February of 1945, seven months before the surrender. This was done in his famous (or notorious) communiqué proclaiming that "Manila is ours," when actually the battle was just starting, and announcing that his battle cry was "on to Tokyo." Subsequently, Roosevelt named him supreme commander for the scheduled military invasion of Japan, and after accepting the surrender he became Supreme Commander of Allied Powers, or SCAP.

There are several versions of how Japan got its new constitution, which MacArthur's assistants hailed as "the greatest event in the world since Pearl Harbor"—well they might, since they wrote it. Originally, MacArthur directed the Japanese cabinet to prepare a constitution but they stalled and haggled for four months, and he finally became impatient with their efforts to revise the old Meiji constitution. On a piece of yellow legal paper torn from a pad, MacArthur himself wrote a memorandum: "Four points for constitution." This historical piece of paper has since been lost, but, as best remembered by the man to whom it was handed in Tokyo, it said:

"1. Emperor shall be dynastic. Hereditary monarch. Symbol of state. Never shall exercise powers of government.

"2. Forever renounce war and sovereign rights of belligerent nation.

"3. Legislature responsible to people. Universal suffrage.

"4. Pattern budget after British system."

These four points became the basis for the constitution, which was largely written by the American Government Section in Tokyo after what MacArthur called, "painstaking investigation and frequent conferences between members of the Japanese government and this headquarters following my initial direction to the Cabinet five months ago."

MacArthur's personal popularity with the Japanese met and survived two severe tests; his failure to make a strong showing in the 1948 American presidential primaries and his dismissal from command. The latter brought strong avowals of gratitude from many Japanese, and far from forgetting him after his departure, the Japanese are planning to make him "guest of the state for life . . . for meritorious service in the peaceful and democratic rehabilitation of the country." Numerous other honors are also being prepared for him.

By contrast, his own government rewarded him for his brilliant and devoted work in Japan by refusing to make him an official participant in the signing of the peace treaty in San Francisco, which was not only an unbelievably petty snub of MacArthur but a stupid propaganda error which was bound to have repercussions throughout Japan and the Far East.

MACARTHUR'S STAFF

One of the most frequent criticisms of MacArthur concerns the character of the men closest to him, the members of his staff. It is often said disparagingly that MacArthur gave and demanded complete loyalty from those who worked for him, but this particular criticism obviously has no validity; no executive or commander could possibly work with subordinates who doubted his ability or his intentions—as MacArthur himself discovered when he was dismissed from command. There is an equally false impression that MacArthur was surrounded by "yes" men who never ventured to disagree. The fact is that throughout his military career he has welcomed and listened attentively to the opinions of his staff. General Eisenhower, the only staff officer to emerge from the towering shadow of MacArthur into individual greatness, has stated that he argued with his commander throughout the nine years they were together.

As a matter of accuracy, it should be pointed out that most criticisms of MacArthur's "staff" do not really apply, nor are they intended to, to the great majority of his top-ranking associates, or even to their subordinates. Through popular usage, it has become customary to use the term "staff" to refer to a small group, five to ten men, who have been particularly close to him in recent years not only on a professional basis, but also personally. Of these men it is frequently (and largely truthfully) said that they share several common characteristics—each carries a chip on both shoulders, is highly and sometimes childishly sensitive, and is convinced that the General is the greatest man who ever lived. Given their way, MacArthur would be judged not as an ordinary mortal with the personal foibles and idiosyncrasies that contribute to his total character and therefore affect all of his actions, but as if he existed in some perfect idealistic vacuum—the soldier-statesman as distinct from the man. Fight as they may among themselves over preference or power, the men of the staff unite to present a solid wall to the outside world whenever MacArthur is criticized. Anyone who refuses to accept in toto the concept of a perfect MacArthur is classed by the staff as an "enemy" and treated accordingly; everyone in the world is either "for" or "against" the General and no deviation, no elasticity of judgment is acceptable to the staff.

It will be interesting to watch whether this attitude changes as MacArthur and his close friends become acclimated once again to America; it is my opinion that their attitude is in great measure due to long absence abroad when, almost imperceptibly, the nuances of American life are lost and a picture of "home"—true in general outline but false in detail—is built up in the mind of the exile.

The sensitivity that was so noticeable in Japan and which they brought home with them in 1951 is a product of the Bataan-Corregidor-Australia days of World War II when MacArthur communicated to those around him his extreme bitterness over the "callous abandonment" of the Philippines by Washington and the subsequent "starvation" of his Southwest Pacific Area. As other officers joined the staff, they came to share the conviction that MacArthur was being thwarted by political and personal enemies back home who were determined to destroy him. In order to counteract this supposed conspiracy, it became necessary to "protect the General" in both his present reputation and his place in history. During the war this protection took the form of a censorship of propaganda and special pleading for his area, and the chief public relations officer took the position that the function of correspondents was to help "glorify" MacArthur. When Japan was finally reached, this officer expressed his appreciation to the reporters for "helping me achieve my goal of having General MacArthur made commander in chief here."

The same officer or members of his staff looked at every still or motion picture taken in MacArthur's area and edited them for reasons far beyond those of military security. Any showing MacArthur in a less than commanding pose were destroyed. In contravention of War Department orders that all film be sent unedited to Washington, one motion picture showing an amphibious landing was sharply cut. This was at Morotai, where there was a miscalculation in the tides and the landing forces disembarked in water up to their necks. Because this film would have made

MacArthur appear somewhat less than perfect as a tactician, the public relations officer cut out the footage showing a colossal pile-up on the beach. In the case of another film which had already slipped past censorship and gone to Honolulu, a special courier was dispatched by air to retrieve it.

The determination to "protect the General" was carried on into Japan, where any criticism of MacArthur brought forth a prompt and thunderous reply. No publication was too small or obscure to catch the eagle eye of someone on MacArthur's staff, and replies ranged from a brief note to a 6,000-word letter to *Fortune* magazine, signed by the General himself. When MacArthur returned home after his dismissal, these tactics were continued; and his spokesman issued statement after statement in the first days of his arrival. Friends advised the General that it was ludicrous and undignified to take note of every trivial criticism, and the replies have since been confined to major matters. In fairness to MacArthur, it is little wonder that he is annoyed by some of the ridiculous or outrageous misconceptions printed about him, especially in the liberal press. But many of his replies (or those of his staff) missed their mark by being worded in a petulant or wounded manner.

Five of the officers who were closely associated with him in World War II or in Japan have returned with him to the United States. Three remain in the army on the staff provided by the Department of the Army for MacArthur as a five-star general, who always retains active rank even though without assignment. These are Colonel L. E. (Larry) Bunker, his aide; Colonel Sidney Huff, an old friend and one-time naval officer, whose duties are chiefly social and whose wife is a frequent companion of Mrs. MacArthur, and Lieutenant Colonel Anthony Story, the General's pilot, who joined him shortly after Japan's surrender. Two major generals, Charles Willoughby and Courtney Whitney, have retired from the army in order to serve MacArthur. Of this group, Huff and Willoughby were members of the original "Bataan staff" or "Bataan gang" which left Corregidor with MacArthur in 1942.

Born in Heidelberg in 1892 of an American mother and German father named Tscheppe-Weidenbach, Willoughby (who adopted his mother's name) has continental charm of manners and a European accent. He came to America as a young man, enlisted before World War I, acquired something of a reputation as a military author as he rose through the ranks, and between 1941 and 1951 was G-2 (intelligence officer) for MacArthur. In that role he has been accused of three major errors: failing to predict the Japanese attack on the Philippines in 1941 and the North Korean attack in June, 1950, and failing to foresee Red China's entry into the Korean war in November of that latter year. Under close examination, none of those accusations can be completely supported.

Willoughby, as already noted in this book, correctly forecast the strategy of the Japanese assault on the Philippines but was off in his timing—which simply means that he was in a numerous and distinguished company which included nearly every American official from Roosevelt down. As to Korea, he did gather and present to MacArthur correct information on the presence of Red Chinese "volunteers" before the Communists' full-scale intervention. What MacArthur did on the basis of that information is his responsibility, and not Willoughby's. The State Department, Defense Department, and Central Intelligence all were caught flat-footed as to Red China's decision to intervene with full strength and the intelligence failures in this case are not attributable to Willoughby. As MacArthur correctly pointed out, such information should have been gathered on a world level and not left to the limited facilities of a field command.

On the whole, Willoughby has made no grave intelligence mistakes and his work has been sound and thorough. His personality works against him in many cases; his urbanity can change quickly to vindictive harshness. Many officers simply refuse to take him seriously and call him a "librarian," although he has studied at the Sorbonne, Heidelberg, Gettysburg College, and the University of Kansas.

In the natural course of his duties, a G-2 becomes acquainted with spies and agents, and in this line Willoughby came across a fantastic and fascinating spy case in Japan. The story involved Richard Sorge, a German who headed a Soviet Russian spy ring operating in the Far East in the late 1930's and early '40's. Finally trapped by the Japanese, Sorge wrote a long and detailed confession before his execution. Working from this confession, Willoughby made further investigations and composed a lurid report which purported to show that several American Communists had served Sorge. At this writing, Willoughby is scheduled to testify before Congressional committees about his discovery and is also seeking to publish a book about the Sorge case.

Willoughby's poorest showing, I believe, was in Japan, where, in opposition to the general liberal current of the occupation, he showed his own inclination toward centralized, authoritarian control. He has been called the "Senator Joe McCarthy of the occupation." There is some justification in this characterization, for Willoughby countenanced, if he did not instigate, the persecution and blacklisting of good and hard-working American citizens whom he falsely suspected of Communistic tendencies; his suspicions even extended to men of highly conservative background who opposed him on some point of occupation policy.

Contrary to popular opinion, Willoughby did not have an open door to MacArthur. He was required to go through the chief of staff and was always militarily correct in doing this. Frequently during the last years in Tokyo Willoughby was denied access to the Far Eastern commander, and would wait in the hall for MacArthur to start for home or for the men's room and then say with surprise, "Oh, General, are you leaving? I was just coming to see you." MacArthur would invite him back to the office to explain his problem.

Willoughby's admiration for his chief's professional skill is unbounded. He calls MacArthur "a fellow craftsman in a distinguished historical company of great commanders—Napoleon as well as Lee." Of one amphibious campaign he said, "The masterly coordination of ground, sea, and air has not had a more brilliant exhibition in modern times." Right behind MacArthur, Willoughby ranks Generalissimo Francisco Franco, whom he considers "the second greatest living military genius."

Few people who knew Courtney Whitney as a Manila lawyer in the 1930's ever dreamed he would one day become, under MacArthur, political chief of conquered Japan and one of the most liberal leaders of the occupation. In the process he also became MacArthur's closest confidant, his alter ego, and so much like his chief in speech and thought that today it is difficult to tell where MacArthur ends and Whitney begins. A little story is illustrative.

Asked by a Texas chapter of the Red Cross for an inspirational message to support a fund-raising campaign, MacArthur personally dictated and signed a short letter to this effect: "Congratulations on your fine work. Every American should assist so worthy a cause."

Shortly afterward a somewhat petulant letter came back from the Red Cross chairman, who appreciated the fact that MacArthur was an extremely busy man but regretted that he had not been able to give his personal attention to the letter. "We could all tell from the style," wrote the lady chairman, "that you did not write the letter." MacArthur handed this letter to Whitney with a wry smile. "It looks, Courtney," he remarked, "as if I'll have to let you write *all* my letters so that I'll sound like myself."

Similarly, the top Army men who handled messages from the Far East signed by MacArthur could not be certain whether they were written by MacArthur himself or by Whitney. They could always tell whether some other officer on MacArthur's staff had done the writing, but the messages of MacArthur and Whitney were characteristically identical. Some relatively late-comers to the occupation headquarters in Tokyo were completely confused by the Whitney-MacArthur relationship; they were unable to distinguish whether ideas originated with one man or the other; both delivered themselves of identically worded philosophical discourses, both expressed liberal concepts, both used religious sentiments and referred constantly to "Providence" and "Fate." Upon examination of their past records, it seems more likely that Whitney has come to resemble MacArthur than vice versa, and of course Whitney is not the first man to be so thoroughly inspired by MacArthur that he would, gladly and unquestioningly, die in his service.

Whitney, a native of Maryland born in 1897, served in the ranks in World War I, and remained in the Army with an officer's commission. In his spare time as a soldier he studied law (like MacArthur's father) and practiced in the Philippines from 1927 to 1940. With war approaching, he rejoined the Army in the Air Corps. As a lawyer he was shrewd, aggressive, and acquisitive, and before long had purchased or lawyered his way into extensive holdings; some of his practices have been questioned and as a result of a lingering bad taste left from those days many G.I.'s (and others) believed stories that he was engaged in black-marketing; these stories, of course, are completely untrue—he is a man of integrity. On week ends in Manila, Whitney took to prospecting in the mineral-rich mountains, and once discovered a chrome deposit which was successfully mined.

With his reputation as a legal sharpshooter, Whitney had the ideal type of mind (John Gunther described it as "sharp, fluent") to direct an underground organization; and MacArthur summoned him to Australia in 1943 to set up the amazingly successful Filipino guerrilla movement. Whitney's young son left Yale to join it. Like many of MacArthur's officers, Whitney is a man of considerable personal courage and he voluntarily went along on a daring raid deep into enemy territory to rescue internees at Los Banos in the Philippines.

There was nothing in Whitney's background that would seem to prepare him for the role he played in the occupation as a fighter for liberal concepts. Yet an associate in Tokyo—not a member of the Bataan clique—says Whitney was "full of ideas, bristling with ideas" for reforming Japan. He was once heard to tell the Japanese Prime Minister, who had come to protest occupation policies against monopolies, "The only thing that will save your country is a sharp swing to the left." Whether this represented a fundamental change in Whitney's philosophy is not easily answered; having made his own fortune through private and sometimes monopolistic enterprises, Whitney would be expected to feel sympathetic toward them in Japan. The answer may be that Whitney felt the Zaibatsu (big monopolistic combine) in Japan had gone too far and were spoiling a good thing; their excessive practices could not fail to provoke the Japanese people to a swing toward communism.

Whitney was the "most inside" of the MacArthur insiders; his hatchetman and glad hander. He has been with him from three to five hours daily since 1945. Since their return, he is MacArthur's neighbor in the Waldorf Towers. Although Whitney and Willoughby have frequently fought over policy, and possibly over the General's favors, they have remained close personal friends and associates. For instance, when Willoughby reached New York behind the others of the party, Whitney telephoned him, jokingly impersonated a Congressional investigator, and in a heavy-handed imitation instructed the intelligence officer to get ready to testify about the Sorge case.

Whitney, who was unmercifully rapped by the American press for his "communiqués" from "GHQ, Waldorf Towers," immediately after MacArthur's return, has explained that he did not consult MacArthur prior to some of his meetings with the press. "The reporters were assigned by their editors to keep a 24-hour watch," he said. "I went in to see them—feeling sorry for them . . . and offered to answer any questions. They murdered me." One particularly unfortunate statement by Whitney has been widely misrepresented and even distorted into "proof" of a whole fantastic theory that MacArthur confuses himself with Christ. Whitney mentioned

"Doubting Thomases," and someone recognized this as a Biblical reference. Whitney himself was not sure if it was from Luke or Mark or somewhere else, but the sharp reporters looked it up and discovered that the complete reference—going far beyond the everyday expression, "Doubting Thomas"—was to Jesus. The press had a natural field day in making fun of MacArthur, but he is so fond of Whitney that he let him off with a humorous scolding; however, the press conferences were soon afterward stopped.

In the debate and controversy following MacArthur's return, President Truman became convinced that Whitney was an ungrateful man. As Truman tells the story, MacArthur requested him during their Wake Island conference to get a second star (major generalship) for Whitney and the President did so; another and likelier version is that the generous idea came from Truman himself. This promotion made Whitney the equal in rank of Truman's own major general and White House pet, Harry Vaughn. But in the series of forceful statements he issued from the Waldorf Towers, Whitney blasted the President from here to there, and Truman mused over his ingratitude. Incidentally, Vaughn worked under MacArthur in the early days of World War II in Australia, and has a pleasant letter to show for it. No comparison between Truman's major general and MacArthur's major general is called for in these pages; suffice it to say that each is suited to the man he serves.

At this writing, Whitney is supposed to have agreed to work for Remington-Rand. The irreverent, aware of MacArthur's eventual plans to join that company, said that Whitney had "gone to prepare a place for Him." *

The officers who controlled (and those who still control) access to MacArthur are responsible for many of the frictions and antagonism of which the General is sometimes unaware. In World War II Major General (later Lieutenant General) Richard Sutherland as chief of staff was the man who stood between MacArthur and the outside world, did a great deal of his work, and made many important decisions. Sutherland also made a great many enemies by his brusqueness, contempt, and rough handling of subordinates or officers of other services. Sutherland has said that MacArthur was little interested in anything beyond "publicity and politics" and left all details to his staff. But Sutherland also says, "MacArthur has more gray matter and could see farther over the horizon" than any man living.

Sutherland did not share his chief's conviction that democracy—at least in wartime—is the greatest form of government yet devised by man. An illustrative story is recounted by General Kenney (in *The MacArthur I Know*), who tells of Sutherland arguing that democracy was not strong enough to operate as necessary in wartime. MacArthur rebuked him mildly, "The trouble with you, Dick, I am afraid, is that you forget that we

* Both Whitney and MacArthur have evidently changed their minds about Remington-Rand, but the story is too good to leave out.

fight for the principles and ideals of democracy." Historians will certainly find much material in a 200-page memorandum which Sutherland dictated and which is now under lock and key in Washington. Sutherland's record shows him to be a highly capable and ambitious officer—perhaps too ambitious for MacArthur's liking. He did not last long with MacArthur after the latter discovered he was forming a powerful coterie of supporters with GHQ. A personal incident offered a convenient excuse for making it known to Sutherland that it would be a good idea for him to leave Japan and go home, where he retired.

The most famous and far-reaching feud between men under MacArthur will long have repercussions. The principles were Lieutenant General Edward N. (Ned) Almond, who became chief of staff in Japan, and Lieutenant General Walton K. Walker, commander of the Eighth Army. During the investigation of his dismissal, MacArthur testified in effect that the two men were bosom friends. But if this was his real opinion, he simply was unaware of the facts. Almond and Walker (the latter since killed in a jeep accident) disliked each other intensely; they were far too much alike to get along. Both were good field soldiers and brave men, good executives, hard taskmasters, pluggers. Both were uninspired and undiplomatic, with no special ability or brilliance. Each got to the top through association with famous men. Almond was a protégé of General George Marshall, who gave him command of a Negro division in Italy in World War II, while Walker commanded a corps under Patton. Though known as "a Marshall man," Almond got along well with MacArthur when he was sent to Tokyo in the regular routine of War Department transfers, and came to admire his new commander even more than he does Marshall.

In the pre-Korea chain of command in Tokyo, Almond was a major general and Walker a lieutenant general commanding the Eighth Army. But to reach MacArthur, it was necessary for Walker to go through Almond and this proved a difficult task. Walker would often be kept fuming for a half hour or longer after the fixed time for an appointment, while Almond read a newspaper or picked his teeth in an otherwise empty office. Informed that Walker was outside, Almond frequently said, "Let the son-of-a-bitch wait." Walker was first to go to Korea with his Eighth Army, and in the Inchon landing Almond followed with the X Corps. Once when Almond was near Walker's headquarters, it was suggested that he pay a courtesy visit. He exploded, "Why should I call on that such-and-such?" Later he grudgingly made the visit. Such was what MacArthur called a friendly relationship inspiring complete teamwork.

When MacArthur ordered his drive to "end the war in Korea" in October, 1950, he placed Walker with the Eighth Army in the center and Almond on the east coast. The two forces were divided by a mountain chain; and although MacArthur testified that they had perfect radio communication, he placed the X Corps directly under his own control in Tokyo, rather than under the Army. Spurred on by the rivalry of their commanders, the two forces began a headlong race toward the border, but recoiled into retreat when they were struck by the massive Chinese Red forces whose advance guards had already been in battle for some time. After the Eighth Army was driven back below the 38th parallel, the X Corps came under Army control. Shortly thereafter Walker's death put an end to the feud, and Almond continued in his command under General Ridgway and later Van Fleet. Officers in the field say that the Walker-Almond enmity had become so bitter that one or the other would have had to be relieved. They guessed that MacArthur would have removed Almond, even though he rewarded him with a third star for the successful evacuation from North Korea.

As with any group of individuals, there is plenty of gossip about MacArthur's staff. One story involves Willoughby's dashing over to Bataan one afternoon and winning the Silver Star for "seizing command of a leaderless company." There was the officer on Corregidor who requested that a correspondent dispatch a "lovey-dovey, umswy-wumsy" message to the correspondent's glamorous woman employer. There was the officer who had been fired from his job as a teacher; there were the drunken colonel and the sad colonel and a number of somewhat faded White Russian beauties—the latter kept carefully out of MacArthur's sight. There was the case of the Australian lady WAAC who campaigned in Australia and the Philippines, and later turned up in San Francisco, to the embarrassment of the State Department. In fact, there were several cases of lady WAACs, who if they chose to do so, may make great contributions to history in their memoirs, not only of the Pacific war but of hostilities in Europe. Pending publication of such volumes, these stories belong in gossip columns rather than in these pages.

No recitation of the personal foibles of the half-dozen or so staff men who were close to MacArthur should be allowed to conceal the fact that they did their jobs and did them well, or were promptly fired. That they did them somewhat eccentrically, that their contacts with the "outside world" were petulant and grieved, that they sometimes made cruel use of their personal power, does not detract from this fact that their work got done.

Nor would it be fair to leave the impression that all the officers closely associated with MacArthur have been mediocrities. Eichelberger and Krueger, his Army commanders, were top men. Highly skilled air generals and admirals have been under his command and have formed extremely high opinions of his professional skill. One admiral said, "He knows more about the use of carriers than any man outside the Navy," and General Stratemeyer of the Air Force declared, "He knows all there is to know about the use of air power. . . . He's the best-informed man I've ever known."

Personal aides like Lloyd Lehrbas were efficient officers, among many others, and in the lower echelon of the fantastically bad public relations organization there were many competent and much abused officers and men.

After the foregoing had been written, a newspaper dispatch from Washington reported the award of the Distinguished Service Cross to Brigadier General Crawford F. Sams, who as a member of MacArthur's staff did a tremendously successful job of public health administration in Japan. Sams won the award by going in disguise behind the enemy lines in Korea and slipping into a military hospital where he made a daring first-hand check on sick North Korean and Chinese Red soldiers, whose armies had been reported suffering from either bubonic plague or smallpox. Sams saw enough to convince him the disease was smallpox, and consequently steps were taken to immunize UN troops and 6,000,000 South Korean civilians. Sams returned safely.

Having said that much, it is permissible on the evidence to conclude that as a rule MacArthur did not select the brightest, most capable, and most promising officers in the Army to serve under him. Most of the men on his staff were never heard of in the Army before they joined him, and never will be again. In general, there is an amazing gap between the brilliance and professional competence of MacArthur and the run-of-the-mine characteristics of those who served him.

MACARTHUR AND THE PRESS

No less than the rest of the world, the reporters and correspondents who worked in MacArthur's area were sharply divided in their opinions about him, and continue to be so since he has come home. Basically, a large part of the complaints of the press were caused by the fact that he was operating in terms of history to be written 2,000 years hence, and the reporters were working against tomorrow morning's deadline. Another thing was that the reporters could not get to see him regularly or even infrequently. On his return to America, the press had the same difficulty and only a few reporters have been granted interviews.

Desiring to report things as they actually were, and not as they might appear in broad outline in history books, the correspondents in Japan ran into constant difficulties with MacArthur's staff. Any stories deviating from the official line aroused wide resentment and retaliation in the form of closing MacArthur's door to the writers, or even barring them from returning to Japan after visits to nearby countries. If a correspondent's paper at home offended by criticizing the occupation, the General did not attempt to win over the representative but barred him from his office, which was already difficult of access. MacArthur's public relations officer in Tokyo wrote stinging letters to home offices accusing seven newspaper correspondents and one broadcaster of "playing the Communist game," by criticism of MacArthur's policies and practices. In fairness, it should be stated that some reporters took a heckling, captious, nagging attitude toward everything the occupation attempted, and some of the reports were so slanted and so inaccurate that they finally got under MacArthur's skin.

It may be difficult to believe, if you have not worked as a reporter in the vicinity of MacArthur, that a great many times he had no idea of what his staff was doing. This is not said in extenuation; he should have known, but the fact is that without his knowledge books were censored in Japan, complaining letters written to publishers, and all sorts of repressive actions taken to restrict freedom of the press and of thought. When it was possible to reach MacArthur, he would immediately rescind these regulations and occasionally rebuke the offending officer—the only time I ever heard him raise his voice in 10 years of off-and-on relationship was to deliver a stinging reprimand to a press officer. However, it was not easy to reach him to voice complaints, and as a general rule MacArthur was inclined to forgive staff officers who were over-zealous in their efforts to protect him.

Throughout World War II MacArthur repeatedly said that he personally did not believe in censorship and would abolish it completely except for War Department regulations. Frankly no reporter believed this. But when the Korean war broke out, MacArthur battled with the War Department against censorship and won his way on the ground that this was a United Nations rather than a U.S. war. He took the position that the reporters were mature men, fully able to do their jobs without disclosing vital secrets to the enemy. Unfortunately, this experiment did not work out too well.

Many of the quickly recruited war correspondents were young, green, eager-beavers, who repeatedly jeopardized the safety of our troops by insisting on reporting what unit was in what village, and in general drawing the complete daily line of battle for the enemy. No doubt accurately, they pictured the early U.S. forces as a beaten, dispirited army. When the Eighth Army headquarters in Korea expelled several reporters in protest against these stories, MacArthur stuck by his guns and promptly reinstated them. Veteran reporters—Handleman, Boyle, Whitehead, Conniff, Downs, Dunn, Morin, Beech and others—realized the damage being done and repeatedly appealed for a responsible military censorship.

As late as October 30, MacArthur was still clinging to his conviction that everything was working well in Korea. In a glowing report to the UN, he even defended the reporters who had yielded to "outcroppings of emotional strain." His point of view is so unusual for a military man, that it is worth reproducing in part: "In evaluating the issue between compulsory and voluntary censorship, one must understand that the sole purpose of either is to safeguard against the premature publication of information . . . which would assist the enemy. . . . No form of censorship can prevent espionage . . . nor is it the proper instrument for the avoidance of factual error. The ability of correspondents . . . to assume the responsibility of self-censorship has been amply and conclusively demonstrated in the course of the Korean campaign. In the many military campaigns in which I have engaged, most of which were covered by a rigid form of news censorship, I have never seen the desired balance between public information and military security so well achieved and preserved as during the

Korean campaign." However, after a few reporters had foolishly disclosed to the enemy full details of the UN evacuation from Hungnam in northern Korea, MacArthur finally installed complete censorship. Once installed, it proved as bad as military censorship always is and continued to be bad even after MacArthur was relieved.

But to reporters in Tokyo, the arrival of General Ridgway to succeed MacArthur as Supreme Commander was like a fresh breeze. Even those correspondents who had almost adored MacArthur and been used by him as mouthpieces, felt spiritually emancipated as they emerged from the hypnotic aura of MacArthur's staff and found themselves working in a normal, low-pressure atmosphere. Ridgway's press officers took the position that their duties were to assist the correspondents in gathering news, and the whole emphasis changed from the familiar "no" of MacArthur's regime to an attitude of helpful co-operation.

CHAPTER

17

Korea: The War MacArthur Won

WE COME NOW TO A CHRONOLOGICAL ACCOUNT OF Douglas MacArthur's last war and of the events that led to his dismissal from command and the termination of his long and brilliant military career under bitterly controversial circumstances. The background should be briefly recalled: In June of 1950, troops of the Communist government of North Korea invaded the Republic of South Korea. The United States—in an action immediately afterwards ratified by the United Nations—determined to meet and repel this aggression with armed force. As commander of United Nations forces, MacArthur successfully drove the North Koreans back toward the border of China and complete military victory was in sight when, in November of 1950, Communist China intervened and drove the UN armies back southward across the 38th parallel. A military stalemate developed which in the summer of 1951 resulted in cease-fire talks as a possible prelude to diplomatic consideration of the Korean problem.

So far as his actions went, MacArthur's connection with the war was wholly military. He did not have any part in policy decisions; he did not influence the original decision to intervene and did not make the subsequent decision to carry the war into the territory of North Korea. But when the war was nearing an obvious condition of stalemate, MacArthur intervened in policy matters to urge the use of American air and naval power to force the Chinese Communists to discontinue their aggression in Korea. The political and military authorities of the United States, together with our allies, refused to support MacArthur's position, fearing that his proposals would provoke Russia into counterattack in defense of China and thus bring on World War III. MacArthur's repeated public protests against this stand—which he considered a policy of appeasement and surrender more likely to bring on a world conflict than the action he proposed—resulted in his dismissal.

Against this background, a glance at MacArthur's state of mind and way of life in the period prior to the war may contribute to understanding of the final denouement. He had now seen the sun rise and set for 70 long years, and by the simple facts of mathematics and the inexorable workings of chemistry, the end of his career could not be far away. The facts of that career had given him great faith in his own destiny and confidence in his own decision; even before him there had been his father, seizing the initiative at Missionary Ridge and charging beyond the ordered objective, while Grant looked on and said, "It will be all right if it turns out all right." There was his own almost single-handed opposition to the General Staff in World War I in his advocacy of the use of citizen-soldiers, who had so bravely proved the correctness of his position, even as the Filipino soldiers and citizens had proved him right in his judgment of their bravery in battle. There was the time in World War I when under protested orders he had halted his troops after breaking through the St. Mihiel salient and getting the enemy on the run. A bloody stalemate had resulted from failure to pursue this advantage. Shortly afterward, without specific orders (but not against them) he had again led his troops to a breakthrough and, sensing that the German enemy was beaten and had fled, he followed through to an important and lifesaving three-mile gain. Alone, he had battled against higher authority to reverse Pacific grand strategy in World War II and make possible the liberation of the Philippines. He had found in Japan a vacuum, not only in the minds of the defeated people but in the attitude of the indecisive Allies toward the conquered country, and he had filled this vacuum with his own brilliantly conceived and strikingly successful revolutionary administration.

On the wall of his office in Toyko there was hung a framed quotation from a Roman general, which his staff referred to as "MacArthur's Credo." It said in part: "If therefore anyone thinks himself qualified to give advice respecting the war which I am to conduct, let him not refuse assistance to the state . . . but come with me to Macedonia. . . . But if he thinks this too much trouble and prefers the repose of the city life to the toils of war, let him not on land assume the office of pilot. The city in itself furnishes abundance of topics for conversation; let it confine its passion for talking to its own precincts . . . we shall pay no attention to any council but such as shall be framed within our camp." In the light of the experiences of MacArthur's life, his long exercise of power, the fact that an absence of policy had on numerous occasions opened the way for him to make decisions and act more or less as an independent authority, the events in the final months of his military career seem natural and perhaps inevitable.

Now in mid-1950, after more than five decades of the most intense and stimulating activity, his life had become essentially passive, an act of waiting, of watching time speed by when there was no longer much time left.

The occupation had become routine and offered few further challenges, and, given his own way, MacArthur would have ended it by 1948. He was (as he still is) acutely though not morbidly conscious of his age and of the fact that he is 58 years older than his son. He wanted to have young Arthur with him every possible moment, but at the same time he fully realized that it was not entirely fair to the boy to keep him indefinitely from the homeland he had never seen.

An obvious solution was for MacArthur to leave active service and return home with his family. But for MacArthur it was unthinkable to leave the work in Japan half finished. Conscious, as always, of his prospective place in history, he regarded it as imperative for him to conclude his life work with a fitting, monumental achievement, and for him that meant the conclusion of a peace treaty which would wipe out the bitter memories of war and bring Japan again into a peaceful brotherhood of nations. But outside of Japan the tensions of the cold war mounted; the problems of the treaty could not be solved quickly, and consequently he stayed on and on in Tokyo and his family stayed with him.

As a result of this situation, MacArthur's underlying mood was one of restless impatience. His life had become a steady routine (broken only by trips to Korea and the Philippines for the inaugural ceremonies of those republics) of home-office-home-office-home for seven days a week, every day in the year, with occasionally a short drive to Haneda airport to meet incoming celebrities. Day after day in luncheon discussions at his home, he told his visitors of his dream of world peace, even though events had already forced him to begin the partial rearming of Japan. He incessantly emphasized his conviction that within 100 years the new Japanese constitution —which outlawed war—would be recognized as one of the great milestones in human history.

During these disquisitions, MacArthur showed his years. His hands trembled and his voice shook. Sometimes he started to talk hesitantly, losing the thread and repeating himself, until suddenly the thoughts straightened themselves out and he went on smoothly and eloquently with all his old power and brilliance.

MacArthur got the news of the North Korean attack in the early morning of June 25, and within hours he was a different man. Responding to the call to action, he changed physically. An aide said, "The added responsibility seems to have peeled 10 years from his shoulders." The shaking disappeared from his hands, his voice firmed, his step became light and strong. His decisions were quick and sure. Watching him work, his chief of staff exclaimed, "God, the man is great! He's the greatest man alive." And his air commander said, in all sincerity, "He's the greatest man in history."

In this transformation, we see MacArthur once more as a symbol—the symbol of schizophrenic man torn between peace and war, good and evil; dreaming of peace eternal but always fighting bigger and more destructive wars; worshiping the ideal of peace—calm, static, philosophical, restful—but responding eagerly and happily to the movement, challenge, and brutal adventure of war. But underneath, MacArthur was still an impatient man who had lived 70 years, still restless to go home, and still determined not to go before finishing his job and bringing his career to a suitable historical climax.

During his five years in Tokyo, MacArthur had watched helplessly while Communism swept over much of Asia, overwhelming the Chinese government of Chiang Kai-shek and driving it to a last island refuge on Formosa. MacArthur—as he has pointed out frequently since his homecoming—strongly opposed official American policy of withholding decisive aid from Chiang Kai-shek on the grounds that his government was something less than perfectly democratic, a policy which resulted in "endangering the paramount interests of the United States," as he said at the time, "by confusing them with an internal purification problem in China."

When the Communists began preparing for an assault on Formosa, MacArthur could no longer hide his concern, nor his conviction that if Formosa fell the whole American outpost line in the Pacific would be breached. The Joint Chiefs of Staff shared his views about the strategic importance of Formosa, but, although it is now futilely denied, our government was taking preliminary steps toward American recognition of Red China and toward handing over Formosa to that regime. As if to emphasize this position, Secretary of State Acheson in January of 1950 drew an "American defense perimeter" which excluded South Korea as well as Formosa, and from later developments it is obvious that his words were given close attention in both the North Korean capital and in Moscow. They were the invitation to the waltz.

Meanwhile, in Korea itself, two regimes had grown up after the defeat of Japan. By military agreement between America and Russia, a line was drawn through Korea at which troops of the two nations—in supervising the surrender of Japanese forces—would eventually meet and stop. This was the 38th parallel, artificially dividing the agricultural south from the industrial north, and it became a permanent division when the Soviets refused to honor an earlier pledge to support a "unified, free, and democratic Korea."

The United Nations then attempted to establish a unified government for all Korea, but its commission was turned back at an "iron curtain" along the 38th parallel. Subsequently a "Democratic People's Republic of Korea," a Communistic police state, was created in the North under Soviet auspices, and in the South a "Government of the Republic of Korea," a Republic with vicious police state overtones, was set up by the United Nations and the United States. At the inaugural ceremonies of this new regime in 1948, Douglas MacArthur was an honored guest. To aged Syngman Rhee, president of the new nation, he made a pledge he was later to fulfill, though it is doubtful that he realized its implications at the time: "I will defend your country," MacArthur promised, "as I would my own."

Soviet troops were first withdrawn from the North in 1948. Then the Allies withdrew from the South six months later, partially under pressure from the South Koreans themselves, partially as a result of Soviet propaganda pressure, and in part because it was the considered opinion of our

Joint Chiefs of Staff that the position there was militarily untenable and that it would be a major error for us ever to become involved in a ground war on the continent of Asia.

When the American forces departed, a military mission was left behind which trained and equipped lightly armed forces for the Republic; their intended mission was to guard the border and help maintain internal order. The North Koreans established similar forces, and for a year before the outbreak of war there were occasional border clashes and growing irritation; but the forces seemed fairly well matched and it looked as if they might settle down to peaceful coexistence after a period of feeling out each other's strength. The United States felt no special concern for the safety of its protégé, the Republic of Korea, and instead there was considerable apprehension that the Republican forces themselves might precipitate an attack aimed at destroying the North Korean regime.

Because of what was generally considered an unalarming situation, the world capitals paid little attention to frequent warnings from the South Koreans of an impending attack from the North.

In the early spring of 1950, MacArthur's own intelligence advised Washington that there were rumors of a possible North Korean attack in June, but the warning was so qualified as to minimize its urgency. No special alarm was felt in May when North Koreans evacuated all civilians from a two-mile stretch along the parallel, nor when, on May 10, Defense Minister Sung Mo of the Southern Republic warned that an invasion by the Northern Reds was imminent. This, again, was not regarded as especially significant. On May 18, MacArthur himself was convinced no world conflict (he meant a general world war) was imminent, and shortly afterward President Truman declared the world was closer to peace than in the previous five years.

Meantime, as hinted in South Korean reports which were not taken seriously by *any intelligence agency* in the free world, a North Korean Red Army had been organized, drilled and trained in Manchuria (a part of Communist China) under direct supervision of Soviet officers. Its heavy equipment was entirely Soviet-made and included modern tanks and field pieces. Its numbers included veterans of European fighting, some of them survivors of a Korean unit which had fought beside the Red Army in the dogged defense of Stalingrad. This was the real strength of North Korea; the lightly armed border forces were simply a blind.

"It was," said MacArthur later of this secret army, "as efficient and as able a force as I have ever seen in the field." Beginning about the 10th of June, this army began to move secretly across the Yalu River and southward toward the 38th parallel. It passed through its own border security forces, and early on June 25 "struck like a cobra" across the frontier and crashed into the South Koreans, whose light forces were completely overmatched by this modern, well-trained, and well-equipped army. Soviet officer "observers" and advisers accompanied these troops, but were kept well behind the front lines to avoid being killed or captured, and identified.

At this point, three things should be made clear:

1. MacArthur had nothing whatever to do with Korea's defense or administration after the withdrawal of American troops. His sole responsibility was with the domiciliary arrangements for the American military mission of about 500 officers and men, and he was also charged with evacuating some 2,000 American nationals from Korea in the event of trouble. The ranking American official in South Korea was a civilian, Ambassador John C. Muccio.

2. MacArthur's intelligence was only incidentally concerned with Korea, and information about North Korean plans should have come—if available at all—through world intelligence agencies of the democratic nations.

3. MacArthur's forces in Japan were occupation troops; the units were skeletonized and equipped for an occupation, not for heavy combat.

AMERICAN INTERVENTION IN KOREA

Ordinarily, it takes a minimum of 10 years and sometimes as much as 200 to learn the behind-the-scenes story of a war. But because of the disclosures made in the investigation of MacArthur's dismissal, which bared our nation's inmost secrets to friend and enemy alike, it is already possible to give a reasonably clear picture of what happened in Korea even while the events are still in progress. This account is reconstructed from the testimony of the leading figures, and while it is recognized that there are conflicting statements whose accuracy can be judged only after the future release of top secret messages, and after perusal of the personal diaries of the participants, the picture as a whole is probably close to accurate. With allowances, of course, for the fact that each of those involved is a partisan desirous of protecting his own record.

The decision to intervene in Korea, which led to the final controversial ending of MacArthur's military career, was the most important in our recent history. It was reached at a series of emergency conferences between President Truman and his top advisers, at which Dean Acheson took the lead in urging that American air and naval forces (under United Nations sanction which was subsequently obtained) be sent into action against the North Koreans. It was also Acheson who reversed his previous stand on Formosa and urged that the American Seventh Fleet "neutralize" the island, safeguarding it against Communist attack while at the same time restraining Chiang Kai-shek from moving against the Communist-held mainland. Both these proposals of the Secretary of State were approved by Truman.

It is a curious fact that the Joint Chiefs of Staff apparently gave no deep consideration to the fact that intervention in Korea meant reversing their previous deliberate estimate that Korea was not of prime strategic importance to our national defense. It is also a fact that this momentous decision was made after only relatively perfunctory consideration of possible retaliatory action by Soviet Russia and Red China. The feeling was that a line must be drawn against Communist aggression, and that to fail to act in Korea would completely undermine the United Nations and have a disastrous effect throughout the world.

As General Bradley put it: "One appeasement leads to another until you eventually make war inevitable. And that is the reason, perhaps, that the people thought we should take action at this time." Parenthetically, the "people" were not consulted about taking action, but when it was taken, it met the almost unanimous approval of the American nation and all the free countries of the world; it was also "wholeheartedly and completely supported" by General MacArthur. Under American sponsorship it was likewise ratified by the UN, although this action was not taken until 24 hours after Truman had ordered the United States forces into action.

Truman told the nation, "We are not at war," but engaged in a "police action" against a "bunch of North Korean bandits." This, as things turned out, was not only a complete underestimation of the conflict but it was a very serious propaganda mistake by Truman's advisers. The words "police action" and "bandits" were the ones used by the Japanese to cover their imperialistic war aims when they conquered Manchuria and North China; and they still have a challenging, insulting effect on Asiatics.

I think some points are worth emphasizing about this decision. The first is that it was a completely unilateral decision, an American decision, a presidential decision without congressional approval,* and a civilian rather than a military decision, in that it was primarily urged by a civilian, Secretary Acheson. The credit or blame, therefore, is largely Acheson's. When subsequently it was urged by MacArthur that we carry the Korean war on to a successful and decisive finish "alone, if necessary," he was denounced as if he were a complete idiot. Yet the original decision to intervene was made by the United States "alone," the original military action was entirely by United States forces "alone," MacArthur did not become UN commander until two weeks after the initiation of hostilities, during which time he commanded United States forces "alone," and throughout the war, the United States Chiefs of Staff "alone"—though as "agents" of the UN—made policy decisions and issued military orders.

Meanwhile, in June, 1950, MacArthur had quickly evacuated the 2,000 American residents of Seoul and in response to orders from Washington he swiftly put American planes into action and started naval units toward Korea. His first instructions were for the planes to stay south of the 38th parallel; later to attack purely military targets north of that line while keeping the planes well clear of the frontiers of Manchuria and Soviet Russia. But the invading forces continued their southward drive, seizing most of

* The President's critics have insisted on calling it "Truman's war," and have stated that the President "needed a war" to cover up the shortcomings of his administration. I have seen no evidence to support this theory, but if it is correct, it would not be the first time in our history that a similar thing has happened. The reader is referred to Theodore Roosevelt's statement, and his conspiracy with Senator Lodge which got us into the war in the Philippines in 1898, as reported in an earlier chapter of this book.

the South Korean army supplies which had been massed in a single dump near Seoul. As it became obvious that planes and ships alone could not stop the attack, MacArthur was instructed to give his recommendations on a further course of action.

Even before he received this message, MacArthur had been preparing to visit Korea to inspect the situation, and determine how it would be possible to carry out his directive, which ordered him to give assistance to the South Korean Republic and "to establish a beachhead in the neighborhood of Pusan."

A few days after the North Korean attack, MacArthur flew over to the Suwon Field, went up to within a mile of besieged Seoul, and made a first hand reconnaissance of the fighting which showed him that the South Korean army was in full flight and near complete disintegration, and "it was entirely problematical whether we could save any remnants." Flying back to Tokyo, he told a passenger in his plane, "The moment I land, I shall send President Truman my recommendation for the immediate dispatch of American divisions to Korea. But I have no idea whether he will accept my recommendation."

Clarification is necessary here. In making this recommendation, MacArthur was not arbitrarily and on his own initiative injecting a new element —the use of American ground forces—to back up the decision already made to use American Navy and Air in Korea. By this time, the UN had supported Truman's original decision to intervene by requesting its members to "furnish such assistance to the Republic of Korea as may be necessary to repel the armed attack and to restore international peace and security in the area." MacArthur's reconnaissance was made pursuant to orders given him by the American JCS in consonance with this resolution. Even before he was asked for his opinion, the possible use of ground troops had already been considered in Washington.

Returning to Tokyo the night of June 30 (Washington time) MacArthur held his first telecon (teletype radio conference) with the JCS in Washington, and recommended the dispatch of two American divisions to Korea. Without ground forces, MacArthur pointed out, the Air and Navy meant nothing—"All would be abortive, nothing would be accomplished"; the ground forces were the anvil without which the hammer blows of the Air and Navy would be hitting into empty air. He told the JCS that the South Koreans were in confusion, incapable of united action, and without artillery, mortars, and tanks could only hope to retard the enemy. The only assurance of holding the Han river line and regaining lost ground would be commitment of United Nations ground combat forces. Accordingly, MacArthur stated, if authorized, it was his intention to move immediately a United States Regimental combat team to the combat area in Korea as the nucleus of a possible build-up of two divisions from Japan for early offensive action in accordance with "*his mission of clearing South Korea of North Korean forces.*" The quote is from General Bradley, the italics mine;

the phrase should eliminate any lingering doubts that MacArthur initiated American intervention in Korea.

Both MacArthur and Washington recognized that his forces in Japan were far below normal strength and equipped only for occupation duties, and he was reminded that these were the only forces on which he could count, and that he must regard the security of Japan as a fundamental and basic policy. At the end of the telecon, Washington was asked if MacArthur desired "any further instructions or advice." His reply: "No."

MacArthur gave assurances that the troops could be safely withdrawn from Japan as far as internal security was concerned, and eventually three divisions of four were sent to Korea and the remaining one so shifted about that at one time there was not a single organized combat company anywhere in the nation. This was the most severe and dramatic test that could have been made of MacArthur's five-year rulership of Japan. It had brilliant results, as he himself said vividly and proudly, "The reaction of the Japanese was magnificent. They not only morally and spiritually supported everything we did, but all of the incidental friction of democracy, such as labor struggles and everything, without any word from me, ceased at once. The entire nation spiritually placed itself behind the United Nations to do what it could. . . ."

The moment his telecon was concluded, MacArthur started troops moving toward Korea. The first units were flown in: two rifle companies, one mortar platoon, four 105-mm. guns from the 24th Division. MacArthur made the grim and perilous decision to commit them piecemeal, taking the chance that they would be cut up and eliminated without accomplishing anything. His own account gives the best description of this early action.

"I threw in troops . . . by air in the hope of establishing a loci of resistance around which I could rally the fast retreating South Korean forces. I also hoped by that arrogant display of strength to fool the enemy into a belief that I had much greater resources at my disposal than I did. I managed to throw in a part of two battalions of infantry who put up a magnificent resistance before they were destroyed, a resistance which resulted, perhaps, in one of the most vital successes that we had. The enemy undoubtedly could not understand that we could make such an effort with such a small force. Instead of rushing rapidly forward to Pusan, which he could have reached within a week, without the slightest difficulty, he stopped to deploy his artillery across the Han. We had destroyed the bridges. It took him days to do that.

"We gained 10 days by that process, before he had deployed in line of battle along the 150-mile front from Suwon as the pivotal point. By that time I had brought forward the rest of the 24th Division, under General Dean . . . [with] orders to delay the enemy until I could bring the 1st Cavalry Division, and the 25th Division over from Japan. He fought a very desperate series of isolated combats in which both he, and a large part of that division, were destroyed." The other two divisions arrived and were moved into the battle line: "I do not think that the history of war will show a more magnificent effort against what should have been overwhelming odds as those two divisions displayed. By that time the Eighth Army command had moved over under a very indomitable leader, General Walker. From that time on, I never had the slightest doubt about our ability to hold a beachhead. And, on July 19, in the first communiqué . . . I issued, I predicted that we would not be driven into the sea."

There was a great deal of criticism of MacArthur in the early days for the performance of those troops and the apparent shortcomings in their equipment. It is certain that the troops, for the most part, were not prepared psychologically for the shock of being whisked overnight from peaceful Japan and thrown into combat. "Some of the boys," said Brigadier General Michaelis, a hero of those days, "were afraid of staying out in the dark, and some officers were seeing green grasshoppers." Their equipment, especially bazookas, was too light to stop the Russian-made tanks. There were not enough troops to hold anything approximating a continuous front —the North Koreans took to the hills to come around strong points and the Americans were forced to fight front, rear, and on the flanks. Many Americans surrendered or were captured after being wounded, and hundreds of them were massacred by the North Koreans while helpless prisoners.

MacArthur had this to say about exaggerated charges that the troops consisted mostly of 18-year-olds with nothing but 14 weeks' basic training: "The Eighth Army had been released (11 months earlier) from its occupation duties and given the mission of being placed in an excellent state of professional efficiency. That was carried out by General Walker with great ability. Those troops had had about 10 months of the most intensive training. They were as good as any troops I have ever known short of the troops that have had combat experience. . . . Under the handicaps that they had, I have looked back with amazement at the success that they achieved."

The truth then, is that some of the first troops were inexperienced youngsters in their teens. Nevertheless, a veteran army was quickly forged in combat and as soon as newer and better equipment could be loaded on ships it was rushed out to the Far East together with the 1st Marine Division and the 5th Regimental Infantry from Pearl Harbor. There were good officers and good men among the first units, and the Republic of Korea force (ROK's) fought spottily but occasionally very well under the stimulus of American leadership. Other UN forces began to come in. The North Koreans, who could have barreled through to Pusan if they had not stopped to deploy, were held first at Taejon and then in late July at Taegu, where General Walker ordered: "Stand or die! There will be no more retreating . . . our soldiers have to be impressed that they must stand or die."

At the end of July, 1950, MacArthur went to Formosa to visit Chiang Kai-shek. A tremendous commotion resulted. The British were alarmed, the Indians outraged, and many Americans as surprised as if MacArthur had conferred with the devil himself. The campaign by our State Department to prepare this country for recognition of Communist China had made such a strong impression on the American public that it was widely assumed that MacArthur had gone without the knowledge of Truman or without orders—which was completely untrue. It was charged that MacArthur had "upset delicate international relations," arrogated to himself the making of foreign policy, and otherwise acted in a rebellious manner. This newspaper criticism—which the White House did nothing to correct for some time—prompted MacArthur to blast, "My visit has been maliciously misrepresented to the public by those who invariably in the past have propagandized a policy of defeatism and appeasement in the Pacific."

This could mean no one but Truman and Acheson. The two men were incensed by MacArthur's statement, and even more angered a few weeks later when a letter from MacArthur to the Veterans of Foreign Wars was inadvertently released for publication after the President had ordered MacArthur to withdraw it. As a result of his visit, MacArthur had recommended a military mission for Formosa; Truman had approved it, and MacArthur was so jubilant over the apparent reversal of American policy of abandoning Chiang Kai-shek that he reiterated his well-known views as to Formosa in his letter to the VFW. From this time on, as he himself said later, Truman began to think about ways and means of getting rid of MacArthur; he might have done it immediately except for the arguments of Defense Secretary Louis Johnson.

The handling of this matter was typical of the double-dealing from Washington of which MacArthur had complained since 1941. Truman had ordered MacArthur to Formosa, had approved a military mission for Chiang Kai-shek—yet the President did not want the country to know it, nor the British to know that his views were changing, and became furious at MacArthur's statement. After MacArthur's visit to Formosa the President dispatched his special ambassador, Averell Harriman, to Tokyo, and the White House "leaked" the inference to the press that he had gone to rebuke the general, which was not true.

THE INCHON LANDING

Meanwhile, although still hard pressed to hold onto the Pusan area, MacArthur decided to take the greatest gamble of his career. He began planning for an amphibious landing at Inchon, far to the north of the battle lines, which, if successful, would decisively change the course of the war. He made the decision while flying over Korea—another example of how first-hand observation is invaluable to a commander—and noting that the rice crop was ready to harvest. He had been considering an amphibious operation, and now he determined to "get that crop and not let the North Koreans have it."

In the first flush of victory after the operation, MacArthur took delight in telling how he had made the decision. He had been recently reading (or had recalled—the versions vary) accounts of the assault by General Wolfe on the heights of Quebec in the month of September, 191 years previously. Wolfe's entire staff argued that the attack was impractical. Believing that if his staff held this opinion, it would also be shared by the French general, Montcalm, and that the French would be taken by surprise, Wolfe made the attack and it was successful.

For his part, MacArthur proposed the Inchon landing to his staff and when they advanced countless objections, his mind was made up: what was good enough for Wolfe was good enough for him. If his own advisers believed the plan was impractical, MacArthur reasoned, the North Koreans would also. On August 12 he issued orders for the attack, after careful personal study of the treacherous tides (he himself is an expert on tides) and consultation with navy experts.

The Joint Chiefs of Staff were concerned over the audacity of the plan and inclined to oppose it, especially as MacArthur tended to treat it as a private matter for his own decision. "Frankly," General Collins said later, "we were somewhat in the dark." Collins and Admiral Sherman went out to Tokyo for first-hand consultations, but were not entirely convinced. On September 7, the worried Joint Chiefs sent a message from Washington giving MacArthur a last chance to change his mind, or alternatively to accept responsibility for failure if the gamble did not come off. Their concern was understandable. What had started out somewhat casually as a minor police action for a noble cause had developed into a full-scale war. As a result, long-standing American policy had been reversed, we were committed in a land struggle on the continent of Asia, already fighting what fitted the description of "the wrong war, at the wrong time, in the wrong place, and against the wrong enemy." The Joint Chiefs had backed MacArthur to the limit, and in doing so had scraped the bottom of the barrel until only one single constituted combat division —the 82nd Airborne—remained in the United States.

They reminded MacArthur of this, and that he was committing his entire Eighth Army reserve. He replied that, in his considered opinion, the landing offered "the only hope of wresting the initiative from the enemy and of creating the opportunity for a devastating blow." He believed that the chance was worth taking; he would accept the responsibility.

MacArthur's military fortune reached its great crest on September 15, 1950, when the landing was made. Destiny smiled strongly on the 71-year-old warrior. Wind, weather, tides, fate itself, favored him. He had expected to lose 100 men in capturing a key island—he lost only 15. Perhaps recalling how Wolfe had died at the moment of his greatest triumph on the Heights of Abraham, MacArthur rashly and deliberately exposed himself to enemy fire at Inchon, but the bullet "had not yet been fabricated" which would strike him in this climactic moment of his career.

His fellow professionals competed with each other to find words of praise for his virtuosity. Admiral Halsey said, "It was the most masterly and audacious strategic stroke in all history." Generals Marshall, Collins, and all the generals and admirals agreed, including MacArthur himself. Optimistically, he predicted the stroke would prevent World War III. He said it was a classic, decisive battle ranking with the greats of war and would stand out in military history.

However, he added with unaccustomed caution, this prediction would be altered if the Chinese Communists entered the war, in which case the landing would be "not one of the short list of decisive battles of the world," but merely a preliminary to that catastrophe. Seoul was taken in a few days and MacArthur restored the civilian government to President Syngman Rhee of the South Korean Republic and (like Stonewall Jackson), in gratitude for the victory, had his officers, soldiers, and visitors at this ceremony repeat the Lord's Prayer in unison. Earlier, MacArthur had wisecracked to Syngman Rhee when they returned to Seoul, "This is where I came in" on his first reconnaissance at the end of June.

The victory was truly a great one. Instantly it transformed a battered and beaten Army—now containing some UN units as well as Americans, but still in numbers predominantly South Korean—into a strong, aggressive force. Before long the cut-off North Koreans below the 38th parallel were destroyed or captured, except for small elements, and the survivors were driven to the north. The entire Republic was cleared of the invaders up to and beyond the 38th parallel. Aggression had been punished. Here, if ever, was the time to sit down and take stock of things.

The American public (if not its officials) was definitely worried about the possible consequences of plunging on into North Korea, and there were many expressions of hope that "MacArthur will stop now." But the news from Korea indicated that MacArthur, while pausing momentarily, had no real intention of stopping. He told the New York *Times* in a message that he would not accept responsibility for security of his troops if ordered to stop at any definite line. He kept his main body of troops south of the parallel, letting South Koreans *only* go northward to reconnoiter. Then after two warnings to the North Koreans, he opened a full-scale drive across the parallel and to the north. The foregoing facts in this paragraph are essentially correct as a skeleton outline, and they account for the totally erroneous impression that MacArthur was responsible for the UN invasion of North Korea.

Nearly nine months later, at the time of truce talks in Korea, it was learned that the decision of Red China to intervene in the war was not made until after "American forces crossed the 38th parallel and drove toward the Yalu River, threatening the borders of China." Therefore, if MacArthur ordered this attack, he is responsible for the subsequent Chinese intervention with its disastrous consequences. But MacArthur did not originate this order. Who did, and who, therefore, is responsible? The record, while still not completely public, gives a reasonably accurate picture:

Nobody told MacArthur to stop at the 38th parallel. Nobody—"except the enemy," as he said later—objected. The Joint Chiefs of Staff knew and approved every move made by his troops in this period, and they were so confident that the attack would sweep all the way to the Yalu River that even before the parallel was crossed in force, they advised MacArthur that "as a matter of policy no non-Korean ground forces will be used in the Northeast provinces bordering the Soviet Union or in the area along the Manchurian border."

In the deliberations of the United Nations, the United States was calling the tune. To President Truman and Secretary Acheson, victory in the South had been heady wine, and they wanted more of it: in another sense, the success in repelling aggression had been so complete that the United Nations, under United States pressure, decided now to proceed to accomplish by force of arms its long-standing purpose of creating a unified Korea—a purpose which had earlier been thwarted by establishment of the Iron Curtain across the 38th parallel.

In later months, the United States would have done almost anything to get the North Koreans into a parley at the 38th parallel; indeed, when the talks were finally held, they were *south* of the parallel. But on September 30, 1950, the UN rejected a Soviet proposal to invite a representative of North Korea to participate in discussion of the independence of Korea. Instead, it decided to take "all appropriate steps"—meaning a military campaign—to "ensure conditions of stability throughout Korea," after which there would be elections for a unified government. Then UN forces would be withdrawn after a glorious victory for the cause of repelling aggression.

The decision of the UN to unify Korea by armed force was taken in the face of warnings that crossing the parallel would result in Chinese intervention. These were fully known to Secretary Acheson, who subsequently admitted, "Well, I think there were some reports indicating they would enter if we crossed the 38th." What Acheson blandly dismissed as "some reports" actually were far more than that. Through the Indian Ambassador in Peiping, S. K. M. Panikkar, word had come to the State Department of threatened Chinese intervention. The Peiping radio was thundering that "the Chinese will not sit idly by while their Korean brothers are being butchered." Acheson's own assistant, Undersecretary Dean Rusk, told the New York *Times*, "Russia is continually urging China to get into a war with the United States. China has already intervened strongly, not only with supplies but with troops. The extent of this intervention will probably increase considerably now." And Air Secretary Thomas K. Finletter expressed himself (October 3) as "extremely worried" about the possibility that "China might intervene almost momentarily in the Korean war."

Meanwhile, under orders from his superiors, MacArthur issued two "cease-fire" appeals on October 1 and October 9. The second was a final ultimatum: "I, as the United Nations Commander in Chief, for the last time call upon you . . . to lay down your arms and cease hostilities . . .

and cooperate . . . in establishing a unified, independent, and democratic government."

There was no answer, and MacArthur—whose position was that of a field commander taking orders from his superiors—started his advance across the parallel, under orders, as he expressed them, "to destroy the North Korean Army and unify the entire nation." So far as is known, he made no objection to these orders or the policy they represented. Indeed, he gave only passing thought to the possibility of Chinese intervention and as to the Russians, he thought the likely time had passed. If they had intended to intervene, the militarily opportune time would have been either in the early days, or with strong air power during the Inchon landings when his forces were afloat and highly vulnerable.* Instead of objecting, he seemed to welcome this opportunity for a decisive victory. Still touched with the magic success of Inchon, he pushed and rushed forward to crush the North Korean Army before the advent of approaching winter.

* Only one Russian had been killed and identified in all this fighting—an aviator shot down when he came too close to an American naval force. His body was recovered, which led to an interesting, if macabre, story. Naval officers were so excited that they rushed a special ship from Korea to Yokohama with the Russian's body, and a messenger hurried to Tokyo to make a breathlessly triumphant report to MacArthur, "We've brought you the body, sir!" MacArthur exploded. "Haven't these old eyes," he roared, "seen enough corpses? Do you expect me to divine what is in Stalin's mind by gazing on this poor lifeless flesh? Now, take this body and give it a soldier's burial. And if any more of the — — come where they have no right to be, shoot them down. Recover the papers. Do what is proper with the bodies. But don't, — — —, bring them here to me!" The Russian aviator now lies buried in the military cemetery at Pusan.

CHAPTER

18

Korea: The War Nobody Won

"TRUMAN LOST HIS TEMPER, MAC ARTHUR LOST HIS job, Acheson lost his war, a million and a half people lost their lives, and Stalin didn't even lose a night's sleep."—Anonymous summary of the final results of what President Truman called "a Korean police action."

The Truman-MacArthur conference at Wake Island came at a time—mid-October, 1950—when UN forces were rolling north from the 38th parallel in pursuit of a seemingly certain victory. Truman's purpose in going to Wake is still not clear unless it involved brief discussion of a subject concealed by censorship. Otherwise the journey was, perhaps primarily, politically useful. MacArthur was riding high, and with the possible exception of Stalin, was for the time being the biggest man in the world—and acting it. His popularity, military reputation, and stature as a symbol of victory were such that Governor Dewey commented, "The Russians have promised not to use the atom bomb against us if we promise not to use MacArthur against them." It was politically sagacious for Truman to associate himself with the General, especially in view of the recent storm created by the President's insult to the Marine Corps, whose "propaganda machine" he had compared to Stalin's.

MacArthur reached Wake first, and, when he greeted Truman, it was less like a meeting between commander in chief and subordinate general than between equal heads of state, as the reporters truthfully but tactlessly noted. MacArthur, towering over the President, strode dramatically to the steps of Truman's plane and gave him his best No. 1 handshake. (No. 1 includes an arm around the shoulder or elbow of the other person, and a firm handclasp. No. 2 is a simple, strong handshake, and No. 3 a limp paw.) "Hello, Mr. President," MacArthur said warmly, and the press noted that he made no move to salute.

"How are you, General," Truman said. "I have been a long time meeting you, General."

In an hour-long talk over breakfast, Truman tactfully informed Mac-

Arthur that his statement to the VFW about Formosa had been upsetting and annoying. MacArthur, disclaiming any such intention, offered his sincere apologies, and in an atmosphere of mutual understanding the two men gathered with their advisers.

Two points raised in the aftermath of this meeting had loud echoes at the time of MacArthur's recall. Going into the general conference, MacArthur inquired of the "President's publicity man," the late Charles Ross, press secretary, whether any record would be made. Ross replied that no stenographer was present and there would be no official record. However, one of those comely government girls who always seems to be taken along on such historic junkets was in the next room. When she heard the men start talking behind the slatted door of the Quonset hut, Miss Vernine Anderson just happened to have a pad handy and "just automatically" started taking note of those portions of the conversation she could hear. Later her record was put together with notations scribbled by General Bradley and others of the President's group and a so-called official report compiled in Washington. When MacArthur learned of this, he roundly denounced it as "surreptitious eavesdropping, stenographic eavesdropping." However, there seems to have been no nefarious intent in making the record; copies were promptly furnished to MacArthur in Tokyo and receipted for without comment. He himself did not even read them.

What was dishonorable was the subsequent release by the White House of these "top secret" notes in an effort to give the public the completely false impression that MacArthur alone was responsible for failing to predict the entrance of Red China in the Korean war.

Actually, the subject was dismissed in a few paragraphs at Wake Island. Truman said nothing whatsoever about the warnings received through the UN, Central Intelligence, and the State Department. Instead, he asked, "What are the chances for Chinese or Soviet interference?"

"Very little," MacArthur replied. "Had they interfered in the first or second months it would have been decisive. We are no longer fearful of their intervention. . . . With the Russians it is a little different." It was his belief that only 50,000 to 60,000 Chinese Reds could cross the Yalu River into Korea, and he was hopeful that "formal resistance" by the North Koreans would end by Thanksgiving. He planned to withdraw the Eighth Army to Japan by Christmas, after completing the destruction of the North Korean forces, and by January he offered to make the 2nd Division available for transfer to Europe. He stated that only Republic of Korea (ROK) troops should be placed along the frontiers with China and with Russia, so as to avoid causing any nervousness in those countries.

When he later fired MacArthur, Truman tauntingly cited these conversations as evidence that the blame was MacArthur's for not having determined and forecast China's intentions. This charge, of course, was absurd. It was the duty of the State Department to put together and evaluate all the information reaching Washington—from foreign diplomatic and intelligence services, through our own Central Intelligence Agency, and from MacArthur's field intelligence. The latter was limited to aerial reconnaissance over the wooded areas of North Korea and to odds and ends gathered from the interrogation of individual Chinese prisoners, who themselves had not the remotest idea of the plans of Mao Tze-tung. MacArthur seemingly failed in properly evaluating his field intelligence, but the larger failure—that of determining the intentions of Communist China—was on a higher level in Washington.

The meeting at Wake ended on a note of harmony that was shattered only two days later. Truman, reporting to the nation on his visit, said he and MacArthur were in complete agreement on Formosa. Whereupon the Far Eastern commander thundered through a spokesman in Tokyo, "there has been absolutely no change on General MacArthur's part in any views he has held as to the strategic value of Formosa." This was one more source of annoyance to Truman, who had been visibly annoyed when MacArthur showed no disposition to linger on Wake for a social visit, and instead departed within an hour and a half after the meeting with a farewell invitation to reporters: "Come on up to Pyongyang, it won't be long now."

Four days later Pyongyang was taken and MacArthur immediately landed at the North Korean capital where he asked jocularly of General Walker, "Have you got any celebrities here to greet me? What about Kim Buck Too?" (Meaning Kim Il Sung, the Red government leader.) MacArthur was a picture of confidence as he declared, "The war is very definitely coming to an end very shortly."

In the next three weeks, MacArthur made every effort to beat the fast approaching winter, bring the war to a victorious close, and present the Chinese Reds with a *fait accompli* that would discourage any interventionist intentions they might have. A parachute drop north of Pyongyang trapped what was believed to be the last large organized body of North Koreans, and in an amphibious operation the bulk of the X Corps was landed at the port of Wonsan. Here, for the first time since his incredible good fortune at Inchon, there were the first slight indications that luck might be turning against the man of destiny. The necessity for clearing Wonsan harbor of thousands of floating mines delayed the landing for two weeks in the face of fast approaching winter weather.

During the Wonsan operation, the X Corps under General Almond was not placed under command of General Walker and his Eighth Army, but held under control of MacArthur in Tokyo. The reasons for this were obvious—both from the standpoint of supply and communication. They were subsequently questioned by amateur strategists, whose doubts were not shared by the Joint Chiefs of Staff. The JCS, as General Collins later testified, "not only didn't question, but we approved" the original decision to divide the X Corps and Eighth Army, with one force attacking in Eastern Korea and the other in the West, because "at that stage of the game there was nothing but North Koreans . . . and it was a wholly reasonable proposition."

What was later questioned was that the division of command was maintained even after the amphibious phases of the operation ended and the two forces—divided by a north-south mountain range that split their fronts—began advancing northward; the chief point of criticism was that direct contact was nonexistent and communications poor between the Eighth Army and X Corps. MacArthur explained that with the number of troops under his command it was impossible to hold a continuous line across the peninsula while attacking, and that he had no choice but to attack along the only geographical routes of approach to the border. To some observers on the spot, however, there were certain indications that the divided-command arrangement was also a concession to the fact—widely known to everyone else in Korea if not to MacArthur himself—that Generals Walker and Almond were far from the best of friends. Whatever the reason, there is no doubt that the arrangement violated two fundamental military textbook precepts against division of command and separation of forces.

To avoid alarming the Chinese and Russians, whose intervention was still considered as a not-very-likely possibility, MacArthur announced that his main forces would stop 40 miles short of the Yalu, and only ROK troops would go up to the frontier. Almond similarly stated that his X Corps would move "toward" (not to) the sensitive northeastern frontier which partially borders Siberia only a short distance from the Soviet base at Vladivostok.

With ROK forces in the van, the UN troops advanced almost unopposed up toward the frontier until October 24, when "foreign troops," identified for the first time in dispatches as Chinese, joined with the North Koreans and stiffened their resistance. Some of the ROK units were wiped out, and MacArthur quickly saw that it would be impossible to clear North Korea "without maximum employment" of American and other UN troops.

Consequently, *without prior consultation of Washington,* MacArthur took all the wraps off his troops. He directed his field subordinates to "use any and all ground forces at their command, as necessary, in order to capture all of North Korea." After he had given this order, he notified the JCS of it in his usual daily report, and they thus learned only after the fact that he had disregarded the previous understanding—on which our Allies placed great importance—that ROK forces alone would be used at the border. Militarily, there is no doubt that his decision was justified. Politically, it had no effect on China's decision to intervene—this had been reached long before. But the fact that he acted without letting the JCS know beforehand seems inexcusable and inexplicable, and can be understood only in the light of his optimistic belief that the war could be "ended very shortly," and his deep-seated desire to wrap up the campaign posthaste, unify and pacify Korea, and get home as soon as possible. In other words, it seems highly likely that he feared that if he consulted the JCS before issuing his orders, they might have turned them down.

In response to his informative message, the JCS advised him that he was not acting "in accordance with previous instructions." They added with the deference they always showed him, and especially since his demonstrated mastery at Inchon, that "while they realized he undoubtedly had sound reasons . . . they would like information of these reasons, since the action contemplated was a matter of concern to them."

MacArthur replied that it was a matter of military necessity; the ROK forces were not sufficiently strong nor sufficiently well led to handle the situation. He said he fully understood the intention of avoiding provocation of the Chinese or Russians and would take all precautions; however, tactical hazards could occur from using ROK's and the result might be to provoke the very dangers which everyone wished to avoid.

The JCS accepted this and ordered no change whatsoever, even though they later were to cite the incident as one case which showed MacArthur was "not in consonance with basic policies, that led us gradually to fear that just as he violated a policy . . . without consulting us, perhaps the thing might be done in some instance of a more serious nature."

With all restraints lifted from other UN forces, the ROK's resumed their advance and promised "not to pause until we bathe our sabers in the Yalu." One spearhead did reach the river at the town of Choyan on October 28, but a few days later they and other elements of the Eighth Army were hit by a strong counterattack in which organized Chinese Red Army units took part. It was still uncertain whether these troops were "volunteers," as was announced by Peiping, or whether their appearance was a forerunner of full intervention by the two armies known to have moved up from the Shanghai area and to be massed in Manchuria.

Consequently, MacArthur made no mention of the Peiping government in a special communiqué of November 5 in which he charged "Communists" with "one of the most offensive acts of lawlessness of historical record" by intervening and in effect renewing hostilities after the North Korean Army had been practically destroyed.

"A new and fresh army faces us," MacArthur announced. He reported that "Communists" had moved "alien forces across the Yalu" without notice of belligerency, and were massing other great concentrations in the "privileged sanctuary" of Manchuria. Still hoping that Chinese intervention would be limited to so-called volunteers, he attempted to reassure the Peiping government by declaring, "Our present mission is limited to the destruction of those forces now arrayed against us in North Korea."

But volunteer or not, Chinese intervention was a fact, and any doubts were removed when the Chinese Air Force joined the battle with Russian-made Yaks and jet-powered MIG's. In retrospect it is obvious that at this point new decisions should have been made to deal with this fact of Chinese participation, either by a withdrawal or by military countermeasures, But the United States and the UN feared that attacks on Manchurian air fields and troop concentrations would bring Russia into the hostilities on the side of Red China, and consequently no retaliation was ordered. Absolutely nothing was done to meet an entirely new military situation.

The first concrete indication of the Allies' indecision in dealing with Chinese aggression—which was surely more flagrant than the original North Korean aggression—came when MacArthur requested permission for his pilots to follow Chinese planes across the border in "hot pursuit." The proposal was fully approved by the JCS and the Department of State in Washington, but was turned down after consultation with six nations of the 13 UN countries which had contingents fighting in Korea. On receipt from these six nations of "unanimously adverse and very disturbed replies," Washington told MacArthur to keep his planes south of the frontier, despite his complaint that the reserves and supplies of the Chinese Reds were "beyond the limits of our present sphere of military action." He raised the question of bombing Manchuria's "privileged sanctuary" (although he did not specifically request authorization to bomb), and he pointed out that American naval and air potential were being only partially used. In a report to the UN he told of Chinese antiaircraft guns firing from across the border against American planes, and declared the Communists were "protected solely by a barrier imposed by the democracies' desire to limit the conflict."

The first Chinese "volunteer" offensive ended as suddenly as it had begun. MacArthur's headquarters announced the Chinese were "demoralized" by their first repulse, and he ordered the UN forces on November 12 to start a slow, cautious advance. This probing attack failed to develop any substantial resistance, and on November 21 U.S. troops reached the border and began digging in south of the Yalu. Once again the UN made reassuring gestures toward the Chinese, whose newspapers and broadcasting stations were still talking of "volunteer" action in Korea. The UN reaffirmed its intention of "holding the Chinese frontier inviolate and fully to protect legitimate Chinese and Korean interests." Red China was invited to discuss the Korean question, but refused unless the UN would also discuss "armed intervention in Korea and aggression by the United States." Hints were given by Washington that if the Reds refrained from further fighting, this country might be willing to discuss the question of admitting Peiping to the UN.

The JCS, who were under strong European pressure to avoid any action that might bring on a general conflict, "suggested" (without ordering) that MacArthur "stop in terrain dominating the approaches to the valley of the Yalu," that he should use "principally ROK troops" in approaching the river, and that he spare the North Korean dams which furnish hydroelectric power to Manchuria. Provided the Chinese did not attack in force —and this possibility was mentioned by the JCS only in passing—MacArthur was directed to go ahead with the task of setting up a government for all Korea.

MacArthur's own belief that the end was near was strengthened by reports from the Central Intelligence Agency, which felt there was little chance for any major intervention by the Chinese. In reply to the JCS "suggestions," MacArthur stated that barring Red intervention the war was practically over and he hoped to clear up the situation in a short time. He said that to carry out his basic directive of unity and peace for all Korea, he would have to destroy all enemy forces within Korea; that this could not be done with ROK's alone, and that the approaches suggested to the Chinese and Russian frontiers would be more likely to promote general conflict than to avoid it. He would have to use American forces to occupy positions along the Yalu but would then replace them as soon as possible with ROK's, would announce the return of American forces to Japan, and take other steps as directed by the UN. He felt that "as soon as UN military objectives had been reached prompt implementation of his plan would effectively appeal to the reason in the Chinese mind." The JCS had no objections to offer.

Satisfied by nearly three weeks of cautious probing and extensive aerial reconnaissance that no new major forces had come south of the Yalu, MacArthur on November 24 ordered his troops to push off in an "end the war offensive." He visited the front and told General Church of the 24th Division, "I have already promised the wives and mothers that the boys of the 24th will be back (apparently in Japan) by Christmas. Don't make me a liar. Get to the Yalu and I will relieve you." The offensive got under way in snowy, bitter, 15-degree-below-zero weather. For two days the advance continued against desultory resistance. Front dispatches said new Chinese units were now along the frontier, but MacArthur himself flew up to the Yalu and saw few signs of Chinese troops. As a precaution, he ordered one of the most unusual military operations ever attempted—the bombing of the southern *half* of the Yalu bridges; his planes were instructed not to bomb beyond the midway point in the river.

The Eighth Army rolled along in gains of more than 15 miles, and everything was going smoothly, when suddenly the roof fell in. Chinese troops in massive numbers hit the Korean II Corps on the right of the Eighth Army, rolled on through, and pushed division after division into the gap until they had penetrated 20 miles behind the UN front lines. The Eighth Army immediately began what generals call a "retrograde movement" (the public calls it a "retreat") that continued for the next seven weeks with occasional pauses for delaying actions. Great quantities of matériel were abandoned and losses were heavy, but the withdrawal was far from a rout, being carried out, as MacArthur stated, in accordance with "plans previously prepared against any such eventuality," and without loss of cohesion and with all units remaining intact.

Across the mountains from the Eighth Army, the X Corps was hit simultaneously by the Chinese, but at first in lesser force. Three of its four spearheads quickly completed withdrawals to the coast. The fourth force, consisting of the 1st Marine Division and units of the 7th Infantry Division, had penetrated to the Changjin reservoir. If it could advance westward over the mountains, this force would be in a position to menace the supply lines of the Chinese divisions attacking the Eighth Army, and Mac-

Arthur ordered the Corps commander, General Almond, to make this attack.

For four days, the Marines kept pressing forward through wild mountain country and against opposition which became steadily stronger until it was evident that they were facing total destruction. Still Almond did not countermand his orders (nor did MacArthur), and the Marines were finally halted only by their own commander, after their situation was already desperate. Almond then ordered them to fight their way out. This they did in an epic action, fighting and marching more than 60 miles in bitter cold along a narrow, sharply curved and ice-covered road while under attack from 80,000 to 100,000 Chinese troops. The survivors, bringing their dead and wounded with them, eventually reached Hungnam on the coast and were evacuated by ship on Christmas Eve. They went back in at Pusan and rejoined the Eighth Army, which meantime had rolled backward in a fighting withdrawal that carried it all the way past the 38th parallel and below Seoul before a line was finally established and held. MacArthur refused to regard as disastrous the loss of some 250 miles of ground and the sudden creation of an "entirely new war" from what had been anticipated as brief mopping up operations.

"In its broad implications," he said later, "I consider that these operations initiated November 24 and carried through to this redeployment have served a very significant purpose. . . . Possibly in general result the most significant and fortunate of any conducted during the Korean campaign." However, it looked in early January as if the "redeployment" would not stop until the UN forces had been driven completely out of Korea.

The Communists naturally were elated by their success, and the Peiping radio proclaimed, "MacArthur's great offensive ends in wild flight." Their claims were echoed by MacArthur's ever active detractors in the United States, whose sorrow over our setback was tempered by their delight that MacArthur had gotten it in the neck. A chorus started, led by some war correspondents, and administration senators like Robert Kerr of Oklahoma.

The events of this campaign will long be debated by historians and military experts. The situation in the last eight days of November and early December, 1950, was this:

1. Both MacArthur and his superiors knew that an estimated fifty to sixty thousand Chinese (believed to be volunteers) were already in Korea, with a half million more massed across the Yalu. Despite the fact that the Chinese had already caught him by surprise early in November, MacArthur believed he had "demoralized" these volunteers. It was his firm opinion that Red China would not intervene further. The JCS shared his belief.

2. Tactically, as seen on a flat map, MacArthur's forces appeared to be split from hell to breakfast. The X Corps was extended all over northern and eastern Korea, in spearheads which were necessarily weak because of long and difficult supply lines. The Eighth Army and X Corps were on

opposite sides of a mountain range, with no contact except radio liaison. Both were in communication with Tokyo.

3. The JCS made no objections to MacArthur's dispositions until after the Chinese hit, and then they offered suggestions rather than orders. Four days after the Chinese attack, the JCS requested information concerning coordination of operations between the two UN forces and expressed concern at their growing separation. MacArthur replied that the presence of the X Corps threatened the main supply lines of the Chinese attacking the Eighth Army, and that the Chinese would have to divert men from their main attack to cope with the X Corps. He said he would contract the X Corps, as enemy pressure developed, into a beachhead and evacuate it. The JCS told him to go ahead and do it, and it was done.

4. Both Generals Bradley and Collins were mildly critical of MacArthur's tactics when they testified at the investigation of his dismissal. Both said they believed they would have handled the situation "a little bit differently." But both qualified their comment by insisting that the commander on the spot must have the last word. The two generals refused to accuse MacArthur of major errors of tactics or judgment even under the constant prodding of administration questioners seeking to discredit him.

5. Amateur second-guessing of generals is a hazardous business at best, but some things are evident: All of MacArthur's dispositions, plans, and intentions (all of them okayed by the JCS, or at least not countermanded) were based on destroying the North Korean troops. He had already warned early in November that Chinese troops were crossing the Yalu in great numbers, yet three weeks later he proceeded (as he later testified) to make dispositions that were based "not [on the possibility of Chinese intervention] but upon the basis of the enemy that existed and the orders that I had to defeat them . . . to clear out all North Korea, to unify it and to liberalize it. The number of troops I had was limited, and those conditions indicate the disposition of the troops I had. . . . Even if I had known the Chinese were coming in, I don't see how I could have done it differently."

What has been the subject of both amateur and professional criticism was MacArthur's (or Almond's) failure to withdraw the 1st Marines until long after it was evident that they not only were unable to attack, but were facing annihilation.

6. MacArthur not only underestimated the number of Chinese troops that could cross the Yalu but also their fighting qualities. He overestimated the effect of air attacks on their ability to move and supply themselves. The fact that these troops could cross the border and reach the front in a single night's march made observation virtually impossible, but even so—as General Bradley testified—someone "should have picked up" the Chinese concentration on the right flank of the Eighth Army by air reconnaissance and patrolling. Bradley added, "That is up to the field commander [meaning Eighth Army commander], and I certainly would not blame him [MacArthur] or G-2 or anyone else for the fact he did not

get it, and the fact that he may have had certain information and may have evaluated it wrong."

7. MacArthur's attack did not violate any order, directive, or instructions. Nor did it cause Chinese intervention.

8. History may yet agree with MacArthur's contention that he saved his command from destruction by catching the Chinese off balance and forcing them to attack before they were ready. Indeed, his explanation would probably have been readily accepted by the public except for the optimistic "win-the-war" statements he made before the reverse. His explanation is this: his attack was "a reconnaissance in force to develop the strength of the enemy. If it was not sufficient to resist us, it would have been an all-out assault and would have undoubtedly destroyed the remnants of the North Korean forces.

"We had three alternatives: One was to ascertain the truth of the strength of what he had; the other was to sit where we were. Had we done that, he would have built up his forces, and undoubtedly destroyed us. The third was to go in precipitate retreat, which would not have been countenanced, I'm quite sure. What we actually did was to move forward to ascertain the strength of the enemy's forces. When we moved forward, I had already prepared, and the troops had in their hands the order for retreat if we found the enemy in force. What we did was really a reconnaissance in force. It was the only way we had to find out what the enemy had and what his intentions were." *

Meanwhile, the news of the Chinese attack had created consternation in Washington and other allied capitals. On November 28, Bradley phoned Truman, "a terrible message has come in from General MacArthur." In effect, the message reported what MacArthur announced publicly, "We face an entirely new war. This has shattered the high hopes we entertained that the intervention of the Chinese was only of a voluntary nature. This situation, repugnant as it may be, poses issues beyond the authority of the UN military command, issues which must find their solution within the councils of the UN and the chancellories of the world." Truman told his staff, "MacArthur says he's stymied. He says he has to go over to the defensive. It is no longer a question of a few so-called volunteers. The Chinese have come in with both feet."

Temporarily rattled, Truman declared on December 1 that UN forces in Korea would fight to the end, and if necessary to insure victory, he would authorize use of the atom bomb, letting MacArthur choose the targets; he added that Chinese Communist bases in Manchuria would be at-

* Here is the comment of one high-ranking general who was in Korea at the time: "If the Chinese had waited for us to deploy along the Yalu and then attacked, they would have destroyed us with ease. MacArthur is correct in saying that he had to feel out the enemy, and that by forcing their hand he averted a greater disaster. What was unusual was that he threw everything—reserves and all—into his so-called reconnaissance in force. Looking back, it can be said that he should have held a line, Pyongyang-Wonsan, with his main forces, while carrying out his reconnaissance. But then, the Chinese might have reacted differently———."

tacked if the UN branded Peiping the aggressor. This threat to use the A-bomb startled and terrified the world, and the President "clarified" his statement next day to mean that "active consideration" of its use involved only "routine, regular consideration" of the use of all weapons.

From that time on, although the war in Korea went on, a state of paralysis gripped Washington; for weeks MacArthur continued to fight under his first, now meaningless, directives and orders, and the only really positive action taken thereafter by the administration was to attempt to silence MacArthur, and when that failed, to fire him.

For his part, MacArthur was far from paralyzed. He began roaring, in the first of a series of public statements, interviews, and inspired newspaper stories which continued right up until hours before his relief. First he warned against undue pessimism. Next he said "a million" Chinese were facing his army. He declared he had never seriously intended to hold out hope of getting the troops "home by Christmas," but had been misquoted by reporters who heard him make "informal comments to field commanders . . . in a jocular vein." He replied to numerous radioed newspaper inquiries, asserting emphatically that he was not to blame for the reverses and pointing out that "no authoritative source has ever suggested he stop short of the border and every move had been approved."

This last was in reply to charges—especially from Britain and other European nations with small contingents in Korea—that MacArthur had provoked Chinese intervention by making an unauthorized advance to the border. The European countries were understandably worried. They had been more or less dragged into the Korean adventure in the first place by American action and they were fearful that further action now by MacArthur would touch off World War III and bring immediate Soviet attack against their countries. Their fears, sometimes accompanied by implied threats to weaken support of the Atlantic Defense Alliance, were conveyed to Washington, and it was this pressure that had considerable influence in solidifying opposition to MacArthur's proposals for countering Chinese force with maximum force.

MacArthur—who later was to urge that America force a settlement in Korea "alone, if necessary"—took note of this European reaction in one of his press messages. In response to an inquiry from Hugh Baillie, United Press president then in Paris, he asserted that Europeans failed to realize he was acting by UN direction, approved by their governments, and that "in success or adversity this command has proceeded unerringly in compliance with controlling policies and directives . . . [although] under an enormous handicap without precedence in military history." Emphasizing his conviction that the Communist armed force must be checked by force wherever it struck, in Europe as well as in Asia, MacArthur declared, "Any breach of freedom in the East carries with it a sinister threat to freedom in the West. The issue is a global one and failure to comprehend this fact carries the germs of freedom's ultimate destruction. If the fight is not waged with courage and invincible determination to meet the challenge here, it will indeed be fought, and possibly lost, on the battlefields of Europe."

In messages like this MacArthur began the campaign which he waged in private and public for the next four months and which eventually led to his relief. His idea, later to become so widely known, was that the Chinese aggression must be defeated by force, and whatever measure of force was necessary must be applied to compel them to cease their attacks. To accomplish this he advocated:

1. Aerial reconnaissance of Manchuria, later broadened to include destruction by bombing of China's war industries.

2. A naval blockade of China.

3. Taking the wraps off Chiang Kai-shek and his Nationalist troops by changing the mission of the U.S. Seventh Fleet, which was instructed to prevent their leaving Formosa. "The slightest use that was made of these troops would have taken the pressure off my troops," he said later. "It would have saved me thousands of lives up there, even a threat of that." Earlier he had opposed Chiang Kai-shek's offer to send troops to Korea because the military situation at the time made it inadvisable, but now he favored it. He also advocated "logistical support" to enable the Nationalists to land wherever they pleased on the Chinese coast and fight the Communists, but he strongly opposed sending American troops into China: "Anybody who advocated that," he said, "should have his head examined."

4. Economic sanctions.

The ban on supply of strategic materials was later enforced, but each of the other points was disapproved by the American government. Its position was that aerial reconnaissance (or bombing) of China would not prove decisive and might provoke war with Russia, in view of the Soviet treaty with Red China. Similarly, it was contended that the blockade would not be complete, and might provoke war with Russia. Use of Chiang Kai-shek's troops might drag us into land war in China, would not be decisive, and might provoke war with Russia.

In other words, fear of provoking Soviet intervention dictated Washington policy from that time on; the war policy became one of matching UN flesh and blood against the bodies of Chinese soldiers in the hope of eventually discouraging the Communists. At this writing it seems that the Communists have at last become discouraged. A truce may be near, and history may show that by their restraint and coolness, by paying the immediate bloody price in Korea instead of using military advantages to force China into submission, Truman and his advisers at least temporarily forestalled World War III. This may be so, but MacArthur does not believe it; it is his conviction that the "timidity and fear" of our leaders, far from discouraging aggression, can only encourage new aggression; that even as World War II is now recognized to have begun way back in 1931 with appeasement of Japanese aggression at Mukden—a few miles north of the Yalu River—so history may recognize that World War III resulted from "appeasement on the battlefields" of Korea in 1951—a few miles south of the Yalu.

When Washington recovered from the first stunning shock of the Chinese attack, officials began to consider means for silencing MacArthur's propaganda campaign to force acceptance of his views. On December 6, 1950, a presidential directive was issued. It was aimed at MacArthur alone, but diplomatically (or timidly) was sent to all important government officials at home and abroad, instructing them to submit for clearance in Washington all statements on policy. MacArthur promptly submitted a military communique for approval and was advised that this was not necessary; thereafter he submitted no statements, either military or political, to Washington, and failure to do this was later given as one of the reasons for his relief.

As the Chinese continued to press their attack in early December, there was serious consideration by both MacArthur and Washington of the possibility of evacuation from Korea. On the sixth, fears of a general war became so acute that Washington ordered American Navy units to put to sea in the Mediterranean, and 10 days later Truman declared a national emergency. MacArthur himself believed that unless certain positive steps were taken, it would be tantamount to surrender and withdrawal of his command would be necessary. These steps, as he informed the Chiefs of Staff, were enforcement of the blockade, bombing of Manchurian bases, unlocking the handcuffs on Chiang Kai-shek's forces, and reinforcement for his own army. The JCS, summing up the military situation, likewise realized that unless some such action were taken it would be possible for the Chinese—provided they accepted the necessary losses—to compel us to evacuate or, if we succeeded in holding, to force us into a long and bloody stalemate. Being unwilling to approve the action advocated by MacArthur, the JCS likewise studied the possibility of evacuation.

During the congressional investigation of MacArthur's dismissal, there were attempts by his opponents to show that he had first thought of evacuation, and by his partisans to demonstrate that the JCS had first considered this step. It was intimated that whoever first suggested the possibility was guilty of a disgraceful or cowardly act. General Marshall, apparently seeking to leave the implication that MacArthur alone had suggested evacuation, produced one single message—out of a series—and introduced a sharply shortened and misleading paraphrase at the hearing. For his part, MacArthur declared, "The Joint Chiefs were not sure we could stick in Korea. It was my opinion that we could." Actually, the subject was discussed in numerous messages exchanged between MacArthur and Washington, and far from being reprehensible, it would have been inexcusable military stupidity to have ignored consideration of any possibilities arising from the Chinese attack. In these messages, both MacArthur and the Joint Chiefs seem to have shifted at times in their views.

Apart from the question of evacuation, what is incontestable is that the Joint Chiefs were wavering and indecisive in dealing with the whole new situation resulting from Chinese intervention, and that is the basic fact behind the dispute that led to MacArthur's relief. It was not until December 29, more than a month after the overpowering Chinese assault, that the Joint Chiefs modified MacArthur's basic directive, which had been to furnish "assistance to the Republic of Korea and repel attack and restore to the area security and peace." In modifying this directive, the JCS started by saying that the Chinese Communists appeared "capable of forcing evacuation by forces of the UN," and then went on ". . . your directive now is to defend in successive positions, subject to the safety of your troops as your primary consideration, inflicting as much damage to hostile forces in Korea as is possible. . . . You should consider your mission of defending Japan and the limitation on troops available to you."

Dissatisfied with such contradictory instructions, MacArthur on January 10 asked point blank for a decision: What was he ordered to do—stay in Korea indefinitely, for a limited period, or evacuate at once? He reported that UN troop morale was bad and would become a threat to battle efficiency unless the troops were given full delineation of "the political basis upon which they are asked to trade life for time." He asked for a decision on the highest national and international level and declared the situation, "really boils down to the question of whether or not the United States intends to evacuate Korea. . . . Therefore my query amounts to this: Is it the present U.S. political policy to minimize losses by evacuation as soon as it can be accomplished, or to maintain a military position in Korea indefinitely or for a limited time? Under the extraordinary limitations and conditions imposed upon the command in Korea, as I have pointed out, its military position is untenable, but it can hold, if overriding political considerations so dictate, for any length of time, up to its complete destruction. Your clarification requested."

The JCS replied that on the basis of MacArthur's and other estimates, "We are forced to the conclusion . . . it is unfeasible under existing conditions, including a sustained major effort by Communist China, to hold the position in Korea for a protracted period." But, in effect, they didn't say "yes" and they didn't say "no" about evacuation. They suggested "that maximum practicable punishment be inflicted on Communist aggressors" and that Korea "be not evacuated unless actually forced by military considerations." They wanted to "gain some further time" for consultation of UN countries; and in addition it was important for the North Atlantic Pact and to America's prestige worldwide, and the organization of anti-Red resistance in Asia, that he hold on for awhile.

Several things happened the second week in January, in addition to a slowing down of the Red offensive after the Chinese had driven well below the 38th parallel and captured the South Korean capital, Seoul. On the UN front, the United States instructed its delegate to agree as part of a cease-fire move to discussion of admission of Communist China to the United Nations, and handing over Formosa to the Red regime. This was denounced by the public as appeasement and surrender, and Secretary

Acheson later explained that there was a joker—he was sure the proposal would not be passed, hence the American vote was meaningless. This, in turn, was denounced as treachery and double dealing. On the Washington front, Truman publicly praised MacArthur on January 13, informing him that "the entire nation is grateful for your splendid leadership in the difficult struggle in Korea." MacArthur replied tersely, "I'll do my best." At this time, in response to questions from reporters, Truman also denied that there were any limitations on MacArthur's right to speak freely and publicly about the Korean war.

On the same January 13, Truman dispatched a long private "political background" message to MacArthur, emphasizing that it was not a directive but merely for his guidance. This message fully reflected the indecision and loss of control that had taken hold of Washington after the Chinese intervention. It was a classic example of buck-passing, so ambiguous and equivocal that when it was studied together by Generals MacArthur, Collins, and Vandenberg, they were unable to agree on whether it meant for MacArthur to stay on in Korea or prepare to evacuate. MacArthur and Vandenberg were convinced it meant he should fight, Collins thought it meant to evacuate. MacArthur was so certain his interpretation was correct that he flew over to Korea to instruct the Eighth Army to "tear the word 'evacuation' out of its dictionary."

Collins and Vandenberg had arrived by air in Tokyo on the 13th, taking with them a 14-point *study* which the JCS had drawn up to be effected in the event of either stabilization or evacuation from Korea, and which included the four main points advocated by MacArthur for military action against the Chinese. Due to some inexplicably inefficient handling in the Pentagon, the preface that indicated that this was a study and not a final decision was eliminated from the final copy, and even though he discussed the document with Collins, MacArthur apparently never clearly understood this. He was convinced—as he stated in his speech to Congress after his dismissal—that the JCS agreed with him on his military program, and it was his understanding that they had later been overruled by General Marshall.

Collins and Vandenberg also made quick trips to Korea where they found that General Matthew B. Ridgway had done a superb job since taking command shortly after General Walker's death in a jeep accident and soon after the surging Chinese had crossed the 38th parallel on Christmas Day. Walker had handled his troops with great skill during the retreat, and his personal courage was a factor in holding his forces together and preventing greater disaster. But at the time of his death his army was to a large extent demoralized, as MacArthur had reported. David McConnell, an experienced war correspondent, called it a "badly defeated and frightened army." The spirit was one of "bug-out" (evacuate), and some officers were prone to "push the panic button" and head for the rear. "There is something radically wrong with the American boy today," Mc-

Connell wrote. "He won't fight. He gladly takes a whipping, thinking only of running away."

Ridgway came into this crumbling situation with supreme confidence. He had been MacArthur's "own selection and recommendation," and MacArthur held him "in the highest esteem, not only as a soldier but as a cultured gentleman and one of the most magificent characters I have ever been acquainted with." At a time when the Chinese were gathering their second wind and massing for a new general assault, Ridgway gave his reorganized army a new spirit; there was no longer any division of command. Almond's X Corps, successfully evacuated from Hungnam and brought around to join the Eighth Army, was under the direct control of Ridgway, instead of MacArthur in Tokyo. Ridgway went from command post to command post tearing down maps showing terrain to the rear of front-line positions; he told the officers to look forward, not behind them. He walked into one regimental CP and abruptly asked the commander, "What are tanks for?"

"To kill Chinese," the other answered.

"That's right," said Ridgway, and walked away.

Ridgway's army absorbed the Chinese attack, rolled with the punch, and then went forward itself in what he called "operation killer." He said he had "only one objective—to kill Chinese and save ourselves," and instructed his troops to "keep throwing that scrap iron at them." He was not interested in "real estate," gaining ground, but in killing Chinese, and this expression became the nearest thing to American "policy" for Korea. But Ridgway knew the facts of life, and death, in Korea, and before long he was issuing statements which echoed those later cited as reasons for MacArthur's dismissal. Privately, Ridgway urged the use of Chiang Kai-shek's troops (just as MacArthur had done) and publicly he frankly discussed the basic realities of the war.

During the fighting of January, February, and March, the combat developed into what MacArthur graphically called "the accordion war." One side advanced until it reached the limit of its supply lines; the advantage then shifted to the enemy, and the other side briefly took the offensive. There were long pauses between the massive Chinese attacks—periods required for fresh troops to walk several hundred miles down from the frontier, each soldier carrying his own rice and beans and a portion of them carrying rifles. Once assembled despite incessant UN air attacks, the Chinese attacked in waves—human seas that reminded our soldiers of the crowds pouring out of stadium tunnels after a football game. The Chinese were slaughtered by the tens of thousands by our artillery, automatic weapons, and air power, but sometimes the sheer weight of bodies overwhelmed UN positions and we took our losses too; one gallant British brigade was overrun and nearly annihilated at the same time that supplies for the Chinese Reds—40 million dollars' worth in one three-weeks' period —were pouring into China through the British port of Hongkong. Perhaps the most terrible thing about this slaughter was that there was no hatred in it; no emotion, it was cold, unfeeling—and as MacArthur saw it, pointless—mass killing. Each side treated prisoners humanely; once a Chinese was captured he followed the Americans around like a friendly dog. But still the slaughter went on.

Ridgway discovered methods of meeting and checking the Chinese after they had broken through weak points in his line and after absorbing the weight of the massive assaults, his troops would counterattack and regain their old positions. After one such advance early in March, MacArthur warned in a report to the UN, "There should be no illusions in the matter, however. In such a campaign of maneuver, as our battle lines shift north the supply position of the enemy will progressively diminish, thus in turn causing his numerical ground superiority to become of increasing battlefield significance. Assuming no diminution of the enemy's flow of ground forces and material to the Korean battle area, a continuation of the existing limitation upon our freedom of counteroffensive action, and no major additions to our organizational strength, the battle lines cannot fail in time to reach a point of theoretical military stalemate. Thereafter our further advance would militarily benefit the enemy more than it would ourselves."

Months later, looking back at the predictions of "theoretical military stalemate" he had made early in 1951, MacArthur confirmed his own judgment of the situation. "I couldn't have been any more accurate," he declared, "if I had been looking at it all in a crystal ball."

At the time, MacArthur found the situation increasingly intolerable. He saw nothing ahead but a long, bloody, indecisive stalemate. There was no certainty that in fact Russia, and not *our* side, was taking advantage of the time being bought in Korea "at the tremendous expense of American blood." Fear of Russia had become the dominating factor in our policy, and—as MacArthur saw it—we had "reached that degree of moral trepidation that we paid tribute in the blood of our sons to the doubtful belief that the hand of a blustering potential enemy may in some way be stayed." MacArthur was revolted by the whole Washington attitude toward war—"a Korean skirmish," as one general called it, "with ground rules." A "skirmish," MacArthur hotly retorted at a later date, in which a million soldiers and perhaps a million civilians had died.

It was intolerable to MacArthur to go on fighting a war in which no victory was possible, and he was angered at some of the obviously absurd beliefs held in Washington—notably the opinion that Russia would stand passively by while we slaughtered the whole Chinese nation—provided we did it *south* of the Yalu River—but would instantly spring to arms if we attacked those same Chinese *north* of that river, before they had an opportunity to come down and attack our soldiers. Worst of all, in MacArthur's opinion, was that in the continuing, seemingly pointless slaughter, the original strong and decisive high moral tone of the intervention had completely disappeared. He was willing to listen to any plan to bring a quick and honorable end to this situation. But no other plans were offered, and in this vacuum he pressed forward with his own plan of applying superior military strength to force the Chinese to discontinue their aggression. Failing approval of the military measures he proposed—and which he believed would force the Chinese to withdraw from Korea in four months' time—he believed that the war must be ended by a truce. He felt something must be done to end this nightmare situation in which Washington timidly and uncertainly acquiesced to "this continuing slaughter," as he called it.

MacArthur insisted after his dismissal that in speaking out against the dreadful indecision in Washington he did not violate any directives nor disobey any orders. But the conclusion seems inescapable that even if he had known absolutely that he would be relieved from command, he still would have felt it necessary, for what he conceived to be the good of the nation, to act as he did. It seems equally true that, the situation being what it was, he had to be fired. Whether or not he realized it, he had for a long time been not in open revolt but certainly in semi-open disagreement with Washington. He was waging a campaign not only in direct, quotable statements and semi-private letters but through friendly correspondents in Tokyo, whose object was to force acceptance of a course of action which he believed would end the Korean fighting and prevent a third world war, but which another set of generals believed might provoke a global conflict.

This does not mean that MacArthur was necessarily wrong in his position and the administration right. Many of the policies he advocated and for which he was dismissed were later adopted as official before the truce talks in Korea. To millions, perhaps to a majority of Americans, what he said made sense. Both the positive course of action advocated by him and the more negative one followed by the administration depend in their final outcome not on a temporary truce in Korea but on decisions to be made eventually in Moscow. Until and unless the first atom bomb explodes over the first American city, it cannot be stated categorically that either MacArthur is right or the administration is right. Meanwhile, however, the speeches made by him since his return and the testimony by him and administration policy makers clearly showed the basic cleavage of opinion to be so great that they could not go on working together. He had to be fired, and if it had not been the Martin letter, some other excuse would have been found. As it was, these are the events which, beginning on March 20, 1951, led to his dismissal three weeks later.

On the 20th of March, MacArthur dictated a more or less casual reply to a letter from Representative Joseph P. Martin, Jr., the House Republican leader. There was nothing startling or new in MacArthur's letter (which is reproduced in this book). More than three months earlier he had said the same thing in his statement to Hugh Baillie of the United Press, and he undoubtedly would have replied in the same vein to a letter from a Democrat or anyone else. Since it was written—and since MacArthur's dismissal—Congress has formally established the right of military leaders to reply to inquiries from senators or representatives.

On the same date, the Joint Chiefs of Staff sent an important radio message to MacArthur informing him of a pending peace move by President Truman. This message said: "State planning presidential announcement shortly that, with clearing of bulk of South Korea of aggressors, United Nations now prepared to discuss conditions of settlement in Korea. Strong UN feeling persists that further diplomatic effort toward settlement should be made before any advance with major forces north of 38th parallel. Time will be required to determine diplomatic reactions and permit new negotiations that may develop. Recognizing that Parallel has no military significance, State has asked JCS what authority you should have to permit sufficient freedom of action for next few weeks to provide security for UN forces and maintain contact with enemy. Your recommendations desired." MacArthur replied, making no comment about the peace appeal, but asking no further limitations on his movements as concerned with the 38th parallel.

Simultaneously, Secretary Acheson circulated to the 13 UN governments with forces in Korea the text of Truman's peace proposals. For a reason not yet explained, no copy of this document was sent to MacArthur, nor has it ever been made public. Presumably the reason for both these omissions is that it contained political proposals—similar to the concessions for which the United States had voted at the UN in January—which would have been unacceptable both to the public and to MacArthur.

On March 24, with no consultation of Washington or of the UN, MacArthur startled the world by announcing his readiness to confer in the field with the Chinese Communist commander in Korea, and he immediately flew over from Tokyo to be ready for the meetings if his offer were accepted. His proposal, which he subsequently asserted had been in preparation for some time—and which had been dropped by the thousands on Chinese positions as an act of psychological warfare—was in three parts: An analysis of the enemy's strategic position; warnings to China of the "risk of imminent millitary collapse" if the UN decided to extend operations to China's coastal areas and interior bases; and finally, the offer of a cease-fire preparatory to settlement of the Korean problem on its merits "without being burdened by extraneous matters . . . such as Formosa and China's seat in the United Nations." MacArthur emphasized that he spoke only in a military capacity.

Despite their surprise, many UN members immediately and enthusiastically welcomed MacArthur's efforts. But in Washington his message caused the utmost consternation, and his own government promptly repudiated it. At once, the United States abandoned Truman's peace proposal because (as General Marshall testified) of "the serious impact of (MacArthur's) statement on negotiations with 13 nations." As explained by Acheson in testifying after MacArthur's removal, this "serious impact" was caused by MacArthur's "implied threat" that the UN might extend the war to China proper. Truman's message supposedly contained no such threat.

Of all MacArthur's acts in the Korean situation, this peace proposal was the most controversial, and consequently it can be interpreted in diametrically opposite fashion from two opposing viewpoints. MacArthur's own guileless explanation was that his March 20 message from the Joint Chiefs had "nothing to do with [his] statement whatsoever . . . not the slightest bearing. . . . The last thing in the world that I would have wished . . . to embarrass the President or anyone else working to bring about peace." He professed his inability to understand why the American government should not welcome any move, of any nature, that would bring peace. "An effort to bring about peace and end bloodshed," he said, "I can't believe that would influence in any way, shape, or manner my recall." He insisted that he was working on an entirely different level from Truman's proposed peace move; he was simply acting in line with the "traditional authority that a commander in the field has to negotiate with his vis-à-vis."

Later, he had other things to add. Discussing the reasons given by Truman for his relief, he declared: "The second reason . . . was that I communicated my readiness to meet the enemy commander at any time to discuss acceptable terms of a cease-fire arrangement. Yet, for this proposal, I was relieved of my command by the same authorities who since have received so enthusiastically the identical proposal when made by the Soviet government."

Now that time has passed and the tempers of those days have somewhat cooled, it is indeed difficult to see why MacArthur should have been fired for attempting to bring about an end to the war. But at the time, the issue was not quite so uncomplicated. By his repeated statements in opposition to American policy (or lack of policy), MacArthur had built up an antagonism against himself among the men in Washington; they had reached a state of mind where everything he said or did was viewed with suspicion; every word was examined for possible malice or signs of rebellion. They hardly knew what to expect next from Tokyo.

MacArthur's truce overtures were thus interpreted in Washington as jumping the gun on Truman, attempting to get ahead of the President's own peace efforts. They were considered as deliberate and direct defiance of the presidential directive of December 6 requiring clearance of "all but routine statements." Highly angered, Truman immediately directed the Joint Chiefs to call MacArthur's attention to that directive and to add a blunt warning, "In view of the information given you 20 March 1951 any further statements by you must be coordinated as prescribed in the order of 6 December." He was additionally instructed to advise the JCS immediately if the Communist military leader requested an armistice.

Seen from the Washington viewpoint, MacArthur was clearly guilty of an improper act. Whether he himself realized this is at least debatable. He denies it, and it is possible that from his distant command post in Tokyo, isolated as he was after 14 years absence from home, carried away by his convictions, he actually did not realize to what extent his independent attitude had already offended the military and political leaders in Washington. The December 6 directive may have slipped far back in his mind; he had made many controversial political statements since then without rebuke or reprimand, and the last intimation from Washington in this connection had been Truman's public assurance in January that MacArthur could say whatever he liked about the Korean war.

In any case, far from considering himself rebuked by the latest message of the Joint Chiefs, he went right on talking. On April 4, he was quoted in a London newspaper interview as saying that "the politicians must face up to the realities of the war in Korea. . . . It is not the soldier who is encroaching on the realm of the politician, but the politician who has encroached on that of the soldier."

Then on April 5, Representative Martin made public his letter from MacArthur and an excited White House aide rushed it to Harry Truman. Up to that time, Truman had been annoyed by several of MacArthur's acts, especially his 1950 statement on the strategic importance of Formosa, but he had held a tight rein on his unpredictable temper. Indeed, he had remained a great deal cooler than many of his advisers. He had accepted in stride the disastrous and (to some in Washington) panic-inspiring setbacks in Korea, and at the most crucial time after the Chinese intervention had said with admirable calmness: "People who don't know military affairs expect everything to go well all the time. They don't understand. A general can't be a winner every day in the week. The greatest of generals have had to take reverses. I advise you to study [their] lives. . . . You'll find they all won most of the time, but they all had their troubles, too. I'm not upset, like most people, about these reverses MacArthur is taking."

But to Truman, the letter from MacArthur to a political opponent of the President was too much to take. He decided firmly and irrevocably that MacArthur must be dismissed from command. In the following brief chapter, we shall see how this decision was put into effect.

If MacArthur had not previously realized how much excitement his statements had caused in Washington, he certainly realized it after publication of the Martin letter. He had completely forgotten the letter itself, but he rapidly became aware of the world-wide furore that it caused. The British press (and officials) attacked him; the American press attacked and defended him, and there was widespread speculation that he would either be fired or reprimanded. When Secretary of the Army Frank Pace visited Tokyo, it was widely believed that he had gone to fire the General, but MacArthur not only denied that there had been any rebuke but pointed out that he had asked Pace for more troops and for greater latitude in waging the Korean war. He let it be known through the press that he would continue to fight for what he considered a sincere belief in a military need, and to force recognition of his conviction that since the Kremlin planned to fight and win, in Asia, the battle for the world, America's future was at stake there.

He was still talking at luncheon in the Tokyo embassy on April 12, expounding his views to two visiting senators, when Mrs. MacArthur was called away from the table and brought back the news that the General had been fired. Momentarily he was stunned and he was still silent when his aide, Colonel Sidney Huff, weeping openly, brought him official confirmation in a brown signal corps envelope stamped in red letters: "Action for MacArthur." The faithful General Courtney Whitney, with tears in his own eyes, reported the scene to the waiting press which flashed the description to the world. "I have just left the General," Whitney said. "He received the word magnificently. He never turned a hair. His soldierly qualities were never more pronounced. I think this has been his finest hour."

CHAPTER

19

The Firing Squad

HOW DO YOU GO ABOUT FIRING A GENERAL? IN THE CASE of Douglas MacArthur, there were certain factors that made it easy for Truman to bring about his dismissal; the very fact of MacArthur's long prominence, his tendency to play a lone hand, his long record of opposition to the Europe-first generals, his thinly veiled slaps at State Department policy toward Red China—all these things had built up a resentment and dislike among the top members of the President's officialdom. On the other hand, there were delicate aspects to the situation that confronted a president who had lightly condoned the acceptance of favors by his own deep-freeze generals and must now dismiss a general who had devoted a half century to the honorable service of his country. MacArthur, though disliked by millions, was deeply honored and respected by other millions, and even his opponents recognized the superb job he had done in administering Japan.

Harry Truman, who had full authority to fire any general for any reason that pleased him, or for no reason at all, could have handled the dismissal in many ways. He could have brought MacArthur home for the receptions he deserved as a military hero, and then quietly eased him aside. He could have kept him in Japan to complete his work on the peace treaty, while another general took over military command in Korea. He could have relieved him in a face-saving manner. Instead, the dismissal was carried out in a way that was incredibly brutal and callous. MacArthur was placed at the mercy of old enemies in Washington, and they treated him more like a traitor than a loyal and distinguished American. They acted in a manner which seemingly was deliberately intended to insult and humiliate him, and bring to an ignominious end his 52 years of military service.

Because of the public clamor he knew would be aroused, Truman decided to work up a case against MacArthur, even though his own decision had already been reached. Two days after publication of the Martin letter, the President called the first meeting of the MacArthur firing squad. Present at this first session were:

Averell Harriman, Truman's special ambassador and adviser, who played no particular part in the discussions beyond agreeing with the President;

General of the Army Omar N. Bradley, Chairman of the Joint Chiefs of Staff. The General has a splendid memory, as is evident on every page of his best-selling war memoirs *(A Soldier's Story),* but he just couldn't remember who made the phone call summoning him to the conference. An extremely fair-minded man, Bradley had been concerned over MacArthur's recent pronouncements on policy matters, but according to his own testimony had never considered nor ever discussed the possibility of his dismissal;

Secretary of State Dean Acheson, who had never met MacArthur but had worked with him harmoniously at long distance in framing a peace treaty for Japan. Outside of that area of agreement, Acheson's basic desire to establish working relations with the Communist government of China and his other opinions on Far Eastern policy were almost completely opposite to the viewpoint held by MacArthur. Acheson had recently been under heavy anti-MacArthur pressure from the British, whose opposition to the American general was based on two factors: (1) he was sponsoring a "soft" peace which would enable Japan to regain her Far Eastern and world markets in competition with Britain; (2) he stood in the Far East as a symbol of anti-Communism, whereas Britain was maintaining formal and friendly relations with Red China and carrying on a profitable trade through Hongkong, even while Red Chinese soldiers were killing British soldiers in Korea;

General of the Army George C. Marshall, the fifth conferee at this first White House meeting. The Secretary of Defense for years had been MacArthur's prime antagonist among the Army's top brass. As Chief of Staff, envoy to China, Secretary of State, and Secretary of Defense, Marshall had followed policies to whose chief Pacific and Far Eastern aspects MacArthur was completely and fundamentally opposed.

Other meetings followed in rapid succession and General Bradley was instructed to "obtain the views" of the Joint Chiefs of Staff. If the testimony of the Joint Chiefs (Generals Collins and Vandenberg and Admiral Sherman) is to be taken at face value, the news that MacArthur was about to be dismissed must have come as a great and shocking surprise when they met with Bradley. Up until that time, so General Collins later testified, they had never discussed either informally nor formally any possibility of removing MacArthur. Why not, if he had been guilty of such grave acts as to justify his dismissal? "Because," Collins answered that question, "I did not know the Commander in Chief had apparently reached the point where he was fed up." In any case, once the removal had been suggested, they promptly jumped on the band wagon and within two hours of "informal discussion" had put together a set of "purely military considerations" which would justify the firing of MacArthur, an act in which they "concurred." These military reasons were not committed to writing at this or a subsequent meeting, nor until approximately 10 days later, when they were set down as "the best recollection" of those concerned. Later, Truman showed scant gratitude to his generals for working so hard to strengthen his case. In future discussions, he completely ignored the "military reasons" and, after citing various supposed misdeeds by MacArthur, eventually revealed that his own actual reasons were the MacArthur statement on Formosa, the letter to Martin, and the General's proposal to confer in the field with the Communist commander.

It is a curious fact that at this meeting of Bradley with the Joint Chiefs of Staff and a subsequent meeting with General Marshall, not one of the generals spoke up in favor of making the blow as easy as possible for MacArthur. It was only an Annapolis officer, the late Admiral Sherman, who urged that no drastic action be taken that would discredit MacArthur and set the world in turmoil. He suggested that a five-star general—Marshall himself—travel out to Tokyo, explain to MacArthur in a face-to-face meeting the concern that had been caused by his statements, and get him either to change his course or advise him that he would be removed from his command. But the generals turned him down so flatly and coolly that Sherman dropped his suggestion and did not press it after that first occasion.

The week end of April 6-8 was a busy one for Truman's military advisers, and they had everything in readiness by the morning of Monday, April 9, when the top group of four, Harriman, Acheson, Bradley and Marshall, met again with the President. Truman heard the Joint Chiefs of Staff's views from Bradley, polled the individual opinions of Acheson, Harriman, and Marshall, and then formally announced that he had come to a decision to relieve MacArthur. From this point on, neither Bradley, Harriman, nor the Joint Chiefs had anything to do with events. The President instructed Marshall (with Acheson standing by for any needed assistance) to prepare the papers for changing commands, the directive for MacArthur's relief, and the orders for General Ridgway to succeed him in his four Far Eastern commands.

Over the course of the years, George Marshall and Douglas MacArthur have exchanged many messages, as has been noted in earlier chapters of this book. All of them were in militarily correct language, though the thoughts underlying some of them were deeply felt and sometimes bitter. But none was as terse, curt, and devastating as the final and culminating order of this long exchange. Marshall's message, prepared for Truman's signature, said:

"I deeply regret that it becomes my duty as President and Commander in Chief of the United States military forces to replace you as Supreme Commander, Allied Powers; Commander in Chief, United Nations Command; Commander in Chief, Far East; Commanding General, United States Army Far East.

"You will turn over your commands, effective at once, to Lieutenant General Matthew B. Ridgway. You are authorized to have issued such orders as are necessary to complete desired travel to such place as you select.

"My reasons for your replacement will be made public concurrently with the delivery to you of my foregoing order, and are contained in the next following message. Harry S. Truman."

Truman approved this order and the following public statement, and left to Marshall the manner of effecting the relief and transfer of command. Marshall decided to instruct Secretary of War Frank Pace, then in Korea on an inspection trip, to take the order of relief in person to MacArthur at the embassy in Tokyo, rather than at his office. However, this plan fell through—"the radio at Pusan was to blame," Marshall testified—and on the grounds (as Marshall said) that a "leak was feared in Washington," it was decided to advance the date of the announcement by 20 hours. Acheson was not informed of this change, although he had given his approval to the plan of having Pace deliver the message.

The White House summoned an emergency press conference at 1 A.M. on April 11 and made the announcement which startled the world. MacArthur got the news from the radio.

If the original arrangements had been carried out, the effect might have been to soften some of the impact of the dismissal and to cause less of a shock to the public. But regardless of the method of notification, nothing could alter the summary language of the order, nor the implication that after his many years of service MacArthur had become a terrible threat to the security of the United States, so dangerous that he must at one instant be stripped of all command and power; such a peril that he could not be treated with ordinary decency and customary military protocol.

In explaining why he had taken this action, which was without precedent in the American army, General Marshall declared he had feared the "affair . . . might be still more serious. . . . (The) necessity for his immediate relief was felt by all concerned. . . . The issue was getting too complicated to go on. . . . It was necessary to relieve General MacArthur immediately."

From the minute he received the order, MacArthur had no further responsibility or authority. He could not discuss the peace treaty on which he had been working intensively for months. He could not address a farewell message to his troops or to the Japanese people he had governed so successfully. He could not discuss the military situation with General Ridgway, who was 350 miles away in Korea, nor carry out directives on which he had already started work. "I don't think there is any question," MacArthur said later, "that the interest of the United States was jeopardized in such a summary mode of turning over great responsibilities which involved the security of our country."

But, MacArthur added with his tremendous self-confidence, the decision of his relief "was the judgment of one individual. The final judgment will be made by public opinion and the historical future." As these closing lines are written, public opinion has reached no clear-cut judgment, even though MacArthur has already been partially vindicated by official adoption of several of the steps he was dismissed for advocating.

And whatever the verdict of the historical future, it will certainly find much of interest in the complex character and long career of Douglas MacArthur.

A Pictorial Biography

MacArthur's Heritage and Early Years

1880–1899

Born in Little Rock, Arkansas, 26 Jan. 1880; baptized in Christ Episcopal Church, Little Rock, 16 May 1880; brother, Malcolm MacArthur, age 5, died in 1883; attended various public and private schools in Arkansas, New Mexico, Texas, Missouri, and District of Columbia, 1885 to 1895; cadet at West Texas Military Academy, San Antonio, Texas, Sept., 1895-June, 1897.

Brother, Arthur MacArthur III, graduated from United States Naval Academy, Annapolis, Maryland, and commissioned Ensign, USN, June, 1896; grandfather, Judge Arthur MacArthur, 81, died in Atlantic City, New Jersey, 24 Aug. 1896.

Studied with private tutors and at West Division High School, Milwaukee, Wisconsin, Sept., 1897-June, 1899; received appointment to United States Military Academy from Rep. Theobald Otgen (D.—Wis.), June, 1898; passed scholastic examination but failed physical examination for entrance to United States Military Academy, June, 1898; father, Arthur MacArthur, Jr., promoted to major general, USA, 13 Aug. 1898; re-examined and passed physical examination for admission to United States Military Academy, June, 1899.

In June of 1893, Major Arthur MacArthur said to his wife, "I think there is the material of a soldier in that boy." He nodded toward 13-year-old Douglas, seated erectly in a Washington photographer's wicker chair. With hands, face, and hair shiny clean, and his tweeds in perfect neatness, Douglas MacArthur looked ready for a General's inspection. His brother, Arthur, Jr., Jr., was already well-fitted into Annapolis blues. Proud father MacArthur hurried off to find his Wisconsin Congressman to check on that West Point appointment.

The MacArthurs, or Clann Artair, are a branch of Scotland's great Campbells, and trace their descent from the original stock. In the reign of Alexander III, 1249-86, the Campbells broke into two divisions, those of Mac Chaillain and Mac Artair. The latter maintained their right to the chiefship and held it long after they espoused the cause of Robert the Bruce, Scotland's king, who had been deposed by the English in 1307. With Clann Artair's help he retrieved his crown, rewarding them with gifts of the forfeited Mac Dugal estates and castle Dunstaffnage. In 1406, however, James I beheaded the leader, John Mac Artair, and ousted the clan from its high position. The clan chieftain (above) wore the distinctive Gaelic grandee's stole, usually of saffron color with red tunic, containing 20 or 30 yards of pure linen. The Clann Artair armorial bearings (upper right) were adopted about 1250, and carried by Bruce's warriors.

Sarah Barney Belcher was Douglas MacArthur's paternal great great grandmother. She was probably the first of his antecedents to be photographed in America, some time after the invention of the wet-plate process in 1851. Born in Taunton, Mass., June 26, 1771, she married an enterprising young iron foundryman, Benjamin Belcher, when she was 21 and he 26. Settling in Chicopee Falls, Mass., he became a successful hollow-ware manufacturer and a leader in the community's industrial development. In 1815 they built the 11-room house where 30 years later "Sally" Belcher saw her great grandson, Arthur MacArthur, born. She lived 96 years, burying her husband, son and his wife, and Arthur's mother, Aurelia Belcher MacArthur. She was the common ancestor of cousins (bottom, l. to r.) Franklin D. Roosevelt, Douglas MacArthur, and Winston Churchill. The 3 are related by colonial intermarriages.

Sarah's and Benjamin's son, Benjamin Barney Belcher, married Olive Keep of Somers, Conn., and the union produced a son and 2 daughters. Margaret remained a maiden but Aurelia (top left) was married in 1844 to an ambitious young lawyer and widower, Arthur MacArthur (top right). They moved into her family's home in Chicopee Falls. An entry in the diary of the town's first mayor, Deacon George S. Taylor, still exists. Under the date, June 3, 1845, is noted: "Mrs. MacArthur had her expected baby last night. It was a boy." The boy was named Arthur, Jr., and became Chicopee's outstanding native son a half century later (bottom right). Far to the south, in Herbertsville, Va., 7 years after, Thomas and Elizabeth Hardy had their eleventh child, Mary Pinkney. She grew to be a beautiful and sensitive young woman (bottom left). Mary and Arthur were the parents of Douglas MacArthur.

Attorney MacArthur, the Scottish immigrant husband of Yankee Aurelia Belcher, commuted daily to his office in Springfield, 10 miles from his in-laws' Chicopee Falls home (top left). In 1951 the house still stands in excellent repair beside MacArthur Circle. From his term as Judge Advocate of the Western Military District of Massachusetts, MacArthur acquired the title *Judge* which he bore for the rest of his life. He moved his wife and son to Milwaukee, Wis., in 1849 and 6 years later became the state's Lt. Governor. Frail young Arthur (bottom left), approaching his teens, was unimpressed with politics and wanted a navy life, as a result of the uniform he had seen on an older school chum. At 16, however, he was filling a lieutenant's uniform (right) in the 24th Wisconsin Volunteers in the Civil War.

Baptisms

Communicants. 230 = June 16/97

DAY. DATE. No. NAMES. CH. Whence Received. Educ...

May 16 1880 Malcolm McArthur Born at New Britain, C...
17th October A.D. 187...

Douglas McArthur Little Rock, Ark
Jany 26th 1880

Parents: Arthur MacArthur Jr U.S.A. Sponsors: Dr A. L. Breysacher
Mrs. Mary Pinkney MacArthur " Miss Cordelia Buste...
" Emily Hard...

Parents: Arthur MacArthur Jr. U.S.A. Sponsors: Dr Edwin Bentl...
Mrs Mary Pinkney MacArthur Mrs Ella Bentl...

In the old federal arsenal (bottom) at Little Rock, Ark., on Jan. 26, 1880, Captain and Mrs. Arthur MacArthur had their third son, Douglas. The arsenal had been newly converted into apartments and the MacArthurs' was one of many consigned to junior officers. Mary and Arthur MacArthur already had 2 boys since their marriage on May 19, 1875, in Norfolk, Va. Arthur, Jr., Jr., had been born in his mother's home town on Aug. 1, 1876, and Malcolm was born on Oct. 17, 1878, while the family was vacationing in New Britain, Conn. Old records of Christ Episcopal Church, Little Rock, show that Malcolm and Douglas were baptized together on May 16, 1880 (top). Dr. Edwin Bentley, who had brought Douglas into the world, and his wife, Ella, were sponsors for Douglas' baptism.

Douglas MacArthur's first portrait (below) was made when he was about 6 months old in the city where his mother and father had first met more than 5 years before. The vivacious Southern belle was visiting New Orleans during the social season of 1874-75 when a hero of the Northern forces of the Civil War, Captain Arthur MacArthur, attended the same ball. After a 6-month fast courtship by slow mail, the 29-year-old professional soldier called at the Hardys' red brick Virginia mansion and married her. Four of her brothers who had fought for the Confederacy refused to attend the ceremony. After Douglas was born at Little Rock, the MacArthurs revisited the gay Louisiana scene of their first meeting. The photo of their newest son was dispatched to the senior MacArthurs in Washington, the Hardys in Norfolk, and Aunt Margaret Belcher, in Chicopee Falls, among whose possessions it was found recently.

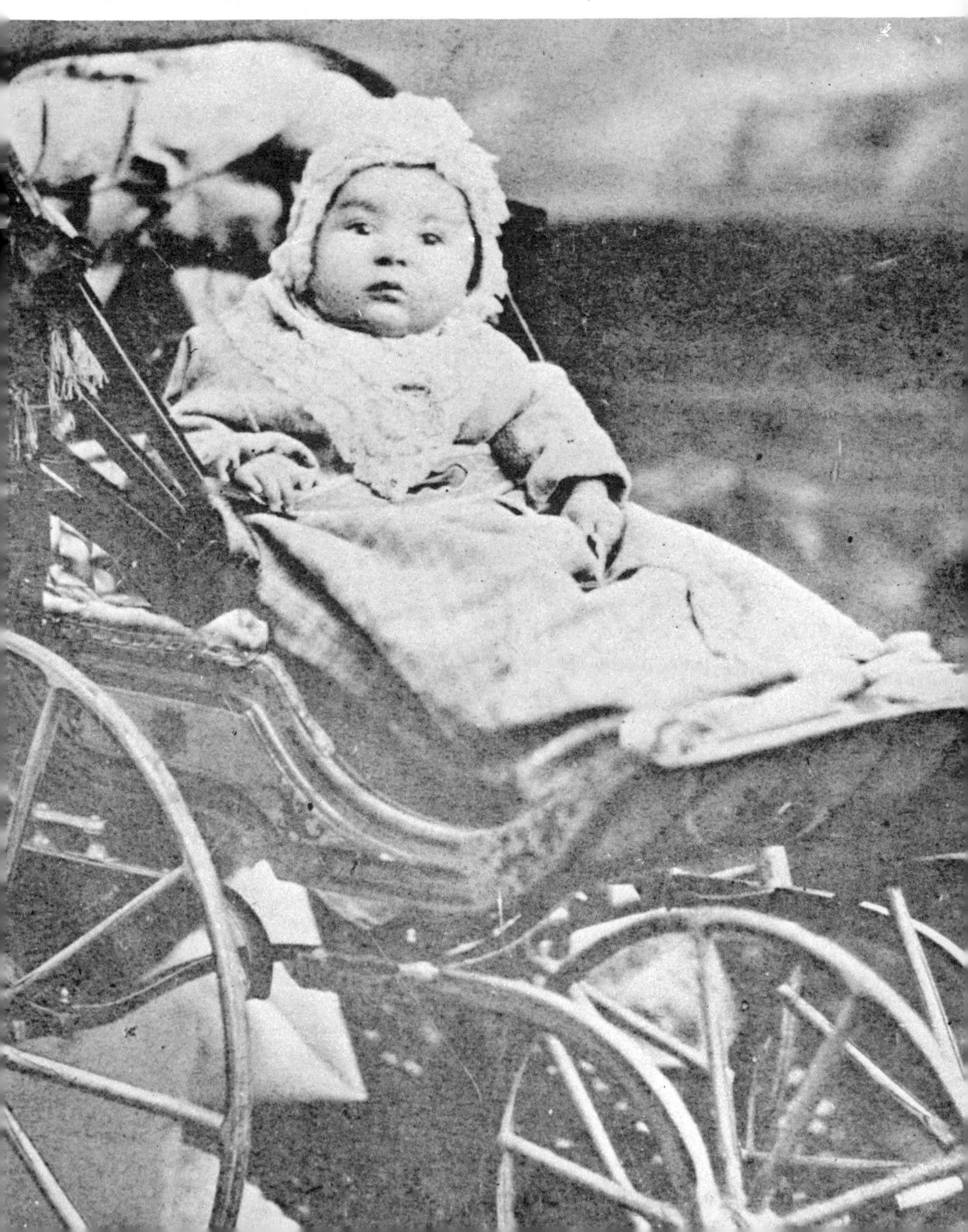

Five-year-old Douglas' predilection for things military was evident when the MacArthurs posed for their first family group portrait (top) in 1885 in San Antonio, Tex. The brown-haired boy insisted on clutching his favorite toy musket when the picture was taken. Older brother Arthur stood between his parents and the quartet created a handsome family scene. The other son, Malcolm, had died 2 years before. After many years as a captain, Arthur MacArthur finally got his majority and became assistant adjutant to Gen. Frank Wheaton in the Army's Southwest Dept. Wheaton's staff photograph (bottom) showed Maj. MacArthur standing at extreme left. The corpulent major was taking 30 years to rise from lieutenant to colonel in the regular army although he had achieved the same promotions in only 3 years as a volunteer in the Civil War. When he joined the regulars his rank had been reduced to lieutenant.

The itinerant military life of the MacArthurs precluded the possession of too many household luxuries such as books. However, the boys read anything and everything they could find and, naturally, most of their reading dealt with wars or soldiers. These became Douglas' lifetime preference. The brothers were inseparable (**below**) although Arthur was 3½ years older. Mother MacArthur kept Douglas' hair long and curled, resembling Little Lord Fauntleroy, until the youngster rebelled with the support of his brother and father. When the news of the dedication of the Statue of Liberty reached their post, Douglas' mother told him he might some day see the wondrous "Lady" from France. The impressed youngster responded by drawing himself to attention and saluting the American flag. Sixty-five years later he encouraged his own son, 13, to take a boat ride around New York and see it himself for the first time.

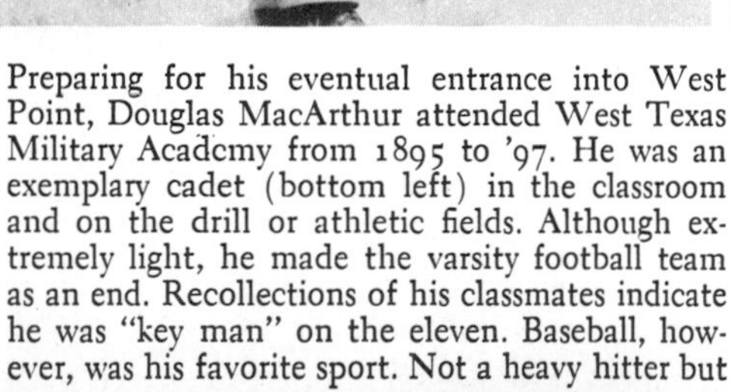

Preparing for his eventual entrance into West Point, Douglas MacArthur attended West Texas Military Academy from 1895 to '97. He was an exemplary cadet (bottom left) in the classroom and on the drill or athletic fields. Although extremely light, he made the varsity football team as an end. Recollections of his classmates indicate he was "key man" on the eleven. Baseball, however, was his favorite sport. Not a heavy hitter but a good bunter, MacArthur held down first base. He was photographed with some of his teammates (top, l. to r.): H. C. Wheeler, Clifton Kinney, Charles Quinn, MacArthur, Lincoln Baker, and Coach Ed Massee. In 1896, brother Arthur (bottom right) was graduated as an ensign from Annapolis, where, as a track star, he had set the Academy record of 2 min., 10 4/5 sec., in the half-mile run.

At the outbreak of the Civil War in 1861, Judge Arthur MacArthur, 2nd Circuit Court of Wisconsin, sat in judgment of his slight 16-year-old son's plea for permission to enlist. "You are an undersized boy, Arthur, very undersized. Soldiers would laugh at you; why your voice squeaks when you get excited. Wait another year, my son, and in the meantime, you might study military strategy." The boy waited. In August of '62 he was appointed a lieutenant in Milwaukee's 24th Regiment and went off to begin one of America's greatest military careers. Returning 3 years later as the "Boy Colonel of the West" (top left), he went on to frontier duty as a regular (top right). In the Spanish-American War, Maj. Gen. MacArthur (bottom left) crushed the Filipino insurrection and in 1905 he was the American army's observer with Marshal Oyama (bottom right) and the Japanese forces which defeated Russia. His son, Lt. Douglas MacArthur, accompanied him.

Douglas MacArthur's mother (top left) was a dominant influence in her husband's and son's lives. Her example of patience, kindliness, and courage—combined with ambition, culture, and pride—stayed with them both throughout their lives. Douglas inherited from his grandfather (top right) qualities of wit, decision, and oratorical ability. A biographer said, "The *Judge* had a wonderful grasp of world affairs and entered into the discussion of every topic with an enthusiasm that was contagious." Of the Judge's 2 sons, Frank, 8 years younger than Arthur, pursued the legal profession in New York after studying at Harvard. The General (bottom left) studied law in his spare time while a major in Washington—but never practiced. Douglas' brother, Arthur (bottom right), was a brilliant and popular naval officer until his early death, of appendicitis, in 1923. He had attained the rank of Captain, U.S.N., after 31 years of service.

In the Philippines, General Arthur MacArthur's campaigns took place in the same area where, 40 years later, his son was both defeated and victorious. The first MacArthur fought in and around Manila as did Douglas in World War II. Gen. Arthur accepted the surrender of Maj. Manuel Quezon, *insurrecto* officer, who—a generation after—became Field Marshal Douglas' intimate friend and "employer." At his headquarters in Manila, shortly after he became a major general, MacArthur posed (top, l. to r.) with three aides: Capt. C. G. Sawtelle, the general, Capt. F. J. Keman, and Capt. Pegram Whitworth. After serving as governor general of the islands he returned to the United States and held various commands including that of the Department of California. At the Presidio of San Francisco, the general enjoyed full-dress ceremonies and relished the opportunity of reviewing troops (bottom) from astride his horse.

During the final decade of the century, the MacArthur family had difficulty keeping track of its few members. From 1896 to 1906, "Dad" had been stationed all over the United States and the Orient. Mother had shuttled back and forth across America many times. Arthur had been at sea and various bases—and had acquired a wife, the former Mary Hendry McCalla, and a son, Arthur IV. Young Douglas traveled from Texas to Wisconsin to West Point (with his mother) and then was assigned to the Philippines, San Francisco, Japan, and other Asiatic countries, and finally, Washington, D.C. Grandfather MacArthur had died in '96 but his kin reunited in the capital at Christmastime 10 years later. The last family photograph (above) was taken December 25. Standing were Lt. and Mrs. Arthur III and Lt. Douglas. Seated and holding her first grandchild, Arthur IV (who died in 1912), was Mrs. Arthur MacArthur, beside the major general.

The Young Soldier in Peace and War

1899–1919

Entered United States Military Academy, West Point, N.Y., as cadet, 13 June 1899; graduated U.S.M.A., and commissioned Second Lieutenant, Corps of Engineers, 11 June 1903; assigned duty as assistant to engineer officer, Philippine Dept., P.I., Oct., 1903; promoted to First Lieutenant, 23 April 1904.

Returned to U.S., assigned duty as assistant and acting chief engineer officer, San Francisco, Calif., Nov., 1904; assigned duty as aide to father, Maj. Gen. Arthur MacArthur, Tokyo, Japan, Oct., 1905; returned to U.S. and assigned to 2nd Battalion Engineers, with duty as aide to President Theodore Roosevelt, Washington, D.C., 15 Sept. 1906; father, Arthur MacArthur, promoted to Lieutenant General, 15 Sept. 1906.

Attended Engineer School of Application, Aug., 1907, graduated Feb., 1908; assigned assistant engineer, Milwaukee, Wis., Feb.,-April, 1908; assigned 3rd Battalion Engineers, Fort Leavenworth, Kan., May, 1908; instructor, Mounted Service Schools, San Antonio, Tex., 1909; promoted to Captain, 27 Feb. 1911; served in Panama Canal Zone, U.S.-Mexico border, and Fort Leavenworth, Kan., 1911-12; father, Lt. Gen. Arthur MacArthur, 67, died in Milwaukee, Wis., 5 Sept. 1912.

Assigned Office of Chief of Engineers, Washington, D.C., Nov., 1912; superintendent State, War and Navy Bldg., Washington, D.C., April-Nov., 1913; appointed member of General Staff Corps and served as assistant engineer officer, Vera Cruz Expedition, April-Sept., 1914; promoted to Major, 11 Dec. 1915; served as Chief of Censors, War Department, Washington, D.C., 1916-17.

Promoted to Colonel of Infantry, 5 Aug. 1917; appointed chief of staff, 42nd Infantry (Rainbow) Division, Camp Albert Mills, Long Island, N.Y., 13 Sept. 1917; departed for France, 18 Oct. 1917; promoted to Brigadier General (National Army), 26 June 1918; appointed commanding general, 84th Infantry Brigade, 6 Aug. 1918, and served in combat operations at St. Mihiel, Essey, Pannes, Woevre, Meuse-Argonne, and Sedan until Armistice, 11 Nov. 1918; wounded in action, 26 March 1918; served as commanding general, 42nd Infantry Division, 11 to 18 Nov., 1918; commanded 84th Infantry Brigade in Occupation of Germany until April, 1919; returned to U.S. and assigned to Office of Chief of Staff, Washington, D.C., until June, 1919.

"Nearly 48 years have gone since I joined the long gray line. As an Army brat it was the fulfillment of all my boyish dreams. The world has turned over many times since that day and the dreams have long vanished with the passing years, but through the grim murk of it all, the pride and thrill of being a West Pointer has never dimmed. And as I near the end of the road, what I felt when I was sworn in on The Plain so long ago, I can still say—'that is my greatest honor.' " (From MacArthur's letter to the Class of 1947, U.S.M.A.)

From West Texas Military Academy, Douglas MacArthur went with his mother to Milwaukee, while his father and brother shipped off to the Spanish-American War. After a semester at West Division High School, Milwaukee, and medical treatment for curvature of the spine, he took his entrance examinations for West Point and scored a remarkable 93.3. On June 13, 1899, he arrived at the Academy and with 144 boys in the class of 1903 (top) began his military service. Mrs. MacArthur decided to live at Craney's Hotel, West Point, for Douglas was her only "family" in the country. She became popular with the cadets as time went on, although in his plebe year her son endured many taunts and jeers about her presence. Hardly a day passed during his West Point career that Douglas did not find a few minutes to visit or walk with her (bottom right).

MacArthur's 4 years at West Point were marked with distinctions. In his yearling year he was made First Corporal, and as a second classman he became First Sergeant. In his final year he was First Captain of the Corps. Ulysses S. Grant III, grandson of the Civil War general, vied for honors with MacArthur in the annual "Order of General Merit" but never surpassed him. Among the officers of the first class (top) MacArthur is second from right and Grant second from left. Douglas played in the outfield on Army's baseball team for two seasons, winning his letter in a victory over Navy. Since he weighed only 145 lbs., he couldn't make the football team, but managed it (bottom). He was graduated on June 11, 1903, with the highest average to have been attained (98.14) in 100 years and commissioned a second lieutenant in the Corps of Engineers.

While Douglas labored over his final examinations at West Point, in May, 1903, his father, in San Francisco, innocently was laying the groundwork for a future military assignment for them both. President Theodore Roosevelt was guest of honor at a luncheon attended by Gen. MacArthur (top). At the guest table were, l. to r., Capt. Henry Glass, TR's Aide; the President; San Francisco's Mayor M. H. deYoung; Secretary of the Navy Moody; Gen. MacArthur; and Adm. Bowman H. McCalla, commandant of Mare Island (and father of Gen. MacArthur's daughter-in-law). Impressed by MacArthur, the President remembered him more than a year later when he needed a seasoned officer and a young, energetic one to act as American observers in the Russo-Japanese War. The MacArthurs got the assignment, which ultimately took the major general (bottom left) and his first lieutenant son (bottom right) throughout the Orient.

Having served in the Philippines as an Engineer 2nd Lieutenant immediately after his commissioning and then with his father in the Orient in 1905, young MacArthur deserved some "stateside duty." From his return until 1913 he successively served as an Engineer with the California Debris Commission, aide to President Roosevelt in Washington, and as student and instructor in service schools. While a captain he saw action on the Mexican border with troops engaged in quelling uprisings and raids by *bandidos* and later with Gen. Frederick Funston in the Vera Cruz expedition of 1914. By this time he had developed a taste for corncob pipes and hats of his own design (top). Returning to Washington, MacArthur, promoted to major, was in the War Department's public relations branch (right) and in 1916 became its chief censor and a member of the General Staff (bottom). He performed these office duties in civilian attire.

After Lt. Gen. Arthur MacArthur died in 1912, his soldier son set out to emulate him. When Congress declared war on Germany in 1917, MacArthur had augmented his combat training with "paperwork" and staff experience. That summer, Secy. of War Baker conceived the idea of creating a division, comprising the best National Guard units, and broached it to one of his bright young favorites, Maj. MacArthur. The 37-year-old officer's eyes sparkled, "Great! It will spread over the country like a rainbow!" Baker jumped at the last word and named it the Rainbow Division—officially the 42nd. He put censor MacArthur on the new duties of organizing it (top) and within a month it was activated with outfits from 26 states and the District of Columbia. MacArthur, now a temporary colonel, was back in the field as its Chief of Staff (bottom right) and hastened to Camp Albert Mills, Long Island, N.Y., to whip it into shape (bottom left).

Command of the Rainbow went to aging Maj. Gen. William A. Mann (left), who gave MacArthur (center) a free hand in the training of its 27,000 men. One of MacArthur's personally selected staff officers was Capt. J. B. Coulter (right) who rose to the rank of lieut. general and served under MacArthur 33 years later in Korea. The careful evaluation and judgment which MacArthur exercised in hand-picking the Rainbow's staff was evident when the division arrived in France in the fall of 1917. Gen. John J. Pershing, commander in chief of the American Expeditionary Forces, took one look at the 42nd's staff roster and then began "raiding" it. Almost every Regular Army officer was finally transferred as a replacement into one of the veteran divisions and the Rainbow's "civilian" officers were promoted to take their places. MacArthur had faith in them, however, and the Rainbow Division became one of the best in the war.

MacArthur took it upon himself to plan every move of the 42nd Division. Many times each day he consulted with his staff (top left) and studied operations maps. Maj. Gen. Charles T. Menoher took over the command from retiring Gen. Mann when the division arrived in France. An artillery specialist, Menoher (bottom right) relied heavily throughout the war on MacArthur's infantry knowledge, strategy, and tactical ability. In June, 1918, MacArthur was made a brigadier general and commanded the division's 84th Brigade. His staff (top right, l. to r.), on steps: Gen. MacArthur; Maj. Walter B. Wolf, chief of staff; Lts. W. H. Wright and W. Hill; on ground: Lts. R. H. Weller, and Louis Bonn; Capt. P. W. Bayard, aide. MacArthur rarely wore a helmet in the war but at Gen. Pershing's insistence, he donned a "tin hat" for the ceremony in which he was awarded the Distinguished Service Medal (bottom left).

A writer once described Gen. MacArthur in this way: "He is the general you read about when you were a kid—when a general was a special kind of person who spent his day on the battlefield instead of behind a desk." MacArthur was always at the front. At St. Benoit en Woevre, before a major assault, he briefed the reconnaissance patrols (top left). He first realized the value of aviation as he watched German observers flying low over his lines (center left). MacArthur attended burial ceremonies (bottom) for Pvt. Dyer J. Bird, 166th Inf., the first Rainbower killed in France. (MacArthur in front of center cross.) He was never without his crop or stick and never wore a sidearm. His distinctive, crushed cap, shining puttees, and heavy muffler created much conversation among the men of MacArthur's outfit. To them he was "The Dude" or "The Stick" (right). Although he was no "hail-fellow," his troops admired and respected him.

When MacArthur determined a course of action and set out to issue a field order (top left) he customarily wrote brief notes of his principal points in longhand. He did not enjoy dictating. His chief of staff and operations officer, Maj. Walter B. Wolf, (top right) detailed and polished the order for release. According to Wolf, "MacArthur worked very early in the morning on his field plans. Alone, he made notes on a card, and by the time we met for a staff discussion he had the plans all worked out. He asked for our opinions but, more often than not, we all concurred with his. His plans invariably covered the optimum situation as well as the minimum. He was meticulous in organization and consummate in planning." MacArthur's muffler (bottom left), a gift from his mother, helped him fight quinsy sore throat, to which he was highly susceptible. One of his men, Sgt. Joseph Cummings Chase, painted his portrait in the field in 1918 (bottom right).

Although he was commander of the 84th Brigade, it was common knowledge among the men of the 42nd that MacArthur "ran" the division. Brig. Gen. Henry Reilly, who commanded the 83rd Brigade, said, "The Division commander occasionally ordered MacArthur and me to talk over with him the plans for the coming attack. Instead of having us come to his post of command, he always went to MacArthur's P.C., where I reported to him. There never was any doubt that MacArthur really commanded, because the Division commander, after briefly stating the situation, would listen attentively while MacArthur, walking around, would analyze it and deduce what should be done, in his typical lucid, vivid and forceful way." In captured St. Benoit Château, MacArthur, the war's youngest general at 38, established a temporary headquarters and luxuriated in the throne-like chair of the castle's original occupant (below).

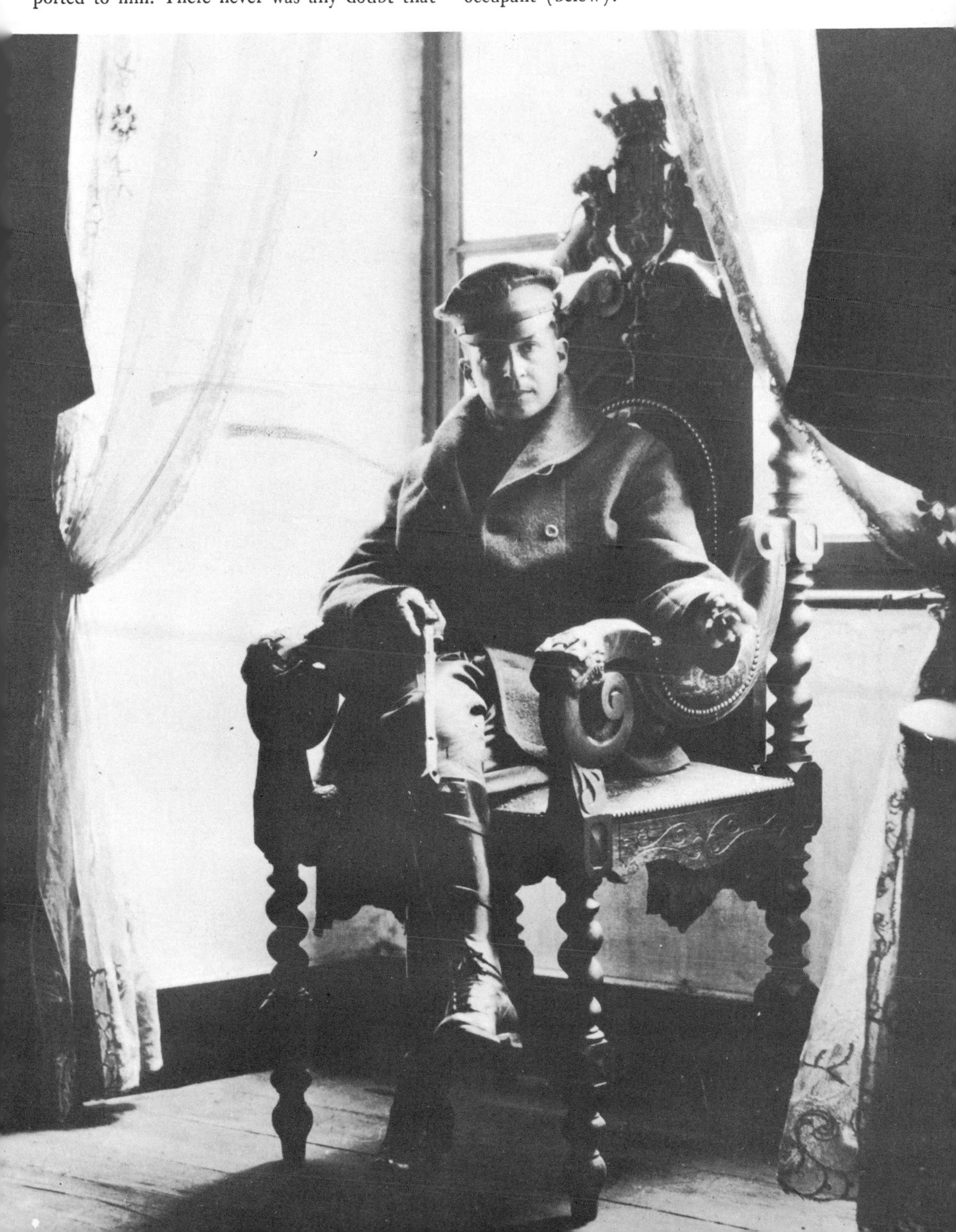

Elements of the Rainbow were often brigaded with the French and from the outset MacArthur had won the esteem of their generals. At the conclusion of a lecture on new tactics given by a veteran French commander, the general turned to MacArthur and gave him a problem on the map. An American who was present reported that "MacArthur's habitual brilliance had fully grasped the new method and he promptly and correctly solved the problem in a way which impressed everyone." In the field with the French (top), MacArthur (left, with stick), usually gave lessons in American tactics. With Gen. de Bazelaire and staff he watched an artillery barrage at Glonville (center left). In the forests, MacArthur and the French staff (center right and bottom) observed combined maneuvers of the Allied troops. (MacArthur at extreme right.)

From the Champagne-Marne defensive through the Aisne-Marne offensive, at St.-Mihiel, Essey, Pannes, Woevre, and the Meuse-Argonne final push—MacArthur survived gassings and was twice wounded. For his "extreme bravery" at Château Thierry, Gen. Pershing again decorated him, this time with the Distinguished Service Cross (top). At MacArthur's left, also decorated, were comrades Col. George Leach, and Lt. Col. William J. "Wild Bill" Donovan. The same day, Pershing reviewed (center) the troops of the battling 42nd with Gen. Menoher and Gen. MacArthur at his left. As the Armistice neared, MacArthur's men continued to push on and broke through the final German defenses. He watched his men take the heights of Barricourt (bottom) with Lt. Col. W. E. Bare, 167th Inf., at his left, and French liaison officer Capt. Chevalier at his right.

Discarding his smashed and battered service cap in favor of a new, stiff one, Brig. Gen. MacArthur returned to the United States, after a short stint as commanding general of the 42nd Division and a brief period in occupied Germany. The men of the Rainbow had begun to idolize him, and their feelings increased with time. Thirty-three years after he left their ranks the Rainbow Division Veterans sent him a message on the day President Truman deposed him from his Pacific commands. Their association's president, Hugh S. Foster, wrote MacArthur: "Because you were our leader, without fear and without reproach, because our hearts were young and fresh, we took you into our hearts and loved you. In days of pain and of peril, in days of glory, this love grew to fill hearts no longer young. Today, General, we have never loved you more."

The Years Between Two World Conflicts

1919–1941

Assumed superintendency United States Military Academy, West Point, N.Y., 12 June 1919; promoted to Brigadier General (Regular Army), 20 Jan. 1920; married Mrs. Henrietta Louise Cromwell Brooks (divorcée) at Palm Beach, Florida, 14 Feb. 1922; assigned to Philippine Dept., Manila, P.I., June, 1922; appointed commanding general Military District of Manila, Nov., 1922; appointed commanding general 23rd Infantry Brigade, Fort McKinley, Manila, P.I., June, 1923.

Brother, Capt. Arthur MacArthur, USN, age 47, died at the U.S. Naval Hospital, Washington, D.C., 2 Dec. 1923; returned to U.S., promoted to Major General, and appointed commanding general 4th Corps Area, Atlanta, Ga., 17 Jan. 1925; commanding general 3rd Corps Area, Baltimore, Md., July, 1925-Sept. 1928; elected president of American Olympic Committee, 18 Sept. 1927; accompanied American Olympic team to Amsterdam, Holland, Olympic Games in summer, 1928; returned to U.S. and assigned command of the Philippine Dept., Manila, P.I., Sept., 1928.

Divorced by Mrs. MacArthur, Reno, Nev., 17 June 1929; returned to U.S. and assigned as commanding general, 9th Corps Area, San Francisco, Calif., 19 Sept. 1930; appointed Chief of Staff, U.S. Army, with rank of General, 21 Nov. 1930; made official military surveys in Europe, 6 Sept.-10 Oct. 1931 and 31 Aug. 8-Oct. 1932; quelled Bonus Expeditionary Force riots and march on Washington, D.C., 28 July 1932; reappointed Chief of Staff by President Roosevelt, 13 Dec. 1934; submitted final report as Chief of Staff, 23 Sept. 1935; relieved as Chief of Staff, reverted to Major General, and appointed Military Adviser to the Commonwealth of the Philippines, 2 Oct. 1935.

Mother, Mary Hardy MacArthur, died in Manila, P.I., 3 Dec. 1935; appointed Field Marshal of the Philippine Army, 20 June 1936; returned to the U.S. with Philippines President Manuel Quezon, 14 Feb. 1937; married Miss Jean Marie Faircloth in New York City, 30 April 1937; departed from San Francisco, Calif., for Manila, P.I., 10 May 1937; retired from U.S. Army as Major General, Manila, P.I., 31 Dec. 1937; son, Arthur MacArthur, born in Manila, P.I., 21 Feb. 1938.

Recalled to active duty, U.S. Army, as Major General, commanding U.S. Army Forces in the Far East, including the Philippine Department and Philippine Army, 26 July 1941; promoted to Lieutenant General, 27 July 1941.

For a score of years after World War I, Douglas MacArthur was to set many records. From West Point, as its youngest superintendent, he went on to become the Army's youngest major general, the nation's youngest Chief of Staff, and later the first American to become a Field Marshal. As Chief of Staff (right), whose duties he performed usually in civilian clothes, he served under 2 presidents, Hoover and Roosevelt, and was the first in that office to be held over for a second tour.

Brig. Gen. MacArthur was appointed superintendent of the U. S. Military Academy at West Point on June 12, 1919, and immediately instituted a number of reforms, such as revising the curricula and adding new methods of instruction to combat Congress' efforts to abolish the Academy. He succeeded so well in modernizing and revitalizing it that the school survived. Among the many distinguished visitors to the Academy's colorful dress reviews was Britain's Prince of Wales (top left) and President Warren G. Harding with his Secretary of War, John Weeks (bottom left). Mrs. T. B. Timberlake, Mrs. Harding, and Mother MacArthur, her son's official hostess, watched from the sidelines (bottom right). New York's Mayor Hylan, Governor Edwards of N.J., and Gen. MacArthur officially opened the 1920 baseball season at the Polo Grounds, where the Giants played the Boston Braves (top right).

"Nothing more quickly than competitive athletics brings out the qualities of leadership, quickness of decision, promptness of action, mental and muscular coordination, aggressiveness, courage . . . and that indefinable spirit of group interest and pride which we know as morale." With those words, MacArthur set to work reorganizing West Point's athletic program with a broad, comprehensive sports-for-all policy. If not a member of an intercollegiate athletic squad, every cadet had to participate in some intramural sport and become reasonably proficient at it. MacArthur had a new, large gymnasium constructed and composed a classic aphorism which in iron letters adorns its entrance (below). Needless to say, his teams were consistent winners.

UPON THE FIELDS OF FRIENDLY STRIFE,
ARE SOWN THE SEEDS
THAT, UPON OTHER FIELDS, ON OTHER DAYS,
WILL BEAR THE FRUITS OF VICTORY.

Commonwealth of the Philippines
Office of the Military Adviser
1 Calle Victoria
Manila

April 18, 1939.

Dear Mr. Cannon:

I have just received your note of March 20th making inquiry as to the authorship of the following inscription above the entrance to the gymnasium at West Point:

"On the field of friendly strife are sown
the seeds that
On other fields and on other days will
bring forth victory."

The general circumstances that surround this inscription were as follows. Shortly after my assumption of the command at West Point, following the World War, a new and enlarged gymnasium was completed. It was desired to appropriately inscribe the entrance to this building. I requested suggested solutions from a number of sources, but rejected them all. Many were splendid from the purely athletic and rhetorical point of view, but none seemed to me to elucidate the great purpose and the great value of athletics to the Army. The training of the athletic field which produces in a superlative degree the attributes of fortitude, self-control, resolution, courage, mental agility, and, of course, physical development, is one completely fundamental to an efficient soldiery. This fact had been recently emphasized by me on the battlefields of France and I wished that this fundamental concept to be the one which animated the athletic training at West Point. To this end I completely reorganized the athletic system and placed it on the broad and comprehensive basis which has been followed in that institution ever since. I, myself, composed the couplet which marks the entrance to the gymnasium.

Very cordially,

Mr. Ralph Cannon,
Assistant to the President,
American Olympic Committee,
11 South La Salle Street,
Chicago, Ill.

President Wilson's Secretary of War, Newton D. Baker, called MacArthur the World War's "greatest front line general," and was immensely pleased that his "protégé" was superintendent of West Point. With Mrs. Baker and the General he attended the Army-Navy baseball game in 1920 (top left). Baker was dwarfed beside MacArthur and tall Chief of Staff Peyton C. March (center) during a ceremony in which France presented a statue to West Point. The General's mother maintained his home (top right) on the Academy grounds. Despite his mother's presence and his active life MacArthur was a lonely man. He once told his adjutant, Col. Hibbs, "When you become a general, Louie, you haven't any friends." Then into the life of the lonely soldier came a young divorcée, Mrs. Henrietta Louise Cromwell Brooks (bottom left). At a West Point ball, the gay society girl captivated MacArthur, and, apparently, the feeling was mutual.

Washington rumors had Mrs. Brooks "almost" engaged to Gen. Pershing, but MacArthur, nevertheless, proposed marriage to her immediately. She later told friends, "If he hadn't proposed, I would have." The daughter of Mrs. E. T. Stotesbury, widow of a millionaire Morgan partner, Mrs. Brooks had attended the finest schools and made her debut at a lavish party. On St. Valentine's Day, Feb. 14, 1922, MacArthur and the 28-year-old Mrs. Brooks were married at her mother's palatial villa, El Mirasol, in Palm Beach. As a brigadier general, the 42-year-old groom received $500 per month. The new Mrs. MacArthur was very wealthy and the newspapers heralded the union: A Marriage of Mars and Millions. After their honeymoon, without a trip, the couple spent their West Point Sundays "at home" to 1700 invited cadets.

There have been many conjectures on the speed with which the newly-wed MacArthurs were ordered to the Philippines a few months after their marriage. The suggestion that Mrs. MacArthur's earlier suitor, Gen. "Black Jack" Pershing had them "exiled" elicited this comment from Pershing: "Damned poppycock." As a matter of fact MacArthur's 3-year tour at West Point was ending anyway. With his bride and her 2 children, Walter and Louise, Gen. MacArthur put in a busy tour of duty, successively, as commander of the Military District of Manila, the 23rd Infantry Brigade (above), and the Philippine Division. After almost 20 years of absence from the scene of his first military assignment, MacArthur had excitedly returned to the Islands to resume his father's old work. For his wife, however, it was dull and unbearable. Here began the breach which eventually widened into the dissolution of their marriage.

At Col. Billy Mitchell's courts-martial in 1925 Gen. MacArthur, the youngest member of the court at 45, posed with the oldest, Maj. Gen. B. A. Poore (top left). Mrs. MacArthur was a daily spectator (top right). The court (bottom) comprised a law member, Col. Blanton Winship, and 9 generals: Edward King, George Irwin, Poore, MacArthur, Robert Howze, Ewing Booth, William Graves, Frank McCoy, and Edwin Winans. It is likely that for 26 years MacArthur carried the memory of Mitchell close to his heart. At his dismissal in 1925, Mitchell said, "My greatest pride in life is to be . . . according to the principles laid down by our forefathers . . . a free American citizen." At his relief in 1951, MacArthur said, "I shall stand . . . for those sacred and immutable ideals and concepts which guided our forefathers . . . I still proudly possess, that to me, the greatest of all honors and distinctions—I am an American."

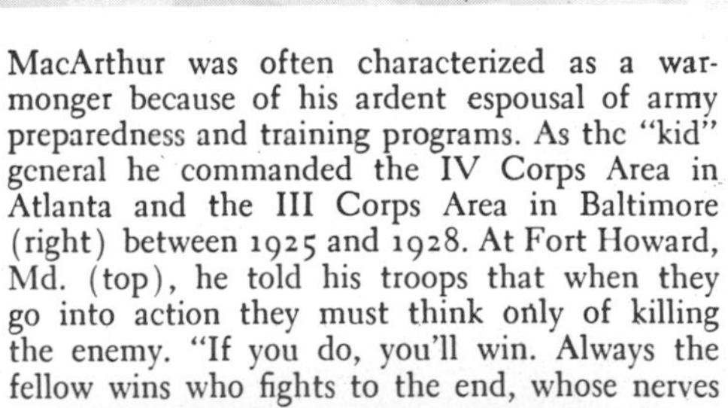

MacArthur was often characterized as a war-monger because of his ardent espousal of army preparedness and training programs. As the "kid" general he commanded the IV Corps Area in Atlanta and the III Corps Area in Baltimore (right) between 1925 and 1928. At Fort Howard, Md. (top), he told his troops that when they go into action they must think only of killing the enemy. "If you do, you'll win. Always the fellow wins who fights to the end, whose nerves don't go back on him, who never thinks of anything but the will to victory." In 1926 he received from the Veterans of Foreign Wars the Lt. Gen. MacArthur Cup, presented by Brig. Gen. F. T. Hines (center left). Recipient of many honorary degrees, MacArthur shared honors with the explorer, Comdr. Richard E. Byrd, at the commencement exercises of Pennsylvania Military College in June, 1928 (bottom left). Byrd left shortly after on his first Antarctic expedition.

Her return to the States from the Philippines restored Mrs. MacArthur to her place in the social world, for she and the General (below) lived in her magnificent estate, Rainbow Hill, near Baltimore and the capital. She and her friends urged the General to retire and to share the bonanza times of easy money in stock trading and real estate. He would have none of it—and when he announced he was assigned again to Manila, to command the Philippine Department, she declined to go. He agreed to a divorce on "any grounds that will not compromise my honor." After he left, she established residence in Reno, Nev. On June 17, 1929, their divorce was granted, Mrs. MacArthur having charged that he had "failed to provide her with the common needs of life." Twelve years later, after she married Lionel Atwill, motion picture star, she remarked when MacArthur was made a 4-star general, "It looks like I traded four stars for one."

Before returning to duty in the Philippines in 1928, MacArthur was elected to head the American Olympic Committee, and he accompanied its team to the Olympic Games of 1928. Aboard the S.S. *President Roosevelt*, en route to Amsterdam, Maj. Gen. MacArthur imbued his team with the same fighting spirit he had developed in his soldiery. Dorothy Poynton, 13-year-old diving star (top) was one of his favorites. The track and field team, which brought home 9 Olympic championships and gave the United States a substantial victory, happily posed (bottom) with their leader (wearing cap, center) on the voyage. On his return, the General submitted to President Coolidge a colorful report of the games, including, "Nothing is more synonymous of our national success than is our national success in athletics. Nothing has been more characteristic of the genius of the American people than is their genius for athletics."

Maj. Gen. Douglas MacArthur's third military assignment in the Philippines, in the fall of 1928, was probably the most decisive period of his life. That tour of duty permitted the severance of his incompatible marriage ties. It also cemented his relations with three Filipino leaders, destined to become the country's first three presidents. To these men (top left), Manuel Quezon, Sergio Osmena, and Manuel Roxas, MacArthur symbolized the benevolent might of their protector, the United States. As commanding general of the Philippine Department, MacArthur began the extensive task of setting up an elementary defense plan with Gov. Gen. Henry L. Stimson (top right). H. R. Davis' portrait of the General was made in Manila, 1928 (bottom left). MacArthur reluctantly bade farewell to the men of his command (bottom right) in September, 1930, and returned to the United States, to await the biggest job in his 30-year career.

At 50, MacArthur attained the pinnacle of military heights; he became the army's chief of staff, the eighth American to wear 4 stars (top left). Only Grant, Sherman, Sheridan, Pershing, Bliss, March, and Summerall had been full generals. MacArthur's father had retired with 3 stars at 64. Maj. Gen. Edward Kreger, Judge Advocate General, administered the oath to Chief of Staff MacArthur on Nov. 21, 1930, as Secretary of War Patrick J. Hurley looked on (top right). When Franklin D. Roosevelt was elected President in 1932, MacArthur in one of his infrequent appearances on horseback led the inaugural parade down Pennsylvania Avenue (bottom right). On another occasion (bottom left) MacArthur, Secretary of War George H. Dern, and Roosevelt chatted amiably at the Presidential car.

To study the military advancements of European powers, MacArthur made an official trip to the Continent on the S.S. *Leviathan* (top right) in 1931. He was intent on learning at first hand what was being done to mechanize and motorize armies, to free them from the immobility and slaughter of trench warfare. At the Arc de Triomphe in Paris, MacArthur signed France's "Golden Book" (top left) and in Warsaw he visited the tomb of Poland's Unknown Soldier (center left). King Carol of Rumania greeted the General in Bucharest and presented him with the Grand Cross of the Rumanian Order of the Star (bottom left). While on the trip he was asked by President Hoover to attend the 1932 disarmament conference. He refused and cabled the President, "The way to end war is to outlaw war, not to disarm."

MacArthur's tour as Chief of Staff was an extremely active one. On an interservice matter he conferred with Secretary of the Navy Claude Swanson (top left). Gen. Pershing presented the Chief of Staff with the Army and Navy Journal's Gold Medal (top right) for his work on the Civilian Conservation Corps movement. At a party given for Col. and Mrs. Charles Lindbergh (center, l. to r.) were Lindbergh, Mrs. Harry Woodring, Secretary of War Dern, the host; William Dern, Mrs. Lindbergh, James Dern, Asst. Secretary of War Woodring, Mrs. Dern, Betsy Dern, Mrs. Harry Baxter, and Gen. MacArthur. The Patrick Hurleys were extremely close friends of MacArthur. With them he attended the theater (bottom left) and when Secretary of War (1929-33) Hurley broke the ground for a new approach to the Tomb of the Unknown Soldier (bottom right) MacArthur was at Hurley's left.

"Since the days of Julius Caesar, showmanship has never in itself prevented one from being a good soldier," a writer once noted. MacArthur's beribboned blouse and polished boots caused more comment in connection with his part in the 1932 Bonus March and riots than the actual quelling of the veterans' "attack" on Washington. Acting on orders from President Hoover, the Chief of Staff called out army troops to subdue the rioters on July 28. With him was his aide Maj. Dwight D. Eisenhower (top left). At Anacostia Flats, MacArthur and a newspaperman (top right) watched while Brig. Gen. Perry Miles' troops carried out the order to "surround the affected area and clear it without delay." The mission was accomplished without any army-inflicted casualties and MacArthur relaxed (bottom) with a container of coffee at the conclusion of "the most distasteful" duty of his career.

In the reviewing stand on Army Day, 1932 (top, l. to r.) were Gen. MacArthur, Mrs. Patrick Hurley, Secretary of War Hurley, President and Mrs. Hoover, and Adm. Sims. MacArthur gave his niece, Mary Elizabeth MacArthur, in marriage (left) to John E. Reyburn in Washington, June 25, 1935. He attended the reception for Italian Gen. Italo Balbo (center right) during the latter's visit to the capital where he was welcomed by Asst. Secretary of War Woodring. From two former comrades of the Rainbow Division, Benson Hough and M. Manning Marcus, Gen. MacArthur received an invitation (bottom right) to speak at the division's 1935 annual reunion. MacArthur accepted and delivered one of his most memorable addresses, in which he prophesied World War II and deplored America's apparent indifference and lethargy to the war clouds gathering in Europe. The speech was printed and widely distributed.

By 1933, the War Dept. staff was a smoothly functioning, competent machine. Appearing in photo are, l. to r., front row—Gens. Andrew Moses, John Dewitt, MacArthur, Asst. Secy. Frederick Payne, Secy. of War Hurley, Asst. Secy. F. Trubee Davison, Gens. George Moseley, Guy Henry, F. W. Coleman; second row—Gens. C. H. Bridges, F. LeJ. Parker, Irving Carr, Blanton Winship, Robert Patterson, Stephen Fuqua, John Preston; third row—Gens. Harry Gilchrist, Samuel Hof, George Leach, John Gulick, Col. Alf Smith; fourth row—Brig. Gen. Charles Kilbourne and Col. Julian Yates. A year later MacArthur personally directed an extensive army training maneuver at Camp Dix and Fort Monmouth, N.J. Meeting (bottom, l. to r.) with him during the maneuvers were Gens. Alf Smith, Andrew Moses, George Simonds, Hugh Drum, MacArthur, Robert Callan, Charles Kilbourne, John Hughes, and Oscar Westover.

At the completion of his 4-year term as Chief of Staff, MacArthur was requested by President Roosevelt to remain on duty until a successor could be appointed. He continued in the post for another year but in the meantime President Quezon of the Philippines had asked FDR to assign a U. S. Military Mission to his country in order to set up the Commonwealth's army and defense program. MacArthur retired as Chief of Staff, reverted to his permanent 2-star rank, and volunteered to head up the Mission bound for Manila. His arrival there in late October, 1935, was cause for a gala reception and parade (bottom). His senior aide, Maj. Eisenhower, stood behind him during the ceremonies. The following summer he was made Field Marshal of the Philippines and early in 1937 he and Pres. Quezon traveled to Washington (top).

MacArthur's beloved mother (top left) died in Manila a few weeks after he became the U. S. military adviser to the Philippines. She had been ill throughout the voyage from San Francisco and had not had an opportunity to meet the vivacious young woman who was to take her place in caring for the General. Jean Marie Faircloth (top right), a Murfreesboro, Tenn. brunette, was en route to Shanghai for a visit with English friends she had met on a previous trip. Gen. MacArthur was smitten from the first. At a stop-over in Honolulu he filled her cabin with roses and by the time they reached Manila he was deeply in love with the Southern belle. She extended her stay for a year, during which the General was her devoted escort. He left Maj. Eisenhower (bottom) in command of the mission when he returned to the U. S.

Jean Marie Faircloth's neighbors and friends in serene Murfreesboro always felt she was an "extra-special" girl, not likely to fall into their quiet uneventful mode of life. The only thing conventional about the petite, brown-eyed girl was her home town, a typical Southern community of shady, maple-lined streets, spacious homes, and a red-brick court house in the middle of the square which memorializes the Confederacy. Patriotism was almost a fetish in her home (top) where crossed flags and swords hung on the walls and buntings were stored carefully in the attic for holiday airings. Her grandfather, Capt. Richard Beard (bottom right), served in the Confederate Army and probably fought against young Arthur MacArthur of Wisconsin. Jean Marie's mother, Sallie Beard Faircloth (bottom left) was divorced from E. C. Faircloth in 1907 and later married a North Dakotan, Frederick Smith.

The lively, gay Miss Faircloth had scores of beaux throughout her youth; she was always the "most popular" in her crowd and was "never known to be jealous, vindictive, spiteful, or cross." Her mother, "Miss Sallie" to all in Murfreesboro, tried to interest Jean Marie in her own love of the theater, but her daughter did not respond. At 4 (top left) she looked like a little actress, however. Her graduation photograph (top center) was made when she finished studying at Soule College, a private school in Murfreesboro. As she blossomed into maturity (top right), Jean Marie's expressive face featured her flashing smile and bright, alert eyes. She attended the fashionable Ward-Belmont School in Nashville (bottom left) for 1 year. Shortly before she met Gen. MacArthur her snapshot (bottom center) was taken in a friend's garden in Murfreesboro. This is one of her most recent portraits (bottom right).

MacArthur's visit to the United States in early 1937 had a dual purpose. While he accompanied President Quezon to Washington for military and economic conferences, he also planned to marry Jean Marie Faircloth in New York. She had left Manila and returned to Tennessee to gather her trousseau and ship her personal belongings back to Manila. She managed this without arousing too much curiosity in her home town and slipped off to New York City to wed the General on April 30, 1937. The couple was married in the Municipal Building (top) and later went to the Hotel Astor for a wedding breakfast of ham and eggs (bottom). MacArthur told a reporter, "This is going to last a long time." After a brief visit to Washington, the couple went to San Francisco and embarked for Manila.

Back in the Islands, the MacArthurs settled in a luxurious penthouse apartment in the Manila Hotel and MacArthur plunged into his work of setting up the Philippines defense program. There were parties and receptions for the bride and groom, among them a lavish affair given by the U. S. High Commissioner and Mrs. Paul V. McNutt (top left). At the end of the year MacArthur officially retired from the United States Army and wrote President Roosevelt, "I will, of course, be just as available for war service when I am retired as I would be on the active list." The General welcomed Gen. George Grunert (top right, beside MacArthur) when the latter arrived in Manila to command the Philippine Department. MacArthur was prevailed upon by Quezon to stay on as Field Marshal and MacArthur decided to do so, saying (bottom) "This is a call of duty I cannot overlook." Quezon and most of his countrymen were overjoyed.

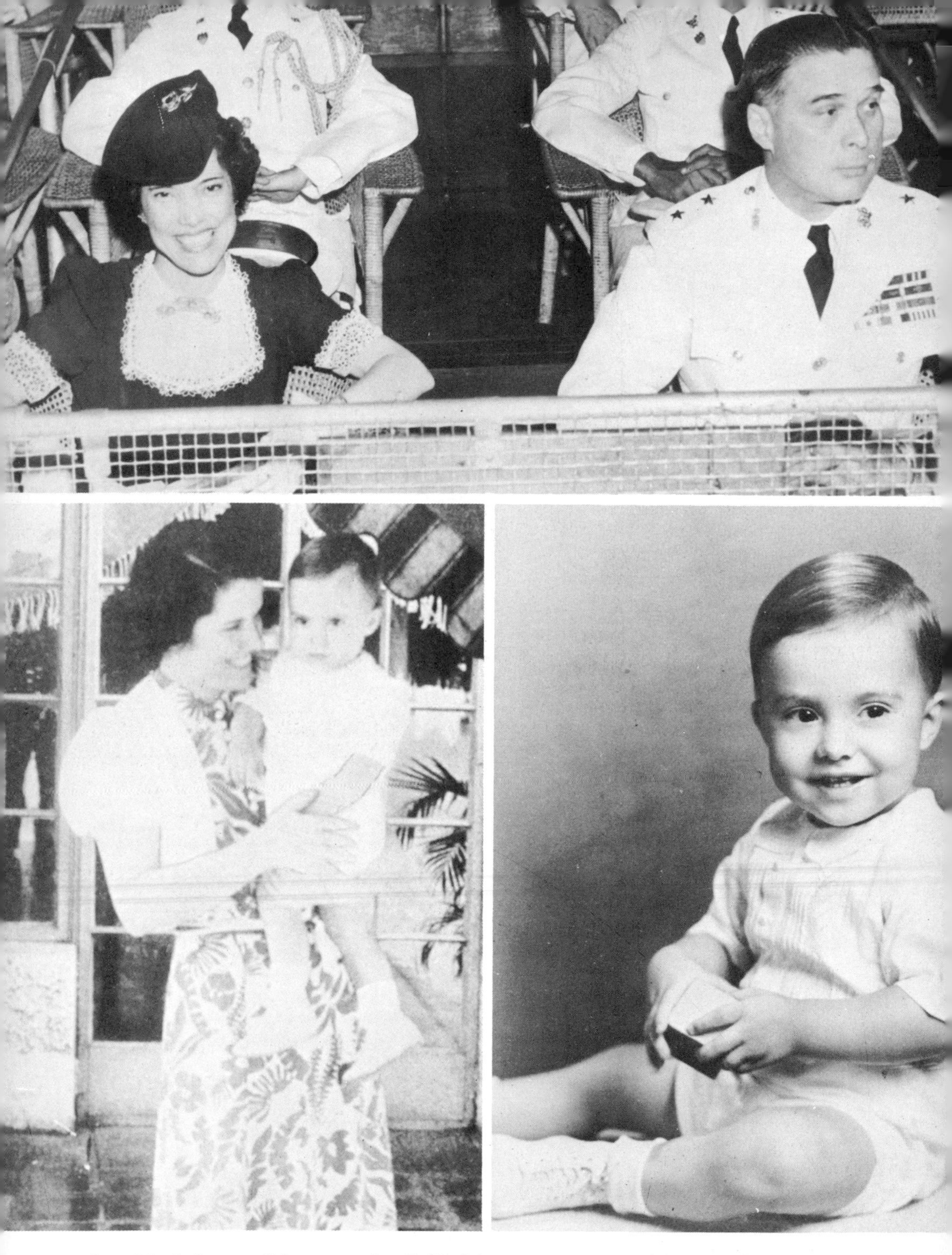

Jean MacArthur, well known and well liked in Manila before her marriage, reduced her social activities considerably when she returned with the General. She was determined to be a wife and homemaker for him inasmuch as he cared little for the gaiety and frivolity of official Manila. On Feb. 21, 1938, she bore him a son who was named Arthur, in the family tradition. The General was delighted that finally, at 58, he had a son to carry on the name. The youngster (bottom, l. and r.) was lively and smart and his aging father was rejuvenated with daily sessions of "piggy back" and close-order drill in his bedroom. Mrs. MacArthur found time, occasionally, to represent the family at public functions, often accompanied by Filipino Chief of Staff, Gen. Basilio Valdez (top) or American officers from the Philippine Department.

The MacArthur home life centered around their fast-growing young son. When Mrs. MacArthur was asked if Arthur would attend West Point when he grew up, she replied, "How can he help it—with such a father?" On Arthur's third birthday a snapshot (top) of the cake-cutting ceremony was dispatched to family and friends in Murfreesboro, where Jean Marie had become the outstanding native daughter. The General's letters always referred to his young son, but late in 1941, his correspondence (bottom) also included prescient references: "if war comes . . . the Army of the Far East will be heard from." On July 26, 1941, President Roosevelt recalled MacArthur to active duty as a major general, commanding the United States Army Forces in the Far East. The following day he was promoted to lieutenant general.

fully cognizant of that.

I have been called back into active service to defend these Islands if war comes. I propose to do so and believe in such an eventuality the Army of the Far East will be heard from.

My little boy is nearly four years old now and needless to say is the complete center of my thoughts and affection. I feel I am very fortunate in having him in the twilight period of my life.

Drop me a line when you have time, telling me of what your plans are and how goes it with your own family.

With affectionate regards,

As ever,

Douglas MacArthur

Colonel Charles H. Patterson,
Headquarters Fourth Corps Area,

President Quezon's answer to the prodding of Japan to rid his country of "that leading Japanophobe, MacArthur," was to hand over (top) the little Philippine army for induction into Lt. Gen. MacArthur's USAFFE. MacArthur was exultant to be back in harness again. The "old soldier" happily accepted his new command (bottom) and said, "I am glad to be able to serve my country at this crucial time. This action of the American government in establishing this new command can only mean that it intends to maintain, at any cost and effort, its full rights in the Far East. It is quite evident that its determination is immutable and that its will is indomitable. To this end both the American and Filipino soldiery can be expected to give their utmost." The size of his force was pitifully small and MacArthur knew that Japan's mobilization program had been tremendous. The Rising Sun was turned toward the islands of the Pacific.

The Tide of Victory in the Pacific

1941–1945

Philippines attacked by Japan, 8 Dec. 1941; declared Manila an open city and transferred USAFFE headquarters to Corregidor, 25 Dec. 1941; departed Corregidor by order of the President, 11 March 1942; arrived Darwin, Australia, 17 March 1942; awarded Congressional Medal of Honor, 25 March 1942; designated Supreme Commander and established General Headquarters, Southwest Pacific Area at Melbourne, Australia, 18 April 1942; established Fifth Air Force, 3 Sept. 1942; established Sixth Army, 16 Feb. 1943; captured areas in Solomon Islands, Bismarck Archipelago, and New Guinea in 1943; captured or neutralized balance of Southwest Pacific Area in 1944; established Eighth Army, 7 Sept. 1944; accomplished landings in Leyte, P.I., 20 Oct. 1944; appointed General of the Army, 15 Dec. 1944; terminated Leyte campaign, 25 Dec. 1944.

Invaded Luzon, P.I., 9 Jan. 1945; entered Manila, P.I., 3 Feb. 1945; restored Commonwealth Government to the Philippines, 27 Feb. 1945; ended Japanese organized resistance in Manila, 3 March 1945; appointed by Joint Chiefs of Staff as commander of all U.S. Army Forces in the Pacific, 3 April 1945; established AFPAC, Manila, P.I., 6 April 1945; terminated Luzon campaign, 4 July 1945.

Potsdam ultimatum issued to Japan, 27 July 1945; first atomic bomb dropped on Hiroshima, Japan, 6 Aug. 1945; Russia declared war on Japan, 9 Aug. 1945; Potsdam ultimatum accepted by Japan, 10 Aug. 1945; unconditional surrender of Japan announced with naming of General of the Army Douglas MacArthur as Supreme Commander for the Allied Powers, 15 Aug. 1945; issued final communiqué from General Headquarters, and first message to Japanese government, 15 Aug. 1945.

MacArthur returns. He had said on the first anniversary of the fall of Corregidor: "Until we lift our flag from its dust we stand unredeemed before mankind. Until we claim the ghastly remnants of its last gaunt garrison we can but stand humble supplicants before Almighty God. There lies our Holy Grail." Crossing Manila Bay, MacArthur faced Bataan and Corregidor.

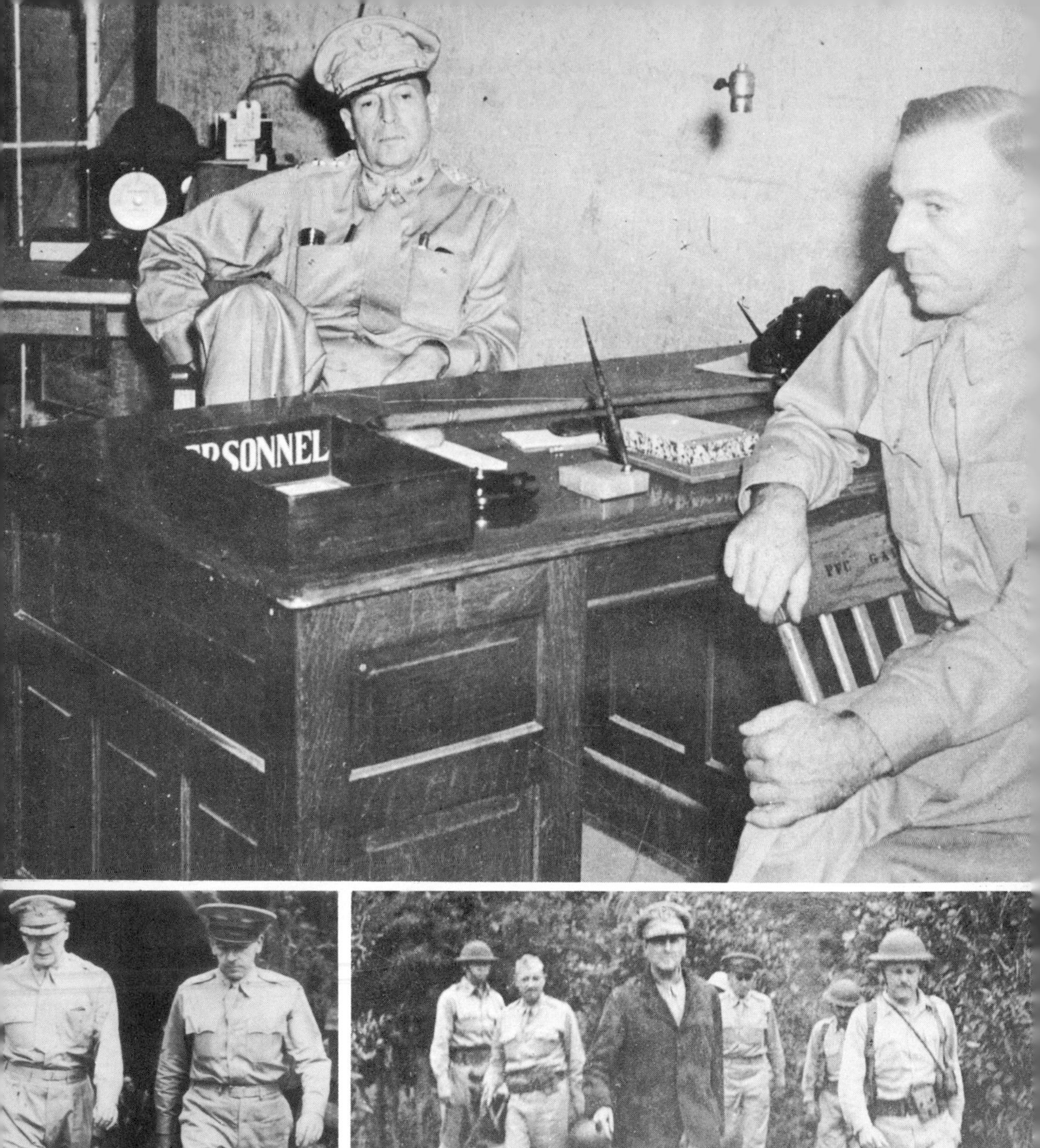

Japan attacked the Philippines cight hours after the blow at Pearl Harbor. On Christmas Eve, 1941, MacArthur declared Manila an open city and moved to Corregidor to direct the defense of that rocky island fortress and of the Bataan Peninsula. From headquarters inside Malinta tunnel, he commanded operations with his chief of staff, Gen. Richard Sutherland (top). In the small house where he lived with his wife and son, MacArthur kept concealed a .38 calibre pistol which his father had carried 40 years earlier in the Philippines. But in the presence of his American and Filipino troops (bottom right) he carried a cane instead of firearms. While not working with Sutherland (bottom left) he spent all possible time with his wife and child.

Father and son MacArthur spent their birthdays under enemy fire on Corregidor. Secretary of War Stimson radioed MacArthur on Jan. 26, 1942, ". . . on your birthday every one of us is inspired to greater efforts by the heroic and skillful fight which you and your men are making." Called "the Sergeant" by his 62-year-old Dad, little Arthur, on his fourth birthday on Feb. 21, celebrated in his favorite khaki overseas cap. Mrs. MacArthur was philosophical about the effect of war's death and destruction surrounding her youngster's life. "If he were older he'd have been frightened, and if he were younger it might have affected him forever," she said. When the Quezon family prepared to leave Corregidor for the safety of the United States, Mrs. MacArthur refused to leave with her son. Firmly, she stated, "We three drink of the same cup."

"We're alone, Jonathan. You know that as well as I. If I get through to Australia you know I'll come back as soon as I can with as much as I can. In the meantime you've got to hold." MacArthur was forced to leave Gen. Jonathan Wainwright in command of his forlorn little army. President Roosevelt had ordered MacArthur to Australia. As Robert E. Sherwood later wrote: "It was ordering the captain to be the first to leave the sinking ship." Wainwright held Bataan valiantly until April 9, and for 27 more days his 11,000 weary men held out Corregidor against the furious attacks of 200,000 Japanese. On May 6 the hopeless carnage ended with his surrender. MacArthur's tearful tribute: "No army has ever done so much with so little. Nothing became it more than its last hour of trial and agony." MacArthur vowed he would redeem the valiant defenders.

The General stalled his departure for Australia as long as he could. With prodding from Washington on March 10, however, he went at one of the most unpleasant tasks of his career—selecting a skeleton staff to accompany him. Somberly reflecting on Julius Caesar's fate, he told the lucky few, "We go with the fall of the moon; we go during the Ides of March." At dusk, March 11, 4 PT boats roared away from Corregidor with MacArthur, his family, and the staff, later dubbed the "Bataan Gang." They were (clockwise from top center): Gens. Richard Sutherland, Harold George, Charles Willoughby, William Marquat, Col. Joseph McMicking, Warrant Officer Paul Rogers, Cols. LeGrande Diller, Francis Wilson, Charles Morhouse, Sidney Huff, Joseph Shaw, Gens. Hugh Casey, Charles Stivers, Richard Marshall, and Spencer Akin.

Leaving behind some of his dearest comrades, MacArthur and his party sped toward Mindanao, 600 miles southeast of Corregidor. Because of Japanese mine fields, naval vessels, and planes the journey was fraught with danger; choppy seas laid everyone low with seasickness. The hardy PTs made it to Cagayan in 36 uncomfortable hours and 3 days later the party flew over 500 miles of enemy-held territory to Darwin, Australia, in 2 Flying Fortresses. Here MacArthur was met by his old friend, Gen. Patrick Hurley, then U. S. Minister to New Zealand (above). "The President ordered me to break through the Japanese lines . . . for the purpose of organizing the American offensive against Japan . . . [and] the relief of the Philippines." Then MacArthur concluded his first press statement, "I came through and I shall return."

MacArthur was hurt and disappointed beyond description on learning that in all Australia there were only 25,000 American soldiers—mostly service and support troops, practically no infantry. "God have mercy on us," he gasped. Nevertheless, he tackled the job of making a fighting force from what he had—plus the veteran Australian 7th Division and the green militia. Visiting their camps he sipped tea with the trainees (top left) and reviewed the more advanced outfits (top right). With Gen. Sir Thomas Blamey, Australian commander, he imbued both Yank and Aussie soldiers with his earnestness: "I have every confidence in the ultimate success of our joint cause, but success in modern war requires more than courage and willingness to die; it requires careful preparation" (bottom). With that he began his campaign to reconquer the Pacific.

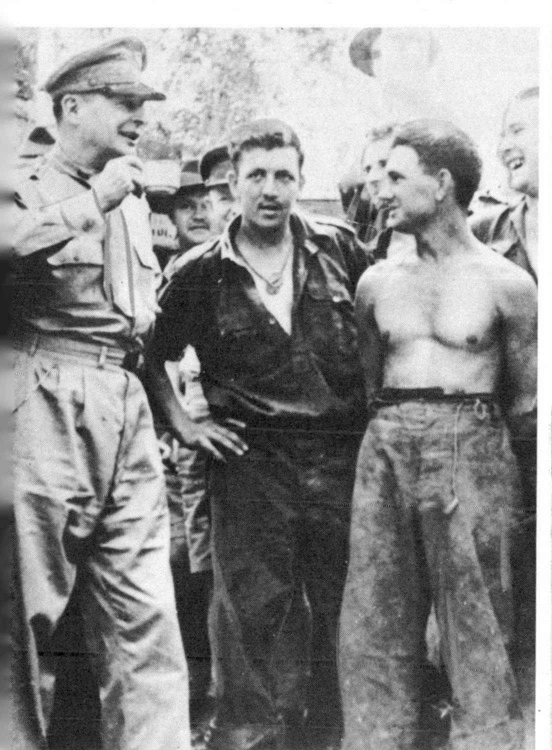

In the spring of 1942 MacArthur had become America's first great hero of World War II. In Indiana a farmer remembered Bataan and named his 2-month-overdue colt "General Mac," because "he held out so long." In Washington the General's bust was unveiled ceremoniously, and Maj. Gen. William Connor accepted it in behalf of West Point. Attending were (top, l. to r.) Connor, William Howard Hoeffer, sponsor; Mrs. Arthur MacArthur, sister-in-law of the General, and sculptor Nison Tregor. In Brisbane MacArthur was briefed on Philippine conditions by 3 newly escaped American officers (center, l. to r.): Maj. William Dyess, Cmdr. Melvin McCoy, MacArthur, and Maj. S. M. Mellnik. Preparing to send his first American units into New Guinea, MacArthur gave them (bottom) a personal send-off: "Kill Japs!"

From the moment he joined MacArthur as air commander, Gen. George Kenney got along well with his new boss (top left). Kenney, more than any man in MacArthur's career, influenced his latter-day enthusiasm for air power. The air chief began his work with only 6 usable heavy bombers in the entire Southwest Pacific Area. U. S. Chief of Staff, Gen. George Marshall, stopped off at MacArthur's New Guinea headquarters (bottom left) for a conference on the progress of the war while he was en route home from Cairo and Teheran. MacArthur continued his policy of studying his men at first hand and in New Guinea he was known to pop up almost anywhere to question a startled GI (top right) or visit a field hospital to cheer the wounded (bottom right). After conversations such as those he often reiterated to aides or staff officers, "I shall keep the soldier's faith," the promise he made when he first arrived in Australia.

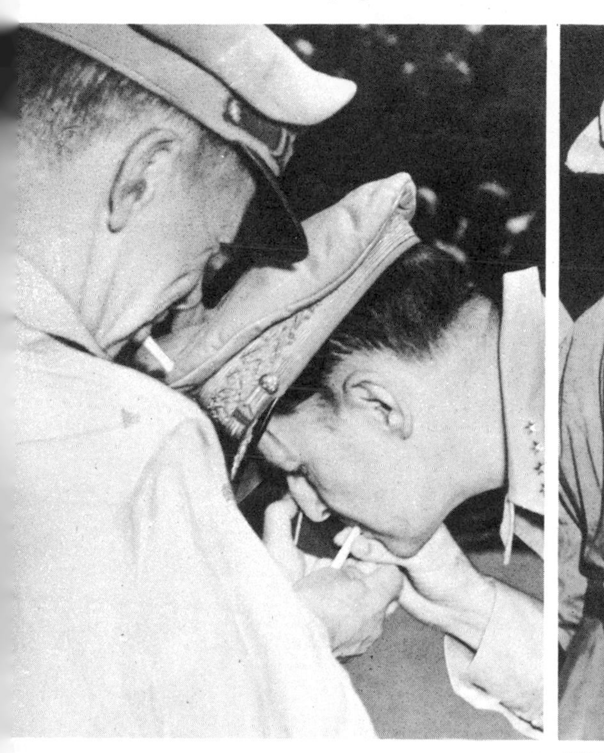

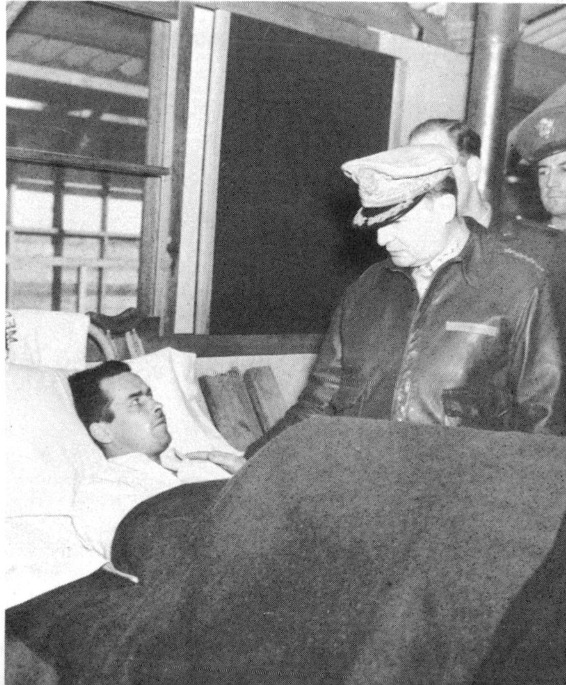

Most of MacArthur's waking hours in World War II were spent in planning his next island-hopping move. Each required long hours with staff officers, field commanders, and interservice liaison personnel. Work horse for MacArthur was his Sixth Army and its commander, Lt. Gen. Walter Krueger (top left). Also close to the General in planning joint Army-Navy operations was R. Adm. Daniel Barbey, commander of the 7th Amphibious Force (bottom left). Before the successful Yank paratroop landing at Lae, New Guinea, MacArthur personally briefed battalion commander Lt. Col. J. J. Tolson of New Bern, N. C. (top right). Every detail of a beachhead landing went under MacArthur's careful scrutiny. With Gens. Krueger and William Rupertus, commander of the 1st Marine Division (bottom right), MacArthur studied a scale relief map prior to the Cape Gloucester, New Britain, invasion in December, 1943.

An Invasion Day with General MacArthur: 1300 Hours, 28 Feb. 1944 (top left)—En route by air from Brisbane to Milne Bay, New Guinea, with Adm. Thomas Kinkaid. Final plans set. Convoy leaves today . . . 1830 Hours (top right)—Aboard Kinkaid's flagship, U.S.S. *Phoenix*, full speed north to the Admiralty Group . . . 0600 Hours, 29 Feb. 1944 (center left)—D-Day! Target: Los Negros Island. Fire! A 2-hour, ear-shattering naval bombardment. Then the troops of the 1st Cavalry Division swarm ashore. Then vehicles. Then supplies . . . 1100 Hours (center right)—On an LCVP chugging into shore with aide Col. Lloyd Lehrbas. Beachhead secure, perimeter established, losses light . . . 1200 Hours (bottom left)—Momote Airstrip taken, antiaircraft defenses set. Well done, men . . . 1300 Hours (bottom right)—Dig in. Bury the enemy dead. "That's the way I like to see them." Now we're ready to hit Hollandia.

We, the undersigned, members of and affiliated with the **Republican** party and qualified primary electors of said **Republican** party, in the State of Illinois, do hereby petition that the name of

DOUGLAS MacARTHUR

who resides at **Plankinton Hotel, 609 North Plankinton Avenue,** in the City of Milwaukee, Milwaukee County, and the State of Wisconsin, shall be printed upon the Primary ballot in the State of Illinois of the **Republican** party as a candidate for the office of

PRESIDENT OF THE UNITED STATES

for the purpose of securing an expression of the sentiment and will of the party voters with respect to candidates for nomination for said office, to be voted for at the Primary Election to be held on the Eleventh day of April, A.D. 1944.

SIGNATURE OF QUALIFIED PRIMARY ELECTOR	RESIDENCE ADDRESS This shall include House Number, Name of Street, City, Town or Village, and Illinois.

11 February 1944.

ersonal

Dear Congressman Miller:

I appreciate very much your scholarly letter of January 27. Your description of conditions in the United States is a sobering one indeed and is calculated to arouse the thoughtful consideration of every true patriot. We must not inadvertently slip into the same condition internally as the one which we fight externally. Like Abraham Lincoln I am a firm believer in the people and if given the truth they can be depended upon to meet any national crises. The great point is to bring before them the real facts.

Our here we are doing what we can with what we have. oI will be glad, however, when more substantial forces are placed at my disposition.

With cordial regard and best wishes,

Douglas MacArthur

DOUGLAS MacARTHUR.

Carrying on successfully against his country's enemies in what he called his "five-and-ten-cent war," MacArthur was not reluctant to complain of the scarcity in men and supplies. Despite the fact that it was marked "personal," his correspondence with an obscure Nebraska Congressman, A. L. Miller, was published and made effective ammunition for attacks on President Roosevelt (bottom). Milwaukeeans, without his permission, circulated petitions seeking his nomination as Republican Presidential candidate (top) and New Yorkers spread stickers (center) advocating a Bricker-MacArthur ticket, also without the General's knowledge. Cognizant of an Army-Navy ruling forbidding members of the armed forces from campaigning while on duty, MacArthur from a beachhead in Hollandia, New Guinea (right), said of the nomination, "I do not covet it, nor would I accept it." Nevertheless, he got one vote at the Republican convention.

Before major operations, MacArthur met with Admiral of the Fleet Chester Nimitz for joint planning (top). Often he inspected jungle advances on the ground (center left) or was high over an invasion in a Fifth Air Force bomber (center right). His last GHQ site before the Philippines campaign was in Hollandia, Dutch New Guinea, where he drew the plans for the assault on Leyte, which crushed Japan's war effort. This was the locale for one of the most widely spread and vicious falsehoods concerning MacArthur: that he had soldier sweat and labor build him a "million dollar mansion" high on a mountain there. The story elaborated further that a "multi-million dollar roadway" led to his palatial home. Actually the house was a standard Army type double "pre-fab," used to house his staff, their offices, conference room, and mess (bottom). The road leading to it was one of the dustiest and most treacherous and uncomfortable in New Guinea.

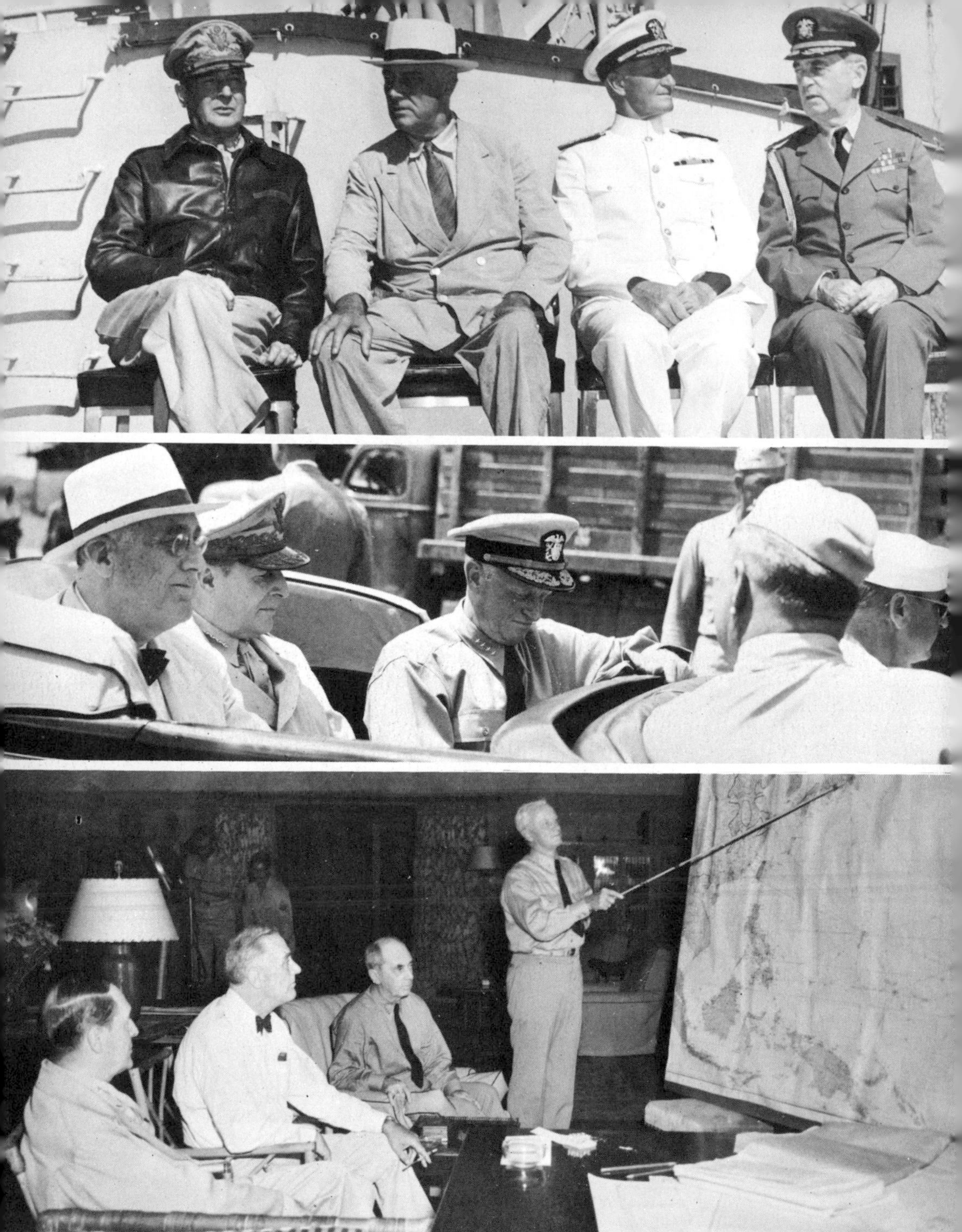

At the end of July, 1944, MacArthur was summoned to a conference in Honolulu to determine the final course of the war against Japan. The participants chatted on the deck of the U.S.S. *Baltimore* (top, l. to r.): MacArthur, President Roosevelt, Adms. Nimitz and William Leahy, chief of staff to the President. Roosevelt noticed that MacArthur's khaki trousers were unfastened as he sat down. The fun-loving President whispered to an aide, "Do you see what I see? Get a photographer, quick!" A historic photograph was lost when MacArthur coincidentally crossed his legs just as the cameraman approached to focus. The group drove through Honolulu (center) to a great ovation and that evening Nimitz earnestly began to summarize his plan for a sea and land assault on Formosa, by-passing the Philippines (bottom).

When MacArthur arrived in Pearl Harbor, the only ammunition he had to sway the President (whom he believed favored Nimitz' proposal) was his expert knowledge, his eloquent oratory, and the intense belief in the necessity of retaking the Philippines. Late that night and for 3 hours the next morning he talked and talked (top). At lunch before Roosevelt announced his decision, the 3 protagonists were glum and dour (center), but after lunch Roosevelt turned to MacArthur (bottom) and closed the historic sessions with, "Well, Douglas, you win! But I'm going to have a hell of a time over this with that old bear, Ernie King." FDR knew that Adm. King, in Washington, assumed the Formosa plan would be adopted. MacArthur flew back to the Southwest Pacific and already began planning his return to the Philippines. En route, however, his happiness was marred by the radioed news that Manuel Quezon had died that day, Aug. 1.

More than 2 years had passed since the MacArthur family arrived in Australia. In that time the General had pushed thousands of miles northwest toward his goals: redemption of the Philippines and victory in Japan. Meanwhile, his wife and son were living in Lennon's Hotel, Brisbane. To her family and friends in Murfreesboro, Jean had sent their first group portrait (top left). With "The Boss" in New Guinea so much of the time she and young Arthur had many opportunities to attend movies, visit Australia's beaches and countryside, and go shopping (bottom left). Arthur's faithful Chinese amah, Ah Chuh, was constantly at his side—even for rides in the General's car (top right) where the youngster continued to wear his faded overseas cap. With the nurse he frequently visited Brisbane's Botanical Gardens (bottom right).

Without an airbase closer to the Philippines than Dutch New Guinca, MacArthur feared for the air support of his invading land forces. Working with a tight timetable, he planned Operation Interlude—the capture of little Morotai Island in the Moluccas Group on Sept. 15, 1944. Engineers, he figured, would hurry the construction of an airstrip and the Leyte invasion would come off on schedule, Oct. 20. If successful, Morotai would cut off the enemy sea lane to New Guinea, flank their movements in Borneo and Java, and bottle up their forces in the Moluccas. It was successful. MacArthur waded ashore 2 hours after H-hour on the Morotai beachhead (top left) and congratulated the troops (top right). He was surrounded by GIs as the American flag was raised (bottom).

Adm. Nimitz offered MacArthur 2 infantry divisions and Adm. William Halsey's Third Fleet from the Central Pacific for the return to the Philippines. With 2 of his own divisions, and others standing by in reserve, MacArthur's force assaulted the east coast of Leyte, after a terrific naval bombardment on the morning of A-day (changed by MacArthur from D-day), Oct. 20, 1944. From the U.S.S. *Nashville* in Leyte Gulf, MacArthur, with Gen. Krueger, watched the waves of men pour on to the beach (top left), and a few hours later he went in (top right) with Philippine President Sergio Osmena at his right and Gen. Carlos Romulo at his left. Wet to the hips, he strode in to the cluttered beach (center) and exultantly proclaimed to the Filipino people, "I have returned. By the Grace of Almighty God our forces stand again on Philippine soil . . ." Disregarding enemy mortar fire, he proudly led the group 300 yards inland to the perimeter (bottom).

The invasion of Leyte was 2 years, 7 months, and 3 days after MacArthur had landed in Australia and promised to return. To intimates he proudly confided also that Oct. 20, 1944, was exactly 41 years to the day that he had arrived in Tacloban, Leyte, as a young Engineers lieutenant on his first assignment after graduation from the Academy. It was probably the happiest day in the General's life. He toured the area of his conquest (top left) and often dismounted from his jeep to encourage his troops and comply with requests for his autograph (top right). Within 48 hours the 1st Cavalry Division had taken the capital, Tacloban, and on the steps of its provincial building (bottom), MacArthur broadcast, "The seat of your government is now firmly re-established on Philippine soil."

"If I should die today or tomorrow," MacArthur once said to his air chief, Gen. Kenney, "and you listen to my last words, you'll hear me say, 'George, bring up the Fifth Air Force.' " MacArthur never forgot how much his "air" helped his victorious push across the Pacific. Top air ace, with an all-time record of 40 enemy planes, Maj. Richard Bong was going home a hero, but MacArthur delayed him long enough to pin the Congressional Medal of Honor to his chest (top left). The troops continued to surge across Leyte to the west and the General kept in close contact with his front-line commanders every day (bottom left). In the field he frequently borrowed a swig from a pleased GI's canteen (top right). For hours each day he conferred with President Osmena on the multiple problems of civilian relief and public administration (bottom right).

In Australia Mrs. MacArthur and the 6-year-old boy anxiously awaited the General's movement to Luzon, and into Manila, where they would join him. Arthur had been taking piano lessons and progressed well (top left) under his mother's eye. His closest chum in Brisbane was Neal Watts, a neighbor, and at Christmas, 1944, Arthur as Santa Claus (top right) presented Neal with a colorful cowboy costume. In Tacloban General MacArthur was preparing to push off for Lingayen Gulf, Luzon, while the youngsters directed their own toy invasion fleet under the Christmas tree. One year, during the war, when the General had been selected "outstanding American father of the year," he cabled home: "My hope is that my son, when I am gone, will remember me not from the battle but in the home, repeating with him our simple daily prayer, 'Our Father Who art in Heaven . . .' "

Before he left Leyte for the invasion of the main island of the Philippines, General MacArthur received word that he had been promoted on Dec. 15 to the highest rank attainable in the Army—General of the Army. With 5 stars adorning his collar, he circled the Philippines and hit Lingayen on Jan. 9, 1945. Fierce Japanese resistance slowed the American march southward to Manila. MacArthur moved his headquarters with his forward echelons, anxious to reach the capital. Often he had to ford streams or cross rivers on planks replacing bombed-out bridges (top). Filipinos volunteered as guerrillas or regulars as fast as they could be signed up and armed. At every opportunity, MacArthur inspired them (bottom) with encouragement and confidence: "There can be no compromise; we shall win or we shall die, and to this end I pledge you the full resources of all the mighty power of my country and all the blood of my countrymen."

At his headquarters, 50 kilometers north of Manila, MacArthur was becoming impatient to enter the city. To Sixth Army commander, Gen. Krueger (top left), and the pressing 1st Cavalry, he ordered, "Get to Manila. Go round the Japs, go through the Japs, bounce off the Japs. I don't care how you do it. Get in there as fast as you can—but save your men—and rescue the internees at Santo Tomas." A few days later, on Feb. 3, the Yanks entered Manila and immediately the walled internment camp. Tears of joy drenched the faces of the freed Americans and hard-bitten GI's choked with emotion. MacArthur blinked sentimentally and moved among his starved and scrawny old Manila neighbors (bottom). At the graves of Bataan's "death marchers" (top right) he reiterated, "I do not know the dignity of their birth but I do know the glory of their death."

MacArthur experienced another hour of impassioned sentiment when he visited retaken Corregidor on the heels of a swift paratroop and beach assault. Returning to the island in a PT boat, the General landed and jeeped (top right) up to "Topside" remarking, "This visit is easing an ache that has been in my heart for 3 years." The island fortress was battle-scarred and its buildings demolished, from both the early Japanese and recent American barrages. MacArthur's party stood silently before the entrance to Malinta tunnel (top left) and the General, alone, moved into its blackness (bottom). The stench of the dead drove him back. He whispered, "Corregidor needs no comment from me. . . I shall always seem to see the vision of its grim, gaunt, ghastly men still unafraid . . . with faith in their hearts and hope on their lips they passed beyond the mists that blind us here. Their yesterday makes possible our tomorrow."

MacArthur knew he was "home," such as it was, when he approached the Manila Hotel (top), a battered, gutted hulk of its former splendor. Many Japanese, in their last-ditch stand south of the Pasig River, had holed up within its walls—but were finally routed with flame-throwers and grenades. The MacArthur penthouse apartment was destroyed and none of its possessions remained. Later, a loyal former servant led him to a chest of the family silverware which the Filipino had buried for safekeeping. In Tokyo, the next year, Mrs. MacArthur took it to a Japanese silversmith for polishing and found that the merchant's grandfather had originally sold it to General Arthur MacArthur in 1905. At Balikpapan, Borneo, in July, 1945, MacArthur got his last taste of battle before the war ended. He went ashore with the victorious Australian 7th Division (bottom).

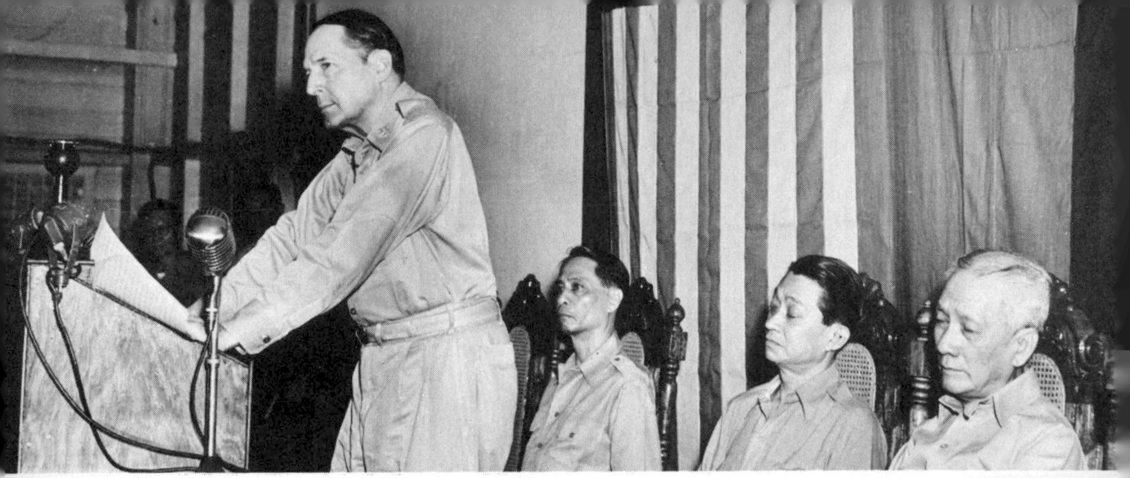

The General restored to the Commonwealth Government its full powers and responsibilities, in a ceremony at Malacanan Palace. Twice he sobbed during the speech, finishing, "Your country is again at liberty to pursue its destiny to an honored position in the family of free nations . . ." Later he addressed the first session of the reactivated Philippine Congress (top and center) in a Manila school auditorium. Legislators from the many islands filled the hall and the ovation for MacArthur lasted 5 minutes. "At that moment," remarked a Filipino newspaperman, "they would have chucked democracy and unanimously elected MacArthur the King." Mrs. MacArthur had returned to Manila, too—although less sensationally—aboard a refrigerator ship. Wherever she went she was besieged by adoring Filipinos. Visiting backstage at a theater, she willingly gave out autographs to the cast (bottom). Her son, Arthur, was rarely seen.

During the hectic days of August, 1945, while the air waves carried surrender negotiations back and forth between Manila and Tokyo, General MacArthur was visited (top left) by Francis Cardinal Spellman (then Archbishop). Already planning the occupation of Japan, MacArthur stated, "The form of government of a country is not nearly so important as whether people hold to the two fundamental beliefs . . . in a Supreme Being (and) in the freedom of man, or, as the Pope so well calls it, 'the dignity of man.'" Another visitor was his war partner in Southeast Asia, Supreme Allied Commander Adm. Lord Louis Mountbatten (top right). From the U. S. on a rehabilitation mission came Sen. Millard Tydings (bottom left). A few days before leaving for Japan MacArthur received an honorary degree from Santo Tomas University (bottom right).

Hours after the atomic bomb blasted Hiroshima, Soviet Russia jumped into the war against Japan. On the day the second bomb was dropped on Nagasaki, Aug. 9, MacArthur was gravely reading the news. "Our men," he later remarked, "died on Bataan early in the war to save Russian lives," while he had waited for "the promised help which never came." The General had insisted 3 years before that Russia declare war on Japan and put pressure on her from the north. Japan's unconditional surrender was announced on Aug. 15, 1945, and MacArthur was named Supreme Commander for the Allied Powers. Preparing for the surrender ceremonies in Tokyo Bay, he added up the score of 3 years' warfare: 300,000 enemy casualties to 60,000 of our own. "From Melbourne to Tokyo was a long road. It was a long, hard road, but this looks like the payoff."

SCAP, Architect of the New Japan

1945–1950

Arrived at Atsugi airdrome, Tokyo, Japan, 30 Aug. 1945; as Supreme Commander for the Allied Powers received formal surrender of Japan, aboard the U.S.S. *Missouri* in Tokyo Bay, 2 Sept. 1945 (V-J Day); established the Occupation of Japan and issued SCAP Directive #1; raised the American flag over the U.S. Embassy, Tokyo, 5 Sept. 1945; surrender of Japanese-held Korea and Japanese forces in the Netherlands East Indies, 9 Sept. 1945; Imperial Japanese General Headquarters inactivated, 13 Sept. 1945; GHQ, SCAP, and AFPAC established in the Dai-Ichi Building, Tokyo, 17 Sept. 1945; attended Independence Day ceremonies for the Republic of the Philippines, Manila, P.I., 4 July 1946; continued as Supreme Commander for the Allied Powers, Supreme Commander of the Army Forces in the Pacific and Commander in Chief of the Far East Command until relieved of same by direction of the President of the United States, 11 April 1951.

"A man of elegance with a corncob pipe," the Supreme Commander for the Allied Powers stood under the symbolic painting of Fujiyama as he deliberated the course of the occupation of Japan. After almost 6 years at the task he said: "I know of no nation more serene, orderly, and industrious, nor in which higher hopes can be entertained for future constructive service in the advance of the human race."

Having already decided in his own mind how to deal with the vastly complicated problem of governing defeated Japan, MacArthur slept peacefully as his C-54, *Bataan*, roared toward Mt. Fuji. Landing at the Atsugi airstrip near Yokohama, on Aug. 30, 1945 the Supreme Commander hitched up his trousers, shoved his long-stemmed pipe between his teeth, and stepped out for a first look at the conquered country. He set the tone of the occupation from the moment he strode—unarmed and obviously unconcerned about his safety—to the waiting group of generals, reporters, and cameramen, some Japanese, and with obvious emotion greeted them, expressed optimism for the occupation, and hurried off to the New Grand Hotel in nearby Yokohama to prepare for the surrender ceremonies 3 days later. It was the event for which he fought 3 long years.

A prisoner-of-war rescue team was returning to Yokohama from Mukden with the man MacArthur had left on Corregidor. When gaunt, sickly Gen. Jonathan Wainwright appeared before him, MacArthur's eyes welled with tears and he embraced him closely, unable to speak for the choking in his throat (left). Both men were silent for almost a full minute. Soon after, Adm. Chester W. Nimitz appeared (top right) to discuss the surrender ceremonies, and the same day Russia's Lt. Gen. Kuzma Derevyanko arrived to present his credentials (center right). The Soviets had been at war with Japan less than a week but hastened to get in on the surrender. Gens. Derevyanko, Krueger, Blamey, Sutherland, Percival, Wainwright, and MacArthur (l. to r., bottom) celebrated their reunion that evening at a private dinner of canned GI rations.

"Today the guns are silent. A great tragedy has ended. A great victory has been won . . . the Holy Mission has been completed." On the broad quarterdeck of the battleship *Missouri*, MacArthur at a great moment in his career conducted the Japanese surrender ceremonies on Sept. 2, 1945. The General, with a slight tremor, signed for all the Allied Powers (top) as Gens. Wainwright and Arthur Percival, British commander who surrendered Singapore, looked over his shoulders. Invited to step up and sign the document in behalf of Japan's Emperor and government, stump-legged Prince Mamoru Shigemitsu nervously studied the papers until MacArthur's voice broke the dead silence, snapping, "Sutherland, show him where to sign!" (bottom left).

Six pens were used for the historic surrender ceremony, including a small, woman's pen belonging to Mrs. MacArthur. Fully decorated and with his Samurai sword clanking at his side, Lt. Gen. Yoshijiro Umezu was the Japanese Army signatory (top). MacArthur whispered to Adm. Halsey, "Start 'em up, Bill," and from out of nowhere the sky was blackened by 1,000 giant B-29 superforts and another 1,000 navy fighter planes. Below, on the deck of the *Missouri,* MacArthur said, "It is my hope, and indeed the hope of all mankind, that from this solemn occasion a better world shall emerge out of the blood and carnage of the past—a world founded on faith and understanding, dedicated to the dignity of man and the fulfillment of his most cherished wish for freedom, tolerance, and justice." MacArthur's eyes were wet, his voice shook.

With the raising of the American flag over the U. S. Embassy the occupation had begun in earnest. MacArthur, with Adm. Halsey and Gen. Eichelberger at his right, saluted as the colors flew (top). "We stand in Tokyo today, reminiscent of our countryman, Commodore Perry, 92 years ago. His purpose was to bring Japan an era of enlightenment and progress . . . It is my purpose." To impress the Japanese in Tokyo, GHQ's Honor Guard company was made up of the top men in the Far East Command. "Spit 'n' polish" was their byword and MacArthur was proud to review them publicly during the occupation years (bottom).

MacArthur's paneled office in the Dai-Ichi Building, Tokyo, was the birthplace of the new Japan. He expected to have only 3 years to complete his job of democratizing Japan before the final peace treaty was executed. Therefore he set his course and went ahead with full steam, slightly left of center. He broke up the trusts—the Zaibatsu—which controlled 80 per cent of Japan's economic life; smashed the secret police organization; freed political prisoners and jailed war criminals; emancipated women; broke up large land holdings; protected and helped develop labor unions; and established free speech and a free press.

During the first month of the occupation, there was much speculation in Tokyo as to when and how MacAthur would meet Emperor Hirohito. MacArthur tactfully waited, respecting the monarch's position and avoiding the humiliation attendant on a "summons" or "invitation." Soon MacArthur was approached by an imperial secretary for an appointment and a few days later the Emperor, in striped trousers and morning tail coat, called at the U. S. Embassy. Hirohito convinced MacArthur that he disapproved of the war and that he had been powerless to stop it. Their relationship was courteous but formal from its beginning and the Emperor made a practice of calling on MacArthur every 6 months until MacArthur's relief.

For his General Headquarters, SCAP (as MacArthur was called during the occupation) chose an imposing marble and granite edifice in downtown Tokyo, the Dai-Ichi Building, home of a Japanese insurance company (bottom). It faces the beautifully kept grounds of the Imperial Palace. At least 4 times every day, MacArthur entered or left the main entrance with an aide (top left with Col. Laurence Bunker). Each time he made an appearance a crowd of hundreds of Japanese (and American servicemen) gaped curiously (center). His Cadillac, with the 5-star insignia, was driven by M/Sgt. Otis J. Edwards of Columbus, Ga., and rarely traveled any route other than that to and from his Embassy home and the office (top right).

MacArthur made only 2 trips out of Japan during the first 5 years of the occupation. His first was on July 4, 1946, to Manila, where he was guest of honor at the Philippines independence day ceremonies. Philippines President Manuel Roxas and Vice President Elpidio Quirino (l. to r., top) paid high praise to MacArthur's role in restoring the commonwealth in 1944. MacArthur (left) addressed the assemblage but it was felt that his popularity in Manila had dimmed noticeably because of the "soft" occupation he was conducting in Japan. Nevertheless, the Filipinos honored him that day with the issue of new silver coins bearing his likeness (bottom center). The MacArthurs met the Paul V. McNutts at the celebration (bottom right), both men having had long careers in Manila, the latter as U. S. High Commissioner.

There were few of high, or low, station whom Jean MacArthur did not meet in her heavy social schedule in Tokyo. Signor Alberto Nogueira, chief of the Portuguese Diplomatic Agency, chatted with her (top left) at a Portuguese reception. She toasted the marriage of Britain's princess Elizabeth in 1947 with Mr. and Mrs. A. D. F. Gascoigne of the United Kingdom Liaison Mission (top right). Mrs. A. B. Otis, Girl Scoutmaster of the American colony, gave her an award at a Scout outing (center left). Popular with enlisted men, she received an orchid from Cpl. Virgil Gillian and Pfc. T. J. Cremmins at the opening of the Tokyo Enlisted Men's Club (center right). Post Exchange officers watched her cut the tape, opening the largest PX in the world in Tokyo (bottom left), and at a Red Cross tea she gave out autographs to Maj. Gen. William Chase's men of the First Cavalry Division, occupying Tokyo (bottom right).

Mrs. MacArthur's only trip to Korea during the occupation took place in August, 1948, 2 years before the Korean war, when she accompanied the General (left) to the inauguration ceremonies of the new Republic. With Dr. Syngman Rhee, first President of the country, MacArthur (top right) watched the celebration and later greeted Korean officials, including Gen. Sung Ho (center right), first commanding general of the Korean constabulary. Before returning to Tokyo with his wife, the General reviewed the 31st Inf. Regt. (bottom) with its commanding officer, Col. Ralph Leighton of Sacramento, Calif. The 31st had been in MacArthur's Philippine command in 1941, at the outbreak of World War II. Many of its men were captured or killed.

The Presidential-election year of 1948 found scattered MacArthur-for-President booms throughout sections of mid-Western United States and in March of that year the General helped them along with his statement from Tokyo: "I would be recreant to all my concepts of good citizenship were I to shrink . . . from accepting any public duty." Japanese MacArthur supporters climbed on the band wagon with hand-painted campaign signs (top left and bottom right). MacArthur's heavy mail quadrupled with letters of Nipponese encouragement (bottom left). All the efforts of his 11 (out of 1,094) Republican convention delegates and a newspaper chain's millions of coupon pledges (top right) failed to stir up enough interest in electing him. Gen. Courtney Whitney told a friend that he was present when MacArthur heard of Dewey's nomination in Philadelphia. Whitney confided that he had never seen the General look so disappointed.

MacArthur, an Episcopalian, was visited by many Catholic prelates during the occupation of Japan. Few, if any, Catholic churchmen could pass through Tokyo without an invitation from the General for a talk in his office or lunch at the Embassy. The late Msgr. E. J. Flanagan, famed as Father Flanagan of Boy's Town, Neb., visited MacArthur (top left) while making a study of juvenile problems in postwar Japan. A newspaperman once remarked that "MacArthur should move his office to Haneda Air Force Base—he spends most of his time there," awaiting visitors and then seeing them off. A frequent visitor to Tokyo from Manila was ambassador to the Philippines, Paul V. McNutt (top right). With the chief of GHQ's Diplomatic Section, William Sebald, MacArthur awaited the arrival of State Dept. officials (bottom left). Under-secretary of State W. H. Draper bade farewell to his Tokyo host (bottom right).

Jean MacArthur told an interviewer in Tokyo: "My whole life is the General and our son, Arthur, and I take care of both of them the best I can." Arthur, with a trace of a British accent absorbed from contact with his tutor, Mrs. Phyllis Gibbons, is a normal boy despite a life of alternating intense excitement and sheltered calm. He showed great interest in the making of silk on a visit with his mother to the Omiya-Katakura plant when he was 9 years old (top left). Like all boys he couldn't resist the electric train displays in the Tokyo PX toy department (top right). Tokyo GIs built and presented him with a complete model railroad. With his mother he viewed the Fourth of July parade at the Imperial Plaza in 1947 (bottom left). His arm was broken at an indoor ice-skating rink. Wearing translation earphones, he was fascinated with the proceedings of Premier Hideki Tojo's war crimes trial (bottom right).

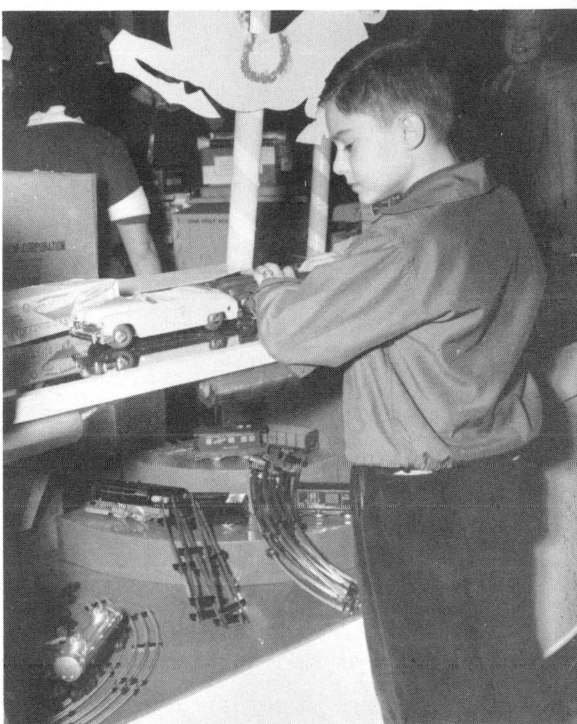

MacArthur, holding himself deliberately aloof for psychological reasons, attended few social functions in the occupation years. In October, 1946, he attended the Russian Revolution Anniversary party at the Soviet Embassy, and was welcomed by Maj. Gen. V. A. Kislenko (top left). Thereafter MacArthur gave Russians in Tokyo the "cold shoulder" treatment, although he could never resist joking with Lt. Gen. Kuzma Derevyanko, of whom he was genuinely fond. Protocol required him to attend a few of the British receptions. With Mrs. MacArthur and Lt. Gen. C. H. Gairdner, British Liaison Officer, he sipped sherry in celebration of Empire Day (top right), and the party-giving Britons lured him also to their celebration of King George VI's birthday in 1947, where he conversed with A. D. F. Gascoigne (bottom left). MacArthur received the Grand Cross of the Legion of Honor from the French Mission (bottom right) in 1946.

Reunion in Tokyo on May 10, 1946, brought together Generals of the Army Dwight D. Eisenhower and Douglas MacArthur when the former was U. S. Chief of Staff. They had not seen each other since "Ike" had left Philippine Field Marshal MacArthur in Manila in 1939 and sailed home as a lieutenant colonel destined for rapid advancement in World War II. Eisenhower chose Douglas MacArthur II, the General's nephew, as his diplomatic attaché in Paris when he set up the North Atlantic Treaty Organization's SHAPE headquarters in 1951. Chairman of the Joint Chiefs of Staff Gen. Omar N. Bradley, MacArthur, and Air Chief Gen. Hoyt Vandenberg (l. to r., bottom) conferred in Tokyo a few months before the Korean war broke out. They admitted in 1951 that none had the slightest intimation of the impending conflict.

In matters concerning her household, Mrs. MacArthur lived her life in Tokyo like every other officer's wife. She stood in line at the PX, the bank, and thc commissary; she shopped wisely with an eye for bargains. With aide Lieut. William Hogan she did most of her Christmas shopping in the big Tokyo PX (top left), and learned how to tell different grades of silk from a sales-girl in a Tokyo department store (center left). When not shopping she made social calls to such centers as the Red Cross canteen where she met ARC worker Emily Hunter and Pvt. Lawrence Tessmer, Melville, Ind. (top right). She attended Episcopal church services weekly, without the General (center right). Native Japanese girls adored her and Ichiko Nakatani presented her with a bouquet from Tokyo businessmen (bottom left), and a Nipponese model happily posed with her during a style show (bottom right) given for Americans by Japanese dress designers.

MacArthur called the occupation of Japan "a milestone in the march of man," and he never failed to report on its success when Washington dignitaries visited him. Louis Johnson, U. S. Secretary of Defense, met MacArthur in June of 1950, just a few days before the attack in Korea. With Gen. Bradley, they saluted as a color guard passed in their honor (top). Extremely friendly with the MacArthurs was the late George Atcheson, Jr., SCAP political adviser. He frequently accompanied them to Haneda to await incoming officials (bottom left). When Korean President Syngman Rhee departed from Japan for the last time before his country was embroiled in war, Mrs. MacArthur and a Korean diplomat waved their farewells vigorously while the General stood calm and silent as though he had been forewarned of the impending crisis in Korea (bottom right). He did not see Rhee again until the war started.

Department of Tactics

UNITED STATES MILITARY ACADEMY
WEST POINT, NEW YORK

6 September 1949

General of the Army Douglas ~~X~~. MacArthur
Commander in Chief, FE
APO 500
% Postmaster
San Francisco, California

Dear General MacArthur:

Representing the Corps of Cadets as "Head Cheerleader" I have been authorized by the Commandant to communicate with you regarding the Army-Navy football rally this year.

As you know, this rally, coming at the climax of our football season, is most important to the team and Corps in assuring a victory over our traditional rival. We would be greatly honored to receive a personal message from you for the occasion. If such a message could be recorded for transmission to the team and Corps at the rally, we are certain that it would assist us greatly in gaining the victory we cherish.

The rally is scheduled for November 23, 1949. I shall be glad to furnish any further details you may desire.

Yours sincerely,

William L. Knapp
WILLIAM L KNAPP
Cdt Lt., 1st Class

From the Far East I send you one single thought, one sole idea — written in red on every beachhead from Australia to Tokyo — there is no substitute for victory!

MacArthur

Nearly 48 years have gone since I joined th
long gray line. As an Army "brat" it was the fulf
of all my boyish dreams. The world has turned o
many times since that day and the dreams have l
vanished with the passing years, but through th
grim murk of it all the pride and thrill of
being a West Pointer has never dimmed. And a
I near the end of the road what I felt when I
was sworn in on the Plain so long ago I ca
still say — "that is my greatest honor".

MacArthur

Thomas E. Stephens, noted New York artist (top), was commissioned by West Point to paint a portrait of MacArthur to be hung in Pershing Hall at the Academy. He detected the General's growing impatience and irritability just before the North Korean attack across the 38th Parallel. Was MacArthur's prescience contributing to his new restless, jumpy nature? Some of his intimates think he sensed the imminence of war weeks before June 25, 1950. The General never failed to answer a request from West Pointers for a note or message of cheer. For the 1949 Army football team he penned his advice at the foot of their letter (bottom left), ". . . there is *no* substitute for victory!" For the Class of 1947 he penciled on a ruled tablet a sentimental message (bottom right), from which he borrowed many phrases for his Congressional speech 4 years later.

The War in Korea

1950–1951

Republic of Korea attacked by North Koreans across the 38th Parallel, 25 June 1950; directed by the President to resist the aggression with U.S. forces in behalf of the United Nations, 26 June 1950; made first inspection trip to Korean battle areas, 29 June 1950; named officially as United Nations Commander and presented with UN flag, Tokyo, Japan, 14 July 1950; visited Formosa for conference with Generalissimo Chiang Kai-shek, 31 July 1950; executed landings at Inchon, 15 Sept. 1950; restored capital city, Seoul, to Republic of Korea, 29 Sept. 1950; conferred with President Harry S. Truman at Wake Island, 15 Oct. 1950; relieved of all commands by direction of the President, 11 April 1951.

Named the first United Nations Commander in the field, Gen. MacArthur accepted the UN flag in Tokyo, July 14, 1950, from U. S. Army Chief of Staff Gen. J. Lawton Collins. Vowing to resist the aggression from the north against the Republic of Korea, MacArthur went at the job wholeheartedly, although he had not been asked for his opinion when both the U. S. and the UN committed themselves. It was to be his last assignment in 50 years of service.

The surprise attack at Korea's 38th Parallel caught the General deep in the work of preparing the Japan peace treaty with John Foster Dulles (top). MacArthur boarded his plane for a personal survey of the Korean situation immediately after he learned that his country was in the war. On his arrival in South Korea he conferred with Brig. Gen. John Church (center), commander of GHQ's advance echelon, on the developments of the first days of warfare. Reporter Marguerite Higgins (bottom) hitchhiked back to Tokyo with the General after his first Korean visit and quoted him as saying: "Give me 2 American divisions and I can hold Korea."

A month after the Korean war started, and after Washington had ordered America's Seventh Fleet to "neutralize" Formosa, stronghold of Nationalist China, MacArthur visited the island and was greeted by Generalissimo Chiang Kai-shek (top). Whether or not the Generalissimo foresaw Communist China's active intervention in the conflict, he pleaded for an opportunity to supply troops to the UN's cause (center), and impressed MacArthur. At the conference table (l. to r.) were Gens. Willoughby, Almond, and Stratemeyer, MacArthur's G-2, Chief of Staff, and air chief, respectively; Madame Chiang Kai-shek, MacArthur, and the Generalissimo. Old friends, MacArthur and Madame Chiang were rapt listeners (bottom).

Host to his bosses, MacArthur personally met Chief of Staff Gen. J. Lawton Collins and Chief of Naval Operations Adm. Forrest P. Sherman, when they flew to Tokyo for a midsummer check on the progress of the Korean war. From Collins, MacArthur had already received the flag and command (bottom left) of the UN, whose declaration he endorsed: ". . . being convinced that complete victory over their enemies is essential to defend life, liberty, independence, and religious freedom and to preserve human rights and justice. . . ." Another visitor to MacArthur was Secretary of the Navy Francis Matthews (bottom right) who received from the General a clear picture of naval requirements throughout the Far East, including the defense of Formosa.

A typical day in the Korean combat zone for MacArthur was a long and arduous one. Near the front he inspected (top left) a knocked-out enemy tank, made in Russia. Viewing dead North Koreans near the 38th Parallel (top right) he cautioned his forces, "The North Korean army should not be discounted . . . professionally . . . an excellent force." Trailed by an entourage of high-ranking officers and newspapermen, MacArthur frequently hiked over newly won roads to gain a vantage point (center). He kept well informed on every maneuver and frequently consulted area maps with Maj. Gen. Edward Almond, CG of X Corps (bottom left). Commanding Gen. Matthew B. Ridgway personally pointed out terrain conditions to MacArthur (bottom right). Ridgway made a point of escorting MacArthur as often as possible.

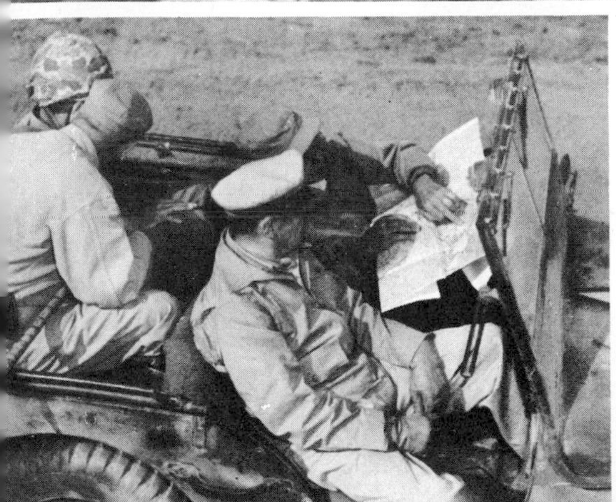

In the boldest move of the war, MacArthur staggered the North Koreans with the UN landings at Inchon, Sept. 15, 1950, followed a few days later by the first recapture of the capital city, Seoul. It was proclaimed a strategic masterpiece. MacArthur himself was in on every minute of the operation. He observed the shelling of the beach (top) from the bridge of the U.S.S. *Mt. McKinley* with Gens. Whitney (left) and Almond (right) . . . cruised about Inchon harbor with Vice Adm. A. D. Struble (center left) . . . congratulated Marine Maj. Gen. Oliver P. Smith on Yellow Beach after the successful landing . . . and sat in with Smith at the initial tactical briefing session of the 1st Marine Division ashore (bottom).

"By the Grace of a Merciful Providence . . ." began MacArthur's solemn address in the Capitol at Seoul on Sept. 29, 1950, as the UN commander turned back to President Syngmam Rhee the government of the Republic of Korea. It was 2 weeks to the day after his Inchon coup, and the weeping Korean audience felt as if they had seen a miracle performed by an American Messiah. Rhee was eloquent in his praise of the UN troops and pledged his people and their meager resources to MacArthur (bottom) in the continuation of the war to the north. The American ambassador to the republic, John Muccio, who had stuck to his post through the bitter first days of the war, was restored to his position in Seoul (top right).

Bent on straightening out the obvious schism between his administration and the UN commander in Korea, President Harry S. Truman met MacArthur on diminutive Wake Island in the mid-Pacific on Oct. 15, 1950. The 2 were apparently affable as the President pinned on the General's breast a fourth oak-leaf cluster to his Distinguished Service Medal and in return MacArthur treated in a comradely way the Commander-in-Chief he had never met before. Ambassador Muccio received the civilian Medal for Merit (bottom right).

While MacArthur has never had the reputation of being a "general's general," most commanders who have served for or with him have respected him highly. He conferred with Air Chief Gen. Hoyt Vandenberg (top left) on air support for his ground troops. He expressed great fondness for the late Lt. Gen. Walton Walker (top right), and worked closely in the field with Maj. Gen. Edward Almond (center right). With the Fifth Air Force commander, Maj. Gen. E. F. Partridge (center left), he personally worked out bombing tactics. His World War I buddy, Lt. Gen. John B. Coulter (bottom left), served under him again in Korea. Gen Matthew B. Ridgway (bottom right) worked in close harmony at all times with MacArthur until he finally replaced him as UN commander. Both are considered "front-line" generals by their subordinates.

Immediately on his arrival in Korea from Tokyo on his many trips to the fighting zone, MacArthur was apprised of the current situation by ranking commanders in the field. Gen. Almond, CG of X Corps (top left), conferred with his superior regularly and the two made extensive use of operations maps. Wrapped in his checkered muffler, MacArthur went over details of the enemy spring offensive in a roadside meeting with Maj. Gen. Robert H. Soule, CG 3rd Infantry Division (top right). "Let's go see the troops. The only way to judge a war is to see the troops in action." That was the usual MacArthur comment after a short briefing by Gen. Ridgway. He toured the entire Suwon front in a jeep with Ridgway (bottom) during the height of the winter freeze in January, 1951. He suffered few colds in the frigid weather, however.

Managing a full-scale war in Korea and administering the occupation of Japan kept the engines of MacArthur's Constellation always hot. En route east to Haneda Air Force Base from a Korean field visit, MacArthur mentally outlined the night's communiqué from his appraisal of the situation. The details would be filled in at GHQ later that night. Always first to greet him as he stepped from his plane (bottom left) was beaming Mrs. MacArthur, with a cheerful "Hi, General," or "Hello, Boss." Before she hustled him off to the U. S. Embassy the news bureau chiefs invariably got their stories. Rarely photographed wearing his reading glasses, MacArthur is shown (bottom) as he dictated from notes on a Korean trip to Earnest Hoberecht of the United Press (seated) and Russell Brines of the Associated Press.

In testimony of our sincere admiration for our Commander-in-Chief
General of the Army

Douglas MacArthur

His commanders in the field, take deep pride in paying him honor respect and affection upon the occasion of the anniversary of his birthday.

His indomitable courage, resolution and understanding in the face of overwhelming odds in the present Korean conflict, during the course of which we have been privileged to serve under his distinguished leadership, have been a source of continuing inspiration not only to all ranks of the combat elements but also to all freedom loving peoples throughout the world.

That we may meet fully his highest approbation in the test of battle is our sincere hope and determined pledge.

Republic of Korea
26 January 1951

안전보장 증명서

북한군 장병들에게

살려면 지금 넘어오시오

국제연합군 쪽으로 넘어오시오。 우리는 당신을 환영하고 잘 대우하겠읍니다. 좋은 음식도 주고 치료도 하겠읍니다。 이 전쟁이 끝나면 집으로 돌아 갈 것입니다. 이 아래 쓴 영문은 맥아더장군이 모든 국제연합군과 대한민국군은 북한군 포로를 잘 대우하라고 한 명령입니다。

SAFE CONDUCT PASS

SOLDIERS OF THE UN FORCES:
This certificate guarantees good treatment to any enemy soldier desiring to cease fighting. Take this man to your nearest officer and treat him as an honorable prisoner of war.

DOUGLAS MacARTHUR
General of the Army
Commander-in-Chief

대한민국 병사에게

이것은 적의 군인으로서 누구나 항복하기를 원하는 자에게 인도적 대우를 보증하는 증명서이다. 이 사람들을 가까이 있는 당신의 상관에게 데리고 가시오. 이사람을 명예스러운 포로로 대우하시오.

맥아더장군 명령

"I have one criticism of Negro troops," General MacArthur once said. "They didn't send me enough of them." M/Sgt. Curtis Pugh of Columbus, Ga., infantryman of the 25th Division, received the Distinguished Service Cross from MacArthur (top left). On the General's seventy-first birthday, Jan. 26, 1951, he received a hand-painted testimonial greeting signed by every one of his field commanders in Korea (top right). MacArthur personally devised the "surrender-and-live-well" leaflets (bottom left) which were credited with bringing in thousands of voluntary prisoners. Gen. Ridgway and MacArthur (bottom right) often "jeeped" as close to the combat line as any vehicle could go in their efforts to get firsthand information.

Since the storm of controversy erupted over MacArthur's letter (top left) to Representative Martin, Congress has formally established the right of military leaders to reply in writing to inquiries from Congressmen. To all appearances the MacArthurs of Tokyo were oblivious of the sizzling powder keg about to go up in Washington. Mrs. MacArthur and son Arthur visited the U.S.S. *Missouri* (top right) with Adm. Struble, while the General conferred with Secretary of the Army Frank Pace (bottom left). MacArthur saluted Pace's departure (bottom right) only a few hours before the news of the President's relief action reached Tokyo. Four days later, in Honolulu, Pace gave credit for the careful planning of the Korean war to MacArthur.

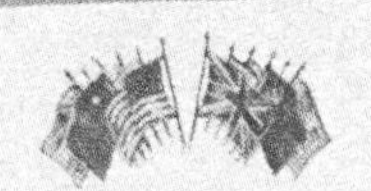

GENERAL HEADQUARTERS
SUPREME COMMANDER FOR THE ALLIED POWERS
OFFICE OF THE SUPREME COMMANDER

Tokyo, Japan.

20 March 1951.

Dear Congressman Martin:

I am most grateful for your note of the 8th forwarding me a copy of your address of February 12th. The latter I have read with much interest, and find that with the passage of years you have certainly lost none of your old time punch.

My views and recommendations with respect to the situation created by Red China's entry into war against us in Korea have been submitted to Washington in most complete detail. Generally these views are well known and clearly understood, as they follow the conventional pattern of meeting force with maximum counter-force as we have never failed to do in the past. Your view with respect to the utilization of the Chinese forces on Formosa is in conflict with neither logic nor this tradition.

It seems strangely difficult for some to realize that here in Asia is where the Communist conspirators have elected to make their play for global conquest, and that we have joined the issue thus raised on the battlefield; that here we fight Europe's war with arms while the diplomats there still fight it with words; that if we lose the war to Communism in Asia the fall of Europe is inevitable, win it and Europe most probably would avoid war and yet preserve freedom. As you point out, we must win. There is no substitute for victory.

With renewed thanks and expressions of most cordial regard,

I am,

Faithfully yours,

DOUGLAS MacARTHUR.

Honorable Joseph W. Martin, Jr.,
House of Representatives,
Washington, D.C.

~~IMMEDIATE RELEASE~~ ~~APRIL 10, 1951~~

ORDER TO GENERAL MacARTHUR FROM THE PRESIDENT

I deeply regret that it becomes my duty as President and Commander in Chief of the United States military forces to replace you as Supreme Commander, Allied Powers; Commander in Chief, United Nations Command; Commander in Chief, Far East; and Commanding General, U. S. Army, Far East.

You will turn over your commands, effective at once, to Lt. Gen. Matthew B. Ridgway. You are authorized to have issued such orders as are necessary to complete desired travel to such place as you select.

My reasons for your replacement will be made public concurrently with the delivery to you of the foregoing order, and are contained in the next following message. (~~See attached~~ Statement by the President.)

The New York Times.
Chicago Daily Tribune
FIRES GEN. M'ARTHUR
Down But Not Out..
THE DAILY COMPASS
MILWAUKEE SENTINEL
TRUMAN FIRES M'ARTHUR
MACARTHUR OUSTED FROM ALL COMMANDS
San Francisco Examiner
A Tragic Day for America
New York Post
MAC IS OUT
New York World-Telegram The Sun
MACARTHUR FIRED BY TRUMAN
New York Herald Tribune
President Ousts Gen. MacArthur
Ridgway Is Named Commander

Sleepy Washington newsmen were aroused after midnight, April 11, 1951, and were handed one of the great news stories of all time—the President's relief of Gen. Douglas MacArthur. Harry S. Truman's reason: ". . . MacArthur is unable to give his wholehearted support to the policies of the United States Government and of the United Nations in matters pertaining to his official duties." Shocked, but by no means silent, the nation's press, radio, and television gave forth the news. In a matter of hours it was no longer Truman and/or MacArthur but the beginning of The Great Controversy, which may well continue for generations to come. The General received the news in Tokyo while at lunch and "he never turned a hair."

Homecoming

1951

Returned to the United States, San Francisco, Calif., 17 April; addressed joint session of Congress, Washington, D.C., 19 April; established residence in the Waldorf-Astoria Towers, New York City, 20 April; testified at the hearings of the joint Armed Services and Foreign Relations committee, U.S. Senate, Washington, D.C., 3-4-5 May.

In civilian clothes for the first time in 10 years, during which he had followed his favorite sport, baseball, from a distance, MacArthur visited New York's Polo Grounds, where he saw the Giants combat the Phillies. The Giants' owner, Horace Stoneham, was at Mrs. MacArthur's left, while the team's effervescent manager, Leo Durocher, erstwhile guest of the General in Tokyo, gripped the guest box. Durocher frequently voices the sentiments of the General, although in less Victorian fashion: "What're we out for except to win? Do I like losing? Hell, no! Anybody can finish second; I want to finish first." MacArthur: "There is no substitute for victory."

Contrasted with the General's jauntiness as he strode to the *Bataan* for his homeward flight, was Mrs. MacArthur's preoccupation as she accomplished her last chore before leaving Tokyo—the closing of the family's bank account in National City Bank of New York. Customarily cheerful, she seemed visibly depressed by the finality of this duty, although she had performed it twice in Manila and once in Brisbane. Heading for Haneda Air Forces Base from their home, the U. S. Embassy, the MacArthurs were bid "sayonara"—farewell—by American honor guards and an estimated 300,000 Japanese lining the route from Tokyo to the field.

While farewell military ceremonies were performed before the MacArthurs' plane took off for Honolulu, the Japanese warmly eulogized their "beloved conqueror" in page one newspaper editorials. Tokyo's *Nippon Times* called MacArthur's removal and departure "perhaps the biggest surprise the Japanese have experienced since the end of the war. Our heart is full when we realize that this General is leaving us. He came as a great reformer . . . he provided the Japanese people with an understanding of the 'dignity of the individual.' It is through our faith in the General that we trust the United States and Western democracy today." En route to a homeland he hadn't seen for 14 years, the General smoked and read and thought. Then he went to work on his forthcoming speech to Congress.

With "humility and great pride . . . with neither rancor nor bitterness in the fading twilight of life," Douglas MacArthur addressed a joint session of Congress on April 19, 1951, and received a tumultuous ovation. By means of radio, television, and newsreels his speech was seen and heard by his countrymen with mixed emotions. He analyzed the Far Eastern situation from his standpoint, then closed his "military career" to "just fade away, an old soldier who tried to do his duty as God gave him the light to see that duty." His critics called him a Barrymore, and even a Bernhardt. His supporters, with worn lungs and palms, began electioneering. Recordings of the speech sold by the millions and "Old Soldiers Never Die" became an overnight hit.

With the Congress' thunderous applause behind them, the schedule-harried MacArthurs began their drive through Washington, D.C., capital of the country which, for that moment, lay at their feet. Already the Pentagon and the White House were preparing their replies to MacArthur's incisive remarks to Congress, and scores of newspapermen, pro and con, were writing their descriptions of his historic speech and spectacular return to Washington. His official welcome (bottom) at the Washington Monument grounds was attended by almost every capital dignitary except President Truman. That night the MacArthurs departed (top right) for their new home —New York City. Young Arthur, bewildered by everyone and everything, was very tired.

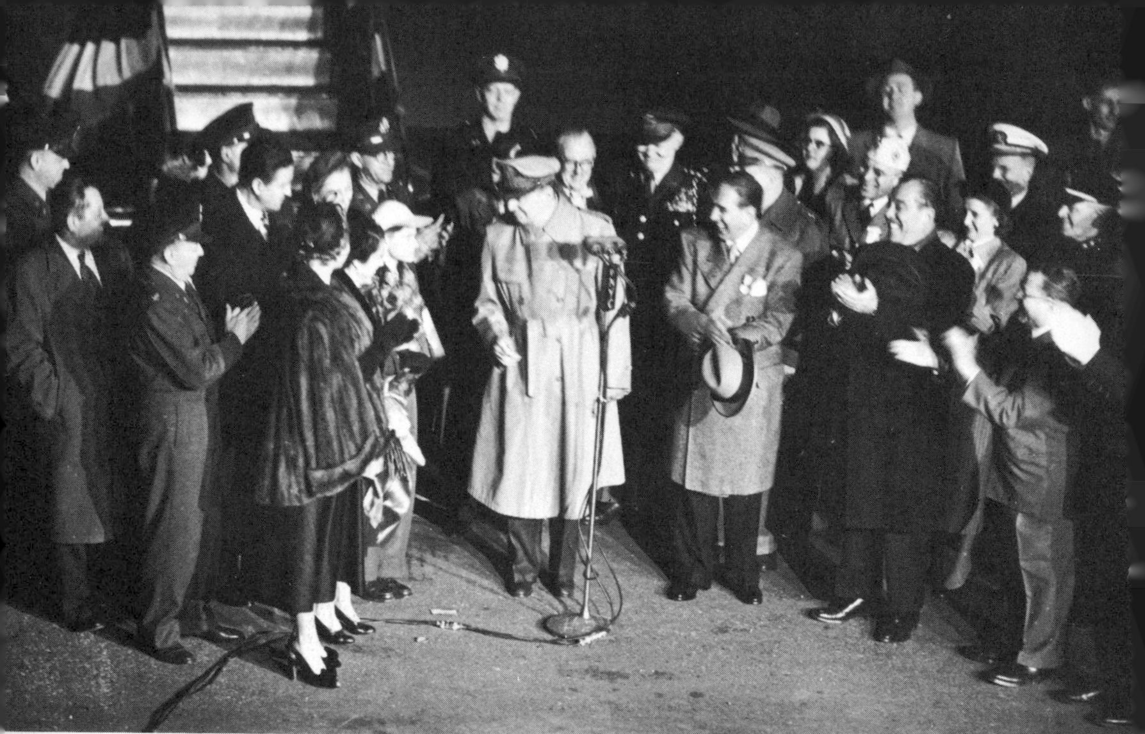

After 14 years of marriage, General and Mrs. MacArthur chose to settle in the city where they were married—New York—and the city's belated wedding party set new records for parades, receptions, and festivities. At New York International Airport, after their tiring day in Washington, the MacArthurs were met by Mayor and Mrs. Vincent Impellitteri and city officials. A New York *Times* editorial headlined it "A Day To Remember" and noted that the General traveled the "hero's route" in parade after parade. During the course of Manhattan's parade, over 3,249 tons of paper were dropped on the motorcade, and it was estimated that over 10 million people saw the General and his family pass on a 20-mile route.

After strenuous receptions in Honolulu, San Francisco, Washington, and New York, the MacArthur trio made a final sweep through the mid-West and 2 hometowns before the General faced Senate committees investigating his dismissal and U. S. policies in the Far East. A long distance cavalcade through Chicago and up Lake Michigan's shore to Milwaukee brought the General back to his parents' home (top) on Marshall Street and to the ovation of his one-time neighbors. On the MacArthurs' fourteenth wedding anniversary they traveled to Murfreesboro, Tenn., "Miss Jean's" Southern hometown, where she was tearfully welcomed (bottom) by her former servant and friend, Mary Ellen Vaughn.

A daily attack by milling photographers, before and after each session of the Senate inquiry into his dismissal, kept the General in condition for the verbal barrage of committee questioners. As the transcript of the hearings filled the air waves and newscolumns, all America took sides on the issues. MacArthur (his aide, Maj. Gen. Courtney Whitney, at his left) extemporaneously answered the Committee's relentless questions hour after hour—day after day, with his usual rhetorical ability. Sen. Richard Russell, Democrat, of Georgia was chairman of the joint committee, comprising 14 Democrats and 12 Republicans. They questioned and heard witnesses for 8 weeks. The official transcript totaled 2,045,000 words—more than twice the wordage in the Bible.

Settled in a tower suite in Manhattan's Waldorf-Astoria Hotel, the MacArthurs turned with obvious enjoyment to the pleasures and comforts which had been denied them for 14 years of overseas life. One of Mrs. MacArthur's first shopping trips took her to a smart Fifth Avenue shoe shop with Lt. Col. Anthony Story (top left). She wears 5½AAA and prefers black. For many years all of her American clothes had been sent to her by friends and a personal shopper in a San Francisco store. By late May, 1951, the MacArthurs were thorough New Yorkers—the General having shed his battle jacket for flannels (top right) and, for their many nights at the theater, evening clothes (bottom).

In a month of sundaes, and sodas, 13-year-old Arthur MacArthur became acquainted with the homeland he was seeing for the first time. He spent every free afternoon after his arrival in the U. S. at a ball park. He was welcomed in the New York Yankees' dugout by Yanks Gerry Coleman, Phil Rizzuto, and Ralph Houk (left to right). Previously, Arthur's only experience with organized baseball was in Tokyo when Japanese teams faced visiting American nines. The General, a loyal Masonic Shriner and member of Seattle's Nile Temple, donned his fez for the Shrine's convention parade in New York, July, 1951. Three "South Pacificans" gathered backstage shortly after the MacArthurs returned to New York and star Mary Martin (right) crossed her fingers wishing luck for all, after a performance of the musical, "South Pacific."

MacArthur continued to satisfy his appetite for the American sports he had missed for so many years and attended Madison Square Garden prizefight with former heavyweight champion, Gene Tunney. Meanwhile a scattered handful of faithful but nonprofessional politicians continued to hope that MacArthur would suddenly attain a political glamour, which his personal appearances had shown him to be lacking. In Washington's permanent MacArthur-for-President headquarters, Erwin Hohensee, self-styled leader of the cause who had never met the General, offered pictures and literature to all seekers. The General, while denying any interest in occupying the White House, embarked on a countrywide speaking tour. At the Alamo, in San Antonio, Texas, he was backed up by 2 of his retired combat generals, Jonathan Wainwright (at Mrs. MacArthur's right) and Walter Krueger (far right).

Thanks are due to the following sources for the photographs appearing in this book:

Jacket photographs: front, Jimmy Carnahan, Ferrell's Studio, Murfreesboro, Tenn.; back, INP.

PART ONE. P. 1: Malcolm MacArthur; p. 2: Mary McCalla MacArthur; p. 3: Malcolm MacArthur, inset left—Army, inset center and right—International News Photos (INP); p. 4: top l.—Andrew Bradley, top r.—Milwaukee Historical Society, bot. l. & r.—Malcolm MacArthur; p. 5: top l.—Frank Bobowski, Fonfara Studio, Chicopee, Mass., bot. l.—Bradley; r.—Milw. Hist. Soc.; p. 6: Army; p. 7: Bradley; p. 8: top—Malcolm MacArthur, bot.—Army; p. 9: Malcolm MacArthur; p. 10: top—INP, bot. l.—Bowman MacArthur, bot. r.—Malcolm MacArthur; p. 11: top l.—Malcolm MacArthur, others—Bowman MacArthur; p. 12: top l.—Harris & Ewing News Photo Service, Washington, D.C., top r.—Malcolm MacArthur, bot. l.—Army, bot. r.—Bowman MacArthur; p. 13: Army; p. 14: Mary Jordan.

PART TWO. P. 1: Bowman MacArthur; p. 2: top and bot. l.—United States Military Academy, West Point, N.Y. (USMA), bot. r.—INP; p. 3: USMA; p. 4: top and bot. r.—Bowman MacArthur, bot. l.—Army; p. 5: top l. and r.—INP, bot. l.—Army; p. 6: top—Harris & Ewing, bot. l. and r.—Bowman MacArthur; pp. 7 through 13: Army; p. 14: Keystone View Company, N.Y.

PART THREE. P. 1: European; p. 2: top l. and r.—INP, cen. and bot. r.—European, bot. l.—Keystone; p. 3: USMA; p. 4: top l., cen. and bot. l.—INP, top r.—USMA, bot. r.—Keystone; p. 5: INP; p. 6: Army; p. 7: top l. and r.—INP, bot.—European; p. 8: bot. l.—INP, others—Army; p. 9: INP; p. 10: top—INP, bot.—American Olympic Committee; p. 11: bot. r.—Air Force, others—Army; p. 12: bot. l.—INP, others—Army; pp. 13 and 14: INP; p. 15: bot.—Keystone, others—INP; p. 16: bot. l. and r.—Harris & Ewing, cen. r.—INP, top—Army; p. 17: Army; p. 18: top—Harris & Ewing, bot.—Army; p. 19: top l. and bot.—INP, top r.—Mary Nelle Morris; p. 20: Mary Nelle Morris; p. 21: top l.—INP, others—Mary Nelle Morris; p. 22: INP; p. 23: Army; p. 24: top and bot. l.—Army, bot. r.—Mary Nelle Morris; p. 25: top—Mary Nelle Morris, bot.—INP; p. 26: Army.

PART FOUR. P. 1: Gaetano Faillace; p. 2: top and bot. r.—Army, bot. l.—INP; p. 3: INP; pp. 4 and 5: Army; p. 6: INP; p. 7 top r. and bot.—Army, top l.—INP; p. 8: top—Harris & Ewing, cen.—Army, bot.—INP· p. 9: Army; p. 10: bot. r.—Marine Corps, others—Army; p. 11: Army; p. 12: right—Navy, others—INP; p. 13: cen. r.—Air Force, others—Army; p. 14: top and cen.—Navy, bot.—Army; p. 15: top and bot.—Navy, cen.—Harris & Ewing; p. 16: bot. l.—INP, others—Army; p. 17: Navy; p. 18: cen.—Army, others—Navy; p. 19: Army; p. 20: top r.—INP, others—Army; pp. 21 through 27: Army; p. 28: Hubbitt Quon.

PART FIVE. Pp. 1 through 3: Army; p. 4: top—Army, bot. l. and r.—Navy; pp. 5 through 8: Army; p. 9: bot.—INP, others—Army; p. 10 top and bot. r.—Army, bot. l.—Navy, inset—INP; pp. 11 and 12: Army; p. 13: bot. l.—Clovis Crummett, others—INP; pp. 14 through 16: Army; p. 17: top—INP, bot.—Army; p. 18: top r.—American Red Cross, others—Army; p. 19: bot. r.—Clovis Crummett, others—Army; p. 20: top—Army, bot l. and r.—USMA.

PART SIX. Pp. 1 through 3: Army; p. 4: bot. r.—Navy, others—Army; p. 5: bot. r.—INP, others—Army; p. 6: top and bot.—Army, cen. l. and r.—Navy; pp. 7 and 8: Army; p. 9: cen. l.—Air Force, others—Army; pp. 10 and 11: Army; p. 12: top r.—INP, others—Army; p. 13: top l. and bot. l.—INP, top r.—Navy, bot. r.—Army; p. 14: top—INP, bot.—Edward F. Dziadzio.

PART SEVEN. P. 1: INP; p. 2: top l.—INP, top r. and bot.—Army; p. 3: Army; p. 4: top and bot. l.—INP, bot. r.—Army; pp. 5 and 6: Army; p. 7: top—Milwaukee "Sentinel," bot.—Jimmy Carnahan, Ferrell's Studio; pp. 8 and 9: INP; p. 10: top and bot. r.—INP, bot. l.—Ira Rosenberg, "The New York Herald-Tribune"; pp. 11 and 12, INP.

mhd00100

MANCHURIA
MUKDEN
YALU R.
RASHIN
HUNGNAM
PYONGYANG
WONSAN
38° PARALLEL
SEOUL
SUWON
INCHON
TAEJON
TAEGU
PUSAN
Yellow Sea
HIROSHIMA
NAGASAKI
SHI
KYUSHU
CHINA
East China Sea
OKINAWA
FORMOSA
PHILIPPINE ISLANDS
LUZON